The Catholic Tradition

REV. CHARLES J. DOLLEN
DR. JAMES K. McGOWAN
DR. JAMES J. MEGIVERN
EDITORS

The Catholic Tradition

Spirituality

Volume 1

A Consortium Book

Library of Congress Card Catalog Number: 79-1977
ISBN: 0-8434-0736-0
ISBN: 0-8434-0725-5 series

The publisher gratefully acknowledges permission to quote from the following copyrighted sources. In cases where those properties contain scholarly apparatus such as footnotes, such footnotes have been omitted in the interest of the general reader.

ABBEY OF GETHSEMANI
Chapters 1-15 from *The Book of St. Bernard on the Love of God* translated by Terence L. Connolly, S.J., Ph.D. Mission Press, copyright 1943.

BURNS OATES & WASHBOURNE LTD.
"On the Contemplative Life" from the *Summa Theologica* of St. Thomas Aquinas, translated by Fathers of the English Dominican Province, 1935.

THE CATHOLIC UNIVERSITY OF AMERICA PRESS, INC.
"The Good of Patience" from *The Fathers of the Church*, Volume 36, *St. Cyprian: Treatises*, translated and edited by Roy J. Deferrari, copyright © 1958; "On Perfection" from *The Fathers of the Church*, Volume 58, *St. Gregory of Nyssa: Ascetical Works*, copyright © 1967; "Confessions: Book Ten" from *The Fathers of the Church*, Volume 21, *St. Augustine: Confessions*, translated by Vernon J. Bourke, Ph.D., copyright 1953.

DOUBLEDAY & COMPANY, INC.
The Imitation of Christ by Thomas à Kempis, pages 31–51. Copyright © 1955 by Doubleday & Company, Inc. Used by permission of Doubleday & Company, Inc.

FABER AND FABER, LTD.
"Four Degrees of Passionate Charity" from *Selected Writings on Contemplation* by Richard of St.-Victor, translated by Clare Kirchberger, 1957; "The Book of Divine Consolation" from *Meister Eckhart:*

Table of Contents

Introduction

The Catholic Tradition is a 14 volume anthology of excerpts from the great Catholic writers from antiquity to the present day. *The Catholic Tradition* is intended for the armchair reader who has not studied theology or church history and has not time to struggle unassisted through 198 books. The publisher's intention is to provide such a reader with a compact home library that will permit him to familiarize himself with the great Catholic writers and their works. The works included in *The Catholic Tradition* are all religious in subject. The publisher did not include fiction or nonfiction books on secular subjects written by Catholic authors.

The Catholic Tradition arranges the writings according to religious subjects. There are seven religious subjects, each of which is covered in two volumes: The Church; Mass and the Sacraments; Sacred Scripture; The Saviour; Personal Ethics; Social Thought; and Spirituality. Within each subject, the writings are arranged in chronological order, which permits the reader to follow the development of Catholic thought across 2000 years.

Each excerpt in *The Catholic Tradition* is preceded by a brief biographical and explanatory introduction to help the reader understand the world in which the writer lived and wrote, and the problems with which he was dealing.

The selection of the excerpts and the writing of the introductions has been a long and difficult process. The task of making the final selections was particularly arduous (as such choices always are); the most modern authors, about whose writing there is yet no final judgment provoking the most debate. The selection of authors was made originally in the publisher's offices and then submitted to the three editors of the series who refined the selection. The editors submitted their selection to an unofficial board of scholars who very kindly made constructive comments.

The process of assembling the many hundreds of books from which to make the final selection was in itself a vast task. Many of the books under consideration were very scarce and not available in bookstores or libraries. The work of collecting the books and then making selections among them stretched over a three year period, and many books were selected for inclusion and later rejected after careful scrutiny and reflection.

The editing of *The Catholic Tradition* was a long and difficult job because the literature of Roman Catholicism is a vast and complex body. Of all the Christian denominations, the Roman Catholic Church is by far the oldest and largest. Its ranks include a tremendous number of saints and scholars, writers and thinkers, mystics and preachers: many of whom felt so strongly about their faith that they were willing to die for it. They have left an incomparably rich legacy of art and writing. Selecting from it is not simple.

The selections that we made are representative of the best of mainstream Catholic writing. Generally, they should be intelligible to a thoughtful layman. Some however, may prove more technical than others, and some of the very recent writers may seem controversial. The reader should bear in mind that some theological questions simply do not admit of facile answers, and that some of the earlier writers were considered controversial in their own days. It is also well to remember that the writings gathered here, brilliant and revered as their authors may be, are not necessarily official statements of Church policy. But they are, all of them, solidly part of the Catholic tradition.

The writers are all Catholics, many of them clergymen, some of them converts to Catholicism. They all wrote as loyal

Introduction

servants of the Church and from a Catholic point of view. When they wrote on personal ethics they proceeded from the assumption that man's goal was to imitate Christ, not simply to follow a secular set of ethical rules. When they wrote on social problems they expressed the need to solve social problems because they loved their neighbors, not for the material enrichment of society. Their writings on Christ reflect an intense struggle to bend human language to divine definition. Taken together, their writings form a literary tradition that is Roman Catholic at heart. That tradition has certain ingredients that are not present in the literary traditions of the other Christian denominations. Particularly, the heritage of liturgical ceremony and mystical contemplation have left an incomparable treasure of literature that is here presented in the volumes entitled *Mass and the Sacraments*, and *Spirituality*.

The whole corpus of Catholic thinking and writing, distilled here in *The Catholic Tradition*, is generally considered by scholars to have three important periods: the ancient, or patristic, period; the high middle-ages, which is the era of St. Thomas Aquinas and sometimes called the scholastic period; finally the time in which we live today, the last 100 years. These three epochs are golden ages of Catholic writing. They are separated from each other by the generally unproductive eras of the dark ages and the Reformation.

Through all these epochs the great Catholic writers have preserved and developed the Christian message: love God; love your fellow man. Each writer wrote conscious of the tradition behind him, conscious that he was building on the work of men before him, adapting their work to changed conditions or continuing their work on the outer edges of human speculation.

The present day writers, those of the third great era of Catholic writing, are the most important part of *The Catholic Tradition*. Here for the first time their thinking is presented along with the work of their predecessors; here can be seen the stunning achievement of today's Catholic writing, and how it follows logically from the writing of the patristic and scholastic thinkers.

The present day writers presented in *The Catholic Tradition* number 114, over half of the total number of writers chosen.

Their writing will probably prove more intelligible to the average reader because they write in today's idiom and they address contemporary problems.

Oddly enough, many if not most of the modern writers are not familiar to the average Catholic. St. Augustine, and St. Thomas Aquinas are household names, but only serious Catholic readers today are familiar with the masterful writings of Karl Rahner, Edward Schillebeeckx, Raymond Brown, and Gustavo Gutiérrez. None the less, these men are representative of a great historical flowering of Catholic writing today and their names may well echo down the ages.

THE PUBLISHER

Clement of Alexandria
150-215

Very little information is available on this Father of the Church who is second only to Origen as a representative of the early development of theology in Alexandria. Clement was well instructed in Greek philosophy, which he used generously in his theological writings. A convert to Christianity, he conducted a school of Christian instruction in Alexandria. He left that city around 202, during a persecution of the Christians. He seems to have spent time in Antioch and Cappadocia before his death.

Clement was deeply concerned with the question of the relationship between Greek philosophy and Christian faith. He clearly strove to bring these two dynamics together in a complementary manner. As the following selection demonstrates, Greek philosophy, and Plato in particular, plays a key role in leading the Christian individual and community to union with God. Clement declares that Greek philosophy provides for the soul the preliminary cleansing and training required for the reception of faith. By welcoming philosophy into the world view of Christian faith, Clement made a positive contribution to the intellectual tradition of Christianity.

Spiritual perfection, for Clement, is a state of union between God, the Author and Organizer of the universe, and the gnostic, i.e., the one who comes to know and see that God is Author and Organizer. The gnostic alone is truly devout, holy, pious, the lover of God. By the term gnostic, Clement does not mean the unorthodox Christian group known as the Gnostics, but simply the person who, through a life of knowledge and prayerful contemplation, comes to love and be loved by God. The true gnostic knows the facts of the Christian religion, accomplishes the will of the Word of God, and has the capacity to impart to others the hidden aspects of truth. The perfection of the true gnostic lies in the unending process of rising from one sphere of vision to another sphere, still higher, until he dwells in transparent clearness and holds communion with God through the great High Priest, Jesus Christ. Perfection is signified through a life of virtue—prudence, temperance, fortitude, justice, high spirit, magnanimity, love. The perfect man is a citizen of the world, not of this world only but of a higher order as well. While moving upward toward union with God by way of knowledge and contemplation, the perfect Christian is at the same time drawn upward by the Father through the Son Who is teacher, source of providence, counsellor to the Father, lover of all mankind.

By way of Clement, several basic Greek themes and images worked their way into a model of Christian spiritual perfection, such as the concepts of union and vision, the constant ascent from orbit to orbit until total perfection is achieved, emphasis on perfection as primarily a search for knowledge, light as a way of speaking both of God and the spiritual life. This particular approach to spirituality became integral to the Christian tradition and continues to play a central role in the Christian quest for perfection.

The selection following is from Book VII of the Stromata *(tapestries, miscellaneous) of Clement. This work, a total of eight books, is Clement's most important writing.*

ON SPIRITUAL PERFECTION

I t is now time for us to prove to the Greeks that the gnostic alone is truly devout, so that the philosophers, learning what sort of person the true Christian is, may condemn their own folly for their careless and indiscriminate persecution of the name of Christian, while they irrationally abuse as atheists those who have the knowledge of the true God. And in addressing philosophers I think one should employ ratiocination as more convincing, since they are better trained to understand it from their previous course of instruction, even if they have not yet shown themselves worthy to participate in the power to believe. Of the sayings of the prophets we will make no mention at present, intending hereafter to avail ourselves of the Scriptures on the fitting occasions. For the present we will only give a summary indication of what is declared by them, in the form of a sketch of the Christian religion, in order that we may not break the thread of the discourse by constant references to the Scriptures, especially when addressing those who do not yet understand their phraseology. When we have shown their general purport, the exhibition of the testimonies shall be superadded afterwards on their believing. And if our words seem to some of the uninstructed to be different from the Lord's Scriptures, let them know that it is from the Scriptures that they draw their life and breath, and that it is their object, taking these as their starting-point, to set forth, not their phraseology, but their meaning only. For further elaboration being unseasonable would with good reason seem superfluous, while on the other hand it would be a very careless and unsatisfactory way of treating the subject if we were to omit all consideration of that which is of pressing importance. And blessed indeed are they who search out the testimonies of the

Lord: with their whole heart they will seek him. Now they which testify of the Lord are the law and the prophets.

It is our business then to prove that the gnostic alone is holy and pious, worshipping the true God as befits him; and the worship which befits God includes both loving God and being loved by him. To the gnostic every kind of pre-eminence seems honourable in proportion to its worth. In the world of sense rulers and parents and elders generally are to be honoured; in matters of teaching, the most ancient philosophy and the earliest prophecy; in the spiritual world, that which is elder in origin, the Son, the beginning and first-fruit of all existing things, himself timeless and without beginning; from whom the gnostic believes that he receives the knowledge of the ultimate cause, the Father of the universe, the earliest and most beneficent of all existences, no longer reported by word of mouth, but worshipped and adored, as is his due, with silent worship and holy awe; who was manifested indeed by the Lord so far as it was possible for the learners to understand, but apprehended by those whom the Lord has elected for knowledge, those, says the apostle, who have their senses exercised.

The gnostic therefore pays service to God by his constant self-discipline and by cherishing that which is divine in himself in the way of unremitting charity. For as regards the service of men, part may be classed as meliorative treatment and part as ministrative service. Thus the medicinal art is meliorative of the body and philosophy of the soul; but that which parents receive from children and rulers from subjects is ministrative aid. Similarly in the Church the meliorative service is imaged in the presbyters, the ministrative in the deacons. As both these services are performed by the ministering angels for God in their administration of earthly things, so they are also performed by the gnostic himself, while on the one hand he serves God, and on the other hand sets forth his meliorative philosophy to men, in whatsoever way he may be appointed to instruct them with a view to their improvement. For he alone is truly devout who ministers to God rightly and unblameably in respect to human affairs. For, as the best treatment of plants is that whereby the fruits grow and are gathered in by the science and art of husbandry, supplying to men the benefit

4

derived from the fruits; so the best ingathering which the devoutness of the gnostic can accomplish by means of his art is the appropriation of the fruits of all who have come to believe through him, as one after another becomes possessed of knowledge and is thus brought into the way of salvation. And if by godliness we understand the habit of mind which preserves the fitting attitude towards God, then the godly alone is dear to God. And such would be he who knows what is fitting both in theory and in life, as to how one should live who will one day become god, aye and is even now being made life to God.

Thus he is before all things a lover of God. For as he who honours his father is a lover of his father, so he who honours God is a lover of God. Hence too the gnostic faculty seems to me to reveal itself in three achievements: (1) in the knowledge of the facts of the Christian religion, (2) in the accomplishment of whatever the Word enjoins, (3) in the capacity to impart to others after a godly manner the hidden things of truth. How then can he who is convinced that God is almighty, and who has learnt the divine mysteries from his only-begotten Son—how can such an one be an atheist? An atheist is one who does not believe in the existence of God, while we call by the name of superstitious him who fears the demons and who deifies everything down to stocks and stones, having brought into slavery the spirit and the inner man which lives in accordance with reason.

CHAPTER II

The first proof that one knows God, after one has put confidence in the Saviour's teaching, is that one in no way does wrong, in the conviction that this befits the knowledge of God. Thus the most excellent thing on earth is the most devout of men, and the most excellent in heaven is the angel, who is nearer in place to the deity and already more purely participant of the eternal and blessed life. But most perfect and most holy of all, most sovereign, most lordly, most royal, and most beneficent, is the nature of the Son, which approaches most closely to the one Almighty Being. The Son is the highest pre-eminence, which sets in order all things according to the Father's will, and steers the universe aright, performing all things with unwearying energy, beholding the Father's secret thoughts through his working. For the Son of God never moves from his watchtower, being never divided, never dissevered, never passing from place to place, but existing everywhere at all times and free from all limitations. He is all reason, all eye, all light from the Father, seeing all things, hearing all things, knowing all things, with power searching the powers. To him is subjected the whole army of angels and of gods—to him, the Word of the Father, who has received the holy administration by reason of him who subjected it to him; through whom also all men belong to him, but some by way of knowledge, while others have not yet attained to this; some as friends, some as faithful servants, others as servants merely.

This is the Teacher who educates the gnostic by means of mysteries, and the believer by means of good hopes, and him who is hard of heart with corrective discipline acting on the senses. He is the source of Providence both for the individual and the community and for the universe at large. And that there is a Son of God, and that this Son is the Saviour and Lord that we assert him to be, is directly declared by the divine prophecies. Thus the Lord of all, whether Greek or barbarian, uses persuasion to those who are willing; for it is not his way to compel one who is able of himself to obtain salvation by the exercise of free choice and by fulfilling all that is required on his part so as to lay hold on the hope. This is he who bestows on the Greeks also their philosophy through the inferior angels. For by an ancient and divine ordinance angels are assigned to the different nations; but to be the Lord's portion is the glory of the believers. Here we have the following alternatives: either the Lord cares not for all men—which might arise from incapacity (but this it is forbidden to say, for incapacity is a mark of weakness), or from want of will on the part of one possessed with power (but such an affection is incompatible with goodness; in any case he who for our sake took upon him our flesh with its capacity for suffering is not rendered indifferent to others' sorrow by self-indulgence)—or he has regard for us all, which also beseems him who was made the Lord of all. For he is the Saviour not on one here and another there, but, to the extent of each man's fitness, he distributed his own bounty

6

both to Greeks and to barbarians, and to the faithful and elect, who were foreordained out of them and were called in their own season.

Neither again could envy be the impelling principle with him, who has called all alike, though he has assigned special honours to those who have shown special faith; nor could the Lord of all be hindered by opposition from without, especially when he is carrying out the will of the good and almighty Father. No, as the Lord himself is absolutely inaccessible to envy, being eternally free from passion, so neither is man's state such as to be envied by the Lord. It is another who envies, who is also acquainted with passion. Nor yet can it be said that the Lord from ignorance did not will to save mankind, because he knew not how to take care of each. For ignorance touches not the Son of God, who was the Father's counsellor before the foundation of the world, the Wisdom in which the Almighty God rejoiced. For the Son is the power of God, as being the original Word of the Father, prior to all created things: and he might justly be styled the Wisdom of God and the Teacher of those who were made by him. Neither indeed could he ever abandon his care for mankind through the distraction of any pleasure, seeing that, after he had taken upon him our flesh, which is by nature subject to passion, he trained it to a habit of impassibility. And how could he be Saviour and Lord, if he were not Saviour and Lord of all—Saviour of those who have believed, because they have determined to know, Lord of those who have been disobedient, until they have been enabled to confess their sins, and have received the grace which comes through him, in the way adapted and corresponding to their state? But all the activity of the Lord is referred to the Almighty, the Son being, so to speak, a certain activity of the Father.

The Saviour then could never be a hater of men, seeing that it was owing to his abounding love for man that he scorned not the weakness of human flesh, but having clothed himself with it, has come into the world for the common salvation of men. For faith is common to all who choose it. No, nor could he ever neglect man, his peculiar work, seeing that into man alone of all animals has an idea of God been instilled at his creation. Neither could there be any better government of men, or one more consonant to the divine nature, than that which has been ordained. At any rate it always belongs to him who is naturally superior to direct the inferior, and to him who is able to manage anything well, that he should have received the government of it as his due. But the true Ruler and Director is the Word of God and his Providence, superintending all things and neglecting the charge of none of her household. And such would be they who have chosen to attach themselves to the Word, viz., those who are being perfected through faith. Thus, by the will of the Almighty Father, the Son, who is the imperceptible power of primaeval motion, is made the cause of all good things. For he was not seen in his true nature by those who could not apprehend it owing to the infirmity of the flesh, but having taken upon him a body which could be seen and handled, he came into the world to reveal what was possible to man in the way of obedience to God's commandments.

Being then the power of the Father, he easily prevails over whomsoever he will, not leaving even the smallest atom of his government uncared for: else the universe of his creation would have been no longer good. And I think the greatest power is shown where there is an inspection of all the parts, proceeding with minute accuracy even to the smallest, while all gaze on the supreme Administrator of the universe, as he pilots all in safety according to the Father's will, rank being subordinated to rank under different leaders, till in the end the great High Priest is reached. For on one original principle, which works in accordance with the Father's will, depend the first and second and third gradations; and then at the extreme end of the visible world there is the blessed ordinance of angels; and so, even down to ourselves, ranks below ranks are appointed, all saving and being saved by the initiation and through the instrumentality of One. As then the remotest particle of iron is drawn by the influence of the magnet extending through a long series of iron rings, so also through the attraction of the Holy Spirit the virtuous are adapted to the highest mansion: but they that are wicked from weakness, having fallen into an evil habit owing to unrighteous greed, neither keep hold themselves nor are held by another, but collapse and fall to the ground, being entangled in their passions. For this is the law from the beginning, that he who would have virtue must choose it.

Wherefore also both the commandments according to the law and the commandments previous to the law, given to those who were not yet under law—for law is not enacted for a just man—ordained that he who chose should obtain eternal life and a blessed reward, and on the other hand permitted him who delighted in wickedness to consort with what he chose. Again they ordained that the soul that at any time improved as regards the knowledge of virtue and increase in righteousness, should obtain an improved position in the universe, pressing onwards at every step to a passionless state, until it comes to a perfect man, a pre-eminence at once of knowledge and of inheritance. These saving revolutions are each severally portioned off, according to the order of change, by variety of time and place and honour and knowledge and inheritance and service, up to the transcendent orbit which is next to the Lord, occupied in eternal contemplation. And that which is lovely has power to draw to the contemplation of itself every one who through love of knowledge has applied himself wholly to contemplation.

Therefore the commandments given by the Lord, both the former and the latter, all flow from one source, for neither did he negligently suffer those who lived before the law to be altogether without law, nor on the other hand did he permit those who were ignorant of the barbarian (i.e., Jewish) philosophy to run wild. For, by giving to the Jews commandments and to the Greeks philosophy, he confined unbelief until the period of his own presence on earth, in which every one who believed not is without excuse. For he leads men by both ways of advance, whether Greek or barbarian, to the perfection which is through faith. But if any of the Greeks dispenses with the preliminary guidance of the Greek philosophy and hastens straight to the true teaching, he, even though he be unlearned, at once distances all competition, having chosen the short-cut to perfection, viz., that of salvation through faith.

Accordingly he made all things to be helpful for virtue, in so far as might be without hindering the freedom of man's choice, and showed them to be so, in order that he who is indeed the One Alone Almighty might, even to those who can only see darkly, be in some way revealed as a good God, a Saviour from age to age through the instrumentality of his Son, and in all ways absolutely guiltless of evil. For by the Lord of the universe all things are ordered both generally and particularly with a view to the safety of the whole. It is the work then of saving righteousness always to promote the improvement of each according to the possibilities of the case. For the lesser things also are managed with a view to the safety and continuance of the superior in accordance with their own characters. For instance, whatever is possessed of virtue changes to better habitations, the cause of the change being the independent choice of knowledge with which the soul was gifted to begin with; but those who are more hardened are constrained to repent by necessary chastisements, inflicted either through the agency of the attendant angels or through various preliminary judgments or through the great and final judgment, by the goodness of the great Judge whose eye is ever upon us.

CHAPTER III

As to the rest I keep silent, giving glory to God: only I say that those gnostic souls are so carried away by the magnificence of the vision that they cannot confine themselves within the lines of the constitution by which each holy degree is assigned and in accordance with which the blessed abodes of the gods have been marked out and allotted; but being counted as holy among the holy, and translated absolutely and entirely to another sphere, they keep on always moving to higher and yet higher regions until they no longer greet the divine vision in or by means of mirrors, but for loving hearts feast for ever on the uncloying, never-ending sight, radiant in its transparent clearness, while throughout the endless ages they taste a never-wearying delight, and thus continue, all alike honoured with an identity of pre-eminence. This is the apprehensive vision of the pure in heart. This, therefore, is the life-work of the perfected gnostic, viz., to hold communion with God through the great High Priest, being made like the Lord, as far as may be, by means of all his service towards God, a service which extends to the salvation of men by his solicitous goodness towards us and also by public worship and by teaching and active kindness. Aye, and in being thus assimilated to God, the gnostic is making and fashioning himself and also forming those who hear him, while, so far as may be, he assimilates to that which is by nature free from passion that which has been subdued by training to a passionless state: and this he effects by undisturbed intercourse and communion with the Lord. Of this gnostic assimilation the canons, as it appears to me, are gentleness, kindness and a noble devoutness.

These virtues I affirm to be an acceptable sacrifice with God, as the Scripture declares that the unboastful heart joined with a right understanding is a perfect offering to God, since every man who is won over for holiness is enlightened into an indissoluble unity. For both the Gospel and the apostle command us to bring ourselves into captivity and put ourselves to death, slaying the old man which is being corrupted according to its lusts and raising up the new man from the death of our old perversion, laying aside our passions and becoming free from sin. This it was which was signified also by the law when it commanded that the sinner should be put to death, viz., the change from death to life, that is, the "apathy" which comes from faith. But the expounders of the law, not understanding this took the law to be jealous, and have thus given a handle to those who without ground endeavour to discredit it.

It is for this reason that we fitly refrain from making any sacrifice to God, who has provided all things for all, being himself in need of nothing; but we glorify him who was consecrated for us, by consecrating ourselves also to ever higher degrees of freedom from want and from passion. For God takes pleasure only in our salvation. Fitly therefore do we abstain from offering sacrifice to him who cannot be swayed by pleasures, bearing in mind also that the smoke of the sacrifice reaches those whom it does reach, i.e., the demons, in some low region far beneath the densest clouds.

The Divine Nature then is neither wanting in anything nor is it fond of pleasure or gain or money, being of itself full and affording all things to every creature which is in need. Nor again is the Divine Nature propitiated by sacrifices or offerings or by glory and honour, nor is it allured by such things:

it shows itself to the virtuous alone, who would never betray justice either on account of threatened terrors or from a promise of greater gifts. Those however who have not observed the freedom of man's spirit and its unfettered action in respect to choice of life, chafe at what is done by unchastened injustice, and disbelieve in the existence of God. Like to them in opinion are they who, from their incontinence in pleasure, being involved both in cross accidents and pains out of the common course, and losing heart at their calamities, say that there is no God, or that, if he exists, he is not the overseer of all. Another class consists of those who are persuaded that the gods of common belief are to be propitiated with sacrifices and gifts, being accomplices, so to speak, in men's own wickednesses, and who are even unwilling to believe that he alone is the true God who is unchangeably the same in his just beneficence.

We are justified therefore in ascribing piety to the gnostic, whose care is first for himself and then for his neighbours with a view to our attaining the highest standard of excellence. For so the son tries to please a good father by showing himself virtuous and like his father, and likewise the subject to please a good ruler; since belief and obedience are in our own power. But the cause of evils one might find in the weakness of matter, and the random impulses of ignorance and the irrational forces to which we fall victims from our incapacity to learn; whereas the gnostic gets the better of these wild elements by his learning, and benefits all who are willing, to the best of his power, in imitation of the divine purpose for men. Should he ever be placed in authority, he will rule, like Moses, with a view to the salvation of his subjects, and will quell what is savage and faithless by showing honour to the best, and by punishing the bad, punishment that is rightly classed under the head of education. For above all things, the soul of the just man is an image divine, made like to God himself, seeing that in it is enshrined and consecrated, by means of obedience to his commands, the Ruler of all mortals and immortals, the King and Parent of all that is noble, who is indeed Law and Ordinance and Eternal Word, the one Saviour both for each individually and for all in common. He is in truth the Only-begotten, the express image of the glory of the universal King and almighty Father, stamping on the mind of the gnostic the perfect vision after his own image; so that the divine image is now beheld in a third embodiment, assimilated as far as possible to the Second Cause, to him, namely, who is the Life indeed, owing to whom we live the true life, copying the example of him who is made to us knowledge, while we converse with the things which are stable and altogether unchangeable.

Being ruler therefore of himself and of all that belongs to him the gnostic makes a genuine approach to truth, having a firm hold of divine science. For the name science would fitly be given to the knowledge and firm hold of intellectual objects. Its function in regard to divine things is to investigate what is the First Cause and what that through which all things were made and without which nothing has been made, what are the things that hold the universe together partly as pervading it and partly as encompassing it, some in combination and some apart, and what is the position of each of these, and the capacity and the service contributed by each: and again in things concerning man, to investigate what he himself is, and what is in accordance with, or is opposed to his nature; how it becomes him to act and be acted on, and what are his virtues and vices, and about things good and evil and the intermediates, and all that has to do with manhood and prudence and temperance, and the supreme all-perfect virtue, justice. Prudence and justice he employs for the acquisition of wisdom, and manhood not only in enduring misfortunes, but also in controlling pleasure and desire and pain and anger, and generally in withstanding all that sways the soul either by force or guile. For we must not endure vices and things that are evil, but must cast them off, and reserve endurance for things that cause fear. At any rate even suffering is found to be useful alike in medicine and in education and in punishment, and by means of it characters are improved for the benefit of mankind.

Forms of manhood are fortitude, high-spirit, magnanimity, generosity, magnificence. It is owing to this that the gnostic takes no notice either of blame or of ill-repute from the world, nor is he in subjection to good opinions or flatteries of others. In the endurance of labours he shows himself amongst other men as a man indeed, being always occupied in some good work at the same time that he is manfully surmounting difficulties of every kind. Again he is temperate owing to his abiding good sense combined with tranquillity of soul; his readiness to take to himself the promises as his own being in proportion to his shrinking from base things as alien. He is a citizen of the world, and not of this world only, but of a higher order, doing all things in order and degree, and never misbehaving in any respect. Rich he is in the highest degree because he covets nothing, having few wants and enjoying a super-abundance of every good, owing to his knowledge of the absolute Good. The first effect of his justice is that he loves to be with those of kindred spirit, and to commune with them, both on earth and in heaven.

For this reason also he is ready to impart to others of all that he possesses: and being a lover of men he has a profound hatred of the wicked through his abhorrence of every kind of evil doing, having learnt that one should be faithful both to oneself and to one's neighbours, as well as obedient to the commandments. For he who is willingly led on by the commandments may be called God's servant; but he who is already pure in heart, not because of the commandments, but for the sake of knowledge by itself—that man is a friend of God. For neither are we born virtuous, nor is virtue a natural after-growth, as are some parts of the body (for then it would have been no longer voluntary or praiseworthy); nor yet is it acquired and perfected, as speech is, from the intercourse of those who live with us (for it is rather vice which originates in this way). Nor again is knowledge derived from any art connected with the supplies of life or the service of the body, nor yet from the ordinary course of instruction: for we might be well satisfied if this could but prepare and sharpen the soul. The laws of the state, it is true, might perhaps be able to restrain evil practices. Again, mere persuasive arguments are too superficial in their nature to establish the truth on scientific grounds, but Greek philosophy does, as it were, provide for the soul the preliminary cleansing and training required for the reception of the faith, on which foundation the truth builds up the edifice of knowledge.

Here it is we find the true wrestler, who in the amphitheatre of this fair universe is crowned for the true victory over all his passions. For the president is God Almighty, and the umpire is the only-begotten Son of God, and the spectators are angels and gods, and our great contest of all arms is not waged against flesh and blood, but against the spiritual powers of passionate affections working in the flesh. When he has come safe out of these mighty conflicts, and overthrown the tempter in the combats to which he has challenged us, the Christian soldier wins immortality. For the decision of God is unerring in regard to his most righteous award. The spectators then have been summoned to view the contest; the wrestlers are contending in the arena, and now the prize is won by him amongst them, who has been obedient to the orders of the trainer. For the conditions laid down by God are equal for all, and no blame can attach to him; but he who is able will choose, and he who wills prevails. It is on this account also that we have received the gift of reason, in order that we may know what we do. And the maxim "Know thyself" means in this case, to know for what purpose we are made. Now we are made to be obedient to the commandments, if our choice be such as to will salvation. This, I think, is the real *Adrasteia,* owing to which we cannot escape from God.

Man's work then is submission to God, who has made known a manifold salvation by means of commandments, and man's acknowledgment thereof is God's good-pleasure. For the benefactor is the first to begin the kindness, and he who accepts it heartily, keeping due reckoning, and observes the commandments—such an one is faithful; but he who goes on to return the kindness to the best of his power by means of love, rises to the dignity of friend. And the one most appropriate return from man is to do those things which are pleasing to God. Accordingly the Master and Saviour accepts as a favour and honour to himself all that is done for the help and improvement of men, as being his own creation and in a certain respect an effect akin to its Cause; just as he accepts the wrongs done to those who have believed upon him, regarding such wrongs as instances of ingratitude and dishonour to himself. For what other dishonour poet Philemon. "When I behold," says he, "a slave on the watch to see who sneezes, or who speaks, or who comes out of his house, I offer him at once to the first bidder. It is to himself that each of us walks and speaks and sneezes, and not to all the city. Things happen as 'tis their nature to." And then we find them praying for health when sober, but bringing on diseases by cramming and drinking themselves drunk at the festivals. Many too have a superstitious fear of the mottoes that are written up.

It was a witty remark of Diogenes, when he found the house of a man of bad character bearing the inscription, "Here dwells the victorious Heracles: let no wickedness enter": "How then," said he, "is the master of the house to enter?" And the same people worship every stock and every shining stone, as the phrase is, and are in awe of red wool and grains of salt and torches and squills and brimstone, being bewitched by the sorcerers according to certain impure purifications. But the true God regards nothing as holy but the character of the just man, nothing as polluted but what is unjust and wicked. At any rate you may see the eggs, which have been removed from the body of those who have undergone purification, hatched by warmth, and this could not have happened, if they had contracted the ills of the person purified. And so the comic poet Diphilus pleasantly satirizes the sorcerers in these words: "He purifies the daughters of Proetus with their father, the son of Abas, and an old crone besides to make up five—so many mortals with a single torch, a single squill, and brimstone and asphaltus of the boisterous surge, gathered from the deep pools of the soft-flowing ocean. But, O blessed Air, send Anticyra from heaven that I may change this bug to a stingless drone."

Menander too says well, "If you were suffering from any real evil, Pheidias, you ought to have sought a real remedy for it. But as that is not so, I have devised a remedy as imaginary as the evil: simply imagine that it does you some good. Let the women rub you down and fumigate thoroughly: then sprinkle yourself with water from three springs, throwing in salt and beans." Every one is pure whose conscience is free from guilt. So in the tragedy we read:

"Orestes, say, what canker saps thy life?
Conscience, which tells me of a dark deed wrought."

For indeed purity is no other than the abstaining from sin. Well therefore says Epicharmus, "If your mind is pure your whole body is pure too." Certainly it is our rule to begin by cleansing our souls from bad and wicked opinions by means of right reason, and then, after that, to turn to the mention of the more excellent principles; for so too, in the case of those who are about to be initiated, it is thought right to apply certain purifications before the communication of the mysteries, on the ground that the godless opinion must be got rid of before they are ready to have the truth communicated to them.

CHAPTER V

Surely it cannot be denied that we are following right and truth when we refuse to circumscribe in a given place him who is incomprehensible, and to confine in temples made with hands that which contains all things. And what work of builders and masons and of mechanic art could be called holy? Were not they more in the right who held that the air and the circumambient ether, or rather the whole world and the universe itself, were worthy of the divine dignity? It would indeed be ridiculous, as the philosophers themselves say, that man being but a toy of God should make God, and that God should come into being through the play of human art. For that which is produced resembles, and is indeed the same as, that from which it is produced: thus, what is made of ivory is ivory, and what is made of gold is golden; and in like manner statues and temples executed by the hands of mechanics, being composed of lifeless matter, must themselves also be lifeless and material and profane; and even though you should carry your art to perfection, they still retain something of the mechanical. This being so, we cannot regard works of art as sacred and divine.

Again, among the heathen enshrinement is supposed to be essential to deity. But what is it which could be localized in a shrine, if there is nothing unlocalized to start with (on the assumption that all things are in space)? And further, that itself, when it becomes an altar closely connected with the precious smoke. Hesiod somewhere says that: "Zeus, being outwitted in some division of the flesh of the sacrifice by Prometheus, chose the white bones of the ox craftily concealed in the glistening lard: and from that time the tribes of men on earth burn to the immortals white bones on fragrant altars." Still they altogether deny that God's partaking of nourishment could be explained by the craving which grows out of want. Accordingly they must suppose him nourished without appetite like plants or hibernating bears. At all events they say that these are not impeded in their growth, whether it be that they are nourished from the density of the air, or even from the exhalation arising from their own body. And yet, if they hold that the Deity is nourished without needing it, what is the use of nourishment to one who needs it not? But if the Deity, being by nature exempt from all need, rejoices to be honoured, we have good reason for honouring God by prayer, and for sending up most rightly this sacrifice, the best and holiest of sacrifices when joined with righteousness, venerating him through whom we receive our knowledge, and through him glorifying him (i.e., the Father) whom we have learnt to know. At any rate our altar here on earth is the congregation of those who are devoted to the prayers, having, as it were, one common voice and one mind.

As to the kinds of nutrition received through the sense of smell, though they may be less unworthy of the deity than those received through the mouth, still they witness to respiration. What then is the worshippers' idea as to the breathing of God? Is it by means of transpiration as in the demons? or by inspiration only, as in fishes through the dilatation of their gills? or by circumspiration, as in insects, through the pressure of the membranes on the waist? No, they would not liken God to any of these, if they were in their senses. But as for creatures that live by respiration, they draw in the air by rhythmic beats corresponding to the counter-dilatation of the lungs against the chest. Then if they assign viscera and arteries and veins and sinews and members to God, they will exhibit him as in no respect differing from man. The word "conspiration" is that which is properly used of the Church. For the Church's sacrifice is indeed speech rising, like incense, from holy souls, while every thought of the heart is laid open to God along with the sacrifice. They are fond of talking about the purity of the most ancient altar at Delos, that altar which, we are told, was the only one approached by Pythagoras, because it was unpolluted by slaughter and death: will they then refuse credence to us when we say that the truly hallowed altar is the righteous soul, and the incense which ascends from it, the prayer of holiness? Sacrifices, I believe, are an invention of mankind to excuse the eating of flesh, though, even apart from such idolatry, it was always possible for one who wished it to partake of flesh. The Mosaic sacrifices symbolize Christian piety; for instance the dove and the pigeon offered for sins show that the purging away of the irrational part of the soul is acceptable to God. But if any of the righteous refuses to weigh down his soul by the eating of flesh, he does this on some reasonable ground, not as Pythagoras and his school from some dream as to the transmigration of souls. Xenocrates in a special treatise on animal food and Polemon in his book on Life according to Nature, seem to lay it down clearly that a flesh diet is inexpedient, as it has already passed through a process of digestion and been thus assimilated to the souls of irrational creatures.

On this ground especially the Jews abstain from swine's flesh, considering that this animal is unclean because it roots up and destroys the fruits more than any other. But if it is argued that the animals have been given to men, we too agree in this, only we say that they are not given entirely, nor indeed all, for the purpose of eating, but only those that do no work. Wherefore the comic poet Plato in his play *The Feasts* well says: "Hereafter 'twere well to kill no beast but swine, for they are excellent eating, and we get nothing out of them but bristles and mire and squealing." Hence it was well said by Aesop that "the reason why pigs make such an outcry when they are being dragged away is because they are conscious that they are good for nothing but to be sacrificed." And so Cleanthes says that in them the soul takes the place of salt to prevent the flesh from putrefying. Some then eat it because it is useless, and others because it injures the fruits; while others again abstain from eating it because of its immoderate salacity. For the same could affect God? Wherefore it is impossible for so great a gift to make a return in full, corresponding to the benefit received from God, as measured by the worth of salvation. But, as they who injure the cattle put a slight on the owners, and those who injure the soldiers put a slight on their captain, so it shows disrespect for the Lord, when injury is done to those who are devoted to him. For as the sun not only lights up the heaven and the whole world, shining on land and sea alike, but also darts his rays through windows and every little cranny into the innermost chambers, so the Word being shed abroad in all directions observes even the minutest details of our actions.

CHAPTER IV

But the Greeks assume their gods to be human in passions as they are human in shape; and, as each nation paints their shape after its own likeness (according to the saying of Xenophanes, the Ethiopians black with turned up nose, the Thracians with red hair and blue eyes), so each represents them as like itself in soul. For instance, the barbarians make them brutal and savage, the Greeks milder, but subject to passion. Hence the conceptions which the wicked form about God must naturally be bad, and those of the good must be excellent. And on this account he who is a gnostic and truly royal in soul is both devout and free from superstition, persuaded that the only God is alone meet to be honoured and reverenced, alone glorious and beneficent, abounding in well-doing, the author of all good and of nothing that is evil. As for the superstitions of the Greeks I think sufficient evidence has been adduced in my discourse entitled *Protrepticus,* where the necessary investigation is given at great length.

What need is there then "the tale once clearly told to tell again"? But as we are on this topic it will be enough just to give a small sample for proof, with a view to show that those are atheists who liken the Divinity to the worst of men. For either they make the gods injured by men, which would show them to be inferior to man as being capable of receiving injury from him; or, if this is not so, how is it that they are embittered at what is no injury, like an old shrew losing her temper, as they say Artemis was wroth with the Aetolians on account of Oeneus?

Being a goddess, how did she fail to reflect that it was not from contempt for her, but either from forgetfulness, or because he had previously sacrificed, that he neglected her worship? Again, Augé, in pleading against Athena, because she was wroth with her for having given birth to a child in her temple, well says:

> Spoils of dead mortals thou delight'st to see
> And corpses strewn: these thou dost not abhor:
> But this new birth thou deem'st a sacrilege.

And yet no fault is found with other animals when they bring forth in the temples.

In their dealings therefore with beings who are so quick to wrath men naturally become superstitious, and think that whatever happens is a sign and cause of evil. "If a mouse digs through an altar of clay or gnaws through a sack for want of something better, or if a cock that is being fattened begins to crow in the evening, they take it as a portent of something." Menander ridicules a fellow of this stamp in his play entitled *The Superstitious Man*. "Heaven send me good luck! In putting on my right shoe I broke the thong. Of course you did, you noodle, because it was worn out, and you were too miserly to buy a new pair." That was a pleasant saying of Antiphon's, when one made an omen of a sow's devouring her young: seeing that the sow was a mere skeleton from her owner's niggardliness, "Well for you," said he, "that the omen did not take the form of her devouring your own children in her hunger." And, "What wonder is it," says Bion, "if the mouse, finding nothing to eat, gnawed through the sack? The wonder would have been if, as Arcesilaus jestingly retorted, the sack had eaten the mouse."

Excellent too was the reply of Diogenes to him who marvelled because he found the snake coiled round the pestle. "Marvel not," said he, "for it would have been far more surprising if you had seen the snake erect and the pestle coiled up round it." For the irrational animals too have to run and eat and fight and breed and die; and these things being according to nature for them can never be unnatural for us. "Moreover many birds beneath the sunlight range," from which omens may be derived. Follies of this sort are caricatured by the comic which is enshrined has received enshrinement from something else, being itself previously unenshrined. If then God has received enshrinement from men, he was previously unenshrined and therefore non-existent. For by the hypothesis it is only the non-existent which was unenshrined, seeing that it is always the non-existent which undergoes the process of localization by enshrinement. And that which exists could not be localized by that which is non-existent, nor yet by anything else that exists: for it is itself also in existence and therefore already localized in common with all other existing things. It remains therefore that it must be enshrined by itself. But how is a thing to beget itself? Or how is the self-existent to localize itself in a shrine? Was it formerly unlocalized and did it afterwards localize itself? No, in that case it could not even have existed, since it is the non-existent which is unlocalized. And how could that which is supposed to have been localized make itself subsequently what it already was? Or that to which all existing things belong, the self-existent Deity, be itself in need of anything?

Again, if the Deity is in human shape, he will need the same things as man needs, food and covering and a house and all things belonging to them. For beings of like form and like passions will require the same kind of life. And if the word "holy" is taken in two senses, as applied to God himself and also to the building raised in his honour, surely we should be right in giving to the Church, which was instituted to the honour of God in accordance with sanctified wisdom, the name of a holy temple of God, that precious temple built by no mechanic art, no, nor embellished by any common vagabond, but made into a shrine by the will of God himself. I use the name Church now not of the place, but of the congregation of saints. This is the shrine which is best fitted for the reception of the greatness of the dignity of God. For to him who is all-worthy, or rather in comparison with whom all else is worthless, there is consecrated that creature which is of great worth owing to its pre-eminent holiness. And such would be the gnostic, who is of great worth and precious in the sight of God, he in whom God is enshrined, i.e., in whom the knowledge of God is consecrated. Here too we should find the likeness, the divine and sanctified image—here in the righteous soul, after it has been itself blessed, as having been already purified and now performing blessed deeds. Here we find both that which is enshrined and that which is in process of enshrinement, the former in the case of those who are already gnostics, the latter in those who are capable of becoming so, though they may not yet be worthy to receive the knowledge of God. For all that is destined to believe is already faithful in the eye of God and consecrated to honour, an image of virtue dedicated to God.

CHAPTER VI

As then God is not circumscribed in place, nor made like to the form of any creature, so neither is he of like passions, nor lacks he anything after the manner of created things, so as from hunger to desire sacrifices for food. Things that are capable of suffering are all mortal; and it is useless to offer meat to that which is in no need of sustenance. The famous comic poet Pherecrates in his *Deserters* wittily represents the gods themselves as finding fault with men for their offerings. "When you sacrifice to the gods, first of all you set apart what is customary for the priests first among you, and then—shame to say—do you not pick the thigh-bones clean to the groin and leave the hip-joint absolutely bare, assigning to us gods nothing but the dogs' portion, a back-bone polished as with a file, which you then cover with thick layers of sacrificial meal to save appearances?" And another comic poet, Eubulus, writes as follows about the sacrifices: "To the gods themselves you offer nothing but the tail and the thigh, as though they were en-amoured of these." And, where he brings on Dionysus in his *Semele,* he represents him as distinguishing: "First of all, when any sacrifice to me, they sacrifice blood and bladder—don't mention heart or caul—the gall and thigh-bones are no food for me." And Menander has written of "the scrag end of the rump, the gall and dry bones, which," says he, "they set before the gods, while they consume the rest themselves." Why, the smoke of burnt sacrifices is intolerable even to the beasts. If, however, this smoke is really the meed of the gods of Greece, no time should be lost in deifying the cooks also (since they are deemed worthy of the same happiness) and in worshipping the stove reason the law never requires the sacrifice of a goat except with a view to banishing evils, since pleasure is the fountainhead of vice. Further, they tell us that the eating of goats' flesh conduces to epilepsy. And they say that the largest amount of nutriment is supplied from pork, for which reason it is of use to those who practise bodily training, but, owing to the sluggishness produced by eating flesh, it is of no use to those who try to encourage the growth of the soul. A gnostic might therefore abstain from flesh, both for the sake of discipline and to weaken the sexual appetite. For, as Androcydes says, "wine and fleshly gorging make the body strong, but the soul more sluggish." Such a diet does not tend to precision of thought. Wherefore also the Egyptians in their purifications forbid their priests to eat flesh, and they themselves live on fowl as the lightest diet and abstain from fish for various fanciful reasons and especially from the idea that such food makes the flesh flabby. Besides this, the life of beasts and birds is supported by breathing the same air as our souls, their soul being akin to the air; but we are told that fishes do not even breathe our air, but that air which was infused into water, as into the other elements, on its first creation, which is also a proof of the fact that air pervades all matter.

"It is not then expensive sacrifices that we should offer to God, but such sacrifices as are dear to him," viz., that composite incense of which the Law speaks, an incense compounded of many tongues and voices in the way of prayer, or rather which is being wrought into the unity of the faith out of divers nations and dispositions by the divine bounty shown in the Covenants, and which is brought together in our songs of praise by purity of heart and righteous and upright living grounded in holy actions and righteous prayer. For (to add the charm of poetry) "what man is there so unwise and beyond measure credulous as to expect that, at the burning of bare bones and gall, which even hungry dogs would refuse, the gods would all rejoice, and accept this as their due meed"; aye, and would show their gratitude to the celebrants, though they might be pirates or robbers or tyrants? The Christian teaching is that the fire sanctifies, not flesh or sacrifice, but sinful souls, understanding by fire not the all-devouring flame of common life, but the discerning flame which pierces through the soul that walks through fire.

Origen
185-253

Origen is one of the most fascinating personalities of early Christianity. His intellectual abilities and accomplishments are astounding; his apostolic zeal knew no bounds. He received an excellent education in the city of his birth, Alexandria. By the age of eighteen he was the head of that city's catechetical school. Throughout his lifetime he journeyed widely, to places such as Rome, Arabia, Cappadocia, Palestine. Wherever he went, his objective was to clarify and communicate his understanding of the Word of God.

It is difficult to say what stands out as Origen's greatest contribution to the Christian tradition. He is best known for his scholarly work in Scripture, his theological writings and his wide use of philosophy, particularly Platonism, to develop Christian doctrine. Sustaining and enriching both his biblical scholarship and his theological speculation was a life of prayer. Origen was an unusually devout Christian. He spent his life seeking the unknowable depths of the love of God. His insatiable drive, anchored in prayer, to penetrate the divine mystery gave direction to his intellectual and apostolic life. It also enabled him, a few years before his death, to withstand brutal torture for the name of Christ during the persecution of Emperor Decius.

Origen clearly influenced the development of Christian spirituality. His commentaries on various books of Scripture are filled with spiritual theology. Given the Platonism that he accepted and used, it was natural for Origen to see the human as a being moving steadily toward fullness of knowledge in God. It is by intellect that man can become one with God. Spiritual growth and perfection are proportionate to man's degree of knowledge of God.

Yet Origen counterbalanced his tremendous emphasis on the intellect as the most important human faculty with the conviction that prayer plays a vital role in shaping the Christian's life. He seemed to sense that the intellectual life and prayer life are interrelated processes, neither of which can function nor mature without the other, that radically they are one in the life of the Christian.

The treatise On Prayer, from which we have taken the following passage, fits into Origen's theory of spirituality. It was written for the beginner in the devotional life, to serve as a kind of practical guide to prayer. Immediately, Origen insists that knowledge of the great things of existence and true wisdom are beyond man's capacities. They require the grace of God, poured out upon mankind through Jesus Christ and the Holy Spirit. Origen moves on to discuss the power of prayers, various problems that may arise and their resolution, the divisions of prayer, the proper disposition, posture, place and time. Central to the work is a commentary on the Lord's Prayer. By way of this treatise Origen set a tremendous ideal before the reader, viz., through a simple life of prayer to reach out beyond the ordinary cares and needs of life and to seek the great things, such as God's presence in time and the accomplishment of the divine will. Then one's needs will be taken care of. Such prayer requires fixed attention on God and a spirit of forgiveness. The simplicity of all of this is disarming. It also reveals the secret of Origen, a man who touched people not only by his brilliant intellect but also by his Christian love.

COMMENTARY ON
THE LORD'S PRAYER

CHAPTERS XVIII – XXVI

E nough has been said by us in the foregoing examination of the problem of prayer, "according to the grace given," as we were able to receive it, by "God" through his Christ (and we trust also, in the Holy Spirit—which, if it be so, you who read this book will judge). Now we shall proceed to the next task: for we desire to consider the prayer outlined by the Lord, with what power it has been filled.

The texts of the Lord's Prayer (Chapter XVIII, 2, 3)

2. And first of all we must note that Matthew and Luke might seem to most people to have recorded the same prayer, providing a pattern of how we ought to pray. But the text of Matthew runs as follows: "Our Father which art in heaven, Hallowed be thy name. Thy Kingdom come. Thy will be done, as in heaven, so on earth. Give us this day our daily bread. And forgive us our debts, as we also have forgiven our debtors. And bring us not into temptation, but deliver us from the evil one." Luke's text, on the other hand, runs thus: "Father, Hallowed be thy name. Thy kingdom come. Give us day by day our daily bread. And forgive us our sins; for we ourselves also forgive every one that is indebted to us. And bring us not into temptation."

3. But we must reply to those who take this view, in the first place, that the words, although they have some resemblances, nevertheless appear to differ in other points, as our investigation of them will establish; and, in the second place, that it cannot be the same prayer which was spoken on "the mountain," to which "seeing the multitudes he went up," when, "having sat down, his disciples came unto him, and he opened his mouth and taught them" (for this prayer is found recorded in Matthew in the context of the recital of the Beati-

tudes and the commandments which follow), and that which, "as he was praying in a certain place, when he ceased," was spoken to "one of his disciples," who had asked to be "taught to pray, even as John also taught his disciples." For how can it be possible that the same words were spoken by themselves apart from any previous inquiry and also delivered at the request of a disciple? Perhaps, however, someone will say to this that the prayers are virtually the same and were spoken as one prayer, on one occasion in an extended address, and on another to one of the disciples who had made the request, probably because he was not present when the prayer recorded in Matthew was spoken, or because he had not retained what was said. Perhaps, however, it is better to take the view that the prayers are different, though they have some parts common. We searched also the Gospel of Mark, in case the record of something equivalent there should escape us, but we found no trace whatever of the prayer in it.

The Introduction to the Prayer in Matthew (Chapters XIX to XXI)

XIX, 1. Since, as we said above, he who prays must first be settled and disposed in a certain manner and then afterwards so pray, let us consider the words that were uttered by the Saviour on this subject before the prayer as it is given in Matthew. They are as follows: "When ye pray, ye shall not be as the hypocrites; for they love to stand and pray in the synagogues and in the corners of the streets, that they may be seen of men. Verily I say unto you, They have received their reward. But thou, when thou prayest, enter into thine inner chamber, and having shut thy door, pray to thy Father which is in secret, and thy Father which seeth in secret shall recompense thee. And in praying use not vain repetitions, as the Gentiles do: for they think that they shall be heard for their much speaking. Be not therefore like unto them: for your Father knoweth what things ye have need of, before ye ask him. After this manner, therefore pray ye."

2. Our Saviour in many places clearly ranks vainglory as a deadly passion: as he has done also here, when he deters us from acting at the time of prayer as hypocrites do. For it is to act the hypocrite to wish to pride oneself before men for piety or

liberality. Those who remember the saying, "How can ye believe, which receive glory of" men, "and the glory that cometh from the only God ye seek not?" must despise all glory from men, even though it be reckoned to have been given for a good cause, and must seek the true glory that is properly so-called, which comes from him alone who glorifies him who is worthy of glory in a manner fitting to himself and beyond the deserts of the recipient of glory. And that which would be reckoned as good in itself, and is reckoned to be praiseworthy, is sullied when we do it that we "may have glory of men," or "that" we "may be seen of men": therefore no recompense from God follows us for this. For every word of Jesus is true; and, if one may use a forced expression, is truer, when it is spoken with his accustomed oath. He says of those who for the sake of vainglory seem to do good to their neighbour or "pray in the synagogues and the corners of the streets, that they may be seen of men," the same thing: "Verily I say unto you, They have received their reward." The "rich man," of whom Luke speaks, received as his reward "the good things in" his own mortal life, and because he had received these he was no longer able to obtain them after this present life. Similarly, he who "has received" his own "reward," either for giving something to someone or for his prayers, inasmuch as he did not "sow unto the Spirit," but "unto the flesh, shall reap corruption," but "shall" not "reap eternal life." Now that man "sows unto the flesh" who "in the synagogues and the streets, that he may have glory of men, doeth alms" with "a trumpet before" him, or he who "loves to stand and pray in the synagogues and corners of the streets, that" he "may be seen of men" and be reckoned as pious and holy by those who see him.

3. Moreover, everyone who travels along "the wide and broad way that leadeth to destruction," which has nothing clear or straight but is altogether full of twists and corners (for its straightness has been very much broken into curves), stands in it not otherwise than he who "prays in the corners of the streets," through love of pleasure frequenting not one but several streets, where are to be found those who are "dying like men" because they have fallen from their deity: who praise and count happy those in the streets who are wont to commit iniquity in their

company. And at all times there are many who in their praying are manifestly "lovers of pleasure rather than lovers of God," in the midst of banquets and at carousals behaving drunkenly in prayer, truly "standing in the corners of the streets" and "praying." For everyone who lives according to pleasure, having loved "the broad" path, has fallen from "the narrow and straitened way" of Jesus Christ—a way with not the slightest bend and absolutely no corners at all.

XX, 1. If there is a difference between the Church and the synagogue (the Church properly so called "not having spot or wrinkle or any such thing," but "being holy and without blemish": into which neither he that is "born of fornication entereth," nor the "eunuch," nor an "emasculated" person, nor yet "an Egyptian" or "an Idumaean," save that "sons born to them" of "the third generation" may scarcely join "the assembly," nor yet the "Moabite" or "Ammonite," unless the tenth "generation" is fulfilled and "the age" is accomplished; the synagogue, on the other hand, being "built" by "a centurion," who did this in the times before the sojourn with us of Jesus, when as yet witness had not been borne to him that he had such "faith" as the Son of God "found not in Israel"), he who "loves to pray in the synagogues" is not far from "the corners of the streets." But the saint is not such a one: for he does not "love [φιλεῖ] to pray," but rather has a deep concern [ἀγαπᾷ] to do so, and not "in synagogues," but in churches, and not "in corners of streets," but in the straightness of "the narrow and straitened way"; nor yet again that he "may be seen of men," but that he "may appear before the Lord God." For he is a male person, perceiving "the acceptable year of the Lord," and keeping the commandment which says: "Three times in a year shall all thy males appear before the Lord thy God."

2. We must pay careful attention to "they may be seen," since "nothing that is seen is good," being in appearance, as it were, and not truly, deceiving the imagination and not forming a distinct or true image. The actors of a drama in the theatre are not what they say they are or what they appear to be in accordance with the character they assume. Similarly, those who simulate in appearance an impression of the good are not

32

righteous but are actors of righteousness, and are themselves acting in their own theatre, "the synagogues and the corners of the streets." But he who is not an actor, and on the contrary puts aside everything that is not his own, and prepares to delight himself in a place that is greater and far surpasses any of the theatres mentioned above, "enters into" his own "inner chamber, shutting" himself in upon the riches laid up in store, "the treasure of wisdom and knowledge." And never bending outside nor gaping at the things outside, he "shuts" every "door" of the faculties of sense, so that he may not be enticed by the impressions of sense and their image may not penetrate into his mind. Thus he prays to the Father, who does not flee from or abandon such a secret place, but rather "dwells" in it, his only begotten being also present with him. For, says he, "I and the Father will come unto him and make our abode with him." It is evident that if indeed we pray thus, we shall make intercession not only with the righteous God but also with the Father, as One who is not absent from his sons but is present in our secret place, and watches over it, and increases what is in "the inner chamber," if we "shut the door" of it.

XXI, 1. In praying, however, do "not" let "us use vain repetitions," but rather let us speak to God. Now we "use vain repetitions" when we fail to examine for blemishes either ourselves or the words of prayer we offer up, and so speak of corrupt deeds or words or thoughts, which are mean and blameworthy and alien from the incorruptibility of the Lord. Indeed, he who "uses vain repetitions" in "praying" is actually in a worse case than those who frequent "the synagogues," of whom we spoke above, and in a more grievous condition than they who stand "in the corners of the streets," since he does not preserve a trace of even a pretence of good. According to the text of the Gospel, they who alone "use vain repetitions" are "the Gentiles," who have no notion whatever of great and heavenly requests, but offer up every prayer for bodily and outward things. Therefore he who requests things of below from him who dwells in the heaven and above the highest heaven, even the Lord, is like unto a "Gentile using vain repetitions."

2. It seems indeed that he who speaks much "uses vain repetitions," and he who "uses vain repetitions" speaks much.

For no material or bodily thing is single: but every one of them, though reckoned single, is split up and cut in pieces and divided into several parts, having lost its unity. Virtue is one, vice is many; truth is one, falsehood is many; the wisdom of God is one, the wisdoms "of this world," and "of the rulers of this world, which are coming to nought," are many; the word of God is one, those who are estranged from God are many. Therefore no one "shall escape transgression for much speaking," and no one, though "thinking" that he "shall be heard for" his "much speaking," can be heard thereby. And so our prayers must not "be like unto" the "vain repetitions" or "much speaking" of "the Gentiles," or to whatever else they may do "after the likeness of the serpent." "For" the God of the saints, being a "Father, knoweth what things" his sons "have need of," since they are things worthy of the Father's knowledge. But if a man knows not God, and knows not the things of God, he knows not "what things" he "has need of": for the things which he thinks he "has need of" are entirely wrong. On the other hand, he who contemplates what higher and holier things he lacks, will attain to the objects of his contemplation, which are known by God and have been known to the Father or ever the request was made. Having said so much on the passage which precedes the prayer in the Gospel according to Matthew, let us now go on to see the meaning of the prayer itself.

OUR FATHER WHICH ART IN HEAVEN

(Chapters XXII and XXIII)

XXII, 1. *Our Father which art in heaven*. It is worth while examining with unusual care the Old Testament, as it is called, to see if it is possible to find anywhere in it a prayer in which someone calls God "Father." Though we searched to the best of our ability, up to the present we have found none. We do not mean that God is never called "Father," or that those who were wont to believe in God are never styled "sons of God," but that we have not yet succeeded in finding in a prayer that confident affirmation in styling God as "Father" which was made by the Saviour. That God is called "Father," and that those who have drawn nigh to the word of God are called "sons," may be seen

34

from many passages, as for example in Deuteronomy: "Thou hast forsaken the God who begat thee, And hast forgotten the God who nurtureth thee'; and again: "Is not he thy Father that hath bought thee, and hath made thee and established thee?"; and again: "Sons in whom is no faith"; and in Isaiah: "I have begotten and brought up sons, but they have rejected me"; and in Malachi: "A son will honour his father, and a servant his master: and if I am a father, where is mine honour? and if I am a master, where is my fear?"

2. Therefore, even though God is spoken of as "Father," and those begotten by the word of faith in him as "sons," it is not possible to find in the ancients at any rate a firm and unchangeable affirmation of sonship. For example, the passages we have quoted show that those called "sons" are blameworthy: since, according to the apostle, while "the heir is a child he differeth nothing from a bond-servant, though he is lord of all; but is under guardians and stewards until the term appointed of the father"; but "the fulness of the time" arrived at the sojourn of our Lord Jesus Christ, when those who desire it "receive the adoption of sons," as Paul teaches in the following words: "For ye received not the spirit of bondage unto fear; but ye received the spirit of adoption, whereby we cry, Abba, Father." And in the Gospel according to John: "But as many as received him, to them gave he the right to become children of God, even to them that believed on his name." And because of this "spirit of adoption," we learn in the general Epistle of John as concerning those "who are begotten of God" that "whosoever is begotten of God doeth no sin, because his seed abideth in him: and he cannot sin, because he is begotten of God."

3. Nevertheless, if we consider the meaning of the words "When ye pray, say, Father," as it is written in Luke, we shall hesitate if we are not true sons to address him by this title, lest perchance in addition to our sins we should incur the charge of impiety also. What I mean is something like this. Paul says in his former [epistle] to the Corinthians, "No man can say, Jesus is Lord, but in the Holy Spirit"; and "no man speaking in the Spirit of God saith, Jesus is anathema." He uses "Holy Spirit" and "Spirit of God" as synonymous terms. But what the meaning is of "saying in the Holy Spirit Jesus is Lord" is by no

means clear, for countless hypocrites and numbers of heretics use this title, and sometimes even demons when they are overcome by the power that is in the Name. No one will dare to maintain that any of these "says Jesus is Lord in the Holy Spirit." Nor could they even be shown to say "Jesus is Lord," since those only from the heart say, "Jesus is Lord," who while serving the word of God and while engaged in doing anything whatsoever call none other "Lord" save him. If it be such that say, "Jesus is Lord," it may be that everyone who anathematizes the divine Word in transgressing by his own actions cries out: "Jesus is anathema." Therefore, just as such a one says, "Jesus is Lord," and he of an opposite mind, "Jesus is anathema," so also, "whosoever is begotten of God" and "doeth no sin," through partaking of the "seed" of God, which turns him aside from every sin, says by his deeds: "Our Father which art in heaven," "the Spirit himself bearing witness with" their spirit, "that" they "are children of God," and his "heirs," and "joint-heirs with Christ," since suffering "with him" they have good hope to "be also glorified with him." And in order that such may not only half say, "Our Father," "the heart" also, which is the fountain and source of good works, in conjunction with the works "believeth unto righteousness," and in harmony with them "the mouth maketh confession unto salvation."

4. Every deed and word and thought of theirs, having been formed by "the only begotten Word" after his likeness, imitates "the image of the invisible God," and is "after the image of the Creator," who "maketh his sun to rise on the evil and the good, and sendeth rain on the just and the unjust," so that there is in them "the image of the heavenly," who is himself "the image of God." The saints, therefore, being "an image" of an image (that image being the Son), acquire an impression of sonship, becoming "conformed" not only "to the body of the glory" of Christ, but also to him who is "in the body." They become conformed to him who is in "the body of the glory," as they are "transformed by the renewing of the mind." If such persons in everything say, "Our Father which art in heaven," evidently "he that doeth sin," as John says in his general [epistle], "is of the devil; for the devil sinneth from the beginning." And as the "seed" of God, "remaining in him that

is begotten of God," becomes for him who has been conformed to "the only begotten Word" the cause that "he cannot sin," so in everyone "that doeth sin" the seed of "the devil" is present, and, so long as it is inherent in the soul, prevents him who has it from being able to perform right actions. But since "to this end was the Son of God manifested, that he might destroy the works of the devil," it is possible, by the dwelling in our soul of the Word of God, when "the works of the devil" have been "destroyed," for the evil seed implanted in us to be done away with, and for us "to become children of God."

5. Do not let us think that we are taught to say actual words at a certain fixed time of prayer. If we understand what has been said above in our discussion about "praying without ceasing," our whole life as we "pray without ceasing" shall say, "Our Father which art in heaven": its "citizenship" shall in no wise be on earth but in every way "in heaven," which is the "throne" of God; for the kingdom of heaven is seated in all those who "bear the image of the heavenly," and therefore are themselves heavenly.

XXIII, 1. But when "the Father" of the saints is said to be "in heaven," we are not to suppose that he is circumscribed in bodily fashion and dwells "in heaven"; otherwise, if the heaven contained him, God would be found less than, because contained by, the heaven: but we must believe that by the ineffable power of his Godhead all things are contained and held together by him. And, speaking generally, sayings which taken literally are supposed by simple folk to assert that God is in a place, must instead be understood in a manner that befit grand and spiritual conceptions of God. Such are the following in the [Gospel] according to John: "Now before the feast of the passover, Jesus knowing that his hour was come that he should depart out of this world unto the Father, having loved his own which were in the world, he loved them unto the end"; and, a little further on, "knowing that the Father had given all things into his hands, and that he came forth from God, and goeth unto God"; and later on, "Ye heard how I said to you, I go away, and I come unto you. If ye loved me, ye would have rejoiced, because I go unto the Father"; and again, later on, "But now I go unto him that sent me; and none of you asketh me, whither goest thou?"

If these words are to be taken in a local sense, it is obvious that we must do the same with: "Jesus answered and said unto them, If a man love me, he will keep my word: and my Father will love him, and we will come unto him, and make our abode with him."

2. These sayings do not conceive of a local departure of the Father and the Son to him who loves the word of Jesus, nor are they to be taken in a local sense. But the Word of God, condescending for our sakes and being "humbled," as concerning his own dignity, when he is among men, is said to "depart out of this world to the Father," in order that we also may behold him there in his perfection, returning again to his own "fulness," after the emptiness wherewith he "emptied himself" when he was with us: where also we, using him as our guide, being "made full," shall be delivered from all emptiness. Let the Word of God, therefore, depart to "him that sent him," quitting the world, and let him "go unto the Father." And as for that passage at the end of the Gospel according to John, "Touch me not; for I am not yet ascended unto the Father," let us seek to conceive of it in a mystical sense: the ascent of the Son "unto the Father," when conceived of by us with holy insight in a manner befitting Deity, is an ascent of the mind rather than of the body.

3. I think it necessary to consider carefully these sayings in connection with the words "Our Father which art in heaven," in order to remove a mean conception of God held by those who consider that he is locally "in heaven," and to prevent anyone from saying that God is in a place after the manner of a body (from which it follows that he is a body)—a tenet which leads to most impious opinions, namely, to suppose that he is divisible, material, corruptible. For every body is divisible, material, corruptible. Else, let them tell us that instead of indulging in vain imaginings they claim to conceive clearly how its nature can be other than material. Since, however, before the bodily sojourn of Christ many of the Scriptures seem to say that God was in a place after a bodily manner, it does not appear to me to be inappropriate to quote a few passages from them also, in order to take away all doubtfulness from those whose peculiarity it is, so far as they can, to confine God who is

over all in a small and limited space. And, first, in Genesis, Adam and Eve, he says, "heard the voice of the Lord God walking in the afternoon in the garden: and Adam and his wife hid themselves from the face of the Lord God in the midst of the trees of the garden." We shall ask those who are unwilling to enter into the treasures of the passage, and indeed do not even make a beginning by "knocking at" their "door," if they can maintain that the Lord God who "filleth heaven and earth," who (as they suppose) uses in bodily fashion "heaven" as his "throne" and "the earth" as "the footstool of his feet," is bounded by a place so small in comparison with the whole heaven and earth, that what they suppose is a bodily garden is not completely filled by God, but is so much larger than he, that it contains him as he "walks, a sound" being heard from the treading of his feet. And it is still more absurd, according to them, that Adam and Eve, in awe of God because of their transgression, should hide themselves "from the presence of the Lord God in the midst of the trees of the garden." For it is not even said that they so wished to hide themselves, but that in very truth "they were hidden." And how, according to them, can God ask Adam, saying, "Where art thou?"

4. We have treated these matters at length in our commentaries on Genesis. However, so that we may not now pass over in complete silence so important a problem, it will be sufficient to call to mind the saying of God in Deuteronomy: "I will dwell in them, and walk in them." His "walking" in the saints is of the same kind as his "walking" in the garden, every sinner hiding himself from the presence of God and avoiding his visitation and shunning open speech with him. So also "Cain went out from the presence of God, and dwelt in the land of Nod, on the east of Eden." As, therefore, he dwells in the saints, so also in heaven, whether in every saint "bearing the image of the heavenly," or in Christ, in whom are all the "lights" and "stars" of heaven "who are being saved," or else he dwells there because of the saints in heaven, in accordance with the saying: "Unto thee did I lift up mine eyes, who dwellest in the heaven." And the passage in Ecclesiastes, "Be not hasty to utter any thing before God: for God is in heaven above, and thou upon earth below," makes a deliberate distinction between those who

are still in "the body of humiliation," on the one hand, and the angels and holy powers who are uplifted by the aid of the Word, or Christ himself, on the other. For it is not inappropriate that he is properly the "throne" of the Father, allegorically called heaven, while his Church, given the name of "earth," is "the footstool of his feet."

5. So we have added from the Old Testament also a few sayings which are considered to show that God is in a place, in order that we may persuade the reader by every means "according to the power" given unto "us" to understand the divine Scripture in a loftier and more spiritual sense, whenever it seems to teach that God is in a place. And it was fitting to examine these passages in connection with the words: "Our Father which art in heaven"—words which separate the essence of God from all created things. For to those who do not partake [of his essence] there appertains a certain divine glory and power, and—so to speak—an effluence of his deity.

HALLOWED BE THY NAME

(Chapter XXIV)

XXIV, 1. "Hallowed be thy name." He who prays these words either shows that the object of his prayer has not been achieved, or else having attained it he asks that a result not permanent should be maintained. This is evident enough from the passage here, in which according to Matthew and Luke we are commanded to say, "Hallowed be thy name," as if the name of the Father were not yet hallowed. How, someone might say, can a man ask that the name of God be hallowed, as if it had not been hallowed? What is "the name" of the Father, and what is its hallowing? Let us consider these questions.

2. A "name," then, is a compendious appellation manifesting the individual quality of the being named. For example, Paul the apostle has a certain individual quality: a quality of soul, which makes it of a certain kind; a quality of mind, which makes him capable of contemplating certain kinds of things; a quality of body, which makes it of a certain kind. The individuality of these qualities, which is incommunicable to another (for no being is exactly similar to Paul), is indicated by the name

"Paul." But in the case of men, since their individual qualities, as it were, alter, their names also according to Scripture alter suitably; when the quality of Abram changed, he was called Abraham; and when Simon's, he was named Peter; and when Saul's, the persecutor of Jesus, he was called Paul. In the case of God, however, who is in himself unchangeable, and remaining always unalterable, there is always one name, by which, as it were, he is called, the "I am" spoken of in Exodus, or something of similar import. Since, then, we all have some conception of God, and form some notions of whatever kind about him, but not all conceive what he is (for these are few, and, if I may say so, fewer than these few are those who comprehend his holiness in all things), we are rightly taught that the idea within us of God is holy, in order that we may see the holiness of him as he creates, foresees, judges, chooses, forsakes, receives, turns away from, deems worthy of honour, punishes each one according to his deserts.

3. In these and in similar expressions, if I may say so, the individual quality of God is characterized—what in my opinion is called the "name of God" in the Scriptures: in Exodus, "Thou shalt not take the name of the Lord thy God in vain"; in Deuteronomy, "Let my speech be waited for as the shower; let my words descend as the dew, as the rain upon the young grass and as the copious rain upon the herb: for I called upon the name of the Lord"; in Psalms, "They shall remember thy name in all generations." He who connects the idea of God with things that are not fitting "takes the name of the Lord God in vain," and he who is able to utter speech as the rain, which works together with them that hear for the fruitfulness of their souls, addressing words full of encouragement like dew, and by the power of edification bringing upon the hearers a most profitable shower of words or a most effectual and copious rain, can do these things because of the "name." Therefore, when a man perceives his need of God the perfecter, he calls by himself upon him who is truly the supplier of the above-mentioned blessings; and everyone who clearly sees also the things of God remembers rather than learns them, even though he may seem to hear them from some one or may think that he discovers the mysteries of godliness.

41

4. Even as he who prays ought to note what has been said here and ask that "the name" of God "be hallowed," so also it is said in Psalms, "Let us exalt his name together," the prophet commanding us in full accord with the same mind and the same opinion to haste unto the true and lofty knowledge of the distinctive being of God. For this is to "exalt the name" of God "together," when a man partaking of an effluence of deity "exalts" that very power of God and has conquered his foes, who are unable to exult over his fall. This is indicated in the twenty-ninth psalm by the words: "I will exalt thee, O Lord, because thou didst raise me up, and not make my foes to rejoice over me." And a man "exalts" God when he has dedicated for him a house within himself, as the title of the psalm has it: "A Psalm: A Song at the Dedication of the House"; A Psalm of "David."

5. Further, with regard to "Hallowed be thy name" and the words in the imperative mood that follow, it is to be said that the translators also frequently use the imperative instead of the optative mood, as for example in the Psalms: "Let the deceitful lips be dumb, which speak iniquity against the righteous man," instead of "may they be"; and "Let the extortioner seek out all that he hath, Let him have no helper," in the one hundred and eighth, concerning Judas. For the whole psalm is a request concerning Judas, that this and that may happen to him. But Tatian, failing to understand that "let there be" does not always indicate the optative, but sometimes the imperative, formed a most impious conception concerning him who said, "Let there be light," even God, as if he were praying rather than commanding that there should be light: "since," as he expresses his godless thought, "God was in darkness." To him we must say, how will he take the words: "Let the earth bring forth grass for pasture," and "Let the water under the heaven be gathered together," and "Let the waters bring forth creeping things, creatures that have life," and "Let the earth bring forth a living creature"? Does God really pray that "the water under the heaven" should "be gathered together into one meeting place" in order that he may stand upon a firm foundation? Or, does he pray "Let the earth bring forth" in order that he may partake of the things that are brought forth from the earth? What need

42

has he similar to the need for light on the part of creatures in the water and winged creatures or creatures on dry land, that he should also pray concerning these? But if, according to this author, it would be absurd to pray concerning these—the language used being in the imperative—may not a like thing be said about the saying "Let there be light," since it is not in the optative but in the imperative? I have thought it necessary, since the prayer is expressed in the imperative, to call to mind his various interpretations for the sake of those who have been deceived into accepting his impious teaching. Once upon a time we ourselves came in contact with these persons.

THY KINGDOM COME

(Chapter XXV)

XXV, 1. "Thy kingdom come." If "the kingdom of God," according to the word of our Lord and Saviour, "cometh not with observation: neither shall they say, Lo, here! or, Lo, there!" but "the kingdom of God is within us" ("for the word is very nigh, in" our "mouth, and in" our "heart"), it is evident that he who prays that "the kingdom" of God should come prays with good reason that the kingdom of God should spring up and bear fruit and be perfected in him. For every saint who takes God as his king and obeys the spiritual laws of God dwells in himself as in a well-ordered city, so to speak. Present with him are the Father and Christ who reigns with the Father in the soul that has been perfected, in accordance with the saying which I mentioned a short time ago: "we will come unto him, and make our abode with him." (And I think that by God's kingdom is meant the blessed state of the reason and the ordered condition of wise thoughts; while by Christ's kingdom is meant the words that go forth for the salvation of those who hear them and the works of righteousness and the other virtues which are being accomplished: for the Son of God is "Word" and "righteousness.") But every sinner is under the tyranny of "the prince of this world," since he does not hand himself over to him "who gave himself for" us sinners, "that he might deliver us out of this present evil world," and "deliver us out of" it "according to the will of our God and Father," as is stated in the [Epistle] to the Galatians. He who is under the tyranny of "the prince of this world" through deliberate sin is also ruled over by sin: therefore we are bidden by Paul no longer to submit ourselves to "sin" which desires to "reign" over us; and indeed we are commanded in these words: "Let not sin therefore reign in our mortal body, that we should obey the lusts thereof."

2. But some one will say with regard to these two petitions, that is to say, "Hallowed be thy name" and "Thy kingdom come," that if he who prays prays in order to be heard, and is in fact at some time heard, it is evident that, in accordance with what has been said above, "the name" of God will "be hallowed" at some time for some one, for whom also "the kingdom" of God will be present. But if these things come about for him, how shall he still fittingly pray concerning things that are present already as if they were not present, saying, "Hallowed be thy name; Thy kingdom come"? The reply to this must be as follows. He who prays to obtain "the word of knowledge" and "the word of wisdom" will always fittingly pray for these things, for he will always go on receiving more and more intuitions of "wisdom" and "knowledge" as his prayers are continually heard, howbeit he will "know in part" as much as he is able to receive in this present life; but "that which is perfect, doing away that which is in part, shall then be made manifest when, "face to face," the mind without sense perception comes in contact with spiritual realities. Similarly, "that which is perfect" in the "hallowing" of the "name" of God for each of us and in the coming of his "kingdom" cannot be, unless there "come" also "that which is perfect" as concerning "knowledge" and "wisdom," and, it may be, the other virtues also. And we go on our journey "unto perfection," if "stretching forward to the things which are before" we "forget the things which are behind." As we advance unceasingly "the kingdom of God" that is in us will reach its highest point, when that which was spoken by the apostle is fulfilled, that Christ, when all enemies "have been subjected unto him," shall "deliver up the kingdom to God, even the Father, that God may be all in all." Therefore, "praying without ceasing," with a disposition of the mind that is being deified by the Word, let us say to "our Father which is in heaven, Hallowed be thy name; Thy kingdom come."

3. Moreover, concerning "the kingdom" of God this distinction must also be made, that, as there is no "fellowship" between "righteousness and iniquity," and no "communion" between "light and darkness," nor any "concord" between "Christ and Beliar," so the kingdom of God cannot co-exist with the kingdom of evil. If therefore it is our will to be under the reign of God, "let not sin" in any wise "reign in" our "mortal body," neither let us obey its commandments, when it urges our soul to do "the works of the flesh" and things that are alien from God. Rather, "mortifying the members which are upon the earth," let us bring forth "the fruits of the Spirit," so that the "Lord" may "walk in" us as in a spiritual "garden," reigning alone over us with his Christ, "sitting" in us "at the right hand of" that spiritual "power" which we pray to receive, and seated "until" all his "enemies" within us become "the footstool of" his "feet," and "all rule and authority and power" is "abolished" from us. For it is possible that these things should come to pass for each of us, and that the "last enemy" should be "abolished, even death," so that in our case also it may be said by Christ, "O death, where is thy sting? O Hades, where is thy victory?" Even now therefore let our "corruptible put on" sanctification in holiness and all purity and "incorruption, and" let "the mortal" clothe itself, when "death" has been "abolished," with the Father's "immortality," so that we may be reigned over by God and even now share in the good things of "regeneration" and resurrection.

THY WILL BE DONE, AS IN HEAVEN, SO ON EARTH

(Chapter XXVI)

XXVI, 1. "Thy will be done, as in heaven, so on earth." Luke passes over these words in silence, and after "Thy kingdom come" places "Give us day by day our daily bread." Therefore let us examine the words cited above, as found in Matthew alone, agreeably with preceding context. Let us who pray, being still "on earth," and understanding that "the will" of God is "done in heaven" by all those who dwell in heaven, pray that "the will" of God may be "done" in all things by us also "on earth" even as it is by them: which things will come to pass if we do nothing contrary to his "will." But whenever "the will" of God is accomplished by us who are "on earth as it" in fact is "in heaven," we are made like unto those in heaven, inasmuch as we "bear" as they do "the image of the heavenly," and shall "inherit the kingdom" of heaven, while those who come after us "on earth" will pray to be made like unto us who are "in heaven."

2. But the words "as in heaven, so on earth," to be found in Matthew alone, can be taken with all three clauses, with the result that we are commanded thus to say in the prayer: "Hallowed be thy name, as in heaven, so on earth; Thy kingdom come, as in heaven, so on earth; Thy will be done, as in heaven, so on earth." For "the name" of God has been "hallowed" by those "in heaven," and "the kingdom" of God has come for them, and "the will" of God has been "done" in them: all these things are lacking to us who are "on earth," yet they can become ours as we make ourselves worthy to gain the hearing of God concerning them all.

3. But, with reference to "Thy will be done, as in heaven, so on earth," some one may ask as follows: How has "the will" of God been "done in heaven," where there are "the spiritual hosts of wickedness," whence it comes to pass that "the sword" of God shall be "filled with blood" even "in heaven"? If we pray that "the will" of God be "done on earth as" it is done "in heaven," perhaps we may without knowing it pray that these opposing forces may remain "on earth," to which they came from "heaven"; for there are many evil things "on earth" because of "the" victorious "spiritual hosts of wickedness" which are "in the heavenly places." Anyone, however, will easily resolve the question by allegorizing "heaven," and saying that it is Christ, and that the Church is "earth" (for who is so worthy to be "the throne of God" as Christ? and what is "the footstool of his feet" equally with the Church?); and that every member of the Church ought to pray that he may so achieve "the" Father's "will" as Christ achieved it, who came to "do the will" of his Father and "accomplished" it in its entirety. For it is possible by being "joined unto" him to become "one spirit" with him, in this way achieving "the will," in order that "as" it has been accomplished "in heaven," so it may also be ac-

complished "on earth." For, according to Paul, "he that is joined unto the Lord is one spirit." And I think that this interpretation will not be lightly dismissed by anyone who pays careful attention to it.

4. But an objector to it will quote the saying of the Lord after the resurrection to "the eleven disciples," to be found at the close of this Gospel: "All authority hath been given to me as in heaven so also on earth." For having "authority" over the things "in heaven," he says that there has been added authority "on earth," the things in heaven having been formerly enlightened by the Word, but at "the end of the world" the things "on earth" also will imitate the perfect state of the things "in heaven" over which the Saviour received "authority." Therefore, as it were, by means of prayer he wishes to take as his fellow workers before the Father those who are being "made disciples" by him, in order that he may bring the things "on earth" (in like manner as the things "in heaven" which have been subjected to truth and the Word), when they are emended by the "authority," which he received "as in heaven so" also "on earth," to the blessed end that awaits whatsoever has been placed under his authority. But he who maintains that the Saviour is "heaven" and the Church "earth," alleging that "the firstborn of all creation," on whom the Father rests as on a throne, is "heaven," would find that the "man" whom he put on, when he had fitted him for that power by having "humbled himself" and "becoming obedient unto death," said after the resurrection, "All authority hath been given unto me as in heaven so also on earth," the "man" as Saviour having received "authority" over the things "in heaven," as things that appertain to "the only begotten," in order that he may share them with him, being mingled with his deity and united with him.

5. It still remains to resolve the second difficulty put forward, namely, how "the will" of God is "in heaven," when there are "the spiritual hosts of wickedness in the heavenly places" wrestling against those "on earth." The question may be resolved in this way. It is not because of place but of choice that he who is still "on earth" has his "citizenship in heaven," "lays up treasure in heaven," has his heart "in heaven, bears the image of the heavenly," and "is" no longer "of the earth" nor

"of the world" below, but of heaven and of the heavenly world that is "better" than this one. Similarly, "the spiritual hosts of wickedness" that still reside "in the heavenly places," having their "citizenship on earth," and, by the evil designs wherewith they wrestle against men, "laying up treasure on earth," "bearing the image of the earthy," such as he who "was first formed by the Lord, having been made for the angels to play with," are not heavenly, nor do they dwell "in heaven" because of their evil disposition. When, therefore, it is said, "Thy will be done, as in heaven, so on earth," it is not to be reckoned that they are "in heaven," since they have fallen in mind with him who "fell from heaven" after the manner of "lightning."

6. And perhaps when our Saviour says that we ought to pray that "the will" of the Father be "done, as in heaven," so in like manner "on earth," he is not in any way bidding prayers to be made for those who are in a place "on earth," in order that they are to be made like unto those who are in a heavenly place; but his command to pray arises from his desire that all the things "on earth," that is to say, inferior things, suited to those of the earth, should be made like unto better things, that have their "citizenship in heaven," that is, to all things that have become "heaven." For he who sins, wheresoever he may be, is "earth," and, unless he repent, will be returning somehow to his kindred [earth]. But "he that doeth the will of God and does not disobey the saving spiritual laws is "heaven." If, therefore, we are still "earth" because of sin, let us pray that the "will" of God may extend to us also for our correction, in like manner as it reached those before us who became "heaven" or were "heaven." And if we are reckoned by God not as "earth" but as already "heaven," let us make our request that the "will" of God may be fulfilled "on earth" (I mean, persons of bad character) in like manner as it is "in heaven," for the heaven-making (if I may use the expression) of earth, so that there may no longer be any "earth," but all things may become "heaven." For if, according to this interpretation, the "will" of God is so "done on earth as in heaven," the earth will not remain earth. To take a clearer example. If the "will" of God were to be "done" for the licentious as it had been "done" for the temperate, the licentious will be temperate; or, if the "will" of God is

"done on earth as in heaven," we shall all be "heaven": for "the flesh," which does "not profit," "and blood," which is akin to it, "cannot inherit the kingdom of God," but they would be said to inherit it, were they to change from flesh and earth and dust and blood to the heavenly substance.

St. Cyprian
200-258

St. Cyprian, bishop of Carthage, ended his active career as a martyr during the Valerian Persecution. Exactly when he was born is not known. He was converted to Christianity in 246 and only three years later was the bishop of Carthage. His excellent education, his public speaking talents and his strong leadership abilities contributed to the rapidity with which he rose to such an important position in the church. Cyprian guided his people through the Decian Persecution (250-251). There were times when his outspokenness led to serious tensions between himself and the bishop of Rome. After contributing his talents so generously to the development of the early Church, he went to his death, in imitation of the Word of God, in silence. His great worth was quickly recognized and honored, for his name was listed among the martyrs specifically mentioned in the liturgical canon.

Cyprian is best known for his concept of the Church. He was convinced of the basic unity of the Church and applied this conviction at various levels, viz., the city of Carthage, the region of Africa and the Church universal. There could be but one faith and one charity, and all members were held together in the Holy Spirit. Episcopal collegiality was essential to the living out of church unity. All members of the church, through baptism and the other sacraments, were one in Christ and were called to live out that unity in their daily lives.

Knowing the demands of the Christian commitment, the pressures under which a believer had to live, and the constant temptation to give up and abandon life in Christ, Cyprian exhorted his people to persevere in the way that they had undertaken. The Good of Patience reveals his awareness of the difficulties facing the Christian in the third century and the energy with which he addressed these difficulties. Patience is essential to the Christian life. God Himself, the Source, Origin and Author of patience, manifests this virtue by putting up with the evils and impiety of mankind. Throughout the pre-Christian era, numerous patriarchs, prophets and holy men witnessed to the importance of patience in their efforts to lead the people of God and to communicate His message to them. Christ, above all, taught the value and necessity of patience by both word and example. His passion manifested full and perfect patience. Without patience faith and hope can never reach fruition; without patience charity cannot last. Patience sustains the believer in the face of wickedness and saves us for the good.

The entire treatise is presented here. The major source of inspiration for Cyprian is obviously sacred scripture. Christ appears as perfect example and model, as well as the promise of fulfillment for those who await his coming in patience. The treatise is an exhortation to persons who had committed their lives to Christ to be faithful to that commitment in the face of trials and persecution. Patience, for Cyprian, is the endurance, the long-suffering, the strength by which the Christian perfects across a lifetime the union with Christ that was initiated by baptism.

THE GOOD OF PATIENCE

CHAPTER 1

In speaking of patience, beloved brethren, and in preaching on its benefits and advantages, how can I better begin than by pointing out the fact that now, just for you to listen to me, I see that patience is necessary, as you could not even do this, namely, listen and learn, without patience. For only then is the word of God and way of salvation effectively learned, if one listens with patience to what is being said. Nor do I find, beloved brethren, among all the ways of heavenly discipline whereby we Christians are directed to seek the God-given rewards of our hope and faith, any other thing that is preferable, whether as more useful for life or more significant in attaining glory, than that we who are subject to the precepts of the Lord with an obedient fear and devotion should maintain patience especially and with extreme care.

CHAPTER 2

Philosophers also declare that they pursue this virtue, but their patience is as false as is their wisdom, for how can anyone be either wise or patient unless he knows the wisdom and patience of God? For He Himself warns and states concerning those who think that they are wise in this world: 'I will destroy the wisdom of the wise and the prudence of the prudent I will reject.' Likewise the blessed Apostle Paul, filled with the Holy Spirit and sent to call and to form the Gentiles in the faith, declares and teaches, saying: 'See to it that no one ravages you by philosophy and vain deceit, according to human traditions, according to the elements of the world and not according to Christ, for in Him dwells all the fullness of the Godhead.' And in another place he says: 'Let no one deceive himself. If anyone of you thinks he is wise, let him become foolish in the eyes of this world that he may become wise, for the wisdom of this world is foolishness in

God's sight. For it is written: I will catch the wise in their craftiness, and again: God knows the thoughts of the wise that they are foolish.' Therefore, if their wisdom is not true, their patience cannot be true either. For if that man who is humble and meek is patient, and yet we see that the philosophers are not humble or meek, but very pleasing to themselves, and displeasing to God by the very fact that they are pleasing to themselves, it is evident that patience is not found where there is the arrogant boldness of an affected freedom and the shameless boasting of the proud and half-naked breast.

CHAPTER 3

We, however, beloved brethren, are philosophers not in words but in deeds; we exhibit our wisdom not by our dress, but by truth; we know virtues by their practice rather than through boasting of them; we do not speak great things but we live them. Therefore, as servants and worshipers of God, let us show by spiritual homage the patience that we learn from heavenly teachings. For that virtue we have in common with God. In Him patience has its beginning, and from Him as its source it takes its splendor and dignity. The origin and greatness of patience proceeds from God its Author. The quality that is dear to God ought to be loved by man. The Divine Majesty commends the good which He loves. If God is our Master and our Father, let us strive after the patience of Him who is both our Master and our Father, because it is fitting that servants be obedient and it is not proper that sons be unworthy.

CHAPTER 4

But how wonderful and how great is the patience of God! He endures most patiently the profane temples, the earthly images and idolatrous rites that have been set up by men in insult to His majesty and honor. He makes the day to rise and the sun to shine equally over the good and the evil. When He waters the earth with showers no one is excluded from His benefits, but He bestows His rains without distinction on the just and the unjust alike. We see that, at the will of God, with an indivisible uniformity of patience toward the guilty and the innocent, the religious and the impious, the grateful and the ungrateful, the seasons obey and the elements serve, the winds blow, fountains flow, harvests increase in abundance, the fruits of the vines ripen, trees are heavy with fruit, the groves become green, and the meadows burst into flower. And although God is provoked by frequent, yes even continual, offenses, He tempers His anger and patiently waits for the day of retribution which He once foreordained. And although vengeance is in His power, He prefers to be long-suffering in His patience, that is waiting, steadfastly and delaying in His mercy, so that, if it is at all possible, the long career of malice at some time may change, and man, however deeply he is infected with the contagion of error and crime, may be converted to God even at a late hour, as He Himself warns and says: 'I desire not the death of him that dieth, as much as that he return and live.' [And again: 'Return to Me, saith the Lord.'] And again: 'Return to the Lord your God for He is merciful and loving and patient and rich in pity, and one who turns aside His judgment in respect to the evils proposed.' The blessed apostle Paul, calling back the sinner to penance by reminding him of this, putting the question says: 'Or do you despise the wealth of His goodness and His long-suffering and patience? Dost thou not know that the patience and goodness of God is meant to lead you to repentance? But thou, according to thy hardness and thy unrepentant heart, dost treasure up to thyself wrath on the day of wrath and of the revelation of the just judgment of God who will render to every man according to his works.' He said that the judgment of God is just, because it is delayed; because it is postponed repeatedly and for a long time, so that care and thought may be taken for man's eternal life by the long-enduring patience of God. Punishment is finally paid by the impious and the sinner when repentance of the sin can no longer avail.

CHAPTER 5

And in order that we may be able to understand more fully, beloved brethren, that patience is an attribute of God and that whoever is gentle, patient, and meek is an imitator of the God the Father, when in His gopsel the Lord was giving salutary precepts and in revealing the divine counsels was instructing His disciples unto perfection, He made this pronouncement: 'You have heard that it was said: "Thou shalt love thy neighbor and shalt hate thy enemy." But I say to you, love your enemies and pray for those who persecute you, so that you may be the children of your father in heaven, who makes his sun to rise on the good and evil and sends rain on the just and the unjust. For if you love those who love you, what reward shall you have? Do not even the publicans act thus? And if you salute your brethren only, what are you doing more than others? Do not even the Gentiles do that? You, therefore, will be perfect as your heavenly Father is perfect.' He said that it is in this way that the sons of God are made perfect; He showed that it is in this way that we attain our goal, and He taught that we are restored by a heavenly birth, if the patience of God the Father abide in us, if the divine likeness which Adam lost by sin be manifested and shine in our actions. What glory it is to become like God! What wonderful and what great happiness it is to possess among our virtues what can be put on a par with the divine merits!

CHAPTER 6

And this, beloved brethren, Jesus Christ, our Lord and our God, did not teach by words only, but He also fulfilled it by His deeds. And He who said that He came down for this purpose, namely, to do the will of His Father, among the other miracles of virtue by which He gave proof of His divine majesty, also preserved and exemplified His Father's patience by His habitual forbearance. Accordingly, His every act right from the very outset of His coming is marked by an accompanying patience; for from the first moment of His descent from the sublimity of heaven to earthly things, He did not disdain, though the Son of God, to put on man's flesh, and although He Himself was not a sinner, to bear the sins of others. Having put aside His immortality for a time, He suffered Himself to become mortal, in order that, though innocent, He might be slain for the salvation of the guilty. The Lord was baptized by His servant, and He, although destined to grant the remission of sins, did not Himself disdain to have His body cleansed with the water of regeneration. He, through whom others are fed, fasted for forty days; He felt hunger and starvation so that those who were famished for the Word of God and grace might be filled with the Bread of Heaven; He engaged in conflict with the devil who tempted Him, and content with having vanquished so formidable an enemy, He did not carry the fight beyond words. He did not rule His disciples as a master rules his slaves, but being both kind and gentle, He loved them as a brother, even deigning to wash the feet of His apostles, so that, while He was such a Master to His servants, He might teach by His example the attitude that a fellow servant ought to have toward his companions and equals. We should not wonder then that He was such a one among His disciples, who was able to tolerate Judas, even to the end, with enduring patience, who could eat with His enemy, who could know the foe in His household and not reveal him, who could not refuse the kiss of His betrayer. But what wonderful equanimity in bearing with the Jews, and what wonderful patience in persuading the unbelieving to accept the faith, in winning the ungrateful by kindness, in responding gently to those who contradicted Him, in enduring the proud with mercy, in yielding with humility to persecutors, in wishing to win over the murderers of the prophets and those persistently rebellious against God even to the very hour of His passion and cross!

CHAPTER 7

But in that very hour of His passion and cross, before they had come to the cruel act of His slaughter and the shedding of His blood, what violent abuses He listened to with patience, and what shameful insults He endured! He was even covered with the spittle of His revilers, when, but a short time before, with His own spittle He had cured the eyes of the blind man. He Himself suffered the lash, in whose name His servants now scourge the devil and His angels. He who now crowns the martyrs with eternal garlands was Himself crowned with thorns; He who now gives true palms to the victors was beaten in the face with hostile palms; He who clothes all others with the garment of immortality was stripped of His earthly garment; He who has given the food of heaven was fed with gall; He who has offered us the cup of salvation was given vinegar to drink. He the innocent, He the just, nay rather, Innocence Itself and Justice Itself is counted among criminals, and Truth is concealed by false testimonies. He who is to judge is judged, and the Word of God, silent, is led to the cross. And although the stars are confounded at the crucifixion of the Lord, the elements are disturbed, the earth trembles, night blots out the day, the sun withdraws both its rays and its eyes lest it be forced to gaze upon the crime of the Jews, yet He does not speak, nor is He moved, nor does He proclaim His majesty, even during the suffering itself. He endures all things even to the end with constant perseverance so that in Christ a full and perfect patience may find its realization.

CHAPTER 8

And after such sufferings, He even still receives His murderers if they are converted and come to Him, and with a patience instrumental in saving man, this kind Master closes His Church to no one. Those adversaries, those blasphemers, those persistent enemies of His name, provided they do penance for their offense, provided they acknowledge the crime committed, He not only receives and pardons, but admits to the reward of the kingdom of heaven. What can be called more patient, what more kind? Even he who shed the blood of Christ is given life by the blood of Christ. Such is the wonderful patience of Christ. And unless it were so wonderful in character, the Church would not have Paul the great Apostle.

CHAPTER 9

But if we also, beloved brethren, are in Christ, if we put Him on, if He Himself is the way of our salvation, let us who follow in the salutary footsteps of Christ walk by the example of Christ as John the Apostle teaches, saying: 'He who says that he abides in Christ ought himself also to walk just as He walked.' Likewise Peter, on whom the Lord had deemed it worthy for His Church to be founded, writes in his letter and says: 'Christ also has suffered for you, leaving you an example that you may follow in His steps, "Who did no sin, neither was deceit found in His mouth," who when He was reviled, did not revile in turn, when He suffered did not threaten, but yielded Himself to Him who judged Him unjustly.'

CHAPTER 10

We find accordingly that the patriarchs and prophets and all the just, who set up in their persons the type of Christ as a prefiguration, have treasured nothing in the estimation of their virtues more than the fact that they preserved patience with a strong and stable equanimity. So Abel, as the first one to inaugurate and dedicate martyrdom and the suffering of the just, did not resist or struggle against his brother the parricide, but in humble and gentle patience allowed himself to be killed. So Abraham, trusting God and being the first to establish the root and foundation of faith, when he was tempted in regard to his son, did not hesitate or delay but obeyed the commands of God with a full and devoted patience. And Isaac, prefigured in the likeness of the Lord as victim, was found to be patient when he was offered by his father to be sacrificed. When Jacob was driven from his own land on account of his brother, he departed patiently and, with greater patience afterward, humbly petitioning by means of peaceful gifts, he restored to harmony his still more impious brother and persecutor. Joseph sold by his brothers and banished, not only patiently forgave but even generously and kindly bestowed free grain on them when they came to him. Moses was often scorned by an ungrateful and faithless people and almost stoned, and yet with mildness and patience he prayed to the Lord in their behalf. But what great and wonderful and Christian patience is to be found in David, from whom Christ descended according to the flesh! David often had the opportunity to kill King Saul, his persecutor, who was eager to destroy him. Yet when Saul was subject to him and in his power, David preferred to save his life and did not retaliate on his enemy but, on the contrary, even avenged him when he was killed. In short, many prophets have been killed, many martyrs have been honored with glorious deaths, and all have attained their heavenly crowns through the merit of patience, for a crown for sorrow and suffering cannot be obtained unless patience in sorrow and suffering precede.

CHAPTER 11

But in order that it can be more manifestly and more fully known, beloved brethren, how useful and necessary patience is, let us consider the judgment of God which, at the very beginning of the world and of the human race, was passed upon Adam who was unmindful of God's command and a transgressor of the law that was imposed. Then we shall know how patient we ought to be in this world, we who are born under the condition that we must struggle here under trials and conflicts. 'Because you have listened,' He said, 'to the voice of your wife and you have eaten of that tree from which alone I commanded you not to eat, cursed will be the earth in all your works; in sorrow and mourning you shall eat from it all the days of your life. Thorns and thistles shall it bring forth to you and you shall eat of the food of the field. In the sweat of your brow you shall eat your bread till you return from the ground from which you were taken, since you are earth and shall return to earth.' We are all bound and confined by the bond of this sentence until, having paid the debt of death, we leave this world. We must be in sorrow and lamentation all the days of our life. And we must eat our bread with sweat and labor.

CHAPTER 12

Hence when anyone is born and enters the abode of this world, he begins with tears. Although even then inexperienced and ignorant of all things, he can do nothing else at his birth except weep. With natural foresight he laments the anxieties and labors of this mortal life, and at its very beginning, by weeping and lamentations his young soul testifies to the trials of the world which he is entering. For he toils and labors as long as he lives here. Nothing else can relieve those who labor and toil more than the consolation derived from patience. This is not only proper and necessary for everyone in this world, but even more for us who, through the onslaughts of the devil, are more harassed; who, standing daily in the front of the battle, are wearied by our combats with an old and well-trained enemy; who, in addition to the various and constant attacks of temptations and in the struggle of persecution, must relinquish our patrimonies, who must endure prison, bear chains, give up our lives, who must undergo the sword, beasts, fire, the cross, in short, all kinds of tortures and punishments, relying on our faith and the virtue of patience, for the Lord Himself teaches and says: 'These things I have spoken to you that in Me you may have peace; in the world, however, you will have affliction; but take courage: I have overcome the world.' If, however, we who have renounced the devil and the world suffer trials and the attacks of the devil and the world more frequently and more violently, how much more ought we to maintain patience, with which, as our helper and companion, we may endure all afflictions.

CHAPTER 13

It is a salutary precept of our Lord and Master: 'He who has endured even to the end will be saved.' And again: 'If you abide in My word, you are My disciples indeed, and you shall know the truth and the truth shall make you free.' We must endure and persevere, beloved brethren, so that, having been admitted to the hope of truth and liberty, we can finally attain that same truth and liberty, because the very fact that we are Christians is a source of faith and hope. However, in order that hope and faith may reach their fruition, there is need of patience. For we do not strive for present glory, but for a future one, according to what Paul the Apostle teaches, saying: 'For in hope we were saved. But hope that is seen is not hope. For how can a man hope for what he sees? But if we hope for what we do not see, we wait for it with patience.' Patient waiting is necessary that we may fulfill what we have begun to be, and through God's help, that we may obtain what we hope for and believe. Accordingly, in another place, that same Apostle instructs and teaches the just and those who do works and those who lay up for themselves heavenly treasures from the increase of divine interest to be patient also, for he says: 'Therefore while we have time, let us do good to all men, but especially to those who are of the household of faith. And in doing good let us not grow tired, for in due time we shall reap.' He warns lest anyone, through lack of patience, grow tired in his good work; lest anyone, either diverted or overcome by temptations, should stop in the middle of his course of praise and glory and his past works be lost, while those things which had begun to be perfect, cease, as it is written: 'The justice of the just shall not deliver him in what day soever he shall err.' And again: 'Hold fast what thou hast, that no other receive thy crown.' And these words urge patient and resolute perseverance, so that he who strives for a crown, now with praise already near, may be crowned because his patience endures.

CHAPTER 14

Patience, however, beloved brethren, not only preserves what is good, but also repels what is evil. Devoted to the Holy Spirit and cleaving to heavenly and divine things, it struggles with the bulkwark of its virtues against the acts of the flesh and the body whereby the soul is stormed and captured. Accordingly, let us look at a few out of many of these acts, so that from these few, all the rest may be understood. Adultery, deceit, homicide, are mortal sins. Let patience be strong and stable in the heart, and then the sanctified body and temple of God will not be corrupted by adultery, innocence dedicated to justice will not be infected by the contagion of deceit, and the hand that has held the Eucharist will not be sullied by the blood-stained sword.

CHAPTER 15

Charity is the bond of brotherhood, the foundation of peace, the steadfastness and firmness of unity; it is greater than both hope and faith; it excels both good works and suffering of the faith; and, as an external virtue, it will abide with us forever in the kingdom of heaven. Take patience away from it, and thus forsaken, it will not last; take away the substance of enduring and tolerating, and it attempts to last with no roots or strength. Accordingly, the Apostle when he was speaking about charity joined tolerance and patience to it, saying: 'Charity is magnanimous, charity is kind, charity does not envy, is not puffed up, is not provoked, thinks no evil, loves all things, believes all things, hopes all things, endures all things.' By this he showed that charity can persevere steadfastly because it has learned how to endure all things. And in another place he says: 'bearing with one another in love, taking every care to preserve the unity of the Spirit in the union of peace.' He proved that neither unity nor peace can be preserved unless brothers cherish one another with mutual forbearance and preserve the bond of unity with patience as intermediary.

CHAPTER 16

How then will you be able to endure these things—not to swear or curse, not to seek again what has been taken away from you, on receiving a blow to offer the other cheek also to your assailant, to forgive your brother who offends you not only seventy times seven times, but all his offenses without exception, to love your enemies, to pray for your adversaries and persecutors, if you do not have the steadfastness of patience and forbearance? We see what happened in the case of Stephen. When he was being killed by the violence and stones of the Jews, he did not ask for vengeance but forgiveness for his murderers, saying: 'O Lord, do not lay this sin against them.' So it was most fitting that the first martyr for Christ who, in preceding by his glorious death the martyrs that were to come, was not only a preacher of the Lord's suffering but also an imitator of His most patient gentleness. What shall I say of anger, of discord, of contention, evils which a Christian ought not to have? Let there be patience in the heart and these evil things can not have a place there; or if they attempt to enter, on being quickly driven out, they depart, so that the heart may continue to be a peaceful dwelling where the God of peace may delight to abide. Accordingly, the Apostle admonishes and teaches, saying: 'Do not grieve the Holy Spirit of God, in whom you were sealed for the day of redemption. Let all bitterness, and wrath, and indignation, and clamor, and reviling, be removed from you.' For if a Christian has withdrawn from the fury and contention of the flesh as from the storms of the sea, and has now begun to be tranquil and gentle in the harbor of Christ, he ought not to admit into his heart either anger or discord, for it is not right for him to render evil for evil or to hate.

CHAPTER 17

Likewise, patience is also necessary in respect to the various hardships of the flesh and frequent and cruel torments of the body by which the human race is daily wearied and oppressed. For since in that first transgression of God's command strength of body departed with immortality, and infirmity entered the body by death, and since strength cannot be regained except when immortality shall have been regained, it is necessary to keep struggling and contending in this state of bodily weakness and infirmity; and this struggle and strife can not be endured without the strength of patience. But different kinds of sufferings are imposed on us to test and prove us, and many forms of temptations are inflicted upon us by loss of wealth, burning fevers, torments of wounds, by the death of dear ones. Nothing else distinguishes the unjust and just the more than this, that in adversities the unjust man complains and blasphemes because of impatience, while the just man is proved by patience, as it is written: 'In thy sorrow endure and in thy humiliation keep patience, for gold and silver are tried in the fire.'

CHAPTER 18

Thus Job was examined and proved and raised to the pinnacle of praise because of the virtue of patience. How many weapons of the devil were hurled against him! How many torments were inflicted on him! He suffered the loss of his property, he was bereft of his numerous progeny; a master rich in wealth and a father richer in children was suddenly neither master nor father. Cruel wounds attacked his body and a scourge of devouring worms consumed his dissolving and decaying limbs. And lest anything at all might remain which Job had not experienced in his trials, the devil even armed his wife against him, using that ancient device of his wickedness, as if he could deceive and cheat all men through a woman as he did in the beginning. Nevertheless, Job was not broken by these heavy and continuous assaults, and in spite of these trials and afflictions he extolled the praise of God by his victorious patience. Tobias also, who after his magnificent work of justice and mercy was tempted by the loss of his eyes, endured his blindness with great patience and gained outstanding merit with God through the renown of his patience.

CHAPTER 19

And, beloved brethren, that the good of patience may shine forth more brightly, let us consider, on the other hand, what evil impatience causes. For as patience is a good of Christ, so, on the contrary, impatience is an evil of the devil; and as the man in whom Christ lives and abides is found to be a patient man, so he is always impatient whose mind is possessed by the wickedness of the devil. Accordingly, let us consider the origins of impatience. The devil bore with impatience the fact that man was made to the image of God, and for this reason was the first to

64

perish and cause to perish. Adam, in violation of the heavenly command, was incapable of resisting the desire of the deadly food and fell into the death of sin; he did not preserve, under the guardianship of patience, the grace received from God. Cain was impatient of his brother's sacrifice and gift and killed him. Because Esau put lower things before higher, he lost his birthright through impatience for the lentils. Why was the Jewish people faithless and ungrateful toward the divine blessings? Was it not that this crime of impatience first drew them away from God? When they could not bear the delay of Moses speaking with God they dared to demand profane gods, and to proclaim as leader of their journey the head of a calf and an earthly image. They never abandoned this same fault of impatience, but always impatient of the divine teaching and guidance, by killing all their prophets and all just men, they hastened to the cross and to the shedding of the blood of the Lord. Impatience also produces heretics in the Church, and, after the manner of the Jews, it drives them, as rebels against the peace and charity of Christ, to hostile acts and furious hates. And not to be tedious by giving details, all things without exception which patience by its works builds unto glory, impatience reduces to ruin.

CHAPTER 20

And so, beloved brethren, after the benefits of patience and the evils of impatience have been carefully weighed, let us observe fully and maintain the patience through which we abide in Christ and with Christ are able to come to God. That patience, rich and manifold, is not confined within a narrow compass or restrained by bounds of small extent. The virtue of patience extends widely and its wealth and abundance proceed from a source that has indeed a single name, but with its full-flowing streams it is diffused through many glorious courses, and nothing in our actions can avail towards the full realization of merit which does not take the power for its accomplishment from that source. It is patience that both commends us to God and saves us for God. It is that same patience which tempers anger, bridles the tongue, governs the mind, guards peace, rules discipline, breaks the onslaught of lust, suppresses the violence of pride, extinguishes the fire of dissension, restrains the power of the wealthy, renews the endurance of the poor in bearing their lot, guards the blessed integrity of virgins, the difficult chastity of widows, and the indivisible love of husbands and wives. It makes men humble in prosperity, brave in adversity, meek in the face of injuries and insults. It teaches us to pardon our offenders quickly; if you yourself should offend, it teaches you to ask pardon often and with perseverance. It vanquishes temptations, sustains persecutions, endures sufferings and martyrdoms to the end. It is this patience which strongly fortifies the foundations of our faith. It is this patience which sublimely promotes the growth of hope. It directs our action, so that we can keep to the way of Christ while we make progress because of His forbearance. It ensures our perseverance as sons of God while we imitate the patience of the Father.

CHAPTER 21

And since I know, beloved brethren, that very many, either because of the weight of their pressing injuries or because of resentment toward those who attack them and rage against them, wish to be revenged quickly, I must warn you before I close, that finding ourselves in these storms of a turbulent world and in the midst of the persecutions of the Jews or of the Gentiles or of the heretics, we should patiently await the day of vengeance. We should not hasten to revenge our pain with an angry speed, since it is written: 'Expect Me, saith the Lord, in the day of My resurrection for a testimony, since My judgment is to the congregations of nations that I may receive kings and pour out My anger over them.' The Lord commands us to wait and to endure with a strong patience the day of future vengenance, and He also speaks in the Apocalypse, saying: 'Do not seal up the words of the prophecy of this book, because now the time is close at hand and those who persevere in doing wrong, let them do wrong, and he who is filthy, let him be filthy still, but let the just man still do more just things, and likewise the holy man, holier things. Behold I come quickly! and My reward is with Me, to render to each according to his works.' Therefore, even the martyrs as they cry out and as they hasten to their punishment in the intensity of their suffering are still ordered to wait and to show patience until the appointed time is fulfilled and the number of martyrs is complete. And He said: 'When he opened the fifth seal, I saw under the altar of God the souls of those who had been slain for the Word of God and for their own testimony and they cried with a loud voice saying: How long, O Lord, Holy and True, dost thou refrain from judging and avenging our blood on those who dwell on the earth. And a white stole was given to each of them and they were told to rest for a little while longer until the number of the fellow-servants and brothers, who are to be slain later even as they had been, should be complete.'

CHAPTER 22

But when the divine vengeance for the blood of the just will come, the Holy Spirit declares through the prophet Malachias, saying: 'Behold the day of the Lord comes glowing as a furnace and all the strangers and all the unjust will be as stubble and the coming day shall set them on fire, saith the Lord.' And we read likewise in the psalms, where it is announced that the coming of God the Judge must be venerated because of the majesty of His judgment: 'God our God shall come revealing Himself and He shall not be silent. A fire shall burn before Him and a mighty tempest shall be about Him. He shall call Heaven on high and earth that he may separate His people. Collect for Him His just men, those who place His testimony in sacrifices and the heavens will announce His justice, for God is the Judge.' And Isaias prophesies the same things, saying: 'For behold the Lord will come like a fire and, like a whirlwind, His carriage, to repay vengeance in anger. For in the fire of the Lord they will be judged and by his sword they will be wounded.' And again: 'The Lord God of Hosts shall go forth and shall threaten war; He shall stir up battle and shall cry over his enemies with strength; I have been silent, shall I be silent always?'

CHAPTER 23

But who is He who says that He was silent formerly and will not always be silent? It is surely He who was led as a sheep to the slaughter and who, like a lamb without making a sound before its shearer, did not open His mouth.' Surely it is He who did not cry out and whose voice was not heard in the streets. Surely it is He who was not stubborn and who did not contradict when He offered His back to the scourges and His cheeks to blows and did not turn away His face from their filthy spittle; He, who when He was accused by the priests and elders, answered nothing and, to the amazement of Pilate, kept a most patient silence. He is the One who, although He was silent in His passion, will not be silent later in the day of reckoning. He is our God, that is, the God not recognized by all but by the faithful and those who believe, and when He comes manifesting Himself in His second coming, He will not be silent. For although He was formerly hidden in humility, He will come manifested in power.

CHAPTER 24

This is the Judge and the Avenger, beloved brethren, that we are to await who, when He revenges Himself, is destined to revenge us, the people of His Church and the number of all the just from the beginning of the world. Let him who hastens and hurries too much to his own revenge consider that He alone who avenges has not yet avenged Himself. [God the Father commanded that His Son be adored and the Apostle Paul, mindful of the divine precept, declares this and says: 'God has exalted Him and has bestowed upon Him that name that is above every name, so that at the name of Jesus all should bend the knee, of those in heaven, on earth, and of those under the earth'; and] in the Apocalypse, when John wishes to adore him, the Angel resists him and says: 'Thou must not do this because I am a fellow servant of you and of your brothers. Adore Jesus the Lord.' How wonderful then is Jesus our Lord, and what great patience this is that He who is adored in heaven is not yet avenged on earth! Let us think of His patience, beloved brethren, in our persecutions and sufferings. Let us show the full obedience that is inspired by our expectation of His coming, and let us not hasten with the impious and shameless haste of a servant to defend ourselves before the Lord. Let us rather persevere and let us labor, watchful with all our heart and steadfast even to total resignation, let us guard the precepts of the Lord, so that when the day of wrath and vengeance comes, we may not be punished with the impious and sinners but may be honored with the just and those who fear God.

St. Gregory of Nyssa
335-394

Gregory of Nyssa is an excellent example of the effort on the part of several writers during the early centuries of Christianity to blend together ideas derived from the Greek philosophical tradition and the teaching of the Bible. The philosophy of Plato particularly influenced his interpretation of scriptural passages. Besides being a respectable philosopher, theologian and spiritual writer, Gregory was a church administrator, at various times the Bishop of Nyssa, Archbishop of Sebaste and Metropolital of Caesarea. His role as a leader was due more to his speculative abilities than to his administrative talents.

Certain basic convictions underlie Gregory's spiritual writings. Man is the image of God. As such, he is lord of the universe and a free being. He is also responsible for his life. By sin, man destroyed his privileged existence as image of God but can recover it by imitation of Christ and a life of virtue. Man's capacity for change and growth is limitless. The goal of the Christian life is union with God.

The following selection, On Perfection, *illustrates Gregory's ability to combine philosophy and scripture. His mood as he approaches the theme of perfection is positive, joyous, optimistic. He declares Christ to be the model of perfection and proceeds to reflect upon various titles of Christ taken from the writings of Saint Paul. The selection reveals a man completely at home in scripture. He moves easily from title to title. But he seeks to do much more than list Paul's titles for Christ. Gregory is convinced that adequate recognition of the true significance of the name of Christ is the way to perfection. The titles become vehicles for meeting the concepts. Suddenly the Christian must incorporate the concepts into his soul, must become the concepts. True knowledge is not a knowledge extrinsic to the Christian, but a knowledge that is his very being. This knowledge is the Christian's life. Thus, the Christian is the concept that is the title that is the name that is the person Christ. And this is the Christian's perfection. It is a highly intellectualized approach to spirituality. Perfection, which identifies ultimately with knowledge of the person Christ, is a process that by its nature cannot end. Rather perfection progresses with the Christian's knowledge of Christ.*

The reader who is familiar with Greek philosophy will immediately recognize several Platonist themes: the concept is, in some way, a reality; to know is to come to see, and this is true life; man arrives at knowledge only through the struggle, comes to light only by travelling through darkness.

Gregory seemed to sense the subtle danger in this approach. One could be tempted to flee to the world of intellect, there to take refuge in such beautiful ideas as Christ the King, the Power, the Wisdom, the Peace, the Light, the Foundation, and so on. Gregory, again faithful to a theme in Plato, insists that knowledge must be realized in virtuous action. By a life of virtue, the Christian conforms himself to the name Christ. In Gregory's terms, each person is the painter of his own life, choice is the craftsman of the work, the virtues are the paints for executing the image.

Gregory's contribution to Christian spirituality is an important one. He knew that the health and maturity of a spiritual life are proportionate to the degree of intellectual insight that feeds into the spiritual life. He dedicated his talents to the development of a rich intellectual structure that could serve the Christian community and its individual members in their unending search for union with God through Christ.

ON PERFECTION

Your zeal to know how anyone may become perfect through a life of virtue so that you may achieve a blamelessness in all things is in keeping with your purpose in life. I could have considered it of great importance that patterns for everything that you are striving for be found in my life, so as to furnish you with the instruction you seek through deeds rather than words. In that way, my guidance towards what is good would have been worthy of belief, because my life was in tune with my words. But, although I pray that this may one day be true, I do not yet see myself as one whose life could be offered to you as an example in place of a treatise. Therefore, in order that I may not seem to be completely useless and incapable of making a contribution to your goal, I have decided to set before you an accurate description of the life towards which one must tend, making this the beginning of my discourse.

Our good Master, Jesus Christ, bestowed on us a partnership in His revered name, so that we get our name from no other person connected with us, and if one happens to be rich and well-born or of lowly origin and poor, or if one has some distinction from his business or position, all such conditions are of no avail because the one authoritative name for those believing in Him is that of 'Christian.' Now, since this grace was ordained for us from above, it is necessary, first of all, for us to understand the greatness of the gift so that we can worthily thank the God who has given it to us. Then, it is necessary to show through our life that we ourselves are what the power of this great name requires us to be. The greatness of the gift of which we are deemed worthy through the partnership with the Master becomes clear to us if we recognize the true significance of the name of Christ, so that when in our prayers we call upon the Lord of all by this name, we may comprehend the concept that we are taking into our soul. We must also understand reverently what we believe He is when He is called upon by this name. When we do understand this, we shall, as a consequence, also learn clearly what sort of persons we should be shown to be as a result of our zeal for this way of life and our use of His name as the instructor and the guide for our life. Accordingly, if we make St. Paul our leader in these two undertakings, we shall have the safest guide to the plain truth of what we are seeking. For he, most of all, knew what Christ is, and he indicated by what he did the kind of person named for Him, imitating Him so brilliantly that he revealed his own Master in himself, his own soul being transformed through his accurate imitation of his prototype, so that Paul no longer seemed to be living and speaking, but Christ Himself seemed to be living in him. As this astute perceiver of particular goods says: 'Do you seek a proof of the Christ who speaks in me?' and: 'It is now no longer I that live but Christ lives in me.'

This man knew the significance of the name of Christ for us, saying that Christ is 'the power of God and the wisdom of God.' And he called Him 'peace,' and 'light inaccessible' in whom God dwells, and 'sanctification and redemption,' and 'great high priest,' and 'passover,' and 'a propitation' of souls, 'the brightness of glory and the image of substance,' and 'maker of the world,' and 'spiritual food' and 'spiritual drink and spiritual rock,' 'water,' 'foundation' of faith, and 'corner stone,' and 'image of the invisible God,' and 'great God,' and 'head of the body of the Church,' and 'the firstborn of every creature,' and 'first-fruits of those who have fallen asleep,' 'firstborn from the dead,' 'first-born among many brethren,' and 'mediator between God and men,' and 'only-begotten Son,' and 'crowned with glory and honor,' and 'lord of glory,' and 'beginning' of being, speaking thus of Him who is the beginning, 'king of justice and king of peace,' and 'ineffable king of all, having the power of the king-dom,' and many other such things that are not easily enumerated. When all of these phrases are put next to each other, each one of the terms makes its own contribution to a revelation of what is signified by being named after Christ and each provides for us a certain emphasis. To the extent that we take these concepts into our souls, they are all indications of the unspeakable great-ness of the gift for us. However, since the rank of kingship underlies all worth and power and rule, by this title the royal power of Christ is authoritatively and primarily indicated (for the anointing of kingship, as we learn in the historical books, comes first), and all the force of the other titles depends on that of royalty. For this reason, the person who knows the separate elements included under it also knows the power encompassing these elements. But it is the kingship itself which declares what the title of Christ means.

Therefore, since, thanks to our good Master, we are sharers of the greatest and the most divine and the first of names, those honored by the name of Christ being called Christians, it is necessary that there be seen in us also all of the connotations of this name, so that the title be not a misnomer in our case, but that our life be a testimony of it. Being something does not result from being called something. The underlying nature, whatever it happens to be, is discovered through the meaning attached to the name. What do I mean? If someone calls man a tree or a rock, will he, on this account, be a plant or stone? Of course not. It is necessary for him, first of all, to be a man, and, then, to be addressed thus in keeping with his nature. For titles based on similarities have no validity, as if one could say that a man is a statue or an imitation horse. If anything is named validly and not falsely, his nature completely reveals the form of address as a true one. Wood disguised in any way at all is still called wood, bronze is called bronze, stone is called stone, or any other such substance upon which art, shaping it contrary to expectation, imposes a form.

It is necessary, then, for those calling themselves after Christ, first of all, to become what the name implies, and, then, to adapt themselves to the title. We distinguish a man himself from what is considered a good likeness of him in a picture by noting characteristic differences. The man we call a logical thinking animal, the picture of an inanimate piece of wood which has taken on the form of the man through imitation; so, also, shall we distinguish the true Christian from the one merely seeming to be a Christian through the individual elements in his character. The marks of the true Christian are all those we know in connection with Christ. Those that we have room for we imitate, and those which our nature does not approximate by imitation,

73

we reverence and worship. Thus, it is necessary for the Christian life to illustrate all the interpretative terms signifying Christ, some through imitation, others through worship, if 'the man of God is to be perfect' as the apostle says, and this perfection must never be mutilated by evil.

There are men who fashion mythical creatures in their speeches and writings, constructing bull-headed horses or centaurs or serpent-footed monsters or other such things made up of different species. They do not achieve an imitation in keeping with a natural archetype, and, illogically overstepping nature, they fashion something other than man, fabricating the impossible. We would not say that what they have constructed in this strange synthesis is a man, even if some parts of the figure happen to resemble certain parts of the human body. In the same way, a person cannot accurately be called a Christian if he does not give assent to the faith with his mind, even if he conforms to it in other respects, or if his mind gives assent, but his body is not suited to his way of life, exhibiting the anger of dragons and the bestiality of serpents, or adding to his human character an equine madness for women. In such cases, a man becomes double-natured, a centaur made up of reason and passion. It is possible to see many such people: either they resemble the Minotaur, being bull-headed in their belief in idolatry, although they appear to be leading a good life; or they make themselves centaurs and dragons by combining with a Christian facade a bestial body. Now, since, as in the case of the human body, the Christian should be recognized in his entirety, it is fitting for the characteristics of his life to represent a pledge of all the good qualities connected with Christ. For being in some respects what the name implies, but in others inclining towards the opposite, is to cut onself apart into a battleground where there are two factions, one of good and one of evil, and thus one becomes truceless to oneself and inconsistent. For, says the apostle: 'What fellowship has light with darkness?'

Since there is a distinct and irreconcilable contradiction between light and darkness, the person partaking of both has a share in neither, because of the opposition of the parts drawn up against each other at the same time in his mixed life. His faith provides the lighted part, but his dark habits put out the lamp of reason. Since it is impossible and inconsistent for light and darkness to exist in fellowship, the person containing each of the opposites becomes an enemy to himself, being divided in two ways between virtue and evil, and he sets up an antagonistic battle line within himself. And just as it is not possible, when there are two enemies, for both to be victors over each other (for the victory of the one causes the death of his adversary), so, also, in this civil war brought about by the confusion in his life, it is not possible for the stronger element to win without the other becoming completely destroyed. For how will the army of reverence be stronger than evil, when the wicked phalanx of the opponents attacks it? If the stronger is going to win, the enemy must be completely slaughtered. And thus, virtue will have the victory over evil only when the entire enemy gives way to it through an alliance of the reasonable elements against the unsound ones. Then will be fulfilled what was spoken from the mouth of God through prophecy: 'It is I who bring both life and death.' For it is not possible for the good to exist in me, unless it is made to live through the death of my enemy. As long as we keep grasping opposites with each of our hands, it is impossible for there to be participation in both elements in the same being. For, if we are holding evil, we lose the power to take hold of virtue.

Therefore, let us take up the original argument, namely, that the one road to the pure and divine life for lovers of virtue is knowing what the name of Christ means, in conformity with which we must shape our lives, attuning it to virtue through the emphasis on the other terms which we gathered together in our introduction from the holy voice of Paul. Placing these before us with the prescribed zeal, we shall make them the safest guide for a life of virtue, imitating some of these traits, as we said in the first part, and revering and worshiping others. Let the marshaling of these be a battle line for us. Let us begin with the first: 'Christ,' it says, 'is the power of God and the wisdom of God.' Through this description of Christ, we derive, first of all, notions befitting the divine which make the name an object of reverence for us. Since all creation, both whatever is known through perception and whatever lies beyond observation, came into being through Him and is united with Him, wisdom is necessarily interwoven with power in connection with the definition of Christ, the maker of all things. We know this through the yoking together of the two words, I mean, power and wisdom, because these great and indescribable wonders of creation would not exist if wisdom had not thought of their coming into being, nor would they exist if power, through which thoughts become deeds, had not accompanied wisdom in bringing the thought to completion.

The meaning of Christ is appropriately divided into this double emphasis on wisdom and power in order that, when we behold the greatness of the composition of being, we may recognize His unspeakable power through what we comprehend, and, in order that, when we calculate how all things that did not exist before came into being (the multiform nature in being having been endowed with substance through the divine nod), we then worship the incomprehensible wisdom of the One who thought of these things. Indeed, it is not useless or without benefit to us to believe in the power and wisdom of Christ in connection with the possession of the good. For, when a person prays, he draws to himself through prayer what he is invoking and looking towards with the eye of his soul. Thus, the person looking towards power (Christ is power) 'is strengthened with power upon the inner man,' as the apostle says, and the person calling upon the wisdom which the Lord knows of old becomes wise, as our introduction stated. Indeed, the person synonymous with Christ, who is power and wisdom, having been empowered against sin, will also exhibit wisdom in himself by his wise choice. When wisdom and power are displayed in us, the one choosing what is fair, and the other confirming the choice, a perfection of life interwoven with both of these qualities is achieved.

Recognizing Christ as 'peace,' we shall exhibit the true title of Christian in ourselves through the peace in our life. For the One 'has slain enmity,' as the apostle says. Let us not, therefore, bring it to life in ourselves, but rather show through our life that it is dead. Let us not rise up against ourselves through anger and backbiting what has been rightly deadened for our salvation by God. This would destroy our soul and bring about an evil resurrection of what is rightly dead. But, if we have Christ, who is peace, let us also deaden hatred in ourselves in order to achieve in our life what we believe is in Him. For that One 'has broken down the intervening wall of the enclosure,' and, out of the two elements in Himself, has created 'one new man,' and made peace. Therefore, let us also reconcile, not only those fighting against us on the outside, but also the elements at variance within us, in order that no longer may the 'flesh lust against the spirit and the spirit against the flesh.' Subjecting the spirit of the flesh to divine law, let us live peacefully, having been dissolved into the new and peaceful man and having become one from two. For the definition of peace is the harmony of dissonant parts. Once the civil war in our nature is expelled, then, we also, being at peace within ourselves, become peace, and reveal our having taken on the name of Christ as true and authentic.

Knowing Christ as the 'true light,' 'inaccessible' to false-hood, we learn this, namely, that it is necessary for our lives also to be illuminated by the rays of the true light. But virtues are the rays of 'the Sun of Justice,' streaming forth for our illumination, through which we 'lay aside the works of darkness,' so that we 'walk becomingly as in the day,' and 'we renounce those things which shame conceals.' By doing all things in the light, we become the light itself, so that it 'shines' before others, which is the peculiar quality of light. And if we recognize Christ as 'sanctification,' in whom every action is steadfast and pure, let us prove by our life that we ourselves stand apart, being ourselves true sharers of His name, coinciding in deed and not in word with the power of sanctification.

And learning that Christ is 'redemption' because He gave Himself as an atonement in our behalf, we are taught this knowledge, that when He furnished us with immortality as our particular possession, as if bestowing a certain honor on each soul, He ransomed us from death with His own life. If, then, we become slaves of the One who redeemed us, we shall look exclusively towards our Master, on the grounds that we no longer live for ourselves, but for the One who possesses us, because He gave His life for us. For we are no longer lords of ourselves, but the possessions of Him who, having bought us, is the Master of His own. Truly, the will of the Master will be the law of our life. And as 'the law of sin' governed us when death was prevailing, so now, that we have become the property of life, it is necessary for us to conform to the government in power. Let us, therefore, never turn aside from the will of life and desert through sin to the wicked tyrant of souls of old, I mean to death.

We are assimilated to Christ, also, if we hear from Paul that he is the 'passover' and 'high priest.' For Christ was truly sacrificed as the paschal victim in our behalf. But the priest, bringing in the sacrifice to God, is no other than Christ Himself. For it says: 'He delivered himself up for us, an offering and a sacrifice.' Through these words we learn this, that the person looking towards that One delivers himself as an offering and sacrifice and passover, and will show himself to God as a living sacrifice, 'holy, pleasing to God,' becoming a reasonable 'service.' But the rule of this holy office is: 'Be not conformed to this world, but be transformed in the newness of your mind, that you may discern what is the good and acceptable and the perfect will of God.' If the flesh lives and is not sacrificed according to the law of the spirit, it is not possible for the will of God to be displayed in it: 'For the wisdom of the flesh is hostile to God and is not subject to the law of God.' As long as the flesh lives, which was offered up through the life-giving sacrifice by 'mortifying the members upon the earth' from which passions spring, it is not possible for the pleasing and perfect will of God to be achieved expeditiously in the life of the faithful.

So, also, Christ, being known as 'a propitiation by his own blood,' teaches each one thinking of this to become himself a propitiation, sanctifying his soul by the deadening of his members. And when Christ is spoken of as 'the brightness of his glory and the image of his substance,' we get from these words the idea of His greatness in the act of being worshiped. For Paul, truly God-inspired and God-taught, examining, 'in the depth of the riches of the wisdom and of the knowledge of God,' the unclear and hidden aspects of the divine mysteries, revealed through suggestive phrases the illuminations that came to him from God concerning the understanding of what is incomprehensible and unsearchable because the tongue is no match for thought. According to the report of those who heard his interpretation of mystery, he spoke, as well as reason can, in the service of thought. For, comprehending as much as human power can concerning

the divine nature, he revealed the unapproachable and incomprehensible Logos of substantial being in human terms.

Accordingly, when speaking of the theories concerning the
divine nature as peace and power and life and justice and light
and truth and such things, he maintained that an account of that
nature itself was completely unattainable, saying that God has
not been seen and will not be seen. For he says: 'No man has
seen or can see' Him. Because of this, when he was asking how
to give a name to what cannot be grasped in thought and did
not discover a word expressing an interpretation of the incomprehensible, he called whatever underlies all good, and is not
sufficiently known or spoken of, 'glory' and 'substance.' The
underlying essence of being, he dismissed as unnamable. However, interpreting the unity and inseparability of the Son and
the Father and the Son's being contemplated indefinably and
invisibly with the indefinable and unseen Father, he addressed
Him as 'effulgence of glory' and 'image of substance,' indicating
the unity of their nature by the word 'effulgence' and their
equality by the word 'image.' For, in connection with an effulgent
nature, there is no middle point in a beam of light, nor is there
an inferior part of an image in connection with a substance
determined by it. The observer of the effulgent nature will
know the effulgence in its entirety, and the person comprehending the size of the substance measures it in its entirety
with its accompanying image. So he speaks of the Lord as 'the
form of God,' not belittling the Lord by the idea of form, but
showing the bigness of God through the word, in which the immensity of the Father is contemplated as never exceeding its
own form or being found outside of its specific character. For
there is nothing formless or unadorned in respect to the Father
which does not rejoice in the beauty of the only-begotten Son.
Therefore, the Lord says: 'He who sees me, sees also the Father,'
indicating through this that there is no deficiency and no excess.
But he also means that He upholds 'all things with the word of
His power,' and thus dissolves the difficulty of the busy-bodies
who seek the undiscoverable when they look for an account of
matter and nowhere check their curiosity, asking how the material is experienced by the immaterial, quantity by that without
quantity, form by that without form, color by the unseeable and

the finite by the infinite, and how, if there is no quality connected with the simple and the uncomposed, matter is interwoven with it. He solves all such inquiries by saying that the Logos 'upholds all things by the word of His power' from non-existence to existence. For all things, as many as exist in connection with matter and as many as have received an immaterial nature, have one cause of their substance: the Word of the unspeakable power. From these words, we learn to look to Him as the source of being. If we pass into being from that source and have our existence in Him, there is every necessity to believe that there is nothing outside of the One in whom we exist and from whom we come into being, and back to whom we go. Along with this thought, the blamelessness of our life is likewise established. For what person who believes that he lives 'from Him and through Him and unto Him' will dare to make the One who encompasses in Himself the life of each of us, a witness of a life that does not reflect Him?

The divine apostle also, in calling the Lord 'spiritual food and drink' suggests that he knows that human nature is not simple, but that there is an intelligible part mixed with a sensual part and that a particular type of nurture is needed for each of the elements in us, sensible food to strengthen our bodies, and spiritual food for the well-being of our souls. And just as in the case of the body, the firm and the fluid, mingling with each other, preserve our nature through digestion, in the same way, by analogy, Paul distinguishes the nurture of the intelligible part, using the same terms, food and drink, and adapting them properly to the needs of those assimilating them. For to those who are exhausted and fainting, bread comes to strengthen the heart of a man, but to those who are weary because of the wretchedness of their life and thirsty because of this, wine comes as a joy to their heart.

Now, it is necessary from what has been said to know the power of the Logos by which the soul is nourished according to its need, having received grace from it according to the riddle of the prophet who points out clearly the relief which comes to the weary from the Logos 'in verdant pastures and in restful waters.' And if someone in examining this mystery should say that the Lord is rightly called 'spiritual food and drink,' he is

80

not far from the truth. For His 'flesh is food indeed' and His 'blood is drink indeed.' But, in connection with the thought just mentioned, there is participation in such nourishment for all, since the Logos who becomes food and drink is received and assimilated without distinction by those seeking Him. However, in connection with another idea, the participation in this food and drink is not careless or indiscriminate, for the apostle limits it thus: 'Let a man prove himself and so let him eat of that bread and drink of the cup, for he who eats and drinks unworthily eats and drinks judgment to himself.' The evangelist, also, seems to point this out definitely, at the time of the mystical passion when that good councilor took down the body of the Lord and wrapped Him in spotless and pure linen and placed Him in a new and pure sepulcher. Thus, the command of the apostle and the observation of the evangelist become a law to all to receive the Holy Body with a pure conscience. If there is somewhere some stain from sin, we must wash it out with the water of our tears.

And when Christ is called 'a rock,' this word assists us in the firmness and permanence of our virtuous life, that is, in the steadfastness of our endurance of suffering, and in our soul's opposition and inaccessibility to the assaults of sin. Through these and such things, we also will be a rock, imitating, as far as is possible in our changing nature, the unchanging and permanent nature of the Master. And if the same One is called 'the wise builder and the foundation' of faith and the 'cornerstone,' neither will this be shown to be without profit for us in leading a virtuous life. For we learn through this that the beginning and end of all good government and good learning and practice is the Lord.

And 'the hope' which we know to be the same as the cornerstone towards which all things tend, if they are zealously pursued in virtue, is that One so named by Paul. The beginning of this high 'tower' of life is our faith in Him, upon which we build, putting down the principles of our life as a kind of foundation, and, through our daily achievements, we erect pure thoughts and actions upon it. Thus, the cornerstone of all becomes our cornerstone, fitting Himself diagonally to the two walls of our life which are built out of our body and soul with elegance and correctness. But if one part of the building is deficient, if the external elegance does not correspond to the correctness of the soul, or if the soul's virtue does not balance the outward appearance, Christ, in fitting Himself to a single portion of a double structure, becomes the cornerstone of a half-completed life. For it is not possible for a cornerstone to exist if two walls do not join. The beauty of the chief cornerstone sets off our building when our dualistic existence, straight and true, is harmoniously set up according to the right rule of life by the plumb line of the virtues, having nothing in itself that is bent or crooked.

But when Paul calls Christ 'the image of the invisible God,' meaning the God over all and the great God (and with these words he proclaims the glory of the true Master, speaking of 'our great God and Savior Jesus Christ' and the One 'from whom is Christ according to the flesh, who is over all things, God blessed forever')—saying these things, then, he teaches us what is the One existing forever. It is that thing which only the existing One knows, and, at all times, it exceeds human comprehension in equal measure, even if the person who always 'minds the things which are above' comes near to it in his moral progress. Accordingly, this Person who is beyond knowledge and comprehension, the ineffable and the 'unspeakable' and the 'inexpressible,' in order that He might again make Himself an 'image of God,' because of His love for man, became Himself an 'image of the invisible God' so that he took on the form which He assumed among you, and again, through Himself, He fashioned a beauty in accord with the character of the Archetype. Therefore, if we also are to become an 'image of the invisible God,' it is fitting that the form of our life be struck according to the 'example' of the life set before us. But what is that? It is living in the flesh, but not 'according to the flesh.' The Prototype, 'the image of the invisible God,' living in His virginity, underwent all temptations because of the similarity of His nature to ours, but He did not share the experience of a single sin: 'Who did no sin, neither was deceit found in His mouth.' Therefore, just as when we are learning the art of painting, the teacher puts before us on a panel a beautifully executed model, and it is necessary for each student to imitate in every way the beauty of that model on his own panel, so that the panels of all will be adorned in accordance with the example of the beauty set before them; in the same way, since every person is the painter of his own life, and choice is the craftsman of the work, and the virtues are the paints for executing the image, there is no small danger that the imitation may change the Prototype into a hateful and ugly person instead of reproducing the master form if we sketch in the character of evil with muddy colors. But, since it is possible, one must prepare the pure colors of the virtues, mixing them with each other according to some artistic formula for the imitation of beauty, so that we become an image of the image, having achieved the beauty of the Prototype through activity as a kind of imitation, as did Paul, who became an 'imitator of Christ,' through his life of virtue.

If it is necessary to distinguish the individual colors through which the imitation comes about, one color is meekness, for he says: 'Learn from me, for I am meek and humble of heart.' Another color is patience which appears quantitatively in 'the image of the invisible God.' A sword, clubs, chains, whips, slaps in the face, the face spat upon, the back beaten, irreverent judgment, a harsh denial, soldiers mocking, the sullen rejection with jests and sarcasm and insults, blows from a reed, nails and gall and vinegar, and all of these terrible things were applied to Him without cause, nay, rather, in return for innumerable good works! And how were those who did these things repaid? 'Father, forgive them, for they do not know what they are doing.' Was it not possible for Him to bring the sky down upon them, or to bury those insolent men in a chasm of the earth, or to throw them down from their own mountains into the sea, or to inundate the earth with the depths of ocean, or to send down upon them the Sodomitic rain of fire, or to do any other angry deed in revenge? Instead, He bore all these things in meekness and patience, legislating patience for your life through Himself. Thus, it is possible to see all the features of the Prototype, the image of God. Looking towards that image and adorning our own form clearly in accordance with that One, each person becomes himself an 'image of the invisible God,' having been portrayed through endurance.

But learning that Christ is the 'head of the Church,' let this be considered before all else, that every head is of the same nature and the same essence as the body subordinate to it, and there is a unity of the individual parts with the whole, accomplishing by their common respiration a complete sympathy of all the parts. Therefore, if any part is divorced from the body, it is also altogether alienated from the head. Reason tells us through these words that whatever the head is by nature, this the individual parts become, in order to be in communion with the head. But we are the parts who make up the body of Christ. If, then, anyone removes one of the members of the body of Christ and makes it 'the member of a harlot,' hurling unrestrained madness at Him like a sword, through this evil emotion, he alienates the member completely from the head. So, also, all the other instruments of evil become swords through which the members are cut off from the body and separated from the head by the emotions which effected the cutting. In order for the body, therefore, to remain whole in its nature, it is fitting for the separate parts to be in communion with the head; for example, if we assume purity to be logically an essential quality of the head, it is altogether necessary for the members subordinate to the head to be pure. And if we know that the head is incorruptible, then, the members also must be incorruptible. And thus, all other notions one has about the head must necessarily be applied to the members: peace, holiness, truth, and all such things. These similar qualities in the members testify to their union with the head. The apostle says that One is 'the Head,' but 'from Him the whole body (being closely joined and knit together through every joint of the system according to the functioning in due measure of each single part) derives its increase.' And it is fitting for this to be taught through the word 'head,' for, just as in the case of animals, the impulse towards action is given to the body from the head. The movement of the feet and the action of the hands control each act through sight and hearing and, if the eye is not directing or the ear not receiving guidance, it is not possible for any of the necessary actions to come about. Thus, it is necessary for us, also, to move our bodies in accordance with the true Head towards every action and undertaking, wherever 'he that formed the eye' or 'He who shaped the ear' leads. Moreover, since the

Head looks 'to the things above,' it is entirely necessary for the members being in harmony with Him to follow His lead and to be inclined to the things above.

But, when we hear that He is 'the firstborn of every creature' and 'firsborn from the dead,' and 'the firstborn among many brethren,' let us, first of all, dismiss the heretical assumptions, since the shameful dogmatic implications of these have nothing to do with those phrases. And, after that, let us determine the ethical implication of these words for our life. For when those who are fighting against God say that the 'only-begotten' God, 'the creator of all,' the One 'from whom and through whom and unto whom all things are,' is the work and creation and product of God, and, on this account, interpret the phrase 'the firstborn of every creature' as meaning that He is the brother of every creature, taking precedence because of the rights of the eldest in time, as Reuben does over his own brothers, and that He is placed first, not because of His nature, but because of the rights of the eldest, this must, first of all, be said to them, that it is not possible for the same person to be believed to be the only-begotten and the firstborn. For the only-begotten is not thought of as having brothers and the firstborn is not thought of apart from his brothers, but, if one is only-begotten, he does not have brothers; and, if he is the firstborn of brothers, it is altogether impossible for him to be or to be spoken of as an only-begotten. Therefore, these words do not coincide and have no common application to the same person, since it is not possible for the same person to be called the two things, only-begotten and firstborn. And yet it is said in the Scripture concerning the Logos that He is an 'only-begotten' God and, again, in Paul, that he is 'the firstborn of every creature.' Therefore, it is fitting to distinguish each of these phrases, analyzing them accurately by the criterion of truth. The Logos existing before time is 'only-begotten'; but, since all creation after this came into being in Christ, the Logos made flesh is 'the firstborn' of creation. And whatever thought comes to us when we learn that He is the 'firstborn from the dead' and the 'firstborn among many brethren,' let us understand it as following upon the concept of Him as 'the firstborn of every creature.' Indeed, 'the firstborn of the dead' becomes the One born as 'the first fruits of those who have fallen asleep,' in order to provide for the resurrection of all flesh. Through His engendering from above, and through His making us 'children of the day and children of light,' born 'of water and the Spirit,' although we are those 'who were by nature children of wrath,' He Himself acts as our guide in this birth in the water of the Jordan, sprinkling on us the grace of the Spirit in accordance with the first fruits of his nature. Thus, all those brought into life by this spiritual rebirth are called brothers of the One born before them 'through water and the spirit.' In the same way, also, thinking of Him as the firstborn of every 'new creature in Christ,' we do not go beyond a reverent interpretation. For when the old creature transgressed and became useless through sin, the new creature necessarily took on the role of those who had disappeared, having been formed through the rebirth and 'the resurrection from the dead.' Because He is considered the leader in this life, He is and He is called 'the firstborn of every creature.' How necessary it is to have truth as a self-sufficient ally could easily be demonstrated to the attentive by the few words that have been said. But, how these words appear to contribute to a virtuous life, we shall explain briefly.

Reuben was the firstborn of those born after him, and their resemblance to him bore witness to their relationship to him, so that their brotherhood was not unrecognized, being testified to by the similarity of appearance. Therefore, if, through the same rebirth 'by water and the spirit,' we also have become brothers of the Lord, He having become for us 'the firstborn among the many brethren,' it follows that our nearness to Him will show in the character of our life, because 'the firstborn of every creature' has informed our life. But what have we learned from Scripture that the character of His life is? What we have said many times, that: 'He committed no sin, nor was deceit found in his mouth.' Therefore, if we are going to act as brothers of the One who gave us birth, the sinlessness of our life will be a pledge of our relationship to Him and no filth will nullify our union with His purity. But the firstborn is also justice and holiness and love and redemption and such things. So if our life is characterized by such qualities, we furnish clear tokens of our noble birth, and anyone, seeing these qualities in our life, will bear witness to our brotherhood with Christ. For He Himself opened the door of the resurrection and, on this account, became 'the firstborn of them that sleep.' He indicated this, that we shall all rise 'in the twinkling of an eye, at the last trumpet,' and He did this for those who were with Him and the rest who are conquered by death.

Nor in the life after this will there be the same resurrection for all who rise from the tomb of earth, for it says: 'They who have done good shall come forth unto resurrection of life; but they who have done evil unto resurrection of judgment.' So that if someone's life tends toward the fearful judgment, that person, even if he happened to be numbered among the brethren of the Lord through the birth from on high, belies the name and denies his nearness to the firstborn because of his evil form. But, 'the Mediator between God and men' who through Himself joins the human being to God connects to God only that which is worthy of union with Him. For just as He in Himself assimilated His own human nature to the power of the Godhead, being a part of the common nature, but not being subject to the inclination to sin which is in that nature (for it says: 'He did no sin, nor was deceit found in his mouth'), so, also, will He lead each person to union with the Godhead if they do nothing unworthy of union with the Divine. But, if anyone is truly 'the temple of God,' containing no idol or shrine of evil in himself, this person is given a share in the Godhead by the Mediator, having become pure through the reception of His purity. 'Into a soul that plots, evil wisdom enters not,' as Scripture says, nor does 'the clean of heart' see anything else in himself except God, and, cleaving to Him through incorruptibility, he receives the whole of the good kingdom within himself. What has been said becomes clear to us if we take as an adjunct to it the message of the Lord sent to the apostles through Mary (Magdalene); He says: 'I ascend to my Father and your Father, to my God and to your God.' It is the Mediator between the Father and the disinherited who says this, the One who reconciled the enemies of God to the true and only Godhead. For when, according to the prophetic word, men were alienated from the life-giving womb through sin, and went astray from the womb in which they were fashioned, they spoke falsehood instead of truth. Because of this, the Mediator, assuming the first fruit of our common nature, made it holy through His soul and body, unmixed and unreceptive of all evil, preserving it in Himself. He did this in order that, having taken it up to the Father of incorruptibility through His own incorruptibility, the entire group might be drawn along with it because of its related nature, and in order that the Father might admit the disinherited to 'adoption' as sons, and the enemies of God to a share in His own Godhead. And just as the first fruit of dough was assimilated through purity and innocence to the true Father and God, so we, also, as dough in similar ways will cleave to the Father of incorruptibility by imitating, as far as we can, the innocence and stability of the Mediator. Thus, we shall be a crown of precious stones for the only-begotten God, having become an honor and a glory through our life. For Paul says that: 'Having made himself a little lower than the angels because of his having suffered death, he made those whose nature had previously become thorny through sin into a crown for himself, transforming the thorn through suffering into honor and glory.' And yet, once He has 'taken away the sins of the world' and taken upon His head a crown of thorns, in order to weave a crown of 'honor and glory,' there is no small danger that someone be discovered to be a burr and a thorn, because of his evil life, and then placed in the middle of the Master's crown because of sharing in His body. The just voice speaks directly to this one: 'How didst thou come in here without a wedding-garment?' 'How were you, a thorn, woven in with those fitted into my crown through honor and glory?' 'What harmony is there between Christ and Belial? What part has the believer with the unbeliever?' 'What has light in common with the darkness?' In order that none of these charges be made against our life, we must take care to avoid every thorny deed and word and thought throughout our entire life, so that having become an honor and glory through a pure and innocent regimen, we ourselves shall crown the Head of all, having become, as it were, a treasure and a possession for the Master. 'The Lord of Glory' cannot be and cannot be called the Lord of any dishonored person. Therefore, the person free from unseemliness and shamelessness in the hidden and visible man makes his won master the One who is and is called 'the Lord of Glory' and not the lord of dishonor.

And He is also a 'beginning.' But a beginning of anything is no different from what comes after itself. If someone defines the beginning as life, what comes afterwards will also be considered life. And if the beginning is light, what comes after the beginning will also be considered light. But what benefit do we derive from believing that He is the beginning? We become ourselves what we believe our beginning to be. For the beginning of darkness is not called the light, nor do we consider death a continuation of what is referred to as the beginning of life. But, unless a person is of the same nature as what produced him, i.e., connected with the beginning through innocence and virtue, the One who is the 'beginning' of being would not be his beginning. 'The ruler of darkness' is the beginning of the dark life, the one having power over death is the beginning of death-bringing sin. Truly, it is not possible for the person who is allied with the beginning of darkness because of his wicked life to say that his own beginning is the beginning of all good. And his being called 'the king of justice and peace' imparts the same notion for those who accept the words of the divine Master for their own good. For, according to the teaching on prayer, the person who prays that the kingdom of God may come to him, once he has learned that the true king is the 'king of justice and peace,' will set up justice and peace completely in his own life, in order that the king of justice and peace may be his king. Every virtue of the king is thought of as part of a military force; for I think it is necessary to think of all virtues in connection with justice and peace. If, then, a person having left his post in God's expedition enlists in the ranks of a different group and becomes a soldier of the inventor of evil, putting off the breastplate of justice and peace and all peaceful armor, how can this one be stationed under the king of peace after having thrown away the shield of truth? For it is clear that the device on one's armor will show who one's king is, and the leader is revealed by the character of one's life, instead of by the emblem sketched on the armor. How blessed is he who is drawn up under the divine generalship and enlisted in the ranks of the thousands and thousands of men armed against evil with virtues which are imprinted with the image of the king.

And why was it necessary to prolong the discourse by bringing in the sequence of phrases by which the name of the Lord is interpreted, those phrases, which can lead the way to a life of virtue, each name, by its particular emphasis, accomplishing something for us in the perfecting of our life? I say that it is good for these things to be remembered and reviewed so that there may be some guidance for us in the scope of the discourse which we proposed in the beginning, when we asked how anyone can achieve perfection in himself. For I think that if a person always keeps this in mind, that he is a participant in the revered name, when he is called a Christian according to the teaching of the apostles, he will also necessarily show in himself the power of the other names by which Christ is thought of, since through his life he is a sharer in each of them.

What do I mean? Three things characterize the life of Christ: action, word, thought. For thought is the beginning of every word; second, after the thinking, is the word which reveals through the voice the thought coined in the soul; and action has the third rank after mind and thought, bringing what is thought to action. So, when the sequence of life brings us to any one of these, it is good to examine accurately these divine ideas of every word, deed, and thought by which Christ is known and called, lest our deed or word or thought be carried beyond the power of those high terms. As Paul says: 'All that is not from faith is sin,' as can be shown clearly from the following. Every word or deed or thought that does not look to Christ looks completely to the adversary of Christ. For it is not possible for what is outside of light or life not to be completely in darkness or in death. If, then, what is not done or spoken or thought in accordance with Christ is akin to the adversary of the good, what is revealed through these words is clear to all, namely, that the person outside of Him rejects Christ by what he thinks, does, or says. Therefore, the voice of the prophet speaks the truth when it says: 'I have accounted all the wicked of the earth as dross.' For, just as one who denies Christ in his pursuits is a sinner against the revered name, so, also, if someone rejects truth or justice or holiness and incorruptibility; or if, in the moment of his fight with his passions, he casts from his life any of the other qualities considered virtues, he is called a sinner by the prophecy, sinning

90

through each of these in his life. What, then, is it necessary to do to be worthy of the name of Christ? What else than to distinguish in one's self the proper thoughts and words and deeds, asking whether they look to Christ or are at odds with Christ. Making the distinction is very easy. For whatever is done or thought or said through passion has no agreement with Christ, but bears the character of the adversary, who smears the pearl of the soul with the mud of the passions and dims the luster of the precious stone. What is free from every passionate inclination looks to the source of passionlessness, who is Christ. Drawing from Him as from a pure and uncorrupted stream, a person will show in his thoughts such a resemblance to his Prototype as exists between the water in the running water or stream and the water taken away from there in a jar. For the purity in Christ and the purity seen in the person who has a share in Him are the same, the One being the stream and the other drawn from it, bringing intellectual beauty to his life, so that there is agreement between the hidden and the visible man, since the graceful bearing of our life coincides with our thoughts which are put into motion in accordance with Christ.

This, therefore, is perfection in the Christian life in my judgment, namely, the participation of one's soul and speech and activities in all of the names by which Christ is signified, so that the perfect holiness, according to the eulogy of Paul, is taken upon oneself in 'the whole body and soul and spirit,' continuously safeguarded against being mixed with evil. But what if someone should say that the good is difficult to achieve, since only the Lord of creation is immutable, whereas human nature is unstable and subject to change, and ask how it is possible for the fixed and unchangeable to be achieved in the changeable nature? We reply to such an argument that one cannot be worthily crowned 'unless he has competed according to the rules.' For how can there be a lawful contest if there is no opponent? If there is no opponent, there is no crown. Victory does not exist by itself, without there being a defeated party. Let us struggle, therefore, against this very unstable element of our nature, engaging in a close contest with our opponent, as it were, not becoming victors by destroying our nature, but by not allowing it to fall. For does man make a change only towards evil? Indeed, it would not be possible for him to be on the side of the good if he were by nature inclined only to a single one of the opposites. In fact, the fairest product of change is the increase of goods, the change to the better always changing what is nobly changed into something more divine. Therefore, I do not think it is a fearful thing (I mean that our nature is changeable). The Logos shows that it would be a disadvantage for us not to be able to make a change for the better, as a kind of wing of flight to greater things. Therefore, let no one be grieved if he sees in his nature a penchant for change. Changing in everything for the better, let him exchange 'glory for glory,' becoming greater through daily increase, ever perfecting himself, and never arriving too quickly at the limit of perfection. For this is truly perfection: never to stop growing towards what is better and never placing any limit on perfection.

St. Augustine
354-430

The Confessions *of St. Augustine is a source of great joy and encouragement to the Christian world. It is the story of the human spirit searching for God and of a specific human who sought and found that God. It assures the Christian of his human value, invites him to overcome the fears and anxieties that hold him prisoner, urges him on toward the freedom of love in God. Few books have had as great an impact on Christianity as the* Confessions. *Though written as a kind of spiritual autobiography by Augustine at the close of the fourth century, it is the common property of all mankind.*

Augustine is one of those exceptional human beings who seems to be beyond the barriers of space and time. Yet his autobiography reveals a humanness that makes the reader feel at ease with him immediately. The general lines of his life are well known. He was born in 354, was well-educated, lived a life of sensual pleasures for several years, was constantly searching for truth and intellectual fulfillment, underwent a dramatic conversion process, and developed into the most influential theologian in the western Christian tradition. He died as Bishop of Hippo, Africa, in 430. His was a life that voyaged through darkness and light, that knew joy and sorrow, that drifted downward into the abyss of sin and soared up to unimaginable heights of graceful union with God. His brilliant intellect explored the depths of the human soul in an effort to capture its mysterious origin. This was the search that led him to exclaim, "You have made us for yourself, and our heart is restless until it rests in you." (Confessions, I.1)

God, transcendent yet ever present, was quite real to Augustine. He was the Source and Creator of all existing beings and the whole of existence was moving toward union with God through the God-man Jesus Christ. Meditation on the writings of St. Paul and St. John enabled Augustine to mature in this basic insight and to build his entire spirituality on it.

In the Confessions, *one meets this spirituality in a highly personal manner. Augustine is in dialogue with his God. He reviews before God his childhood and teenage years, his involvement with the Manichaean heresy, his experiences in Rome and Milan. He tells of his intellectual problems, of his struggle with belief and his conversion. The final books of the* Confessions *treat the themes of time and eternity, form and matter, and the creation of the world.*

Taken as a whole, the Confessions *constitute a rare lesson in Christian spirituality. Their timeless appeal is due to the fact that Augustine touched fundamental aspects of the human condition. He brought to light the human need for purification, for love, for union. He made it possible for mankind to enter fearlessly into intimate conversation with God, to recognize the fact of sin, and to accept with gratitude the redeeming and unifying grace of God.*

Augustine's influence becomes operative each time a human being becomes aware of a strange restlessness of the heart and sets out to know and love a divine being who, though dwelling far beyond the realms of the human, is already present within the human soul.

CONFESSIONS

BOOK TEN

CHAPTER 1

I shall know Thee,' O Knower of mine, 'I shall know Thee even as I have been known.' Virtue of my soul, go deep into it and make it fit for Thee, that Thou mayset have and possess it 'without spot or wrinkle.' This is my hope and that is why I speak, and in this 'hope I rejoice,' when my joy is sound. As for the other things of this life: the more tears they receive, the less are they deserving of tears; the less tears are shed over them, the more do they deserve tears. 'For behold Thou hast loved truth.' since 'he who does the truth, comes to the light.' I desire to do this in my heart, before Thee in confession; and in my writing before many witnesses.

CHAPTER 2

Even if I were unwilling to confess unto Thee, what could be hidden in me from Thee, O Lord, to whose eyes the abyss of human conscience is naked? I should but hide Thee from myself, not myself from Thee. Now, indeed, that my groaning is a witness that I am displeased with myself, Thou art refulgent, pleasing, lovable and desirable, that I may be ashamed of myself, reject myself and choose Thee, and that I may be pleasing neither to Thee nor myself, except on account of Thee.

Before Thee, then, O Lord, I lie unconcealed, whatever I may be. Yet, I have already said what is the fruit of my confessing to Thee. Nor am I doing it with fleshly words and speech, but with the words of the soul and the clamor of cogitation, which Thy ear doth recognize. For, when I am bad, to confess to Thee is nothing but to be displeased with myself; when I am good, to confess to Thee is simply not to attribute this to myself. For, Thou, O Lord, dost bless the just man, but first Thou dost rectify him from his impiety. And so, my confession, O my

God, is made silently to Thee in Thy sight, yet not silently. It is silent in relation to noise, but, in the sphere of feeling, it cries aloud. Nor do I say any right thing to men which Thou hast not heard before from me, nor dost Thou hear any such thing from me which Thou hast not previously said to me.

CHAPTER 3

But, what business have I with men that they should hear my confessions, as if they could become the healers 'of all my diseases?' A race interested in finding out about the other man's life, slothful in amending their own! Why do they seek to hear from me what I am, when they do not wish to hear from Thee what they are? And how do they know whether I am telling the truth when they hear about me from myself, since no one 'among men knows what goes on in a man, save the spirit of the man which is in him?' But, if they hear about themselves from Thee, they cannot say: 'the Lord is lying.' For, what is it to hear about oneself from Thee, but to know oneself? Who, then, can know himself and say: 'It is false,' unless he himself lies? But, because 'charity believes all things,' certainly among those whom it makes one, in intimate union with each other, I, also, O Lord, do even confess to Thee in such a way that men may hear, though I cannot prove to them that the things I confess are true. But, they whose ears charity doth open unto me, they believe me.

Do Thou, however, my inner Physician, make clear to me with what profit I am doing these things. For, the confessions of my past evils (which Thou hast 'forgiven and covered up,' so that Thou mightest make me blessed in Thee, changing my soul by faith and Thy Sacrament) may, when they are read and heard, excite the heart so that it will not lie in a torpor of despair and say: 'I cannot,' but will rather wake up in the love of Thy mercy and in the sweetness of Thy grace, whereby every weak man is made strong, provided he becomes aware through it of his own weakness. It is a joy for good men to hear of the past evils of those who are now free from them; not that joy arises from the fact that there are evils, but from the fact that they were, but do not now exist.

With what profit, therefore, O my Lord, to whom my conscience confesses daily, being more secure in the hope of Thy mercy than in its own innocence—with what profit, I ask, do I also confess to men through these writings, in Thy presence, not what I have been, but what I am. Now, the profit of confessing of the past I have observed and noted. Yet, what I now am, right at this very time of my confessions, many people desire to know, both those who know me and those who do not. They have heard something from me or about me, but their ear is not close to my heart, where I am whatever I am. They wish, then, to hear me confessing what I am within myself, where neither eye nor ear nor mind can reach in; they wish this as believers, for how could they know it? Charity, whereby they are good, tells them that I do not lie in confessing about myself, and it, being present in them, believes me.

CHAPTER 4

But, to what profit do they wish this? Do they desire to join me in giving thanks, when they hear how near I approach Thee through Thy grace, and to pray for me, when they hear how much I am retarded by my own weight? I will reveal myself to such people. For, it is no small profit, O Lord my God, that 'thanks will be given by man on our behalf,' and that Thou shouldst be implored by many for our sake. Let the brotherly mind love in me what Thou dost teach to be worthy of love, and lament in me what Thou dost teach to be worthy of lament.

Let the mind doing this be brotherly, not alien, not 'of strange children, whose mouth hath spoken vanity: and their right hand the right hand of iniquity,' but a brotherly one which, approving me, rejoices for me, disapproving me, becomes sad for me, because, whether approving or disapproving me, it loves me. To such people, I will reveal myself. Let them breathe easily over my good deeds, breathe anxiously over my evil ones. My good deeds are Thy arrangements and Thy gifts; my evil ones are my own offenses and Thy judgments. Let them breathe easily over the former and anxiously over the latter, and let hymns and weeping ascend in Thy sight from brotherly hearts,

Thy censers. But do Thou, O Lord, delighted with the scent of Thy holy temple, 'have mercy on me according to Thy great mercy' because of Thy Name, and, in no wise forsaking Thy undertakings, bring my imperfections to perfection.

This is the fruit of my confessions, that I should confess, not what kind of man I was, but what kind I am; and this, not only before Thee in hidden rejoicing with trembling, and in hidden grief with hope, but even unto the ears of believers among the sons of men, of the companions of my joy and the colleagues of my mortality, of my fellow citizens and the pilgrims in my company, those who have gone before and those who go after, and those who share my company on the way. These are Thy servants, my brethren, whom Thou didst desire as Thy sons, my masters, whom Thou didst command me to serve, provided I wish to live with Thee and from Thee. And this Word of Thine would amount to little, if it prescribed to me by words only and did not first lead the way by deeds. I serve these men by words and deeds; I do so 'under Thy wings,' with every great risk, except for the fact that my soul is protected under Thy wings and my weakness is known to Thee. I am very little, but my Father lives forever and My Protector is adequate for me. For He is the same Being, He who has generated me and who protects me. Thou Thyself art all my goods, Thou omnipotent Being who art with me even before I am with Thee. So, I will reveal myself to such men, the kind whom Thou has commanded me to serve—showing not what I was, but what I now am, and what I am still. However, 'I do not even judge myself.'

Thus, then, may I be heard.

CHAPTER 5

For it is Thou, O Lord, who dost judge me. Because, though no one 'knows the things of a man save the spirit of the man which is in him,' there is nevertheless something in a man which even the very spirit of the man does not know which is in him; but Thou, O Lord, knowest all about him, Thou who hast made him. In fact, though I despise myself before Thy sight and consider myself but earth and ashes, yet I do know something about Thee which I do not know about myself.

Truly, 'we see now through a mirror in an obscure manner,' not yet 'face to face.' And so, as long as I am a wanderer away from Thee, I am more present to myself than to Thee, and yet I know that Thou canst in no way be affected from without. But, in fact, I do not know what temptations I may be strong enough to resist and what ones I cannot. Yet, there is hope, for Thou 'art faithful, Thou wilt not permit us to be tempted beyond what we can bear, rather Thou wilt also with the temptation provide a way out that we may be able to bear it.'

Therefore, I will confess what I know of myself and what I do not know of myself, since even what I do know about myself I know by virtue of Thy enlightenment of me, and what I do not know about myself I remain ignorant of, until my 'darkness shall become as the noonday' in Thy sight.

CHAPTER 6

I love Thee, O Lord, not with doubtful but with assured awareness. Thou hast pierced my heart with Thy Word and I have loved Thee. The heaven and earth, also, and all things which are in them, see how, on all sides, they tell me to love Thee. Nor do they cease to tell to all men 'that they may be without excuse.' More profoundly, however, 'wilt Thou have mercy on whom Thou wilt have mercy, and wilt Thou show pity, to whom Thou wilt show pity:' otherwise, heaven and earth speak Thy praises to the deaf.

But, what do I love, when I love Thee? Not the prettiness of a body, not the gracefulness of temporal rhythm, not the brightness of light (that friend of these eyes), not the sweet melodies of songs in every style, not the fragrance of flowers and ointments and spices, not manna and honey, not limbs which can be grasped in fleshly embraces—these I do not love, when I love my God. Yet, I do love something like a light, a voice, an odor, food, an embrace, when I love my God—the light, voice, odor, food, embrace of my inner man, wherein for my soul a light shines, and place does not encompass it, where there is a sound which time does not sweep away, where there is a fragrance which the breeze does not disperse, where there is a flavor which eating does not diminish, and where

99.

there is a clinging which satiety does not disentwine. This is what I love, when I love my God.

And what is this?

I asked the earth, and it answered: 'It is not I.' Whatever things are in it uttered the same confession. I asked the sea, the depths, the creeping things among living animals, and they replied: 'We are not Thy God; look above us.' I asked the airy breezes, and the whole atmosphere with its inhabitants said: 'Anaximenes is mistaken; I am not God.' I asked the sky, the sun, the moon, the stars: 'Nor are we the God whom you seek,' they said. And I said to all these things which surround the entryways of my flesh: 'Tell me about my God, since you are not He; tell me something about Him.' With a loud voice, they cried out: 'He made us.' My interrogation was looking upon them, and their reply was their beauty.

Then, I turned to myself and said: 'Who art thou?' And I answered: 'A man.' Here are the body and soul in me, standing ready to serve me; the one without, the other within. From which of these should I have sought my God, whom I had already sought in the realm of body from earth to sky, as far as I could send out the messenger rays of my eyes? But, the better is what is interior. To it, indeed, as to an overseer and judge, all the messengers of the body send back their messages concerning the answers of heaven and earth, and all things in them, which say: 'We are not God,' and: 'He has made us.' The interior man knows these things through the help of the exterior man; I, the interior man knew these things, I, I, the mind through the senses of my body. I asked the whole frame of the world concerning my God and it replied to me: 'I am not He, but He has made me.'

Is not this beauty evident to all whose sense perception is intact? Why does it not speak the same thing to all men? Tiny and large animals see it, but they cannot interrogate it—for reason is not placed above the message-carrying senses in them, as a judge. But, men are able to ask, so that 'they may clearly see the invisible attributes of God, being understood through the things that are made, but through love they are made subject to these things and, being thus subjected, are not able to judge. These things do not reply to questioners unless these latter are capable of judging. Not that they change their voice, that is, their beautiful appearance, if one being simply sees, while another sees and interrogates, so that it appears one way to the first and another way to the second—but, appearing just the same to both, it is mute to one, while it speaks to the other. Rather, it speaks to all, but the latter understand, for they take in its voice from outside and compare it with the truth within. Now, the truth says to me: 'Thy God is neither sky, nor earth, nor any body.' This, their own nature states. Men see: it is a thing with bulk, smaller in its part than its whole. Now, you are better—I am talking to you, my soul—since you activate the bulk of your body, giving it life, which no body confers on a body. God, however, is even for you the Life of life.

CHAPTER 7

What, then, do I love, when I love my God? Who is He, above the head of my soul? I shall go up through my soul itself to Him. I shall pass beyond my life-force, whereby I cling to the body and fill its frame with life. I do not find my God by that force, for 'the horse and the mule, who have no understanding,' would find it likewise, since it is the same force by which their bodies also live.

There is another force, by which I not only vivify but also sensify my flesh which the Lord has framed for me, commanding the eye not to hear, the ear not to see, but assigning to the former through which I may see and to the latter through which I may hear and to the other senses, according to their organs and functions, their proper objects respectively. I, being one mind, do these different things through them. I shall also pass above this force of mine, for the horse and mule have this, too; they also sense through the body.

CHAPTER 8

So, I shall also pass above this power of my nature, ascending by degrees toward Him who made me, and I come into the fields and broad palaces of memory, where there are treasures of innumerable images, brought in from all sorts of sense objects. There is stored away whatever we cogitate on, too, either by adding to, or taking away from, or changing in any

way the things which sense perception has contacted, and anything else kept or put back there, which forgetfulness has not
yet engrossed and buried.

When I am in it, I can request that whatever I wish be
brought forward. Some things come forth immediately; others
are hunted after for a longer time, yet they are dug out as it
were from some more concealed containers; still others rush
out in a mob, when something else is sought and looked for,
jumping forth in the middle as if to say: 'Would we do, perhaps?' These I drive away from the face of my remembrance
with the hand of my heart, until what I want becomes clear
and enters into sight from the secret places. Other things come
up as they are required, in easy and uninterrupted sequence.
The first ones give way to those which follow and, in leaving,
are stored up to come forth again when I desire it. All of this
goes on, when I recite something memorized.

In it, all things are kept distinct and classified. They are
carried in, each by its own channel—light, for instance, and all
colors and shapes of bodies through the eyes; through the ears
all kinds of sounds; all odors through the channel of the nostrils;
all flavors through the channel of the mouth; and then, by the
sensitivity of the whole body, what is hard or soft, hot or cold,
smooth or rough, heavy or light, whether outside or inside the
body. All these the great recess of memory, and its indescrib-
ably hidden and mysterious chasms, take in, to be called to
mind and reviewed, when need arises. All these things go in,
each by its own gateway, and are there stored away. The
things themselves do not go in, of course, but the images of
sensible things are ready, there, for the cogitation which recalls
them.

Just how these are fashioned who can say, though it is
evident by which senses they are caught up and stored away
within? For, even while I dwell in darkness and silence, I can,
if I wish, produce colors in my memory, and distinguish between white and black and between any others as I wish. Nor
do sounds rush in and disturb the object drawn in through the
eyes, when I am considering it; yet, they are there, also, and
life hidden in separation, as it were. I can summon these, too,
if it pleases me, and they are present at once; with tongue at

rest and silent throat, I can sing as much as I wish. The images of colors, despite the fact that they are present, do not intervene or break in when another store, which has flowed in through the ears, is reviewed. Thus, I can remember at will the other things which have been taken in and piled up through the other senses. I can distinguish the fragrance of lilies from that of violets, while smelling nothing, and I can prefer honey to a decoction of musk, smooth to rough, and not by tasting or touching anything at the time, but by recollecting.

I do this inside, in the immense palace of my memory. In it, sky, earth, and sea are present before me, together with all the things I could perceive in them, except for those which I have forgotten. In it, I even encounter myself and I bring myself to mind: what, when and where I did something, and how I felt when I did it. In it are all the things which I remember, either those personally experienced or those taken on faith. Out of the same supply, even, I can take now these, now those likenesses of things (whether those experienced or those derived from experience) and combine them with things of the past, and from these I can even think over future actions, happenings, and hopes—and all these, again, as if in the present. 'I shall do this or that,' I say within myself in this huge recess of my mind, filled with the images of things so many and so great, and this or that follows in consequence. 'Oh, if this or that could happen!' 'May God prevent this or that!'—I say these things to myself, and, while I say them, the images of all the things I am saying are present from the same storehouse of memory. I could not say anything at all about them, if they were lacking.

Great is this power of memory, exceeding great, O my God, a vast and unlimited inner chamber. Who has plumbed its depths? Yet, this is a power of my mind and it belongs to my nature; I myself do not grasp all that I am. Is, then, the mind too narrow to hold itself, so that the questions arise: Where is this thing which belongs to it, and it cannot grasp? Would it be outside it, and not in it? How, then, does it not grasp it? A mighty wonder rises before me, and on this point astonishment seizes me.

Yet, men go to admire the mountains' peaks, giant waves in the sea, the broad courses of rivers, the vast sweep of the ocean, and the circuits of the stars—and they leave themselves behind! They feel no wonder that I did not see with my eyes all these things when I was talking about them. Yet, I could not have talked of them unless I could see within, in my memory, in their vast expanses, as if I were seeing them externally, the mountains, waves, rivers, and stars which I have seen, and the ocean which I take on faith. Yet, I did not, by vision, take these things into me, when I saw them with my eyes. They are not themselves with me, but just their images. And I know for each what was impressed on me by each sense of the body.

CHAPTER 9

These are not the only things which the vast capacity of my memory bears. Here, also, are all those things which have been grasped from the liberal disciplines and which have not yet been forgotten—put aside, as it were, in an inner place which is not a place. Nor do I carry the images of these, but the things themselves. For, what literature is, what skill in discussion is, how many kinds of questions there are, whatever things like this I know, are present in my memory in a special way. I have not left the thing outside and just retained the image—nor has it existed as a sound and then passed away, like a spoken word impressed through the ears, through a vestigial image, by which in recollection it again sounds, as it were, when it is not actually sounding—nor, as an odor, while passing and disappearing on the breezes, affects the sense of smell from which it sends in its image to the memory, for us to recall when remembering—nor, as food, which, of course, causes no taste when already in the stomach, yet is tasted, in a way, in memory—nor, as some object perceived by touching it with the body, which the memory pictures even when it is separated from us. In fact, these things are not introduced into the memory, but their images alone are grasped with marvelous speed, and are put away in wonderful compartments, and come forth in a wondrous way through remembering.

CHAPTER 10

However, when I hear that there are three kinds of questions—Whether a thing is? What it is? What kind it is?—I keep the images of the sounds by which these words are constituted, of course, and I know that they have passed away through the air, accompanied by noise, and now do not exist. But, the things themselves, which are signified by these sounds, I did not attain by any sense of the body, nor did I see them anywhere else than in my mind; yet, I have stored up in memory, not their image, but the things themselves.

If they can, let them tell me whence these things have come into me. For, I have gone over all the entrances of my flesh and have not found out by which one they came in. Of course, the eyes say: 'If they are colored, we have reported them'; the ears say: 'If they emitted sound, they have been made known by us'; the nostrils say: 'If they were odorous, they passed through us'; so also the sense of taste says: 'If it is not a matter of taste, do not ask me'; touch says: 'If it has no bodily bulk, I did not touch it; if I did not touch it, I did not make it known.'

From what source, and by what route, did these things enter into my memory? I do not know how. When I learned these things, I did not believe in another man's heart; rather, I recognized them in my own and I approved them as true. I committed them to it as to a repository, from which I could take them out when I desired. Therefore, they were there even before I learned them, but they were not in the memory. Where, then, and why did I know them when they were spoken, saying: 'It is so, it is true,' unless because they were already in memory, but so far removed, buried in its deeper enclosures, that, unless they had been dug out by something that suggested them, I should perhaps have been unable to think them.

CHAPTER 11

Therefore, we find that to learn things of this kind—whose images we do not acquire through sensation, but which we discern in themselves within us, without images and as they

105

are—is nothing else than, by cogitation, to make a kind of collation of the haphazard and unarranged contents of memory, and, through one's act of awareness, to command that they be placed close at hand, as it were, in this same memory, where they formerly lay scattered about and unnoticed, that they may eventually come easily to the attention of a mind already familiar with them.

How many things of this kind my memory holds which are already found out, and, as I say, placed ready at hand, as it were—things which we are said to have learned and to know! If I cease to recall them to mind for even a short period of time, they are again submerged and slip off, as it were, into the more removed recesses, so that they must again be excogitated, as if new, from the same place as before—there is no other place for them—and they must be drawn together [cogenda] again, so that they may be known. That is, they must be collected as if from a condition of being dispersed; hence, one speaks of cogitating. For, cogo [draw together] and cogito [cogitate] are related as are ago [do] and agito [do constantly] and as facio [make] and factito [make frequently]. But the mind has made this word its own property, so that what is collated, that is, drawn together, in the mind, but not in any other place, is now properly said to be cogitated.

CHAPTER 12

Again, memory contains the reason and innumerable laws of numbers and dimensions, none of which any bodily sense impresses; for, these are neither color, nor resonant, nor odorous, nor tasty, nor tangible. I have heard the sounds of words by which they are signified when there is a discussion about them, but these sounds are one thing and the objects are another. For, the sounds are different in Greek from what they are in Latin, but the things are neither Greek nor Latin, nor do they belong to any kind of language. I have seen the lines of craftsmen—even the thinnest ones, like a strand from a spider's web; but these [mathematical lines] are quite different. They are not the images of those lines which my fleshly eye has reported to me. They are known by whoever recognizes them interiorly, without cogitation about any body whatever. I have

106

perceived, also, the numbers which we reckon in all the bodily senses, but the ones *by which* we do the counting are quite different. They are not images of these, and so, they really exist. Let him laugh at my saying this, the man who does not see them. I shall pity him for laughing at me.

CHAPTER 13

I hold all these things in memory, and I also remember the way I learned them. I have heard and keep in memory the many things most falsely said against them in arguments. Now, even though they are false, the fact that I remember them is not false. I remember, too, that I distinguished between those truths and these errors which are said in opposition. In one way I see that I am now distinguishing these two things, and in another way I remember that I have often made this distinction when I cogitated on them. Therefore, I both remember that I have often understood these things and, as for the fact that I now perceive and understand them, this I store up in memory, so that afterwards I may remember that I now did understand. And so, I remember that I remembered, just as later, if I recall that I could now remember these things, I shall certainly recall it through the power of memory.

CHAPTER 14

The same memory contains also the feelings of my mind, not in the way that the mind itself possesses them, when it undergoes them, but quite differently, in the way that the power of memory is related to itself. For, I can remember having experienced joy, yet not be joyful; I recall my past sorrow, without being sorrowful; I recollect that I formerly was in fear, without present fear; and I have remembrance of former desire, without present desire. Sometimes, on the contrary, I reminisce about my departed sorrow with present joy, and my joy with present sorrow.

There is nothing to be wondered at in this, in regard to the body; the mind is one thing, the body another. Thus, if I remember with joy a past pain of the body, that is not so astonishing; however, this is different with the mind, since the mind is memory itself. Thus, when we give something to be memorized, we say: 'See that you keep this in mind'; and when we forget, we say: 'It was not in my mind' and 'It slipped my mind'—for we call the memory itself, mind.

Since this is so, then, how is it that, when I remember with joy my past sorrow, my mind possesses joy and my memory sorrow? And, when the mind is joyful from the fact that joy is present in it, how is it, then, that the memory is not sorrowful from the fact that sorrow is present in it? Does memory, perhaps, not belong to the mind? Who would claim this?

Without doubt, memory is something like a stomach for the mind; so, joy and sorrow are like sweet and bitter food. When they are committed to memory, conveyed down, as it were, into the stomach where they come to be stored, they cannot be tasted. It is ridiculous to consider these things similar, yet they are not entirely dissimilar.

But, look, when I say that there are four passions of the mind, I bring forth from memory desire, joy, fear, and sorrow. Whatever I could say in a discussion about them, by dividing each into the species within the genus of each and by defining them, it is in the memory that I find what to say and from there that I bring it forth. However, I do not suffer any of these passions when I take note of them by remembering. Yet, before they were recalled by me and reviewed, they were there. For that reason, it was possible to draw them out of it through remembrance.

It may be, then, that these are produced from memory, in the process of recall, just as food is from the stomach in the process of rumination. But, why is the sweetness of joy, or the bitterness of sorrow, not perceived in the mouth of cogitation by the man engaged in discussion, that is, the man who is reminiscing? Is this the point of dissimilarity, since they surely are not wholly alike? Who would willingly speak of things of this sort, if every time we mention sorrow or fear we were forced to undergo sorrow or fear? Yet, we would not speak of them unless we found in our memory not only the sounds of their names according to images impressed by the senses of the body, but also the notions of the things themselves which we did not receive through any avenue of the flesh. The mind itself, in sensing, through the experience of its own passions, committed them to memory; or, the memory retained them for itself, even though they were not committed to it.

CHAPTER 15

Whether through images or not, who can easily say? In fact, I can name a stone, I can name the sun, while the things themselves are not present to my senses. Of course, their images are at hand in my memory. I can name bodily pain, and it is not present in me when there is no suffering. Yet, unless its image were present in my memory, I would not know what I am talking about, and I would not distinguish it from pleasure, in a discussion. I can name the health of the body, while I am healthy in my body; the things itself is indeed present in me. Yet, in fact, unless its image were also present in my memory, I would not recall at all what the sound of this name meant. Nor would sick people know what was said, when health is named, unless the same image were kept by the power of memory, although the thing itself were absent from the body.

I can name the numbers by which we count; see, they are in my memory: not their images, but themselves. I can name the image of the sun and it is present in my memory. I do not recall an image of an image, but simply the image; it is present to me when I remember. I can name the memory and I recognize what I am naming. Where do I recognize it unless in memory itself? Now, could it be present to itself through its own image, and not through itself?

CHAPTER 16

Now, when I name oblivion, and likewise recognize what I am naming, what would be the source of my recognition if I did not remember it? I am not talking about the sound of the name, but the thing which it signifies. Now, if I had forgotten this meaning, I should not be able at all to recognize what the sound's function is. Therefore, when I remember my memory, the very memory is present to itself in itself, but, when I remember oblivion, both memory and oblivion are present— memory, as that from which I recall; oblivion, as that which I recall. But, what is oblivion except the privation of memory? How, then, can it be present, so that I may remember it, when I cannot remember while it is present? But, if we keep in memory what we remember, and if, without remembering oblivion, we could not possibly know the meaning of this word when we heard it, then oblivion is retained in memory. Therefore, it is present so that we will not forget, and, when it is present, we do forget.

Or, is one to understand from this that it is not present in memory through itself, when we remember it, but rather through its image—because, if oblivion were present in itself, would not the result be that we would forget, not that we would remember? Now, who will eventually work this out? Who will understand how it is?

Certainly, O Lord, I am working hard on it, and my work is being done on myself; I have become unto myself a soil of difficulty, and of too much sweat. For, we are not now gazing curiously at the sky's expanses, nor are we measuring the distances between the stars, nor are we trying to weigh the earth; I am the one who is remembering, I am the mind. It is not so astonishing if whatever I am not is far distant from me, but what is nearer to me than myself? And, notice, the power of my memory is not understood by me, yet, at the same time, I cannot speak of myself without it. What should I say, when it is a certitude to me that I do remember oblivion? Or, should I say that what I remember is not in my memory? Or, should I say that oblivion is in my memory just for this—that I may not forget? Both are most absurd.

What of a third possibility? On what basis may I say that the image of oblivion is kept in my memory, not oblivion itself, when I do remember it? On what basis, too, may I say this, since, when any image of a thing is impressed on memory, it is first necessary for the thing itself to be present, from which the image can be impressed? For, thus do I remember Carthage; thus, all the places where I have been; thus, the faces of the men I have seen and the things reported by the other senses; thus, the health of the body itself or its pain. When these things were at hand, my memory took the images from them, which, as being present, I might see directly and review in my mind when I remembered the things in their absence.

If, then, oblivion is held in memory through its image and not through itself, it must certainly have been present itself, in order that its image might be grasped. Now, when it was present, how did it write its image in the memory, when oblivion erases, by its presence, even what it finds already known? Yet, I am certain that I do remember in some manner or other, though this manner be incomprehensible and inexplicable, even oblivion itself, whereby the object we remember is consigned to destruction.

CHAPTER 17

Great is the power of memory; its deep and boundless multiplicity is something fearful, O my God! And this is the mind, and I am this myself. What, then, am I, O my God? What is my nature? A life of many aspects and many ways, strikingly immeasurable.

Look into the fields, hollows, and innumerable caverns of my memory, filled beyond number with innumerable kinds of things, either by means of images as in the case of all bodies, or by means of their own presence as in the case of the arts, or by means of some sort of notions or impressions as in the case of the feelings of the mind (which the memory keeps even when the mind is not undergoing them, though whatever is in the memory is in the mind!). I run through all these things, and I flit here and there. I even go as deep as I can, yet there is no limit. So great is the power of memory, so great is the power of life in man who lives mortally!

What shall I do, Thou true Life of mine, O my God? I shall pass over even this power of mine which is called memory; I shall pass over it to reach Thee, sweet Light. What dost Thou say to me? Behold, going up through my mind to Thee, who dwellest above me, I shall even pass over this power of mine which is called memory, desiring to attain Thee where Thou canst be attained, and to cleave to Thee where it is possible to be in contact with Thee.

For, even beasts and birds have memory; otherwise, they could not find their lairs and nests, or the many other things to which they become accustomed. And they could not grow accustomed to any thing, unless through memory. Therefore, I shall even pass over memory to attain Him who has set me apart from the four-footed beasts and made me 'wiser than the fowls of the air.' I shall even pass over memory, so that I may find Thee—where, O truly good and serene Sweetness—where shall I find Thee? But, if I find Thee without memory, I am without remembrance of Thee. And how, indeed, may I find Thee, if I am without remembrance of Thee?

CHAPTER 18

The woman who had lost her drachma and looked for it with a lamp would not have found it, unless she retained some remembrance of it. For, when it had been found, how would she know whether it was the one, if she retained no remembrance of it? I remember many lost things which I have looked for and found. From this, I know that, when I was looking for one of them, and people would say to me: 'Perhaps this is it? Maybe this one?' I would continue to say: 'It is not,' until the thing I was seeking was shown to me. Unless I had some remembrance of it, whatever it was, I should not have found it, even if it were shown to me, for I should not have recognized it. That is always the way it is, when we look for some lost thing and find it. Yet, of course, when by chance something is lost from sight, not from memory—any visible body, for example—its image is retained within, and it is sought until it comes back within view. And, when it is found, it is recognized from the image which is within. We do not say that we have found what we lost, if we do not recognize it, and we cannot recognize it, if we do not remember it. It disappeared, indeed, from before our eyes, but it was retained in memory.

CHAPTER 19

What? When the memory itself loses something, as happens when we forget and try to remember, pray, where do we look for it, unless in the memory itself? And in it, if one thing is presented in place of another, we reject it until the thing we are looking for turns up. When it does turn up, we say: 'This is it.' We would not say that unless we recognized it, and we would not recognize it unless we remembered. Yet, we certainly had forgotten it.

Or, had it disappeared, not completely, but only in part? And is the other part sought, by means of that which is retained, because the memory felt that its object of consideration was not as complete as usual, and, feeling the defect in a habit which was, as it were, defective in some part, it strove to get back what was missing?

For instance, if a man who is known comes before our eyes or into our thoughts, and we are trying to recall his name, which we have forgotten, then, any other name which occurs fails to be connected, because it has not been customary for our thought of him to go along with it; hence, it is rejected until that name occurs which our customary way of thinking of the man accepts as not inappropriate. And, from what source does it occur, if not from memory itself? For, when we recognize it, on being reminded by someone else, it is from there that it comes. So, we do not accept it as something new, but, in recalling it, we judge that what has been said is the right name. But, if it is entirely wiped out of mind, then we do not remember even when reminded. And, if we even remember that we have forgotten it, then we have not yet completely forgotten. Therefore, we would not be able to look for something that has been lost, if we had altogether forgotten it.

CHAPTER 20

Now, how do I look for Thee, O Lord? When I look for Thee, my God, I am looking for the happy life. May I seek Thee, so that my soul may live. For, my body has life from my soul, and my soul has life from Thee. How, then, do I seek the happy life? It is not mine, until I can say: 'Enough, there it is.' Here, then, I ought to say how I do look for it, whether through remembrance, as though I had forgotten it and I still retained the fact that I had forgotten, or through a desire to learn it as something unknown, either something I never knew, or which I have so forgotten that I have no remembrance even that I have forgotten it. Surely, the happy life is this: what all men desire and [such that] there is absolutely no one who does not desire it? Where did they know it, this object which they desire in such a way? Where did they see it, to love it so? Certainly, we do possess it, but how I know not.

There is one certain way whereby each man, when he possesses this object, is then happy, and there also are those who are happy in hope. The latter possess it in an inferior way, compared to those who are already really happy, yet they are better off than those others who are happy neither in reality nor in hope. Still, unless this third kind of people possessed it, in some way, they would not desire to be happy; that they have such a desire is most certain. Somehow or other they came to know it, and so they possess it in some kind or other of knowledge. My problem concerning this is whether it may be in the memory; for, if it is there, then we were at one time happy, either all individually, or all in that man who was the first to sin, in whom also we all died, from whom we are all born amidst unhappiness. I do not ask this question now, but I do ask whether the happy life is in the memory.

Now, we would not love it, unless we knew it. We hear this word and we all admit that we seek this thing, for we are not delighted merely by the sound. When a Greek hears this word in Latin, he is not delighted, for he does not know what has been said. Yet, we Latins are delighted, as he is, too, if he hears it in Greek, for the thing itself is neither Greek nor Latin, this thing which Greeks and Latins and men of every tongue yearn to obtain. So, it is known to all men who, if they could be asked whether they desire to be happy, would reply in one voice, without any hesitation, that they do. This would be impossible, unless the thing itself, of which this is the name, were kept in their memory.

CHAPTER 21

Now, is this the same as the case of the man who, having seen Carthage, remembers it? No! The happy life is not seen with the eyes, since it is not a body.

Is it like the example of our remembering numbers? No! One who possesses these in knowledge does not seek to obtain further, but we possess the happy life in knowledge, and so we love it, yet wish to attain it further so that we may *be* happy.

Is it like the instance where we remember the art of oratory? No! For, though, when this word has been heard people recall to mind the thing itself, even those who are not yet eloquent—and many do desire to be (whence it is apparent that eloquence exists in their knowledge), but, on the other hand, they have observed through the senses of the body that other people are eloquent and they are delighted and long to be likewise; they would not be delighted except from interior knowledge and they would not desire to be likewise unless they were so delighted. However, we do not have personal experience of the happy life in other people, through any sense of the body.

Is it like the way in which we remember joy? Perhaps so. For, I remember my joy even when sad, just as I do the happy life when I am unhappy, and I have never seen, or heard, or smelled, or tasted, or touched my joy by any sense of the body, but I have experienced it in my mind when I have been joyful. Its knowledge stuck in my memory, so that I am able to remember it, sometimes with contempt, sometimes with longing, depending on the difference between the things from which my joy came, as I remember it. For, I have been imbued with a certain joy arising from shameful things, and, as I now recall this, I feel disgust and curse it; at other times, it arises from good and virtuous things, and I recall it with longing, even though, perhaps, they are no longer available, and therefore I am saddened as I recall my former joy.

Where, then, and when did I experience my happy life that I should now remember, love, and desire it? Not just I alone, or in the company of a few people, but absolutely all people want to be happy. Unless we knew it with certain knowledge, we would not will it with such a certain act of will. But, how is this? If the question be asked of two men whether they wish to serve in the army, it is quite possible that one of them may reply that he wants to, the other that he does not. But, if they are asked whether they wish to be happy, both will say at once and without hesitation that they do desire it. Nor is there any different reason why one wishes to enter military service and the other does not, than that they wish to be happy. One man, perhaps, finds his joy in one thing, another man in another? Even so, they agree that they all wish to be happy, just as they would agree, if asked the question, that they wish to possess joy. This joy they call the happy life. Even though one man attains it here, another there, still it is but one thing which all men strive to reach, so that they may be joyful. Now, since this is a thing which no man can deny experiencing, it is therefore recognized as found in the memory, when the name, happy life, is heard.

CHAPTER 22

Far be it, O Lord, far be it from the heart of Thy servant who is confessing to Thee, far be it that I should consider myself happy by virtue of just any joy which I experience. For, there is a joy which is not given to the wicked, but rather to them who serve Thee for Thine own sake; for such people, Thou Thyself art Joy. And this is the happy life, to rejoice unto Thee, from Thee, on account of Thee: this it is and there is none other. They who think that there is another pursue a different joy, and not the true one. Yet, their will is not turned away from some representation of joy.

CHAPTER 23

Is it, then, uncertain that all men wish to be happy, because those who do not wish to find their joy in Thee—and this is the only happy life—do not, in point of fact, desire the happy life? Or, do all desire this, but, because 'the flesh lusts against the spirit, and the spirit against the flesh . . . so that they do not do what they wish,' they descend to that of which they are capable and are content with it, for they do not desire that for which they have insufficient capacity, to the extent that their desire would render them capable of it?

Now, I ask all men whether they would prefer to get their joy from truth rather than from falsity? They will hesitate as little to say that they prefer it from truth as they hesitate in saying that they wish to be happy. Indeed, the happy life is joy arising from truth. For, this is the joy coming from Thee, who art the Truth, O God; Thou art 'my light,' the salvation of my countenance, O my God. This happy life all men desire;

this life, which alone is happy, all men desire; the joy arising from truth all men desire.

I have been acquainted with many men who wished to deceive, but not one who wished to be deceived. Where, then, did they get their knowledge of this happy life, unless where they got their knowledge of truth, too? For they love the latter, also, since they do not wish to be deceived. And, when they love the happy life, which is nothing other than joy arising from truth, they certainly love truth, also. Nor would they love it, unless some knowledge of it were in their memory.

Why, then, do they not take their joy from it? Why are they not happy? Because they are more keenly concerned with other things which have greater power to make them unhappy than this, which they faintly remember, to make them happy. 'Yet a little while the light is' in men; let them walk, walk, lest darkness overtake them.

But, why does 'truth engender hatred' and Thy man who speaks the truth has become a enemy to them, when a happy life is loved and it is nothing but joy arising from truth? Is it that truth is so loved that, whoever love something else, they wish this object of love to be the truth, and, since they did not want to be deceived, they do not want to be shown that they have been deceived? Therefore, they hate the truth because of the same thing which they love in place of truth. They love truth when it enlightens; they hate it when it reproves. Since they not wish to be deceived, and they do wish to deceive, they love it when it reveals its own self, and they hate it when it reveals themselves. Its retribution upon them stems from this: they who do not wish to be revealed by it, it both reveals against their will and is not itself revealed to them.

Thus, thus, even thus is the human mind, even thus is it blind and weak; it wishes to lie hidden, a foul and unattractive thing, but does not wish anything to be hidden to it. What befalls it is the contrary: it is not hidden before the truth, but the truth is hidden before it. Nevertheless, even while it is in such unhappiness, it prefers to rejoice in true things rather than in false. It will be happy, then, if, with no hindrance interposed, it will come to rejoice in that through which all things are true, in the only Truth.

CHAPTER 24

See how much I have traveled about in the spaciousness of my memory while looking for Thee, O Lord, and I have not found Thee outside it. Nor have I found anything about Thee which I did not keep in memory, ever since I learned of Thee. For, from the time that I learned of Thee, I did not forget Thee. Now, wherever I found truth, there did I find my God, Truth Itself, and from the time that I learned of the Truth, I have not forgotten. Therefore, from the time that I learned about Thee, Thou dost dwell in my memory, and there do I find Thee when I remember Thee and delight in Thee. These are my holy delights which Thou hast given me in Thy mercy, having regard to my poverty.

CHAPTER 25

But, where dost Thou dwell in my memory, O Lord; where dost Thou dwell there? What resting place hast Thou fashioned for Thyself? What sanctuary hast Thou built for Thyself? Thou hast granted this favor to my memory, to dwell in it, but in which part of it Thou dost dwell, this I now consider. When I recalled Thee to mind, I went above those parts of it which the beasts also possess, for I did not find Thee there among the images of bodily things. So, I came to the parts of it in which I keep my mental feelings, but I did not find Thee there. So, I entered into the seat of my very mind, and there is one for it in my memory, since the mind also remembers itself, and Thou wert not there. Because, just as Thou art not a bodily image, nor the felling of a living being, such as occurs when we are joyful, sorrowful, longing, fearful, mindful, forgetful, or anything else of this kind, so, too, Thou art not the mind itself. For, Thou art the Lord God of the mind, and all these things are mutable, but Thou dwellest as an immutable Being above them all. So, Thou hast deigned to reside in my memory, from the time that I have learned about Thee.

And why do I look for the place in it where Thou dost dwell, as if there really were places in it? What is certain is that Thou dwellest in it, for I remember Thee from the time that I have learned about Thee, and I do find Thee in it when I recall Thee to mind.

CHAPTER 26

Where, then, did I find Thee in order to learn about Thee? For, Thou wert not already in my memory before I learned of Thee. Where, then, did I find Thee in order to learn about Thee, unless in Thyself above me? Yet, there is no place. We go backward and we go forward, yet there is no place. O Truth, Thou dost preside over all things, even those which can take counsel with Thee, and Thou dost answer in the same time all who consult Thee, however diverse their questions. Thou dost answer clearly, but all do not hear clearly. All seek counsel concerning what they wish, but they do not always hear what they wish. He serves Thee best who does not so much expect to hear the thing from Thee which he himself desires, but rather to desire what he hears from Thee.

CHAPTER 27

Late have I loved Thee, O Beauty so ancient and so new, late have I loved Thee! And behold, Thou wert within and I was without. I was looking for Thee out there, and I threw myself, deformed as I was, upon those well-formed things which Thou hast made. Thou wert with me, yet I was not with Thee. These things held me far from Thee, things which would not have existed had they not been in Thee. Thou didst call and cry out and burst in upon my deafness; Thou didst shine forth and glow and drive away my blindness; Thou didst send forth Thy fragrance, and I drew in my breath, and now I pant for Thee; I have tasted, and now I hunger and thirst; Thou didst touch me, and I was inflamed with desire for Thy peace.

CHAPTER 28

When I shall cleave to Thee with all my being, sorrow and toil will no longer exist for me, and my life will be alive, being wholly filled with Thee. At the present time, however, because Thou dost lift up whomever Thou fillest and I am not filled with Thee, I am a burden to myself. My joys, which are to be lamented, struggle against my sorrows, which are cause for joy, and I know not on which side victory may stand.

My evil sorrows struggle with my good joys, and I know not on which side victory may stand. Alas for me! Have mercy on me, O Lord! Alas for me! Behold, I do not hide my wounds: Thou art the Physician, I am a sick man; Thou art merciful, I am a miserable man. Is not 'the life of man upon earth a trial?' Who would want troubles and hardships? Thou dost command that they be endured, not loved. No man loves what he endures, even though he loves to endure. For, though he rejoice that he can endure them, he prefers to have nothing to endure. Amid adversities, I long for successes; amid successes, I fear adversities. What is the middle area between these, where the life of man is not a trial? Woe to the successes of this world, once and again, because of the fear of adversity and the corruption of joy. Woe to the adversities of this world, once, twice and thrice, because of the yearning for success, both because adversity itself is hard and because it may break down endurance! Is not 'the life of man upon earth a trial,' without any interruption?

CHAPTER 29

My whole hope is nowhere but in Thy exceedingly great mercy. Grant what Thou dost command and command what Thou wilt. Thou dost command continence for us. 'And as I knew,' a certain man has said, 'that no one could be continent, except God gave it, this also was a point of wisdom, to know whose gift it was.' Through continence, in fact, we are gathered in and returned to the One from whom we have flowed out into the many. For, he loves Thee less who loves something else along with Thee, which he does not love for Thy sake. O Love, who ever burnest and art never extinguished, O Charity, my God, kindle me! Thou dost command continence; grant what Thou dost command and command what Thou wilt.

CHAPTER 30

Certainly, Thou dost command me to refrain from 'concupiscence of the flesh and concupiscence of the eyes and the pride of this world.' Thou hast commanded [restraint] from concubinage and, in regard to marriage itself, which Thou hast permitted, Thou hast advised something better. Since Thou hast granted it, it has been accomplished, and I reached this state even before becoming a minister of Thy sacrament. But, there still live in my memory, and I have spoken much about it, the images of such things which habit has imprinted therein. When I am awake, they occur to me, though indeed they are not strong, but in sleep it is not merely a question of pleasure; it even goes as far as consent and something very much like the deed. So great is the illusive power of an image over my soul and my flesh that these false things, seen while sleeping, influence me in a manner that real things cannot while I am awake. Am I not myself, at such times, O Lord my God? Nevertheless, there is such a great difference between myself at one moment and myself at another, between the moment when I go to sleep and that when I awaken from it!

Where is reason at such a time, which resists such temptations, when I am awake, and remains firm so that I am unaffected even when real temptations are presented? Is it closed up along with my eyes? Does it go to sleep along with the bodily senses? How is it, then, that we frequently offer resistance during sleep, remembering our good resolutions, most chastely adhering to them, and giving no assent to such allurements? Yet, there is so much difference that, when it happens otherwise, we may return to peace of conscience on waking up, this very difference permitting us to find that it is not we who have done this; we regret, however, that it has been done by us in some way or other.

Is Thy hand, O all-powerful God, not strong enough to heal all the diseases of my soul and to extinguish with Thy more abundant grace these lascivious passions, even during my sleep? Thou wilt increase, O Lord, Thy gifts more and more within me, so that my soul, escaping from the viscous snare of concupiscence, may follow me to Thee, so that it may not be in rebellion against itself, and so that during sleep it will also not only refrain from these debasing acts of turpitude which end in pollution of the flesh as a result of sensual images, but will not even consent to them. For, that such a thing may give no pleasure, or only so slight a pleasure that it can be controlled without difficulty even during the sleep of one who is disposed to be chaste, not only in this life, but even at this stage of life—this is no great feat for an omnipotent Being, 'who art able to accomplish all things in a measure far beyond what we ask or conceive.' Now, however, I have told my good Lord what I am at present in this kind of evil of mine, 'rejoicing unto Him with trembling' for what Thou hast given me; sorrowing for the fact that I am still imperfect; hoping that Thou wilt perfect Thy mercies in me unto the plenitude of peace, which my interior and exterior parts will possess with Thee, when 'death is swallowed up in victory.'

CHAPTER 31

There is another 'evil of the day': would that it were sufficient unto it. For, we repair the daily running down of the body by eating and drinking, until Thou dost destroy both food and stomach, when Thou wilt slay my need with a wonderful fullness and clothe this corruptible body with an immortal incorruption.

Now, indeed, the need is sweet to me, yet I fight against this sweetness, lest I be taken over. I wage a daily battle, 'in fastings,' often bringing my body 'into subjection,' yet my sufferings are banished by sensual pleasure. For, hunger and thirst are sufferings of a sort; they burn and kill like a fever, unless the remedy of food comes to the rescue. Since this is at hand, as a result of the consolation of Thy gifts, among which earth, water and sky minister to our weakness, our disability is called delight.

Thou hast taught me this: that I should partake of foods as if they were medicines. But I reach the condition of peaceful satisfaction, passing from the annoyance of need; I am beset in this very transition by the snare of concupiscence. The transition itself is a sensual delight, yet there is no other way of transition than that which necessity forces us to pass over. Since health is the reason for eating and drinking, perilous enjoyment joins its company, like a lackey, and often strives to get in front so as to become the reason for that act which I claim, and wish, to do only for the sake of health.

Now, the measure is not the same for each, since what is sufficient for health is not enough for enjoyment. It often becomes uncertain whether necessary concern for the body seeks still more sustenance, or whether, urged by the treacherous lust for pleasure, the gratification of greed has begun. The foolish soul grows joyous at this uncertainty and makes ready the protection of an excuse based on this fact; it rejoices that what is enough for healthful moderation is not evident, and so it may conceal the business of sensuality under the pretext of health. I strive every day to resist these temptations; I call upon Thy right hand; I turn over my anxieties to Thee, for good judgment about this matter is not yet established in me.

I hear the voice of my God commanding: 'Let not your hearts be overburdened with self-indulgence and drunkenness.' Drunkenness is far from me: Thou wilt have mercy, lest it come nearer to me. Gluttony, however, sometimes sneaks up to seize Thy servant; Thou wilt have mercy, that it may be removed far from me. For, no man can 'be continent, unless Thou givest it.' Thou dost give many things to us when we pray, and whatever good things we received before praying we received from Thee, and the very fact that we later recognize this we have received from Thee. I was never a drunkard, but I have known drunkards who were made sober men by Thee. Therefore, it is Thy doing that those people who never were such should not have been; it was Thy doing that they who were such have not always been so; it is also Thy doing that both should learn whose doing it was.

I have heard another statement of Thine: 'Go not after thy lusts but turn away from thy own pleasure.' And, through Thy help, I have heard still another, which I have loved much: 'Neither shall we have any abundance if we do eat, nor shall we suffer any loss if we do not eat.' That is to say: neither will the former make me rich, nor will the latter make me poor. I have heard yet another: 'For I have learned to be self-sufficing in whatever circumstances I am, and I know how to live in abundance and I know how to suffer want. I can do all things in Him who strengthens me. Behold the soldier of the heavenly camp, not dust such as we are. But remember, O Lord, 'that we are dust' and that of dust Thou hast made man, and 'He was lost and is found.' Nor did he [St. Paul] have this power within himself, for he, too, was of dust, he who said under the influence of Thy inspiration these words which I love: 'I can do all things,' he said, 'in Him who strengthens me.' Strengthen me so that I can; grant what Thou dost command, and command what Thou wilt. This man [St. Paul] confesses that he received it and that,'when he glories, he glories in the Lord.' I have heard another man praying that he may receive: 'Take from me,' he said, 'the greediness of the belly.' From this it is evident, O holy God, that it is Thou that givest, when a thing is done which Thou dost command to be done.

Thou has taught me, O good Father: 'For the clean all things are clean,' 'but a thing is evil for the man who eats through scandal'; and 'every creature of Thine is good and nothing is to be rejected that is accepted with thanksgiving'; and that 'food does not commend us to God'; and that 'no one should call us to account for what we eat and drink'; and 'let not him who eats despise him who does not eat, and let not him who does not eat judge him who eats.' These things have I learned, thanks to Thee, praise to Thee, my God, my Teacher, who dost knock at my ears, who dost illumine my heart: deliver me from all temptation.

I do not fear the uncleanness of food, but only the uncleanness of concupiscence. I know that Noe was permitted to eat every kind of flesh meat which was edible; that Elias was nourished on flesh meat; that John, endowed with a marvelous abstinence, was not made unclean by partaking of living things, namely, the locusts which happened to be available as food. And I know that Esau was led into error by his greed for lentils; that David blamed himself for his craving for water; and that our King was tempted, not by flesh, but by bread. Further, the people in the desert deserved to be reprimanded, not because they desired flesh meat, but because they murmured against the Lord as a result of this desire for meat.

Having been placed among these temptations, then, I struggle daily against concupiscence in eating and drinking. This is not something which I can resolve to cut off at once and never touch again, as I was able to do in regard to sexual indulgence. Thus, the reins on my palate are to be held in a temperate balance between looseness and tightness. And, O Lord, what man is not somewhat carried beyond the bounds of necessity? Whoever he is, he is a great man; let him magnify Thy Name. Yet, I am not he, 'for I am a sinful man.' But, I also magnify Thy Name, and He intercedes with Thee for my sins, He who 'has overcome the world,' numbering me among the weak members of His body, for 'Thy eyes did see His imperfect part, and in Thy book all shall be written.'

CHAPTER 32

With the allurements of odoriferous objects I am not excessively concerned. When they are lacking, I do not need them; when they are present, I do not reject them, being ready to do without them forever. That is the way I appear to myself; perhaps I am mistaken. For, there are these lamentable darknesses in which my capacity which is within me lies hidden to me, so that my mind, questioning itself about its powers, does not regard itself as easy to believe. For, what is in it is often hidden, unless uncovered by experience, and no one should be free of care in this life, which is called wholly a trial, whether he who has been capable of becoming better from a worse condition may not also become worse from the better condition. One hope, one confidence, one firm promise—Thy mercy.

CHAPTER 33

The pleasures of hearing had held me in tighter bonds and had imposed their yoke upon me, but Thou didst break it and deliver me. I admit that, at present, when Thy words are chanted with sweet and well-trained voice in tones to which those words give life, I do take some little pleasure, not so that I am attached to them, but so that I can rise above them when I wish. Yet, in order that they may be admitted, along with the thoughts by means of which they come into life, they seek in my heart a place of considerable dignity, and I can scarcely offer them a fitting one. Sometimes, indeed, I seem to grant them more respect than is fitting, when I perceive that our minds are moved more religiously and ardently toward the flame of piety by these holy words, when they are sung in this way, than if they are not so sung; and that all feelings of our spirit, in its various dispositions, have their own modes in voice and song, which are stirred up because of some hidden affinity with them.

Yet, the bodily delight, which should not be allowed to enervate the mind, often deceives me, when sense does not keep company with reason so as to follow it passively; but, although it owes the fact of its admission to reason, it strives even to run ahead and lead it. So, in these matters I sin without noticing it, but afterwards I become aware of it.

Sometimes, on the other hand, in giving too much attention to the avoidance of this deception, I err on the side of excessive severity. At times, in fact, I could eagerly desire that all the sweet melody of the chants whereby the Psalter of David is accompanied were banished from my ears and from the whole Church. And then it seems safer to me to follow what I remember was often told me about Bishop Athanasius of Alexandria. He had the reader of the psalms use such slight vocal modulation that it was closer to ordinary speaking than to singing.

Yet, when I recall the tears which I shed over the hymns in Thy church at the early period of the recovery of my faith, and now today when I am affected not by the singing, but by the words which are sung, provided they are sung in a clear voice and with the most appropriate modulation, I again recognize the great usefulness of this practice.

So, I waver between the danger of sensual enjoyment and the experience of healthful employment, and, though not, indeed, to offer an irrevocable decision, I am more inclined to approve the custom of singing in church, in order that the weaker mind may rise to a disposition of piety through these delights of hearing. Nevertheless, when it happens that I am more moved by the song than the thing which is sung, I confess that I sin in a manner deserving of punishment, and, then, I should rather not hear the singing.

See my position! Weep with me and weep for me, you who realize some inner good within yourselves from which good deeds follow. For those who do not act in this way, these words will not move you. But Thou, 'O Lord my God, hear, consider and see, and have mercy, and heal me.' In Thy eyes I have become a problem unto myself and that is my weakness.

St. Augustine

CHAPTER 34

There remains the pleasure of these eyes of my flesh. I speak of it in the form of confessions which the ears of Thy temple may hear, brotherly and pious ears, so that we may bring to a conclusion these temptations of carnal concupiscence which still assail me as I groan, 'yearning to be clothed over with that dwelling of mine which is from Heaven.'

The eyes love beautiful and diverse shapes, brilliant and pleasing colors. Let these things not occupy my soul; let God occupy it, who indeed made all these things which are very good, still He is my Good, not these things. Yet, they affect me every day, while I am awake. No rest from them is given me, such as is given from the voices of song, sometimes from all voices, in a period of silence. For, this queen of the colors, this light diffusing all things which we see, wherever I may be throughout the day, flitting about in manifold ways, entices me while doing something else and not noticing her. She forces herself upon the attention so effectively that, if suddenly cut off, she is sought with longing; if absent for any length of time, she saddens the mind.

O Light which Tobias saw, with his eyes closed, as he taught his son the way of life and walked before him with the step of charity and never a mistake; which Isaac saw, when his fleshly eyes were overburdened and closed with old age, and it was granted him, not, indeed, to bless his sons because he recognized them, but, rather, to recognize them as he blessed them; which Jacob saw, when he, also blind because of great age, sent forth rays of light from his glowing heart upon the tribes of people yet to come, as prefigured in his sons, and imposed upon his grandchildren, through Joseph, his hands symbolically crossed, not as their father tried to put it right considering the external appearance, but as he himself saw from within. This is the Light; it is one, and all who see and love it are one.

But, that corporeal light which I was talking about seasons the life of this world with a seductive and perilous sweetness for those who love it blindly. Yet, those who know how to praise Thee for it, also, 'O God, Who hast created all,' they take this light over for use in a hymn to Thee, and are not taken over by it in their sleep: such do I desire to be. I resist the allurements of my eyes, lest they entangle my feet by which I am progressing on Thy way, and so I lift up my invisible eyes to Thee in order that Thou mayest 'pluck my feet out of the snare.' Thou dost repeatedly pluck them out, for they are easily caught. Thou dost never stop plucking them out, while I frequently get stuck in the traps which are spread on all sides, for 'Thou shalt neither slumber nor sleep, that keepest Israel.'

How many seductions without number have men added to the things which entice the eyes, through the various arts and by the work of craftsmen, in the form of clothes, shoes, vessels, and other artefacts of this kind, even in paintings and all sorts of representations—these things far overstep the bounds of necessary utility, moderation, and faithful representation. In this, men become devotees of their external products, while abandoning internally their own Maker and annihilating the things made by Him.

But I, O my God and my Adornment, can even sing a hymn to Thee from this and offer up a sacrifice of praise to Him who sacrifices for me, since the beautiful designs which are transmitted through souls into artful hands come from that Beauty which is above souls, for which my soul sighs day and night. But, those who produce and are devoted to external beauties derive from this Beauty the measure by which they judge them worthy of approval, but they do not get from It a measure by which to use them. Yet, this measure is there and they do not see it: that they may go no farther, but keep their strength for Thee and not scatter it upon enervating delights.

Now I, who am speaking and seeing these things clearly, do get my steps involved in these beautiful things, but Thou dost free me, O Lord, Thou dost free me, 'for Thy mercy is before my eyes.' Indeed, I am caught in my misery, yet Thou dost pluck me out in Thy mercy: sometimes when I am not aware of it, because I had fallen lightly; sometimes with suffering, because I had already stuck fast.

CHAPTER 35

To this, another kind of temptation joins company, one dangerous in many ways. For, over and above the concupiscence of the flesh which finds a place in the enjoyment of all sensations and pleasures, to which they who put themselves far from Thee become slaves unto their perdition, there is present in the soul through the same bodily senses a certain vain and curious desire—cloaked under the name of knowledge and science—not for fleshly enjoyment, but for gaining personal experience through the flesh. Because this consists in the craving to know, and the eyes are the chief agents for knowing among the senses, it has been called concupiscence of the eyes in holy Scripture.

Indeed, the proper function of the eyes is to see. We also use this word in reference to the other senses, when we direct them toward the act of knowing. Indeed, we do not say: 'Hear how it gleams,' or 'smell how it glitters,' or 'taste how it shines,' or 'feel how it glows'—'see' is the proper word in all these cases. Thus, we say not only: 'See how it lights up,' which the eyes alone can perceive, but also: 'See how it sounds; see how it smells; see how it tastes; see how hard it is.'

That is why the general experience of the senses, as has been said, is called concupiscence of the eyes, for even the other senses appropriate to themselves, by way of analogy, the function of seeing, where the eyes hold first rank, whenever they seek out any object of knowledge.

Now, from this, one can more clearly perceive what there is of pleasure and of curiosity in the functioning of the senses. Pleasure eagerly pursues beautiful, melodious, sweet-smelling, attractive-tasting, soft things, but curiosity even seeks the contraries to these, for the sake of trying them, not to undergo any discomfort, but because of a lust for experience and knowledge.

What pleasure is there is seeing a macerated corpse, at which you would stand in horror? Yet, if one is lying around anywhere, people rush to it only to become sad and pale. They are also afraid to see such a thing in their sleep, as if anyone had forced them to see it while awake or some rumor of its beauty had attracted them!

The same holds true for the other senses; it is too long to go over them all. Because of this diseased craving certain monsters are exhibited in shows. From this craving comes the tendency to examine closely the hidden things of nature outside of us; although knowledge of them is of no value, men crave for nothing but to know them. The same craving is responsible if, having in view that same end of perverted science, men use magical arts in their investigations. And it is from the same cause that, in religion itself, God is put on trial, through a demand for signs and wonders, when these are wanted, not for any saving purpose, but simply for the sake of personal experience.

Behold, in this vast forest filled with pitfalls and perils, how many I have cut down and thrust out of my heart, just as Thou hast given me the power to do, O God of my salvation! Still, when can I dare to say, as so many things of this kind noisily intrude on every side around our daily life, when can I dare to say that my attention has not been caught by such a thing, so as to look upon it and be overcome by idle interest?

It is true that theatrical presentations do not now carry me away, nor am I concerned to learn the courses of the stars, nor has my soul ever sought answers from ghosts; I detest all sacrilegious rites. By how many machinations of temptation does the Enemy work with me so that I might ask some sign from Thee, O Lord my God, to whom I owe the humble and simple service of a slave! But, I beseech Thee, through our King and through our simple chaste homeland, Jerusalem, that, however far from me any consent may be, let it be ever farther and farther. But, when I pray to Thee for the salvation of any person, the end of my insistence is quite different: Thou givest and wilt give me to follow voluntarily, while Thou dost what Thou wilt.

Nevertheless, in how many very minute and contemptible things is our curiosity tempted daily, and who can count how often we fall? How often do we at first put up with the tellers of foolish stories, lest we offend the weak, and then by degrees become willing listeners. Nowadays, I do not watch a dog running after a rabbit, when this happens in the circus. But, if I run across it by chance in a field, such a chase distracts me, perhaps, and even draws my attention to itself, away from some important thinking; not through turning off the road on the animal I am riding, but by the inclination of my heart. Unless, through this demonstration of my weakness, Thou dost quickly admonish me either to elevate my thoughts from this sight to Thee through some act of meditation, or to pass on in contempt of the whole thing, I am bemused by it, like an empty-headed man.

When I am sitting at home, and a lizard is catching flies or a spider is entangling them as they rush into his web, how often does it draw my attention? Now, the fact that these are but small creatures, does that mean that the same thing does not go on? From thence, I do proceed to praise Thee, the wondrous Creator and Orderer of all things, but at first my interest is not in this. It is one thing to rise up quickly; it is quite another not to fall.

My life is full of such things, and my one hope is Thy exceedingly great mercy. For, when our heart is made a container for things of this kind and it carries about a welter of copious vanity, this causes our prayers to be frequently interrupted and disturbed. While we direct the voice of our heart toward Thy ears, in Thy presence, frivolous thoughts rush in from somewhere or other, and the important matter is cut short.

CHAPTER 36

Shall we, then, number this among things to be held in contempt, or will anything lead us back to hope except Thy well-known mercy, since Thou hast begun to change us? Thou knowest to what extent Thou hast changed me, Thou who didst originally cure me of the lust for vindication, so that Thou mightest forgive even all my other iniquities, and heal all my diseases, and redeem my life from corruption, and crown me with compassion and mercy, and satisfy my desire with good things, who hast repressed my pride by means of Thy fear and tamed my neck by Thy yoke. Now I bear it and it is light upon me, for thus Thou hast promised and made it. And, in truth, it was so, though I did not know, when I was afraid to come under it.

But, O Lord, who alone dost dominate without pride, because Thou art the only true Lord, who hast no lord, has this third kind of temptation also ceased for me or can it ever cease in this life—to wish to be feared and loved by men, for no other reason than the enjoyment which derives from this, and which is no joy? It is a wretched life and a foul boasting. Here is a principal source of not loving Thee and not living in chaste fear of Thee; therefore, Thou dost 'resist the proud but giveth grace to the humble,' and Thou dost thunder upon the ambitions of the world and the foundations of the mountains tremble.

Because it is necessary to be loved and feared by men, on account of certain functions in human society, the Adversary of our true happiness keeps urging and spreading 'Well done, well done' among his snares for us. The purpose is that, while we are greedily gathering them in, we may be caught in our carelessness and put our joy far from Thy truth and in the fallacies of men; that we may be pleased at being loved and feared, not on account of Thee, but in place of Thee. In this way the Devil would possess those who have been made like unto him, not for concord in charity, but for companionship in chastisement, for he it is who has determined to place his throne toward the north, so that it will be in cold and darkness that they serve the one who mimics Thee in perverted and distorted ways.

But we, O Lord, see, we are Thy 'little flock'; possess us as Thine own. Spread out Thy wings and let us flee under them. Be Thou our glory. Let us be loved for Thy sake and let Thy Word be what is feared in us. He who desires to be praised by men, when Thou dost blame him, will not be defended by men when Thou dost sit in judgment, nor will he be delivered when Thou dost condemn him. However, when it is not 'the sinner that is praised in the desires of his soul, nor the unjust man that is blessed,' but a man is praised because of some gift which Thou gavest him—yet he rejoices more at the praise for himself than at possessing the gift which is the reason for the praise— then, indeed, he is praised while Thou dost blame him, and better then is he who has given praise than he who has received it. For, the gift of God present in a man was what pleased the former, but the gift of a man was more pleasing to the latter than was the gift of God.

CHAPTER 37

We are tempted by these temptations every day, O Lord; we are tempted unceasingly. The human tongue is our daily 'furnace.' Thou dost enjoin upon us continence in this kind of things, also; grant what Thou dost command, and command what Thou wilt. Thou knowest the groaning of my heart to Thee and the flood of tears from my eyes over this matter. I cannot easily gather how for I am purged of this plague, and I have much fear of my hidden parts which Thy eyes know, but mine do not. In the other kinds of temptations, there is some sort of capacity by which I can investigate myself; in this, almost none. For, in regard to the pleasures of the flesh and curiosity to know idle things, I can see how much progress I may have made in the capacity to restrain my mind, when I am without these things, either voluntarily or because they are not at hand. For then I ask myself whether the privation is more or less troublesome for me.

As to riches, which are sought in order to satisfy one of these three lusts, or two, or all of them: if the mind cannot detect whether it regards them with contempt when it possesses them, they can be put aside so that it may test itself.

But, when it comes to praise, what can we do to be deprived of it and to test ourselves in that condition? Are we to live wickedly, so forsaken and abandoned that no one will know us without detesting us? What greater insanity could be mentioned or thought? Yet, if praise both usually and properly accompanies a good life and good works, then the concomitant should no more be foregone than should the good life itself. Now, I cannot perceive whether I can be without something and be either undisturbed or disturbed, except when it is lacking.

So, what can I confess to Thee in regard to this kind of temptation, O Lord? What, except that I am made joyful by praise? But, more by truth itself than by praise. For, if I were given my choice—whether I should prefer, on the one hand, to be out of my mind, or in error about all things and yet praised by all men, or, on the other, constant and most certain in truth and yet blamed by all—I see what I should choose. Nevertheless, I should not desire that approbation from the mouth of a stranger would increase my joy over any one of my goods. But, I admit that it does increase it; not only that, but blame decreases it.

When I am disturbed by this wretchedness of mine, an excuse surreptitiously occurs to me; of what value it is, Thou knowest, O God—it leaves me perplexed. Since Thou hast commanded for us not only continence, that is, from which things we must restrain our love, but also justice, that is, the goal whereto we should direct it, and Thou hast wished not only that we should love Thee, but also our neighbor, I often appear to myself to be made joyful over the progress or promise shown by a neighbor, when I am delighted by the praise of an intelligent man; and again, I am made sorrowful over his evil, when I hear him blame either what he does not know or what is good.

I am also saddened sometimes by praise of myself, when either the things that are praised in me are such that I am displeased with them myself, or else slighter and less important things are judged to be greater than they should be reckoned. But, again, how do I know whether I am so affected because I do not wish my praiser to have a different opinion from my own, and this not because I am moved by his advantage, but because the same good things which are pleasing to me in myself are a greater source of joy to me when they also please another person? For, somehow, I am myself not praised when my judgment of myself is not praised, since these things are praised which displease me, or those are more praised which please me less. Am I not, then, uncertain of myself in regard to this matter?

Behold, O Truth, I see in Thee that I should not be affected because of myself, but because of the advantage to my neighbor, when praise is directed to me. Yet, whether that is my way I do not know. In this matter, I know less about myself than I do about Thee. I beseech Thee, O my God, reveal me to myself, also, so that I may confess unto my brethren, who will pray for me, what wound I can find within myself. Let me again question myself more carefully. If I am moved by the advantage to my neighbor when I am praised, why am I less moved if someone else is unjustly blamed than if I am myself? Why am I more hurt by the reproach which is cast against myself than I am when the same iniquity is blamed on another person in my presence? Am I ignorant of this, too? Is it to be concluded, finally, that I am deceiving myself and that I am not telling the truth before Thee in my heart or on my tongue? Put this madness far from me, O Lord; let not my own mouth be 'the oil of the sinner to fatten my own head.'

CHAPTER 38

'I am needy and poor,' yet it is better to be displeasing to myself in hidden groanings and to be seeking Thy mercy, until my deficiency is repaired and perfected for the peace which the eye of the proud man does not know. But, speech coming forth from the mouth, and deeds which make themselves known to men, present a most dangerous temptation, arising from the love of praise, which gathers approving opinions as a beggar does alms, for the sake of a certain personal importance. The temptation is active even when it is reproved by myself within myself, and for the very reason that it is reproved. Often, a man may become more vainglorious because of his very contempt for vainglory; thus, it is no longer because of contempt for glory that he glories, for, when he glories, he does not contemn it.

CHAPTER 39

Within us again, within us there is still another evil belonging to the same class of temptation. By it, men become so proud that they are pleased with themselves no matter whether they fail to please or even displease others, or do not care to please them. But, pleasing themselves, they displease Thee a great deal, because they not only regard as good what is not good, but also treat Thy goods as their own, or, if they do regard them as rising from their own merits or as rising from Thy grace, they do not rejoice in this grace with others, but envy that grace to others. Among all these and such dangers and trials, Thou seest the trembling of my heart, and I feel that my wounds will be healed by Thee ever and again rather than that they are not inflicted upon me any more.

CHAPTER 40

When hast Thou not walked with me O Truth, teaching what I must avoid and what I must seek, as I brought back my views of lower things to Thee, in so far as I was able, and took counsel with Thee?

I have examined the world outside by means of sensation, in so far as I was able, and I have observed the life with which I animate my body, and the nature of my senses themselves. Then, I have gone into the hidden places of my memory, into those many spacious areas filled in wondrous ways with innumerable supplies, and I gazed and grew pale with astonishment. I could have perceived nothing pertaining to these without Thee, yet I found that none of them is Thou.

Nor was I myself Thou, myself the discoverer, who surveyed all these things: I endeavored to mark them off from each other and to evaluate each of them in regard to their proper worth, taking some from the report of the senses and questioning them, perceiving some that were mingled with myself, distinguishing and enumerating these messengers of my impressions, then, amid the broad resources of memory, scrutinizing some things, storing some away, getting rid of others. Thou wert not myself when I did this, that is, my power whereby I did it, for Thou art an unchanging Light, which I kept looking toward, in regard to all things, as to whether they existed, what they were, how much they were to be valued: and I heard Thee teaching and commanding. And this same thing I do frequently: it gives me joy to take refuge in this pleasure, in so far as I can take a rest from necessary duties. In all these things which I run through in seeking Thy counsel, I find no safe place for my soul, except in Thee, where my scattered parts are gathered together and no portion of me may depart from Thee. Sometimes, Thou dost introduce me to a very unusual inner experience, to an indescribable sweetness, which, if it reaches perfection in me, will be beyond my present knowledge. But, it will not happen in this life, for I fall back among these lower things, pulled down by troublous weights, and I am absorbed again in ordinary affairs. I am held fast and weep a great deal, but I am held quite firmly. So great is the burden of custom! Here, I am able to exist, but I do not want it; these, I wish to be, but I cannot; in regard to both, I am unhappy.

CHAPTER 41

And so, I have considered the diseases of my sins in the three forms of lust and I have invoked Thy right hand for my salvation. I have seen Thy splendor with my wounded heart, and, being dazzled, I have said: 'Who can attain that?' 'I am cast away from before Thy eyes.' Thou art Truth presiding over all things. I, in my miserliness, did not want to lose Thee, but I wanted to possess a lie along with Thee, just as no one desires to say what is false in such a way that he might himself be ignorant of what is true. Thus, I lost Thee, since Thou dost not deign to be possessed along with a lie.

CHAPTER 42

Whom could I find to bring me back to Thy counsel? Should I have gone to the angels? By what prayer? By what rites? Many people who desire to return to Thee and are not strong enough of themselves, according to what I hear, have tried this, and they have fallen into the craving for curious visions and have deserved to be given over to illusions.

Being proud, they have sought Thee in arrogance of learning, thrusting forth their breasts rather than beating them. They have drawn unto themselves, by virtue of likeness of heart, the 'princes of the air about us,' kindred spirits and associates in arrogance. Seeking a mediator through whom they might be purged, when there was none, they were deceived by them through the powers of magic. For, it was 'Satan disguising himself as an angel of light.' He greatly attracted their proud flesh, because he was not existing in a physical body.

They were mortals and sinners, but Thou, O Lord, with whom they proudly sought to be reconciled, art immortal and without sin. A mediator between God and men should possess something like unto God and something like unto men. Were he like men on both counts, he would be far from God; if like God on both points, he would be far away from men; so, he would not be a mediator. Therefore, this false mediator, by whom in Thy secret judgments pride deserved to be eluded, has one point of resemblance to men, namely, sin; he wishes to appear to possess another with God, namely, to make a show of himself as an immortal because he is not garbed in the mortality of flesh. But, since 'the wages of sin is death,' he possesses in common with men that whereby, together with them, he is condemned to death.

CHAPTER 43

However, the true Mediator, whom Thou hast shown to men in Thy secret mercy, and hast sent, so that, by His example, they might learn humility itself, that Mediator between God and men, the Man Christ Jesus, appeared between mortal sinners and the immortal just Being, sharing mortality with men and justice with God, so that, since the wage of justice is life and peace, He might, through justice joined with God, wipe out the death of sinners who have been justified, a death which He desired to possess in common with them. Was this Mediator shown forth to the saints of old, in order that they might be saved through their faith in His coming Passion, just as we are through faith in that Passion which has come to pass? In so far as He is Man, He is a Mediator. But, in so far as He is the Word, He is not an intermediary, because He is equal with God, God along with God, and at the same time one God.

How Thou hast loved us, O good Father, 'who hast not spared even Thy only Son' but hast handed Him over for us wicked men! How Thou hast loved us, for whom He 'thought it not robbery to be equal with Thee and became obedient unto death on the Cross.' He alone was 'free among the dead,' possessing the power to lay down His life and possessing the power to take it up again. He was for us both a Victor and a Victim unto Thee—a Victor because a Victim—for us a Sacrificer and a Sacrifice—a Sacrificer because a Sacrifice—making us change from slaves into sons unto Thee, by His being born of Thee and by becoming our slave. Rightly is my hope strong in

Him, that Thou wilt heal all my diseases through Him, who sits at Thy right hand and intercedes with Thee for us: otherwise, I should despair. Many and great are my diseases, many are they and great, but mightier is Thy medicine. It would have been possible for us to form the opinion that Thy Word is far removed from any union with man, and thus to despair of ourselves, except for the fact that He did become flesh and dwell among us.

Terrified by my sins and by the mass of my wretchedness, I had stirred up the thought in my heart and had contemplated a flight into solitude, but Thou didst forbid and reassure me, saying: Therefore did 'Christ die for all, that they who are alive may live no longer for themselves, but for Him Who died for them.' Behold, O Lord, I cast my care upon Thee, that I may live, and 'I will consider the wondrous things of Thy law.' Thou knowest my inexperience and my weakness: teach me and heal me. He, Thine only Son, in whom are hidden all the treasures of wisdom and science, hast redeemed me by His Blood. Let not the proud speak evil of me, for I think upon my ransom; I eat and drink and distribute It. Myself poor, I desire to be filled with It, among those who eat and are filled: 'and they shall praise the Lord that seek Him.'

John Cassian
360-435

Cassian was introduced to the ascetical life in Jerusalem. From there he travelled to Egypt and Constantinople. By 404 he had moved to Rome and, around 414, to Marseilles where he founded two monasteries. Through his travels he met a variety of Christian personalities. His writings reveal the breadth and depth of his understanding of the human in search of God. They are some of the most important documents available on monasticism in the fifth century.

A rich spiritual life is available to any person who is willing to orient himself toward God. But for Cassian, it is the hermit who, by a life totally dedicated to contemplation, most perfectly enters the Kingdom of God. Human attention and knowledge can be turned in either of two directions. Most people will turn toward material things and multiplicity, with the end result of getting lost in the everyday cares of life. The alternative obviously is to turn one's being toward God, to dwell in a simplicity that elevates the human far above the distractions and cares of the everyday and places it in the presence of God. Though many Christians work out a life style that mediates the two directions, it is only the hermit who can most thoroughly turn his total attention toward God.

Cassian's life was steeped in the Scriptures and in the writings of authors such as Basil, Jerome, Athanasius and John

Chrysostom. The work from which we have taken a selection is The Conferences. *They were designed for hermits, or for persons moving away from a community style of life toward solitude. Actually the insights they contain would be of value to any person seeking a richer understanding of Christian spirituality. By style Cassian claims that he is merely repeating conferences that he and his friend Germanus heard from Egyptian Abbots, e.g., Abba Isaac. Since there is a gap of almost a quarter of a century between his time in Egypt and the writing of* The Conferences, *it is reasonable to assume that they are Cassian's own productions, heavily influenced by his years in Egypt.* The Conferences *treat the concept of Christian perfection, the virtue of discretion, vocation, obstacles to spiritual growth, prayer and various other aspects of spiritual theology.*

Perfect prayer is, for Cassian, the keystone in the archway of all virtue. It is that which gives meaning to the life of virtue, yet it is dependent upon a firm foundation of virtue for its own development. Purity of heart and the virtue of wisdom are particularly necessary for the life of prayer. There are as many kinds of prayer as there are personalities. However, at the level of prayer as activity, it is practical to speak of four basic kinds of prayer, viz., supplication, vow, intercession, and thanksgiving. Beyond these is prayer as a way of existing, the realm of the wordless, where there is neither image nor action. Here begins the life of true and perfect prayer which makes all virtue possible. Cassian proposes that such a life can eventually be lived by anyone who grasps the secret of the phrase, "O God, make speed to save me; O Lord, make haste to help me." (Ps. 70:1)

A spiritual writer with unusual insights into the structures of the human personality, Cassian had great influence on ascetical theory of subsequent centuries, as is revealed, for example, in the teachings of Benedict, Thomas Aquinas and Ignatius of Loyola.

CONFERENCES OF ABBA ISAAC

I f the Lord gives his blessing, the Conferences of Abba Isaac will keep the promise to write about unceasing prayer, which I made in the second book of the Institutes. When I have completed these, I believe I shall have fulfilled the duty which Bishop Castor of blessed memory laid upon me, as well as your request, Bishop Leontius and brother Helladius. First, you will forgive the length of the book. I tried to compress and to omit much, but still it is longer than I planned. That is why I leave out much of blessed Isaac's talk about various monastic teachings and proceed to the latter part of his discourse.

Isaac: "Every monk (who looks for the perfect way) aims at uninterrupted prayerfulness. As far as is possible to a frail man, he struggles for imperturbable peace and purity of mind. This is the reason why we try so unwearyingly to practise the different disciplines of the body and the spirit. The discipline of the body and spirit on the one side, and unceasing prayerfulness on the other, cannot help having a mutual effect upon each other. The keystone in the arch of all virtues is perfect prayer, and without this keystone the archway becomes rickety and insecure. Conversely, without the virtues no one can attain the continual serenity of prayerfulness which I am discussing. Therefore, I cannot rightly and shortly treat of the effect and chief object of prayer (which is perfected in the truly virtuous life), unless first I treat systematically the way of avoiding sin and attaining goodness. As the Gospel parable teaches, the man who is going to build a tower first takes care to estimate and assemble his materials. But it is impossible to build a fine tower upon this prepared material unless the ground is cleared of rotten or dead rubbish and the foundations are built in firm (or 'lively' as they say) soil or on rock. So it is in the realm of the spirit. To build a tower of the spirit, you must clear the soul of its sins and passions, and build firm foundations of simplicity and humility upon the Gospel: this is the only way the tower can rise unshakable, as high as heaven. Then, though the temtests of passion be poured down upon it, though the floods of persecution beat upon it like battering-rams, though the storm of hostile spirits blows upon it, it shall still stand, and stand undamaged.

No one can offer prayer of a proper intensity and sincerity, unless he is seeking to live thus: first, there must be no anxiety about the bodily needs—not only no worry about a piece of business, but not even the recollection of it: no detraction: no gossip: above all, no anger nor wrongful sorrow, for these cannot but disturb the spirit: no lust of the flesh: no love of money.

By clearing the ground—weeding out these and other public sins—a man makes his life pure, and attains the state of simplicity and innocence. Then he must lay a foundation deep enough to support a tower that will reach to heaven: and the only foundation deep and strong enough is humility.

The lower storeys of the building are the other virtues. The soul should be kept from wandering abroad, and then, little by little, will begin to lift its eyes to contemplate God.

Whatever the mind has been thinking about before it prays will certainly come to it while it is praying. Therefore, before we begin to pray, we ought to be trying to be the kind of people whom we wish God to find when we pray. The mind is conditioned by its recent state. In prayer, the mind remembers recent acts or thoughts or experiences, sees them dancing before it like ghosts. And this annoys us, or depresses us, or reminds us of past lust or past worry, or makes us (I am ashamed to say) laugh like fools at some absurd joke or circumstance, or go over again some recent conversation. Whatever we do *not* want to creep into our time of prayer, we must try to keep out of the heart when we are not praying.

St. Paul's words were: 'Pray without ceasing,' and 'In every place lifting up pure hands without wrath or controversy.' To obey this is impossible, unless the mind is purified from sin, is given to virtue as its natural good, and is continually nourished by the contemplation of God.

There is a good comparison between the soul and a delicate little feather. If a feather has not been touched by damp, it is so light that the slightest breath of wind can puff it high into the air. But if even a little damp has weighed it down, it cannot float, and falls straight to the ground. In the same way the mind, if not burdened by sin and the cares of daily life and evil passion, has a natural purity which lifts it from earth to heaven at the least breath of a meditation upon the invisible things of the spirit. The Lord's command is sufficient warning—'Take heed that your hearts be not *weighed down* by surfeiting and drunkenness and the cares of this world.' So if we want our prayers to reach the sky and beyond the sky, we must make sure that the mind is so unburdened by the weights of sin and passion as to be restored to its natural buoyancy. Then the prayer will rise to God.

Yet we should notice the weights of the mind which the Lord selected. He did not mention adultery, fornication, murder, blasphemy, theft, which everyone knows to be damnable sins. He mentioned 'surfeiting and drunkenness and the cares of this world': faults which worldly men do not take trouble to avoid, nor consider damnable, and which (shameful though it is) some people who call themselves monks think harmless or profitable.

Though these three sins, literally committed, weigh down the soul to the earthy, and separate it from God, they are easily avoidable: especially by people like ourselves who are a long way from ordinary life and have absolutely no opportunity to engage in literal overeating or drunkenness or worldly business. But even though we have given away all our property; even though we have not feasted, have not drunk wine; even though we have been living in a hermit's cell—there is another kind of overeating and drinking and anxiety about the world, a spiritual kind which is just as dangerous, is harder to avoid, and which frequently traps us. The heart soiled with sin and passion will be a heart weighted by this drunkenness of the spirit. And anxieties can still afflict us, even though we are not engaged in worldly business. That is proved by the elders' rule that any food which is more than 'unavoidable, necessary, and ordinary' diet must be regarded as 'worldly anxiety.'

For example: suppose that a job with a wage of a shilling would satisfy our needs, and we try to work longer hours for two or three shillings: or suppose that two tunics are sufficient, one for the night and one for the day, yet we become owners of three or four; or suppose a hut of one or two rooms would be adequate, yet we build four or five rooms, and these larger and better decorated than we need—then we are moved by secular pleasure and desire, and are letting worldly passion reign, so far as is possible for people in our situation.

We have practical proof that this happens by the prompting of devils. One day an elder of repute was passing by the cell of a brother who was suffering from this disease of the soul and used to sweat to build and repair buildings which he did not need. From a distance the elder watched him breaking up a rock with a heavy hammer. And he saw a negro standing beside him, putting his hands on the hammer and inciting him to work harder. For a long time the elder stood there, marvelling at the terrible appearances of the demon, astonished that the monk could thus be deceived. For when the monk was exceeding weary and wanted to stop work and rest, he was incited by the demon to pick up his hammer again and go on. And he was so buoyed up that he did not feel the harm which this overwork was doing him. In the end the elder, disturbed by this horrible, satanic, jest, turned aside to the monk's cell, greeted him, and asked: 'What are you doing, my brother?' He replied: 'We are working at this exceedingly hard rock, which we can hardly break at all.' The elder said: 'You are right in saying *we* can't. You were not alone when you hit it, but an unseen person was standing by you, driving you on to hit harder.'

In this way it is no proof that our hearts are not plagued with ambition, if we abstain from worldly occupations in which we could not engage even if we wanted; nor if we despise what would, if we achieved them, render us notorious among worldly men as well as religious men: but only if we eschew everything which ministers to our own power, even when it seems to be clothed in a garment of right.

Truly these things which seem trivial, or which we see other monks allow without a qualm, weigh the mind down more in proportion than the bigger things which normally and in their measure intoxicate the senses of worldly men. For they prevent the monk from leaving the earthly mind behind and concentrating his due attention upon God: and even a little parting from that supreme good must be regarded as an approach to destruction.

When the mind is freed from lust, established in tranquillity, and does not waver in its intention towards the one supreme good, the monk will fulfil the precept of St. Paul, 'Pray without ceasing,' and 'In every place lifting up holy hands without wrath and controversy.' By purity of heart (so to say) the mind is abstracted from earthly feelings and is re-formed in the likeness of an angelic spirit. Then, whatever thought the mind receives, whatever it considers, whatever it does, will be a prayer of true purity and sincerity."

Germanus: "I would I could keep the thoughts of the things of the spirit as easily as I can conceive their first beginnings! I conceive them in my heart through remembering the Scripture or through recollecting spiritual acts or through an intuition of the heavenly mysteries; and then they vanish all too soon; though how, I do not know. And when the mind has found some other opportunity of spiritual experience, other thoughts crowd in upon us and scatter the thoughts we had grasped. The mind has no perseverance, no stable control of its thoughts; even when it does seem to retain them for a while, I believe it happens unintentionally. And if the retention of a thought is not in my power, why should I think the origin of that thought to be so?

But this is a digression. We ought to keep to the plan of your discourse, in order not to delay any further your exposition of the nature of prayer. Leaving this question to its proper place, I ask you to tell us at once the nature of prayer, particularly in the light of St. Paul's command to 'pray without ceasing.' By 'nature of prayer,' I would like first to know what sort of prayer it is that ought *always* to be offered: and secondly, how we can offer this prayer whatever it is. Your explanation confirms our ordinary experience that this cannot be done by any light purpose of heart. For you have defined the goal of the monks, the summit of his moral ascent, to consist in perfect prayer."

Isaac: "I imagine that no variety of prayer can be apprehended fully without great purity of heart and soul, and the illumination of the Holy Spirit. There are as many kinds of prayer as there are different states of soul, as many kinds of prayer as there are souls. Although I know that my dull heart prevents me from experiencing all kinds of prayer, yet so far as my slender experience allows, I shall try to go through them in order.

According to the progress of the mind in purity, the state in which its response to circumstance and its own effort have placed it, its prayers will vary from moment to moment. It is therefore certain that no one can go on sending up a prayer which never changes. A man prays in one way when he is lively; in another when he is weighed down with melancholy or despair; another when he is heartened by success; another when he seeks absolution; another when he asks for increase of grace or a special virtue or the removal of a special sin; another when he is stricken with fear at the prospect of hell and the judgement to come; another when he is longing for the future good; another in need and danger; another in peace and serenity; another when he is enlightened by some revelation of heavenly mysteries; another when he is oppressed by sensations of dryness and barrenness.

I have spoken on the states of prayer, not as much as the subject needs, but as much as the time and my scant abilities warrant. Now I am faced with a greater difficulty: to expound the four kinds of prayer which St. Paul mentioned: 'I exhort therefore first of all that supplications, prayers, intercessions, thanksgivings, be made.' We cannot suppose that St. Paul made this fourfold distinction without good reason.

First we must investigate what he meant by the different words he used, *supplication, prayer, intercession, thanksgiving.* Then we must ask, are they to be used simultaneously? Do they enter into every prayer which is offered, or are they to be offered separately or simultaneously: thirdly, whether St. Paul arranged this order with a view to teaching the hearer something further, or whether he put them in this order without a particular reason.

148

This last suggestion seems to me obviously absurd. I cannot believe that the Holy Spirit uttered anything through the apostle without meaning something by it.

So I begin in the order I have said, and trust in the Lord's help.

'I exhort therefore first of all that supplications be made.' 'Supplication' is a beseeching or petition for sins. In it a person, repentant for his present or past sins, asks for pardon.

'Prayers' are those by which we offer a vow to God. In Greek it is called *Euche*, which is the synonym of *vow*.

We pray in this way, when we renounce the world and vow to mortify every act and earthly relation and to serve God with the whole heart. We pray, when we promise to despise secular honours and wealth, and follow the Lord with contrite heart and poverty of spirit. We pray, when we promise to be chaste in body, and to suffer unwearyingly; or when we vow to tear from the heart the roots of anger or the sorrow that brings spiritual death. If we are guilty of sloth, if we fall again to our old sins, we shall be before the judgement seat about our prayers and vows, and it will be said of us 'It is better not to vow, than to vow and not to pay': or, as it is in Greek 'It is better for thee not to pray, than to pray and not to pay.'

The third kind, intercession, is customarily offered, in moments of fervour, for other men and women—our family, the peace of the world. To use St. Paul's words, we pray 'for all men, for kings, and all in authority.'

The fourth kind, thanksgiving, is when the mind recollects what God has done or is doing, or looks forward to the good which he has prepared for them that love him, and so offers its gratitude in an indescribable transport of spirit. Sometimes it offers still deeper prayers of this sort; when the soul contemplates in singleness of heart the reward of the saints and so is moved in its happiness to pour forth a wordless thanksgiving.

From each of these four kinds rise other opportunities of richer prayer. Whether the prayer is expressing repentance, or is pledging the heart in the confident trust of a pure conscience, or is expressing the intercessions which spring from a charitable heart, or is rendering thanks in the sight of the great and loving gifts of God—we have known prayers dart up like sparks from a fire. It is therefore clear that all men need to use all four kinds. The same person according to his diversity of affective states will use prayers of repentance or offering or intercession or thanksgiving.

Nevertheless, the first kind seems particularly suitable to beginners, who are still smarting under the recollection of their sins. The second kind seems particularly suitable to people who have already attained a certain progress towards goodness. Intercession seems particularly suitable to people who are fulfilling the pledges of self-offering which they made, see the frailty of others, and are moved by charity to intercede for them. Thanksgiving seems particularly suitable for those who have torn out of their hearts the sins which pricked their conscience and are at last free from fear of falling again: and then, recollecting the generosity and the mercy of the Lord, past or present or future, are rapt away into that spark-like prayer which no mortal can understand or describe.

Yet sometimes the mind which is advancing to the true state of purity and has begun to be rooted in it, can conceive all these kinds of prayer in a single action; it cannot be understood, but may be compared to the leaping of a flame. It consists of a powerful and wordless pouring forth of prayer to God, which the spirit, with groanings that cannot be uttered, sends up though not conscious of its content. In that moment it conceives and puts forth what no one can describe, and which the mind apart from that moment cannot remember.

So it happens that, whatever state of life a man has reached, he sometimes can offer pure and devout prayer. Even in the lowliest place where a man is repenting from fear of punishment and the judgement to come, his 'supplications' can enrich him with the same ardour of spirit as the man who has attained to purity of heart, gazes upon God's blessing, and is filled with an ineffable happiness. As the Lord said, he begins to love the more, who knows he has been forgiven the more.

Yet, in progress towards goodness, we ought to aim at those kinds of prayer which are offered from the vision of future good or from charity—or at least (to speak in a way more appropriate for beginners) which are directed to acquiring a virtue or eradicating a sin. We cannot attain the higher kinds of prayer unless our mind has little by little been elevated by an advance in the sort of petition which it offers.

The Lord himself deigned to be the author, by his example, of these four kinds of prayer—in this, too, is fulfilled the text: 'the things which Jesus began both to do and teach.' He used *supplication* when he said: 'Father, if it be possible, let this cup pass from me': or, as is sung in his person by the Psalmist: 'My God my God look upon me; why hast thou forsaken me?' and texts like these. He used *prayer* when he said: 'I have magnified thee upon the earth, I have finished the work which thou gavest me to do': and 'For their sakes I sanctify myself, that they also may be sanctified in the truth.' He used *intercession* when he said: 'Father, those whom thou hast given me, I will that they also may be with me, that they may see my glory which thou hast given me': and 'Father, forgive them, for they know not what they do.' He used *thanksgiving* when he said: 'I confess to thee, Father, Lord of heaven and earth, that thou hast hid these things from the wise and prudent, and hast revealed them unto babes. Even so, Father: for so it seemed good in thy sight': and 'Father, I thank thee that thou hast heard me. But I knew that thou hearest me always.'

Although he used these four kinds separately and at different times, accommodating himself to the measure that we understand, he showed that in a perfect prayer they can be offered simultaneously; in the long prayer which he offered and which we read at the end of St. John's Gospel. The text is too long to insert here: but the careful reader will find this to be so. St. Paul in the Epistle to the Philippians said the same, though slightly changing the arrangement, and showed that they ought sometimes to be offered altogether in one ardent offering—'In everything by prayer and supplication with thanksgiving, let your requests be made known to God.' Here he particularly wanted to teach us that even in prayers of penitence and self-offering, thanksgiving should not be absent.

Out of these four kinds of prayer rises the loftier state of prayer, formed by the contemplation of God alone and by a charity that burns like fire. Here the mind throws itself into love for God and converses familiarly with him as with its own Father. The first words of the Lord's Prayer, 'Our Father, teach us to strive for this state. When we confess the God and Lord of all Creation to be our Father, we confess that we have been called from a state of slavery to the state of adopted sons.

'Who are in heaven': we pray that we may shrink from the earthly life, in which we live as pilgrims, and which divides us so far from our Father, and may long for that country where we know him to dwell; that we may avoid everything unworthy of our sonship, everything that might deprive us of our inheritance and make us liable to his severity. In this loving state of sonship, we shall direct our minds to our Father's glory instead of our own interests; thus:

'Hallowed be thy name': we declare that our desire and our joy is his glory: and in this we imitate our Lord who said: 'He who speaketh for himself, seeketh his own glory. But he who seeketh the glory of him who sent him, the same is true and there is no unrighteousness in him.' This was St. Paul the chosen vessel's feeling when he wished that he could be accursed of Christ if only Christ's family might be multiplied, and the people of Israel be saved to God's glory. The man who knows that death is not the end is confident in his wish to die for Christ. Again, 'We rejoice when we are weak but ye are strong.' It is no wonder if St. Paul, for the glory of Christ and the conversion of his brother-Jews and of the Gentiles, should want to be accursed of Christ, when even the prophet Micah wanted to be a liar and to lose the inspiration of the Holy Spirit if the Jews could escape the punishment and destruction which he had prophesied— 'Would that I were not a man that hath the Spirit, and that I rather spoke a lie.' And there was the case of the lawgiver, Moses, who did not refuse to perish with his brothers who were doomed to die, but said: 'I beseech thee, O Lord, this people hath sinned a heinous sin; either forgive them this trespass, or, if thou do not, blot me out of thy book which thou hast written.'

'Hallowed be thy name' may appropriately be taken thus: the hallowing of God is our own sanctity. So when we pray this prayer, we are saying: 'Make me the kind of person worthy to understand and take thy great holiness to myself; make my spiritual life such that in it thou canst be seen to be hallowed.' This is what happens when men 'see our good works and glorify our Father who is in heaven.'

"Thy kingdom come'—the second petition of a pure heart, that the Father's kingdom may come at once. There is a present kingdom, where now Christ reigns within his saints: and in us this comes to pass when we eradicate wickedness and cast the devil's rule from our hearts, and God begins to rule in us, in fragrant goodness, in chastity instead of adultery, in serenity instead of rage, in humility instead of pride. And there is a future kingdom, which is promised in due time to all the perfect, to all the children of God, when Christ shall tell them: 'Come, ye blessed of my Father, inherit the kingdom prepared for you from the beginning of the world.' To this kingdom the soul turns its gaze and its desires, and prays 'Thy kingdom come.' By the witness of its conscience, the soul knows that when he shall appear, it will share his glory. No guilty person would dare to want or pray 'Thy kingdom come': for no guilty person would want to face the tribunal of the Judge, knowing that at his coming he would receive prompt and condign punishment instead of reward.

'Thy will be done on earth, as it is in heaven': a petition of sons. There can be no greater prayer than the prayer that earth may be like heaven. To pray 'Thy will be done in earth, as it is in heaven' is to pray that men may be like angels, that as angels fulfil God's will in heaven, men may fulfil his will, instead of their own, on earth. No one can say this sincerely except one who believes that every circumstance, favourable or unfavourable, is designed by God's providence for his good, and that he thinks and cares more for the good of his people and their salvation than we do for ourselves. It may be understood thus: the will of God is the salvation of all men, according to that text of St. Paul: 'who willeth all men to be saved and to come to the knowledge of the truth.' It is of this saving will that Isaiah speaks in the name of God the Father, 'And all my will shall be done.' When we pray: 'Thy will be done in earth, as it is in heaven,' we are praying in other words that all the dwellers upon earth may be saved, like the citizens of heaven, through the knowledge of thee, our Father.

'Give us this day our bread,' which is ἐπιούσιος which means 'supersubstantial': bread which another evangelist calls 'daily.' *Supersubstantial* means that its quality is noble beyond other substances, that its magnificence and holiness exceed that of other creatures. *Daily* means that without it we cannot live a spiritual life for a single day.

The word 'this day' shows that we must receive it daily, that yesterday's supply is inadequate: the word suggests that we should offer this prayer at all times. There is no day on which we do not need to strengthen the heart of the inner man.

Perhaps the word 'this day' can be understood of 'this life': while we are mortal men, give us this bread. Though we know that it is given to those who shall hereafter deserve it from thee, we ask thee to grant it to us 'this day'—unless a man has deserved to receive it in this life, he shall never partake of it in the life to come.

'Forgive us our debts, as we also forgive our debtors.' Unspeakable mercy of God! He has given us a form of prayer, has taught us a way of moral life acceptable to himself: has given with the form the command to pray always, and so is eradicating the roots of anger and sorrow: and, above all this, to men who pray he has provided an opportunity, and revealed a way by which they may move God to pronounce a merciful judgement upon them. You might say that he has given a power to make the judge's sentence lenient, because by forgiving others their offences we can draw him to forgive ours—'Forgive us, as we also have forgiven.' And so with the confidence of faith a man may ask pardon with this prayer—if he has been merciful to his own debtors rather than the debtors of his Lord.

Some of us, regrettably, are inclined to be serene and merciful about sins, however grave, committed by others against God, and inexorable debt-collectors when others commit trifling wrongs against ourselves. The man who from his heart forgives not his brother who has offended, by this prayer calls down, not forgiveness, but judgement, and out of his own mouth asks to incur severer punishment: saying: 'Forgive me as I also have forgiven.' If his request is answered, surely he will be treated after his example, with an implacable sentence. If we want to be judged with mercy, we must be merciful to those who have sinned against us. Only so much will be forgiven to us, as we have forgiven those who have injured us, however wickedly they have injured us.

There are some people who are so dreadfully aware of this that they silently omit the clause whenever the Lord's Prayer is recited congregationally in church: afraid that they are binding instead of excusing themselves. They do not understand how fruitless is the attempt, with quibbles like these, to make the Judge of all men lenient. He has willed to reveal to men who pray to him the way in which he will judge. Because he wills not to be harsh and inexorable towards them, he has declared his plan of judgement, that we must judge our brother, if he sins against us, in just the way in which we wish him to judge us. 'He shall have judgement without mercy on him who hath shown no mercy.'

'And lead us not into temptation.' About the meaning of this clause there is much discussion. If we pray not to be allowed to be tempted, how shall we have any power of resistance? There is a text: 'Everyone who is not tempted is not proved': and 'Blessed is the man that endureth temptation.' The clause 'Lead us not into temptation,' therefore does not mean 'Do not allow us to be tempted,' but, 'do not allow us to fall when we are tempted.' Job was tempted, but was not 'led into temptation': for he did not call God foolish, nor did he consent to the blasphemy to which the devil sought to lure him. Abraham was tempted, Joseph was tempted, but neither was 'led into temptation' because neither gave way to the tempter.

So finally, 'deliver us from the evil one': let us not be tempted of the devil above our capacity, but with the temptation make 'a way of escape that we may be able to bear it.'

You see the method and pattern of prayer put before us by the judge to whom we pray. It contains no request for riches, no thought of honours, no petition for power, no mention of physical health or length of life. The author of eternity would have us ask nothing ephemeral, nothing paltry, nothing transient. He who neglects these petitions for eternity and prefers to ask for the evanescent, insults the generous majesty of God; meanness in prayer offends the judge instead of propitiating him.

The Lord's Prayer, given to us with his authority, seems to include the very pattern of a perfect prayer. Yet it carries those who use it to the higher state of prayer which I mentioned before, to that spark-like and ineffable prayer which very few men know by experience. It transcends the senses; is marked by no vocal expression, whether silent or aloud; but the mind, illuminated by an outflowing of light from heaven, does not define it in the narrow limit of human language. With the senses unified, it pours forth prayers, almost with violence, as a spring pours forth fresh water, and in a second's time darts up a prayer of such richness that afterwards the mind, returned to normality, cannot easily describe it. This state of prayer our Lord typified in those pattern prayers which he is said to have offered in silent retreat upon the mountain, and when (though here he give an example impossible to imitate) in an agony of prayer he let drops of blood fall upon the ground.

Can anyone, however experienced, explain adequately the origins and causes and diversities of compunction in spirit, which strikes the spark in the mind and elevates it to prayer of fervent purity? I will now give a few examples of these occasions of compunction, so far as I can by God's aid remember them at the moment.

Sometimes the verse of a psalm which we are singing sets off the spark. Sometimes the beauty of the cantor's voice rouses the dull mind to a concentrated prayer. I know that the clarity and solemnity of the reader of the psalms can contribute to the fervour of the congregation. Often the address or conference of some holy man has been fruitful in stirring the affections of the hearers. I have known myself snatched away into true compunction of spirit by the death of a brother monk or of a dear friend or relative. Sometimes the memory of my own half-heartedness and carelessness has elevated my soul. No doubt there are countless occasions of this sort, which can rouse the mind, through God's grace, from its drowsiness and half-heartedness.

It is just as difficult to describe how these compunctions arise from the inner sanctuary of the soul. Sometimes it happens because the soul is filled with an indescribable joy and cannot help breaking out into ejaculations, and even the occupant of the next cell feels the power of the happiness in the heart. Sometimes the mind withdraws into a kind of secret abyss of silence, sudden illumination leaves it speechless, the awestruck spirit locks its feelings within or loses feeling altogether, and pours out its longings to God in groanings that cannot be uttered. Sometimes a compunction of grief overwhelms it, and the only way to express it is by a release of tears."

Germanus: "I have very little experience, but even I have experienced something of this compunction of spirit. Sometimes tears will rise when I remember my sins, and then I am visited by the Lord and refreshed by the unspeakable joy which you have described: and the joy, by its very power, has given me the assurance not to despair of forgiveness. I believe there is no loftier state of prayer than this. But the trouble is that it cannot be created when we choose. Sometimes, when I am struggling as hard as I can to excite a compunction of penitence, and I have decided to imagine my sins, I fail altogether in the effort: my eyes remain as dry as a flint and I cannot squeeze a drop of moisture out of them. When I am granted tears, I am happy. But when I cannot call them at will, I am cast down."

Isaac: "Not all varieties of weeping are evoked by the same feeling. There is a weeping because the heart is pricked by sin. There is a weeping which springs from contemplating eternal good and longing for future light, and tears of joy and desire cannot help but break out; as the soul is athirst for the mighty living God, saying: 'When shall I come to appear before the presence of God? My tears have been my meat day and night.' There is a weeping which rises, not from the consciousness of mortal sin, but still from the fear of hell and the terrible judgement; and the soul makes its own the prophetic prayer: 'Enter not into judgement with thy servant: for in thy sight shall no man living be justified.' There is a weeping caused, not by self-knowledge, but by awareness of others' sins and their lack of repentance. So Samuel is said to have wept for Saul; and the Lord in the Gospel, and Jeremiah before him, are described as weeping for the city of Jerusalem, 'O that my head were water and mine eyes a fountain of tears! And I will weep day and night for the slain of the daughter of my people.' And then there are the tears of the 101st psalm: 'I have eaten ashes for my bread and mingled my cup with weeping.' This was not caused by the same feelings as those of the penitent in Psalm 6, but arose from the anxieties, poverty and suffering of this life, the common lot of the righteous in the world.

You can squeeze tears out of dry eyes and with a hard heart, but this is quite a different kind of weeping. I do not believe that this sort of weeping is altogether without profit, for the intention is good, especially in people who have not yet been able to reach perfect knowledge or to be thoroughly purified of past and present sin. But in people who have already progressed so far that they love goodness, this kind of weeping never ought to be extracted unnaturally. Even if it succeeds, it cannot rival spontaneous weeping as an occasion of elevated prayer. It is more likely by the failure of the effort to depress the soul and drive it away from that intention towards heaven in which the prayerful and reverent mind ought to be stable. It will force the soul to relax its concentration and instead go feebly after a weeping which is forced and futile.

To teach you the feeling of true prayer, I will give you, not my opinion, but that of St. Anthony. I have known him sometimes so long at his prayers that the sun rose before he had finished. And I would hear him, still in a rapture of spirit, cry out to the sun: 'Why do you hinder me? The rising of your light draws my mind away from the true light.' And St. Anthony also uttered this heavenly, inspired, saying on the end of prayer: 'That prayer is not perfect in which the monk understands himself and the words which he is praying.'

I hardly dare to add anything from my own slender experience. But so far as I can I will now point out how you can tell whether a prayer is one which the Lord hears.

If we pray unhesitatingly, without any touch of hopelessness to weaken the confident faith of the petitioner—if in the act of earnest prayer we feel ourselves to have obtained our request—we should not doubt that our prayers have effectively reached God. A man will deserve to be heard in proportion as he believes that God is looking upon him and that God can grant his prayer. It is impossible to minimize the Lord's declaration—'Whatsoever ye ask when ye pray, believe that ye shall receive, and it shall come to you.' "

Germanus: "I am sure that this confident faith in being heard springs from a clear conscience. But sin yet pricks my heart; I have no merit to plead for me. How can I have this faith so confident as to presume that my prayers will be heard?"

Isaac: "The Gospels and the prophets teach us that prayers are heard for different reasons according to the different condition of the praying souls.

The Lord declares first, that if two agree, their prayer will be heard: 'If two of you shall agree upon earth touching anything for which they shall ask, it shall be done for them of my Father which is in heaven.'

He declares, secondly, that prayer in fulness of faith (which he compared to a grain of mustard seed) is heard. 'If ye have faith as a grain of mustard seed, ye shall say unto this mountain, Be thou removed, and it shall be removed; and nothing shall be impossible to you.'

Again, persevering prayers, which the Lord called importunity, will be heard. 'Verily I say unto you, that if not because of his friendship, yet because of his importunity he will rise and give him as much as he needs.'

Again, almsgiving will be heard. 'Shut up alms in the heart of the poor, and it shall pray for thee in the time of tribulation.'

A reformed life, or works of mercy, will be heard. 'Loose the bands of wickedness, undo the bundles that weigh down,' and (after a few words which castigate the uselessness of a sterile fast) 'Then thou shalt call and the Lord shall hear thee; thou shalt cry, and he shall say, Here am I.'

Sometimes, the sufferer's prayer of agony is heard. 'When I was in trouble I called unto the Lord, and he heard me,' and 'Afflict not the stranger, for if he crieth unto me, I will hear him, for I am merciful.'

You see how many different ways prayer may be made so that it is heard. A hopeless conscience should make no one despair of being granted requests for a good which is saving to eternity. And as I look at our plight I grant that we possess none of the virtues—the right agreement between two people, faith like a grain of mustard seed, the works of charity which the prophet deserves—yet cannot we have that importunity which he supplies to all who want it? And to mere importunity he has promised that he will answer.

We must pray, then, without faithlessness and believe that merely by keeping at our prayer we shall be granted what we have asked in accordance with God's will. Wanting to grant us the everlasting good of heaven, the Lord encourages us to constrain him by our importunity. He does not scorn nor reject the importunate, but welcomes and praises them, and with his generosity promises to give them what they hopefully persevere to win. 'Ask, and ye shall receive: seek, and ye shall find: knock, and it shall be opened.' And 'all things, whatsoever ye shall ask in prayer, believing, ye shall receive,' and 'nothing shall be impossible to you.' So even if all the other grounds for confidence are lacking, at least we can rouse our importunities; for anyone, without either merit or difficulty, can do this.

The man who prays must not doubt that he will certainly not be heard so long as he doubts whether he is heard. The example of blessed Daniel, whose prayer was answered twenty-one days after he began to pray, teaches us how unwearyingly we must petition the Lord. If we think the answer is slow in coming, we should not cease from the intention with which we began. It is possible that the Lord is postponing his gracious reply for some useful reason, or that the angel who was bringing us God's gift was delayed by the devil's resistance after he left the Almighty's presence. Certainly the angel cannot bring the gift if he finds that we have stopped wanting it. This could surely have happened to Daniel unless he had persevered so courageously to the twenty-first day.

A sense of hopelessness must not weaken our confident faith, even when we imagine that our request has been refused. Let us wholeheartedly accept the Lord's promise: 'All things, whatsoever ye shall ask in prayer, believing, ye shall receive.' We should consider the text of the evangelist, St. John, where he removes all doubt about the matter: 'This is the confidence which we have in him, that whatsoever we ask according to his will, he heareth us.' He commands us to have this full unhesitating confidence in requests which suit not our own convenience and comfort, but the Lord's will. The Lord's Prayer teaches us to include this in our prayers—'Thy will be done'—Thy will, not our will.

Remember the words of St. Paul: 'We know not what to pray for as we ought.' Hence we understand that sometimes we ask for a thing which would militate against our salvation; and that our request is refused by one who perceives our good more accurately and truly than we do ourselves. This was clearly what happened to St. Paul when he prayed to be freed from Satan's messenger, who was permitted by the Lord to buffet him for his good: 'For which I besought the Lord thrice that he might depart from me. And he said unto me, My grace is sufficient for thee, for strength is made perfect in weakness.' Even our Lord felt this in his human person (here giving us an example in prayer as in all else) when he prayed, 'Father, if it be possible, let this cup pass from me: nevertheless, not as I will but as thou wilt'—though his will was certainly not discordant with his Father's will. 'For he had come to save what was lost, and to give his life a ransom for many,' and 'No man taketh my life from me, but I lay it down of myself. I have power to lay it down, and I have power to take it again.' The will of the Father and the will of the Son is everywhere one.

Instructed by this example of our Lord, we ought to end every prayer with the proviso: 'Nevertheless, not as I will, but as thou wilt.'

Everyone is aware that the person who is praying with concentration cannot observe the three profound inclinations which are usual at the end of the office in monastic congregations.

Above all we ought to observe the teaching of the Gospel, to enter into our closet, and shut the door, and then pray to our Father. This has a spiritual meaning. We pray 'in the closet' when we have driven from the heart the turmoil of thoughts and cares, and are offering our prayers like friends whispering intimately. 'The shut door' means that we are praying silently, to him who searches the heart and not the lips. 'In secret' means that with a concentrated heart and mind we display our petition to God alone, and no devilish enemy can discover what we are asking.

So we ought to pray in deep silence. This is partly to avoid disturbing monks, praying nearby, with murmur or noise; but partly to prevent the demons, who are especially alert to pounce on people at their prayers, from knowing our intention. In this way we shall obey the command: 'Keep the doors of thy mouth from her who sleepeth in thy bosom.'

Hence we should pray often but shortly. If we dawdle about our prayers, the subtle enemy might be able to sow a seed in our heart.

The true sacrifice to God is a contrite spirit: the saving offerings and libations are the sacrifices of righteousness and praise. The true, acceptable, victims and burnt offerings are those offered by a contrite and humble heart. And if we practise this discipline and concentration of spirit which I have described, we shall be able effectually to sing: 'Let my prayer be set forth in thy sight as the incense: let the lifting up of my hands be an evening sacrifice.'

Dusk reminds me that we ought to join in our evening devotions. In spite of my meagre experience I seem to have discoursed for a long time, however brief it has been in proportion to the profundity and difficulty of the material."

He ended. We felt awe and wanted him to continue. But after we had celebrated Vespers, we received his promise that at dawn he would treat the subject further; and so in happiness at what we had learnt and at his promise of more, we returned to our cells to lie down for a little sleep. We felt that we had been shown the excellence of prayer, but that we had yet to learn fully the method and the power by which we could acquire or preserve the state of unceasing prayerfulness.

CONFERENCE 10

The Second Conference of Abba Isaac

ON PRAYER

I have tried, however unskilfully, to describe with God's help the sublime customs of the hermits. The order of my discourse now forces me to insert a passage which may seem like a pimple on a lovely body. Yet I have no doubt that less educated readers will learn much from it about the image of Almighty God which Genesis describes. So I insert it with a view to a better understanding of a great doctrine which cannot be misapprehended without blasphemy and heresy.

The clergy of Egypt observe the feast of Epiphany as the time of our Lord's birth as well as the time of his baptism, and.

unlike the western Church with its two separate festivals, keep both commemorations upon the same day. They keep a custom of immemorial antiquity that after Epiphany the Bishop of Alexandria sends a letter to every church and monastery in Egypt declaring the dates for the beginning of Lent and Easter Day.

A few days after the first conference with Abba Isaac, arrived the customary festal letter from Bishop Theophilus of Alexandria. Besides declaring the date of Easter, he included in the letter a long refutation of the absurd heresy of the Anthropomorphites. Nearly all the monks in Egypt, being uneducated and therefore holding wrong ideas, received this with bitterness and hostility: and a large majority of elders from all the ascetic brotherhood decreed that the bishop was guilty of a grave and hateful heresy, because (by denying that Almighty God was formed in the fashion of a man, when Scripture bears clear witness that Adam was created in his image) he seemed to be attacking the text of Holy Scripture. Even the hermits in the desert of Scete, who were more educated and more spiritually advanced than any other Egyptian monks, rejected the letter of Theophilus. The priests who were presiding over three of the four churches in Scete would not allow the letter to be read at their meetings: and the only exception was Abba Paphnutius, who was the priest of my own congregation.

Among those caught by the error was a monk named Sarapion, who had for many years lived a life of strict discipline and had achieved the leading of a truly good life. Almost first among monks in merit and in years in the desert, equally he was almost first in his ignorant prejudice against orthodox believers. The saintly priest, Paphnutius, used many exhortations to bring him back to the true belief, but unsuccessfully. To Sarapion the view seemed a novelty, not found in tradition.

It chanced that a deacon of great learning, named Photinus, arrived from Cappadocia with the object of visiting the brothers in Scete. Paphnutius gave him a warm welcome. And to support the doctrine contained in the letter of Bishop Theophilus, he led Photinus into the middle of the congregation, and in the presence of all the brothers, asked how the Catholic Churches of the East understood the text in Genesis: "Let us make man after our image and likeness." Photinus explained how all the leaders of the churches understood the text spiritually, not literally nor crudely, and made a long speech adducing numerous proofs from Scripture. "That unmeasurable, incomprehensible, invisible majesty cannot be limited by a human frame or likeness. His nature is incorporeal, uncompounded, simple, and cannot be seen by human eyes nor conceived adequately by a human mind."

At last old Sarapion was moved by the numerous and convincing assertions of this learned man, and consented to the traditional faith of Catholics. Abba Paphnutius and the rest of us felt great joy at his assent; joy that the Lord had not allowed a man of such age and goodness, who had erred in simple ignorance, to end his days unorthodox in the faith.

When we stood up to give thanks to the Lord in prayer, the old man felt mentally bewildered at having to pray, because he could no longer sense in his heart the anthropomorphic image of God which he had always before his mind's eye when praying. Suddenly he broke into bitter weeping and sobbing, and throwing himself prostrate on the ground with groans, cried: "Woe is me! They have taken my God away from me, and I have none to grasp, and I know not whom to adore or to address."

Germanus and I were deeply moved by this scene. And with the effect of the last Conference still in our hearts, we returned to Abba Isaac. When we reached his presence we addressed him thus:

"Your last Conference on prayer stirred our desire to put aside all else and return to you. But this new incident has strengthened the desire still further. Abba Sarapion, misled by skilful demons as we believe, fell into grave error. And this has cast us down into a state of hopelessness. We are thinking how for fifty years he has so admirably lived as a great ascetic in this desert, and yet through ignorance not only lost the merit of that life but incurred a risk of eternal death. So, first, we want to know how and why this grave error crept upon him.

Secondly, we ask you to teach us how we can reach the state of prayer of which earlier you taught us at length, and so finely. Your earlier conference made us admire that state, but did not show us how to achieve or secure it."

Isaac: "It is not surprising that a very simple man who had never received any instruction on the being and nature of God could be caught and deceived, even until now, by an error which he mis-learnt a long time ago. This error is not, as you suppose, a modern illusion of demons, but an inheritance from the ignorance of the old heathen. They used customarily and erroneously to worship demons fashioned in the likeness of men, and even now they think to worship God in his majesty—the incomprehensible and indescribable—in the limited form of some statue. And they suppose they have nothing to worship unless they have in front of them a statue, which they can continually address in their devotions, can mentally conceive, and can keep in front of their eyes. Against this error is directed the text: 'And they changed the glory of the incorruptible God into the likeness of the image of corruptible man.' And Jeremiah says: 'My people have changed their glory for an idol.'

This is the way in which this error has been implanted in some men. Nevertheless, in people whose souls have never been polluted by heathenism, the error is contracted by ignorance, under cover of this text: 'Let us make man in our image and likeness.' Hence the so-called Anthropomorphite heresy has risen out of the detestable interpretation of this text, a heresy which maintains obstinately and perversely that the limitless and simple nature of God is fashioned in human form and features. Anyone well-instructed in Catholic doctrine will detest the idea as heathen blasphemy: and in detesting it he will come to that pure state of prayer where the person will allow (I need not say) no effigy of God to be mingled in his prayers, and will not even admit the recollection of a saying or an action, or the outline of a character.

I said in my first Conference that every soul attains the kind of prayer proportionate to its purity: for it can abandon the contemplation of the earthy and material only in proportion as its state of purity carries it upwards to see Jesus in the mind's eye—Jesus still in the humility of his incarnate life, or Jesus glorified and coming in majesty. Jesus coming in his kingdom shall not be seen by men who are restrained by a weakness like that of the Jews and therefore cannot say with St. Paul: 'And if we have known Christ after the flesh, yet now we know him so no more.' Only those of purest sight look upon his divinity, men who have climbed up from earthly acts and thoughts and have gone apart with him into a high and lonely mountain. Jesus, untroubled by any earthly thought and passion and sin, exalted in the purity of his faith and goodness, discloses the brightness of his face and likeness to men who can look upon him because their souls are pure.

Inhabitants of cities and villages and hamlets, men engaged in the ordinary and virtuous pursuits of life, sometimes see Jesus: but they cannot see him with the distinctness possible to those who can climb up with him upon the mount of saintliness, as did Peter, James and John. So in the wilderness he appeared to Moses, and spoke with Elijah. He wanted to teach us this and leave us an example of perfect purity. As the source of holiness, a source unpolluted like a spring of fresh water, he did not need to go apart in the wilderness to attain that perfect purity. No dirt, no stain from the crowds of human society could lessen the fulness of his purity of heart, for he it is who cleanses and purges all pollution.

Yet he went apart alone to the mountain to pray. He gave an example of withdrawal, to teach us that if we want to address God with a heart of integrity we should go apart from all crowd and tumult that disturbs our peace; and there, though still mortal men, we may in part succeed in attaining at least the shadow of the bliss promised to the saints in the future, and God may be to us all in all.

Then our Saviour's prayer, wherein he prayed the Father for his disciples, will be truly fulfilled in us: 'that the love wherein thou lovedst me may be in them, and they in us': and 'that they all may be one, as thou, Father, art in me and I in thee, that they also may be one in us.' This unity will be when that perfect love of God, wherewith 'he first loved us' has passed into the affections of our own hearts. So his prayer will be fulfilled, and we believe that that prayer cannot fail of its effect.

Then God shall be all our love, all we desire and seek and follow, all we think, all our life and speech and breath. The

unity which now is between Father and Son shall be poured
into our feelings and our minds: and as he loves us with a pure,
sincere, unbreakable charity we on our side shall be linked to
him by a lasting affection that nothing can spoil. In that union,
whatever we breathe or think or speak is God. So the end of his
prayer is attained in us—'that they all may be one as we are one:
I in them, and thou in me, that they also may be made perfect
in one': and 'Father, those whom thou hast given me, I will that
where I am, they may also be with me.'

This should be the aim and purpose of the solitary: to seek
to possess in some measure, even while mortal man, the first
bridal gifts from the heavenly country and its glory. I repeat:
this is the end of all true goodness, that the mind may every day
be lifted beyond the material sphere to the realm of spirit, until
the whole life and every little stirring of the heart becomes one
continuous prayer."

Germanus: "We were bewildered by the first conference
and returned to you for further explanation. But now our be-
wilderment has grown. Certainly this doctrine stirs us to long
for the bliss of heaven; but the more we yearn, the more we
despair. For we still do not know how to achieve the sort of
disciplined life which can enable us to reach this lofty goal. I beg
you to be patient and allow me to explain (perhaps at some
length) what we had begun to consider during our daily meditations in our cell. I know that you are unused to being troubled
by the silly questions of weak brothers like ourselves. Yet is is
worth bringing these silly questions into the open, so that the
absurdity in them may be corrected.

We think that every art or science must begin with rudi-
ments easy and suitable for the uninitiated. A man must be
trained, so to speak, on the milk of the intellect, and thereby
may grow, step by step, from ignorance to education. First he
acquires the more obvious principles, passes the gateway to
his subject, and thereby can climb without difficulty to the
pinnacles of knowledge. A boy cannot frame sentences until he
has learnt the alphabet properly. He cannot become a quick
reader unless he can first read short and simple nouns. The man
ignorant of grammar will never be able to write elegant prose or
to become a sound philosopher.

This higher discipline in which we learn to cleave to God continually, must doubtless have first principles, foundations on which a man may build to raise the lofty tower. I think, though hesitantly, that its first principles consist in learning by what meditations God may be grasped and conceived; and then, how to preserve this thought, whatever it is, uninterruptedly: and I am sure that this uninterrputed preservation is the true perfection of the discipline.

We want you to show us material for this recollectedness by which God is conceived in the mind and the conception is retained permanently. Thereby we may keep it in front of us; and, when we feel we have fallen away, may at once be able to return, without any delay or ignorant meandering of the thoughts.

Sometimes, when my mind has wandered away from contemplating God, I wake up as if from a sleep as sound as death; I look round like a drowsy man just out of bed, for the subject-matter to recreate recollectedness. The process of finding the material distracts and delays me: before I find the vision again, my purpose of heart is beginning to fade. I am sure it happens because I do not keep before my eyes some special intention in the way of a formula to which the wandering mind could be recalled from its travels—so to say, a quiet harbour after a long and stormy voyage. Thus the mind, constantly hampered by this ignorance, teeters to and fro like a drunkard and does not even grasp the spiritual thought which comes to it, unasked and unsought. As it goes on receiving one sensation after another, it is unconscious of their arrival, their origin, or their departure."

Isaac: "Your question is intricate: and the fact that you have asked it proves you to have made headway towards purity of mind. To ask questions, still more to use a delicate introspection in this matter, is only possible to a person who by mental zeal and alertness has reached a stage where he can understand the complications of the problem; to a person whose constant attempts at a disciplined life have given him the experience whereby he may knock at the gates of mental purity. I see that you are no longer standing at the outer gate of true prayer, but are knocking at its inner door, and have already pushed it half open. A visitor who has reached the main hall of a house can easily be shown its inner rooms: and with God's guidance I think it will be easy to bring you to the heart of true prayer. I believe you will allow no obstacle to hinder your self-examination. The man who knows what questions to ask is on the verge of understanding: the man who is beginning to understand what he does not know is not far from knowledge.

So I am not afraid of the charge of speaking irreverently or betraying secrets if I now disclose what I omitted from my earlier Conference. I think that by God's grace your own study would have taught you the way even if you had no words of mine to help you.

You made an admirable comparison between spiritual discipline and the education of children. A child cannot recognize or make letters before he has become used to seeing them every day in wax copies. I must give you the formula for contemplation. If you carefully keep this formula in front of you, and learn to recollect it all the time, you can use it to mount to the contemplation of high truth. Every monk who looks for continual recollection of God uses this formula for meditation, and with the object of driving every other sort of thought from his heart. You cannot keep the formula before you unless you are free from all bodily care.

The formula was given us by a few of the oldest fathers who remained. They did not communicate it except to a very few who were athirst for the true way. To maintain an unceasing recollection of God it is to be ever set before you.

The formula is: 'O God, make speed to save me: O Lord, make haste to help me.'

This verse has rightly been selected from the whole Bible for this purpose. It fits every mood and temper of human nature, every temptation, every circumstance. It contains an invocation of God, a humble confession of faith, a reverent watchfulness, a meditation upon our frailty, a confidence in God's answer, an assurance of his ever-present support. The man who continually invokes God as his guardian, is aware that he is always at hand. The formula contains a fervent charity, a fearful contemplation of the devil's power, a regard for the defender's succour which alone can relieve the beleaguered soul from the devil's siege by day and night. The verse is an impregnable battlement, a shield and coat of mail which no spear can pierce. Souls sunk in accidie or worry or melancholy thoughts of any kind find the cure of despair in this verse, which shows them God's watch over their struggles and their prayers. Souls happy in their spiritual progress, it warns against a bubble-like complacency, assuring them that only with God's protection can they keep what they have won; teaching them not merely to ask his help, but to ask it speedily.

I repeat; each of us, whatever his condition of spiritual life, needs to use this verse. The man who wants to be helped in all circumstances and at all times, shows that he needs God to help him in prosperity and happiness as much as in suffering and sorrow. He needs to be delivered from the one, and maintained in the other. For he knows that frail human nature cannot remain unimparied in either state without God's help.

Suppose I feel gluttonous; I look round for food unknown among hermits; in the middle of the desert I scent the cooking of a dish fit for kings, and against my better will I cannot help hungering for it. Then I must say immediately: 'O God, make speed to save me, O Lord, make haste to help me.' Or I am tempted to eat supper too early, or am struggling to eat no more than the right and customary quantity, I must cry out: 'O God, make speed to save me; O Lord, make haste to help me.' I need severe fasts to quench lust, yet I dare not undertake them through the delicacy or dryness of my stomach. And so to quieten the lust without severe fasting, I must pray: 'O God, make speed to save me: O Lord, make haste to help me.' I go to supper at the correct time and shudder at the food and cannot eat what I must eat to live, then I must sigh: 'O God, make speed to save me: O Lord, make haste to help me.'

Perhaps I want to keep my heart stable by forcing myself to read the Bible. But a headache stops me, by nine o'clock in the morning I have fallen asleep with my head on the page—and I am driven to go to bed before the appointed hour, and so fail to say the full office and the proper series of psalms—again I must say: 'O God, make speed to save me: O Lord, make haste to help me.' Perhaps night after night I suffer some devilish insomnia and am exhausted from lack of sleep, gain no refreshment from my night's rest. I must breathe: 'O God, make speed to save me: O Lord, make haste to help me.'

Perhaps, if I have not yet tamed the flesh, some sudden temptation against chastity comes upon me softly at night: and I must prevent this invading fire from burning up the fragrant flowers of chastity. So I must call: 'O God, make speed to save me: O Lord, make haste to help me.' Perhaps I feel the heat of passion to have cooled. Then this virtue—nay, this grace, for it is a gift of God—I must keep within me by saying carefully: 'O God, make speed to save me: O Lord, make haste to help me.'

Perhaps temptations to anger, or avarice, or melancholy afflict me and force me to disturb my calm state, so pleasant to me. I must prevent myself being bitter by crying aloud: 'O God, make speed to save me: O Lord, make haste to help me.' Perhaps some temptation to accidie, or vanity, or pride, or to despise the half-heartedness of other monks, creeps upon the mind. To stop this devilish suggestion, I must pray with deep contrition: 'O God, make speed to save me: O Lord, make haste to help me.'

Perhaps I have repented long and so have pricked the bubble of pride and gained the grace of humility and simplicity. So that 'the foot of pride' may not again 'come against me,' and 'the hand of the sinner disturb me,' and that satisfaction at my success may not cause still worse moral damage, I must call with my whole heart: 'O God, make speed to save me: O Lord, make haste to help me.'

Perhaps wandering thoughts career about the soul like boiling water, and I cannot contest them, nor can I offer prayer without silly mental images interrputing it; I feel so dry that I seem incapable of spiritual feeling, and many sighs and groans cannot save me from dreariness—I must needs say: 'O God, make speed to save me: O Lord, make haste to help me.'

Perhaps by some joyous rapture I feel that the Holy Spirit has visited me, and I have gained a re-directed purpose, a concentration of mind, a liveliness of heart. And through these overflowing sensations I discern a sudden disclosure by the Lord of sacred truths hidden from me till now. To dwell upon these truths for more than a moment, I must be careful to keep praying: 'O God, make speed to save me: O Lord, make haste to help me.'

Perhaps in the night I am encompassed by appearances of unclean spirits and in my turn am thrown into a despair even of life and salvation. I shall find in the whole-hearted praying of that verse a safe fortress for the fugitive: 'O God, make speed to save me: O Lord, make haste to help me.' Then the Lord restores and consoles me, and I feel that he is garrisoning me with his countless hosts of angels, and suddenly I can dare to go out to face the enemy and provoke them to fight, when a moment before I was trembling with fear of death and shuddering in mind and body at their touch or proximity. To abide by God's grace in this strength and courage, I must say with my whole heart: 'O God, make speed to save me: O Lord, make haste to help me.'

Continuously and ceaselessly, in adversity that we may be delivered, in prosperity that we may be preserved but not puffed up, we ought to send up this prayer. Meditate on it, never stop turning it over within your breast. Whatever work or ministry or journey you are undertaking, go on praying it. While you are going to sleep, or eating, or in the last necessities of nature, think on it. It will be a saving formula in your heart, will guard you from the attacks of demons, will cleanse you from the stains of earthly life, lead you to contemplate the unseen things of heaven, and carry you up to the ineffable glow of prayer which very few have experienced. Sleep ought to catch you thinking about this verse, until you are so moulded by its use that you pray it when asleep. When you wake it should be your first thought, it should force you from your bed to your knees, and thence send you out to your daily work, there to be always with you. You should think on it, in Moses' words, at home or on a journey, going to bed or rising from bed. You should write it on the doors of your lips, the walls of your house, the sanctuary of your breast. Whether you kneel down to pray or whether you rise up from praying and turn to the needs of your daily life, this should be your prayer.

This formula the mind should go on grasping until it can cast away the wealth and multiplicity of other thoughts, and restrict itself to the poverty of this single verse. So you will attain with ease that Gospel beatitude which holds first place among the other beatitudes: 'Blessed are the poor in spirit: for theirs is the kingdom of heaven.' This noble poverty will fulfil the prophet's saying: 'The poor and needy shall praise the name of the Lord.' Truly, what higher or holier poverty can there be than this, that a man knowing he is defenceless of his own, asks help for daily life from another's generosity, and realizes his life and being to depend every moment on God's help. Such a one truly confesses himself 'the beggar of the Lord,' like the Psalmist who said: 'I am a beggar and a poor man: and God helps me.'

So by God's light he mounts to the manifold knowledge of God and thereafter to feed on mysteries loftier and more sacred: the prophet said: 'The high hills are a refuge for the stags, and the rocks for the hedgehogs.' I think this meaning of the text is appropriate for this reason. A man who perseveres in simplicity and innocence, is aggressive to none and content to defend himself from being spoiled by his enemies; like the hedgehog hiding under a rock, he is protected, by his continual recollection of the Lord's passion and meditation upon this verse of the psalms. With the same spiritual intention the book of Proverbs speaks about hedgehogs—'The hedgehogs are a feeble folk, who have made their homes in the rocks.' Nothing is feebler than a Christian; nothing weaker than a monk, who for wrong may take no vengeance nor even indulge mild feelings of annoyance, however concealed within his breast.

The man who in his moral ascent possesses simple innocence and yet the gift of wisdom has Satan crushed like a poisonous viper beneath his feet. And, as a stag browsing upon high pastures, his quick intelligence feeds upon the lofty mysteries revealed by the prophets and apostles.

There, with deep compunction, he will make the thoughts of the psalms his own. He will sing them no longer as verses composed by a prophet, but as born of his own prayers. At least he should use them as intended for his own mouth, and know that they were not fulfilled temporarily in the prophet's age and circumstances, but are being fulfilled in his daily life. There are times when a man understands God's Scriptures with the clarity with which a surgeon understands the body when he opens up the marrow and the veins. These are the times when our experience seems to show us the meaning by practical proof before we understand it intellectually.

For example, if we have the same attitudes of heart wherein the Psalmist wrote or sang his psalms, we shall become like the authors and be aware of the meaning before we have thought it out instead of after. The force of the words strikes us before we have rationally examined them. And when we use the words we remember, by a kind of meditative association, our own circumstances and struggles, the results of our negligence or earnestness, the mercies of God's providence or the temptations of the devil, the subtle and slippery sins of forgetfulness or human frailty or unthinking ignorance. All these feelings we find expressed in the psalms. We see their texts reflected in the clear glass of our own moral experience. And with that experience to teach us, we do not hear the words so much as discern the meaning intuitively. We will not merely recite them like texts committed to memory, but bring them out from the depths of the heart as an expression of moral reality.

So the mind shall attain that purest of pure prayers to which our earlier Conference led, so far as the Lord deigned to grant us; the prayer which looks to see no visual image, uses no mind nor words; the prayer wherein, like a spark leaping from a fire, the mind is rapt upward; and, destitute of the aid of the senses or of anything visible or material, pours forth its prayer to God with groanings and sighs that cannot be uttered."

Germanus: "You have most clearly explained the system of spiritual discipline for which I asked, and perfect prayer itself. There can be nothing more sublime than to fold the recollection of God into the little space of a meditation upon a single verse, to summarize all the prayerful feelings in one sentence.

Now, we beg you to expound our one remaining problem. You have given us this verse as a kind of formula. How can we keep it permanently before us? By God's grace we have been liberated from the stupidities of secular thoughts—how may we grasp spiritual thoughts and never let them go?

When the mind has begun to take the meaning of a psalm, it passes on unawares and unintentionally to some other text of Scripture. When it has just begun to meditate upon that text and has half considered it, its attention is caught by another

174

passage and it forgets all about the earlier matter for meditation. And so it goes on, hopping from text to text, from psalm to psalm, from Gospel to Epistle and thence to a prophetic book and thence to a narrative in the historical books of the Old Testament; meandering vaguely through the Bible, choosing nothing and grasping nothing on purpose, considering no text to its depth; the mind becomes a dilettante, a taster of spiritual meanings, not a creator or owner of them. At the time of the office it totters about like a drunkard, its worship ever inadequate. During the prayers it is thinking about a psalm or lesson. During the singing of the psalter, it is thinking about something quite outside the text of the psalm. During the lesson, it is thinking about something that has to be done, or remembering something that has been done. So it receives or rejects nothing in a disciplined and orderly manner, but seems to be knocked about by haphazard assaults, powerless to keep or to linger over the text which pleases it.

We therefore need to know how to worship adequately by these means, and how permanently to hold this verse which you gave us as a formula. Then our feelings would not rise and fall hither and thither under their own impetus, but would respond to the control of the will."

Isaac: "I think that enough was said on this subject in our earlier discussion. But because you want me to repeat it, I will give a brief summary on how to make the heart stable.

Three things make the wandering mind stop wandering: watching, meditation, prayer, when used purposefully and assiduously. This is only possible if the anxieties and worries of this life are first put away, through tirelessly engaging in work undertaken not for monetary gain, but for the religious needs of the coenobium. This is the only way to obey St. Paul's command, 'Pray without ceasing.'

He prays too little, who only prays when he is on his knees.

But he never prays, who while on his knees is in his heart roaming far afield.

Therefore what we wish to be while praying, we ought to be before we begin to pray. The praying mind cannot help being fashioned by its earlier condition, cannot help its earlier thoughts lifting it upward to heaven or pulling it downward to earth."

Thus far Abba Isaac, to our wonder, gave his second Conference on the nature of prayer. He gave his teaching about meditating on that one little verse, as an outline for beginners. Germanus and I admired the teaching and wanted to follow it, for we believed it to be a short and easy way. But when we tried it, we found it harder to observe than our previous method of wandering haphazardly through the Bible and meditating on a variety of different texts.

However, it is certain that a man is not incapable of perfection or purity of heart because he cannot read. Perfection and purity are available for anyone who uses one brief text—if he uses it with a purpose of heart strong and unwavering towards God.

St. Benedict
480-547

The name of Saint Benedict is almost synonymous with monasticism. The contribution he made to the shaping of the occidental monastic tradition is immeasurable. Born in Italy, Benedict studied in Rome, lived as a hermit somewhere near Subiaco, and eventually, with the disciples who had gathered around him, founded the monastery of Monte Cassino. The legacy he left to his followers is the famous Rule of St. Benedict. *For several centuries during the middle ages, all monks were required to follow this* Rule. *The spiritual families of Benedict continue to flourish today.*

The monastic way of life has traditionally held a privileged place in Christianity. It reaches deep into the quiet regions of the human spirit, calls men and women away from the noise of the everyday world and offers an atmosphere in which the human can pay serious attention to God. As a life-style, it is not meant for everyone. Its demands are as great as its rewards.

Benedict's Rule *was written in response to a need for direction. Monastic life-style was somewhat less than exemplary. Monks roamed freely from town to town, monastery to monastery, having as their law only their own good pleasure. Year after year, building upon his own experience and dedicated life, Benedict constructed the* Rule. *It is designed to enable the members of the monastic community to live out, in an orderly and meaningful manner, the everyday life of the monastery, on the thesis that, if this is fulfilled, the loftier heights of wisdom and virtue will be attained. Besides a series of chapters on the Divine Office and another series on faults and corrections, the* Rule *deals with a variety of items that make up daily life, such as meals, work, clothing and journeys, and the virtues that are essential to monastic life. Benedict was convinced that ordinary tasks, performed for the right reason, can lead to Christian perfection.*

Of the prologue and seventy-three chapters that make up the Rule, *we have chosen the prologue and the first seven chapters for the following reading. The prologue orients and gives meaning to all that follows. It begins with an urgent call to rise up from sleep, to see the light, to hear the divine voice. The atmosphere in which the monk is to dwell is established, viz., as son and servant, ready to obey the father and master. Benedict states that the monk's goal is to "merit to see him who has called us unto his kingdom." The means, though simple, are demanding: faith, good works, guidance of the Gospel. Chapter four presents the tools of good works. Among them are: love God, neighbor, oneself, the enemy; do not kill, commit adultery, steal; practice works of mercy toward the poor, the naked, the sick; learn to hold one's tongue; make peace with one's adversary before sundown; never despair of God's mercy. Such are the tools of the spiritual craft. Properly employed throughout a lifetime, they lead to a life in God.*

The terminology of the Rule *is simple and direct. Benedict understood human nature. He knew that of all those who begin well, very few will continue down the road of everyday routine to a life of perfection. The challenge he issued to anyone who, as a monk, would seek God is valid today. It requires the capacity to empty one's life of all self-interest, of all self-will, of all fear. At this point, one dwells in love and does all for love. And that is the life of perfection.*

THE RULE OF ST. BENEDICT

H earken, my son, to the precepts of the master and incline the ear of thy heart; freely accept and faithfully fulfil the instructions of a loving father, that by the labour of obedience thou mayest return to him from whom thou hast strayed by the sloth of disobedience. To thee are my words now addressed, whosoever thou mayest be that renouncing thine own will to fight for the true King, Christ, dost take up the strong and glorious weapons of obedience.

And first of all, whatever good work thou undertakest, ask him with most instant prayer to perfect it, so that he who has deigned to count us among his sons may never be provoked by our evil conduct. For we must always so serve him with the gifts which he has given us, that he may never as an angry father disinherit his children, nor yet as a dread lord be driven by our sins to cast into everlasting punishment the wicked servants who would not follow him to glory.

Up with us then at last, for the Scripture arouseth us, saying: *Now is the hour for us to rise from sleep.* Let us open our eyes to the divine light, and let us hear with attentive ears the warning that the divine voice crieth daily to us: *Today if ye will hear his voice, harden not your hearts.* And again: *He that hath ears to hear, let him hear what the Spirit saith to the churches.* And what doth he say? *Come, ye children, hearken unto me: I will teach you the fear of the Lord. Run while ye have the light of life, lest the darkness of death overtake you.*

And the Lord, seeking his workman among the multitudes to whom he thus crieth, saith again: *What man is he that desireth life and would fain see good days?* And if hearing him thou answer, "*I am he,*" God saith to thee: *If thou wilt have true and everlasting life, keep thy tongue from evil and thy lips that they speak no guile. Turn away from evil and do good:*

seek after peace and pursue it. And when you have done these things, my eyes will be upon you and my ears open unto your prayers. And before you call upon me, I shall say to you, "Lo, here I am." What can be sweeter to us, dearest brethren, than this voice of our Lord inviting us? Behold in his loving mercy the Lord showeth us the way of life.

Let us, therefore, gird our loins with faith and the performance of good works, and following the guidance of the Gospel walk in his paths, so that we may merit to see him who has called us unto his kingdom. And, if we wish to dwell in the tabernacle of his kingdom, except we run thither with good deeds we shall not arrive. But let us ask the Lord with the prophet: *Lord, who shall dwell in thy tabernacle, or who shall rest upon thy holy hill?* Then, brethren, let us hear the Lord answering and showing us the way to that tabernacle and saying: *He that walketh without blemish and doth that which is right; he that speaketh truth in his heart, who hath used no deceit in his tongue, nor done evil to his neighbour, nor believed ill of his neighbour.* He that taketh the evil spirit that tempteth him, and casteth him and his temptation from the sight of his heart, and bringeth him to naught; who graspeth his evil suggestions as they arise and dasheth them to pieces on the rock that is Christ. Such men as these, fearing the Lord, are not puffed up on account of their good works, but judging that they can do no good of themselves and that all cometh from God, they magnify the Lord's work in them, using the word of the prophet: *Not unto us, O Lord, not unto us, but unto thy name give the glory.* So the apostle Paul imputed nothing of his preaching to himself, but said: *By the grace of God I am what I am.* And again he saith: *He that glorieth, let him glory in the Lord.*

Wherefore the Lord also saith in the Gospel: *He that heareth these my words and doth them, shall be likened to a wise man that built his house upon a rock. The flood came and the winds blew, and they beat upon that house, and it fell not, for it was founded upon a rock.* Having given us these instructions, the Lord daily expects us to make our life correspond with his holy admonitions. And the days of our life are lengthened and a respite allowed us for this very reason, that we may amend our evil ways. For the Apostle saith: *Knowest thou not that the patience of God inviteth thee to repentance?* For the merciful Lord saith: *I will not the death of a sinner, but that he should be converted and live.*

So, brethren, we have asked the Lord about the dwellers in his tabernacle and have heard what is the duty of him who would dwell therein; it remains for us to fulfil this duty. Therefore our hearts and bodies must be made ready to fight under the holy obedience of his commands; and let us ask God that he be pleased, where our nature is powerless, to give us the help of his grace. And if we would escape the pains of hell and reach eternal life, then must we—while there is still time, while we are in this body and can fulfil all these things by the light of this life—hasten to do now what may profit us for eternity.

Therefore must we establish a school of the Lord's service; in founding which we hope to ordain nothing that is harsh or burdensome. But if, for good reason, for the amendment of evil habit or the preservation of charity, there be some strictness of discipline, do not be at once dismayed and run away from the way of salvation, of which the entrance must needs be narrow. But, as we progress in our monastic life and in faith, our hearts shall be enlarged, and we shall run with unspeakable sweetness of love in the way of God's commandments; so that, never abandoning his rule but persevering in his teaching in the monastery until death, we shall share by patience in the sufferings of Christ, that we may deserve to be partakers also of his kingdom. Amen.

CHAPTER 1

THE KINDS OF MONKS

There are evidently four kinds of monks. The first are the Cenobites, that is those who live in monasteries, serving under a rule and an abbot.

The second are the Anchorites or Hermits, that is those who not in the first fervour of their conversion, but after long probation in a monastery, having learnt in association with many brethren how to fight against the devil, go out well-armed from the ranks of the community to the solitary combat of the desert. They are able now to live without the help of others, and by their own strength and God's assistance to fight against the temptations of mind and body.

The third kind of monks is that detestable one of the Sarabaites, who not having been tested, as gold in the furnace, by any rule or by the lessons of experience, are as soft and yielding as lead. In their actions they still conform to the standards of the world, so that their tonsure marks them as liars before God. They live in twos or threes, or even singly, without a shepherd, in their own sheepfolds and not in the Lord's. Their law is their own good pleasure: whatever they think of or choose to do, that they call holy; what they like not, that they regard as unlawful.

The fourth kind of monks are those called Gyrovagues. These spend their whole lives wandering from province to province, staying three days in one monastery and four in another, ever roaming and never stable, given up to their own wills and the allurements of gluttony, and worse in all respects than the Sarabaites.

Of the wretched observance of all these folk it is better to be silent than to speak. Therefore, leaving them on one side, let us proceed with God's help to provide for the strong race of the Cenobites.

CHAPTER 2

WHAT KIND OF MAN THE ABBOT SHOULD BE

An abbot who is worthy to rule a monastery should always remember what he is called and realize in his actions the name of a superior. For he is believed to be the representative of Christ in the monastery, and for that reason is called by a name of his, according to the words of the Apostle: *Ye have received the spirit of the adoption of sons, whereby we cry Abba, Father.* Therefore the abbot ought not to teach, or ordain, or command anything which is against the law of the Lord; on the contrary, his commands and teaching should be infused into the minds of his disciples like the leaven of divine justice. Let the abbot remember always that at the dread Judgement of God there will be an examination of both these matters, of his teaching and of the obedience of his disciples. And let the abbot realize that the shepherd will have to answer for any lack of profit which the Father of the family may discover in his sheep. On the other hand, if the shepherd have spent all diligence on an unruly and disobedient flock and devoted his utmost care to the amending of its vicious ways, then he will be acquitted at the Judgement and may say to the Lord with the prophet: *I have not hid thy justice within my heart: I have declared thy truth and thy salvation; but they have despised and rejected me.* And so at the last, for these sheep disobedient to his care, let death itself bring its penalty.

Therefore, when anyone has received the name of abbot, he ought to rule his disciples with a twofold teaching, displaying all goodness and holiness by deeds and by words, but by deeds rather than by words. To intelligent disciples let him expound the Lord's commandments in words; but to those of harder hearts and ruder minds let him show forth the divine precepts by his example. And whatever he has taught his disciples to be contrary to God's law, let him show by his example that it is not to be done, lest while preaching to others he should himself become a castaway, and lest God should some day say to him in his sin: *Why dost thou repeat my commandments by rote, and boast of my covenant with thee? For thou hast hated to amend thy life and hast cast my words behind thee.* And again: *Thou sawest the speck of dust in thy brother's eye and didst not see the beam in thy own.*

Let him not make any distinction of persons in the monastery. Let him not love one more than another, unless he find him better in good works and obedience. Let not a freeborn monk be put before one that was a slave, unless there be some other reasonable ground for it. But if the abbot for just reason, think fit so to do, let him fix anyone's order as he will; otherwise let them keep their due places; because, whether slaves or freemen, we are all one in Christ and have to serve alike in the army of the same Lord. *For there is no respect of persons with God.* In this regard only are we distinguished in his sight, if we be found better than others in good works and humility. Therefore let the abbot show an equal love to all, and let the same discipline be imposed on all in accordance with their deserts.

For the abbot in his teaching ought always to observe the rule of the apostle, wherein he says: *Reprove, persuade, rebuke.* He must adapt himself to circumstances, now using severity and now persuasion, displaying the rigour of a master or the loving kindness of a father. That is to say, that he must sternly rebuke the undisciplined and restless; but the obedient, meek, and patient, these he should exhort to advance in virtue. As for the negligent and rebellious, we warn him to reprimand and punish them. And let him not shut his eyes to the faults of offenders; but as soon as they begin to appear, let him, as he can, cut them out by the roots, mindful of the fate of Heli, the priest of Silo. Those of gentle disposition and good understanding should be punished, for the first and second time, by verbal admonition; but bold, hard, proud, and disobedient characters should be checked at the very beginning of their ill-doing by the rod and corporal punishment, according to the text: *The fool is not corrected with words;* and again: *Beat thy son with the rod and thou shalt deliver his soul from death.*

The abbot should always remember what he is and what he is called, and should know that to whom more is committed, from him more is required. Let him realize also how difficult and arduous a task he has undertaken, of ruling souls and adapting himself to many dispositions. One he must humour, another rebuke, another persuade, according to each one's disposition and understanding, and thus adapt and accommodate himself to all in such a way, that he may not only suffer no loss in the sheep committed to him, but may even rejoice in the increase of a good flock.

Above all let him not have greater solicitude for fleeting, earthly, and perishable things, and so overlook or undervalue the salvation of the souls committed to him; but let him always remember that he has undertaken the government of souls and will have to give an account of them. And if he be tempted to complain of lack of means, let him remember the words: *Seek ye first the kingdom of God and his approval, and all these things shall be yours without the asking.* And again: *Those that fear him never go wanting.* And let him know that he who has undertaken the government of souls, must prepare himself to render an account of them. And whatever number of brethren he knows he has under his care, let him regard it as certain that he will have to give the Lord an account of all these souls on the Day of Judgement, and certainly of his own soul also. And thus, fearing always the examination which the shepherd will have to face for the sheep entrusted to him, and anxious regarding the account which will have to be given for others, he is made solicitous for his own sake also; and while by his admonitions helping others to amend, he himself is cleansed of his faults.

CHAPTER 3

OF CALLING THE BRETHREN TO COUNCIL

As often as any important business has to be done in the monastery, let the abbot call together the whole community and himself set forth the matter. And, having heard the advice of the brethren, let him take counsel with himself and then do what he shall judge to be most expedient. Now the reason why we have said that all should be called to council, is that God often reveals what is better to the younger. Let the brethren give their advice with all deference and humility, nor venture to defend their opinions obstinately; but let the decision depend rather on the abbot's judgement, so that when he has decided what is the better course, all may obey. However, just as it is proper for disciples to obey their master, so is it becoming that he on his part should dispose all things with prudence and justice.

In all things, therefore, let all follow the Rule as master, nor let anyone rashly depart from it. Let no one in the monastery follow the will of his own heart; nor let anyone presume to contend impudently with his abbot, or to contend with him at all when outside the monastery. Should he presume to do so, let him undergo the discipline of the Rule. The abbot himself, however, should do all things in the fear of God and observance of the Rule, knowing that he will certainly have to render an account of all his judgements to God, the most just Judge. But if the business to be done in the interests of the monastery be of lesser importance, let him use the advice of the seniors only. It is written: *Do all things with counsel, and thy deed shall not bring thee repentance.*

CHAPTER 4

THE TOOLS OF GOOD WORKS

In the first place, to love the Lord God with all one's heart,
all one's soul, and all one's strength.
Then, one's neighbour as oneself.
Then not to kill.
Not to commit adultery.
Not to steal.
Not to covet.
Not to bear false witness.
To honour all men.
Not to do to another what one would not have done to oneself.
To deny oneself, in order to follow Christ.
To chastise the body.
Not to seek soft living.
To love fasting.
To relieve the poor.
To clothe the naked.
To visit the sick.
To bury the dead.
To help the afflicted.
To console the sorrowing.
To avoid worldly conduct.
To prefer nothing to the love of Christ.

Not to yield to anger.
Not to nurse a grudge.
Not to hold guile in one's heart.
Not to make a feigned peace.
Not to forsake charity.
Not to swear, lest perchance one forswear oneself.
To utter truth from heart and mouth.
Not to render evil for evil.
To do no wrong to anyone, and to bear patiently wrongs done
to oneself.
To love one's enemies.
Not to render cursing for cursing, but rather blessing.
To bear persecution for justice' sake.

St. Benedict

Not to be proud.
Not a wine-bibber.
Not a glutton.
Not somnolent.
Not slothful.
Not a grumbler.
Not a detractor.
To put one's hope in God.
To attribute to God, and not to self, whatever good one sees
    in oneself.
But to recognize always that the evil is one's own doing, and
    to impute it to oneself.

To fear the Day of Judgement.
To dread hell.
To desire eternal life with all spiritual longing.
To keep death daily before one's eyes.
To keep constant guard over the actions of one's life.
To know for certain that God sees one everywhere.
When evil thoughts come into one's heart, to dash them at
    once on the rock of Christ and to manifest them to one's
    spiritual father.
To keep one's mouth from evil and depraved talk.
Not to love much speaking.
Not to speak vain words or such as move to laughter.
Not to love much or violent laughter.
To listen gladly to holy reading.
To apply oneself frequently to prayer.
Daily in one's prayer, with tears and sighs, to confess one's
    past sins to God.
To amend those sins for the future.
Not to fulfil the desires of the flesh.
To hate one's own will.
To obey in all things the commands of the abbot, even though
    he himself (which God forbid) should act otherwise:
    remembering the Lord's precept: *What they say, do ye;*
    but what they do, do ye not.
Not to wish to be called holy before one is holy; but first to
    be holy, that one may more truly be called so.

To fulfil God's commandments daily in one's deeds.

To love chastity.
To hate no man.
Not to be jealous.
Not to give way to envy.
Not to love contention.
To shun vainglory.
To reverence the old.
To love the young.
To pray for one's enemies in the love of Christ.
To make peace with one's adversary before sundown.
And never to despair of God's mercy.

Behold these are the tools of the spiritual craft. If we employ them unceasingly day and night, and on the Day of Judgement render account of them, then we shall receive from the Lord in return that reward which he himself has promised: *Eye hath not seen nor ear heard, what God hath prepared for those that love him.* Now the workshop, wherein we shall diligently execute all these tasks, is the enclosure of the monastery and stability in the community.

CHAPTER 5

OF OBEDIENCE

The first degree of humility is obedience without delay. This becometh those who hold nothing dearer to them than Christ. Because of the holy service which they have professed, the fear of hell, and the glory of life everlasting, as soon as anything has been ordered by the superior, they receive it as a divine command and cannot suffer any delay in executing it. Of these doth the Lord say: *He hath listened to me and hath obeyed me.* And again he saith to teachers: *He who listens to you, listens to me.*

Such as these, therefore, immediately abandoning their own affairs and forsaking their own will, dropping the work they were engaged on and leaving it unfinished, with swift obedience follow up with their deeds the voice of him who commands them. And almost in the same moment of time that the master's order is issued, is the disciple's work completed, in the swiftness of the fear of the Lord; the two things being rapidly accomplished together by those who are impelled by the desire of attaining life everlasting. Therefore they choose the narrow way, according to the Lord's words: *Narrow is the way which leadeth unto life;* so that not living by their own will, and obeying their own desires and passions, but walking by another's judgement and orders, they dwell in monasteries, and desire to have an abbot over them. Assuredly such as these imitate that saying of the Lord wherein he saith: *I came not to do my own will, but the will of him who sent me.*

But this obedience itself will then be acceptable to God and pleasing to men, if what is commanded be not done timorously, or tardily, or tepidly, nor with murmuring or the raising of objections. For the obedience which is given to superiors is given to God, since he himself said: *He who listens to you, listens to me.* And disciples should give their obedience with a good will, because *God loveth a cheerful giver.* For if the disciple obey with an ill will, and murmur not only in words but even in his heart, then even though he fulfil the command, his work will not be acceptable to God, who sees that his heart is murmuring. For work such as this he will gain no reward; nay, rather, he will incur the punishment due to murmurers, unless he amend and make reparation.

CHAPTER 6

OF SILENCE

Let us do as saith the prophet: *I said, I will take heed unto my ways, that I offend not with my tongue. I have set a guard to my mouth. I was dumb and was humbled, and kept silence even from good words.* Here the prophet teaches us that if we should at times, for the love of silence, refrain from good talk, we should with more reason still, for fear of sin's punishment, eschew all evil talk. Therefore, on account of the great value of silence, let leave to speak be seldom granted to observant disciples, even though it be for good, holy, and edifying conversations; for it is written: *In much speaking thou shalt not escape sin,* and elsewhere: *Death and life are in the power of the tongue.* For it becometh the master to speak and to teach; but it befits the disciple to be silent and to listen.

And therefore, if there be anything to be asked from the superior, let it be sought with all humility and respectful submission. But as for buffoonery and talk that is vain and stirs laughter, we condemn such things everywhere with a perpetual ban, and forbid the disciple to open his mouth for such conversation.

CHAPTER 7

OF HUMILITY

Holy Scripture crieth out to us, brethren, saying: *Everyone that exalteth himself shall be humbled, and he that humbleth himself shall be exalted.* When it so speaks, it teaches us that all exaltation is a kind of pride; which the prophet shows that he shunned in the words: *Lord, my heart is not exalted nor mine eyes lifted up; neither have I dwelt on high things, nor on marvels that are beyond my reach.* And why? *If I was not humbly minded but exalted my soul with pride; as a child that is weaned from his mother, so wilt thou requite my soul.*

Wherefore, brethren, if we wish to attain to the summit of humility and desire to arrive speedily at that heavenly exaltation to which we ascend by the humility of the present life, then must we set up a ladder of our ascending actions like unto that which Jacob saw in his vision, whereon angels appeared to him, descending and ascending. By that descent and ascent we must surely understand nothing else than this, that we descend by self-exaltation and ascend by humility. And the ladder erected is our life in this world, which for the humble of heart is raised up by the Lord unto heaven. Now the sides of this ladder are our body and soul, into which sides our divine vocation has fitted various degrees of humility and discipline which we have to climb.

The first degree of humility, then, is that a man keep the fear of God before his eyes, altogether shunning forgetfulness. Let him ever remember all the commandments of God, and how hell will burn for their sins those that despise him; and let him constantly turn over in his heart the eternal life which is prepared for those that fear him. And guarding himself always from sins and vices, whether of thought, word, hand, foot, or

190

self-will, and checking also the desires of the flesh, let him consider that God is always beholding him from heaven, that his actions are everywhere visible to the eye of the Godhead, and are constantly being reported to God by the angels. The prophet teaches us this when he represents God as always present in our thoughts: *God searcheth the heart and the reins;* and again he saith: *Thou hast understood my thoughts from afar;* and: *The thought of man shall praise thee.* In order then that he may be careful regarding his wrongful thoughts, let the good brother say constantly in his heart: *Then shall I be spotless before him, if I shall have kept myself from my iniquity.*

We are, indeed, forbidden to do our own will by Scripture, which saith to us: *Turn away from thine own will.* Moreover, we ask God in prayer that his will be done in us.

And rightly are we taught not to do our own will, since we dread that sentence of Scripture: *There are ways which to men seem right, but the ends thereof lead to the depths of hell;* and since we fear also what is said of the careless: *They are corrupt and have become abominable in their pleasures.* And in regard to the desires of the flesh, let us believe that God is always present to us, since the prophet says to the Lord: *All my desire is before thee.*

We must be on our guard, then, against evil desires, for death lies close by the gate of delight; whence Scripture gives this command: *Go not after thy lusts.* So if *the eyes of the Lord behold the good and the evil,* and the Lord is ever *looking down from heaven upon the children of men, to see if there be one soul that reflects and seeks God;* and if our deeds are daily, day and night, reported to the Lord by the angels assigned to us: then, brethren, must we constantly beware, as the prophet says in the psalm, lest God some day behold us falling into evil ways and turned unprofitable, and spare us for this present time, because he is merciful and awaits our amendment, but should say to us in the future: *These things didst thou do, and I was silent.*

The second degree of humility is that a man love not his own will, nor delight in fulfilling his own desires, but carry out indeed the saying of the Lord: *I came not to do my own will, but the will of him who sent me.* It is written also: *Self-will hath its punishment, but necessity winneth a crown.*

The third degree of humility is that a man for the love of God subject himself to his superior in all obedience, imitating the Lord, of whom the apostle says: *He was made obedient even unto death.*

The fourth degree of humility is that, meeting in this obedience with difficulties and contradictions and even injustice, he should with a quiet mind hold fast to patience, and enduring neither tire nor run away; for the Scripture saith: *He that shall persevere to the end shall be saved;* and again: *Let thy heart take courage, and wait thou for the Lord.* And showing how the true disciple ought to endure all things, however contrary, for the Lord, it saith in the person of sufferers: *For thy sake we face death at every moment. We are reckoned no better than sheep marked down for slaughter.* Then, confident in their hope of the divine reward, they go on with joy to declare: *But in all these things we overcome, through him that hath loved us.* And again in another place the Scripture saith: *Thou, O God, hast put us to the proof: thou hast tested us as men test silver in the fire. Thou hast led us into a snare: thou hast bowed our backs with trouble.* And to show that we ought to be under a superior, it goeth on to say: *Thou hast set men over our heads.* Moreover, in adversities and injuries they patiently fulfil the Lord's commands: when struck on one cheek they offer the other, when robbed of their tunic they surrender also their cloak, when forced to go a mile they go two, with the apostle Paul they bear with false brethren, and they bless those that curse them.

The fifth degree of humility is that he humbly confess and conceal not from his abbot any evil thoughts that enter his heart, and any secret sins that he has committed. To this does Scripture exhort us, saying: *Make known thy way unto the Lord and hope in him.* And again: *Confess to the Lord, for he is good, and his mercy endureth for ever.* And further: *I have made known my sin to thee, and my faults I have not concealed. I said: I will be my own accuser and confess my faults to the Lord, and with that thou didst remit the guilt of my sin.*

The sixth degree of humility is that a monk be content with the meanest and worst of everything, and esteem himself, in regard to the work that is given him, as a bad and unworthy workman, saying to himself with the prophet: *I am brought to nothing; I am all ignorance; I am become as a dumb beast before thee; yet am I ever close to thee.*

The seventh degree of humility is that he should not only in his speech declare himself lower and of less account than all others, but should in his own inmost heart believe it, humbling himself and saying with the prophet: *But I am a worm and no man, a byword to all men and the laughing-stock of the people. I have been lifted up only to be humbled and confounded;* and again: *It is good for me that thou hast humbled me, that I may learn thy commandments.*

The eighth degree of humility is that a monk do nothing except what is commended by the common rule of the monastery and the example of his superiors.

The ninth degree of humility is that a monk restrain his tongue and keep silence, not speaking until he is questioned. For Scripture showeth that *in much talking thou canst not avoid sin;* and that *the talkative man shall not prosper on the earth.*

The tenth degree of humility is that he be not ready and prompt to laughter, for it is written: *The fool lifteth up his voice in laughter.*

The eleventh degree of humility is that a monk, when he speaks, do so gently and without laughter, humbly and seriously in few and sensible words, and without clamour. It is written: *A wise man is known by the fewness of his words.*

The twelfth degree of humility is that a monk should not only be humble of heart, but should also in his behaviour always manifest his humility to those who look upon him. That is to say, that whether he is at the Work of God, in the oratory, in the monastery, in the garden, on the road, in the fields, or anywhere else, and whether sitting, walking, or standing, he should always have his head bowed and his eyes downcast, pondering always the guilt of his sins, and considering that he is about to be brought before the dread judgement seat of God.

Let him constantly say in his heart what was said with downcast eyes by the publican in the Gospel: *Lord, I a sinner am not worthy to raise mine eyes to heaven;* and again with the prophet: *I am bowed down and humbled on every side.*

Then, when all these degrees of humility have been climbed, the monk will presently come to that perfect love of God which casts out all fear; whereby he will begin to observe without labour, as though naturally and by habit, all those precepts which formerly he did not observe without fear: no longer for fear of hell, but for love of Christ and through good habit and delight in virtue. And this will the Lord deign to show forth by the power of his Spirit in his workman now cleansed from vice and from sin.

St. Bernard of Clairvaux
1090-1153

Holiness expresses itself through a variety of personalities. Quiet, calm types seem to be more readily accepted as candidates for sanctity. The vehement, explosive personality is often looked upon with some reserve.

St. Bernard was of the latter type. His zeal in seeking out and defending the truth is almost legendary. Born near Dijon, France, he dedicated himself as a young man to the Rule of the Cistercian Order. He established the abbey of Clairvaux before he was 25 years old. By the time he died in 1153 he was responsible for 68 monastic foundations. With equal energy he preached, wrote and challenged enemies of Christianity. The vigor with which he pursued a person like Peter Abelard and his refusal to relent until Abelard was condemned make one wonder exactly what the mystery of Christian love meant to him. Yet it must be admitted that this same Bernard dedicated himself totally and selflessly to the building up of Christianity in the twelfth century. He was a man of prayer. He knew his weaknesses and worked to overcome them. Bernard sought, above all, union with the God whom he loved and served so generously.

The teaching of Bernard is relatively simple. He was at home with the Scriptures, the writings of the Fathers of the Church and the Rule of St. Benedict. Drawing from these sources, he taught that God is love. By love He created all things, man included; by love He redeemed mankind and draws all things to Himself. Bernard completed this doctrine with themes such as the Incarnation, the necessity of grace, humility, and prayer.

The following selection is taken from his treatise On the Love of God. It contains important insights into Bernard's basic vision. Why should God be loved? For one reason only, God Himself. How should He be loved? Beyond measure. From this direct beginning, Bernard moves on to a fuller explication of the theme. The gifts that God has given to mankind are a first reason for loving God. Christians especially, because their lives are completed in Christ, have cause to love God. A further reason is the fact that only in God can man satisfy his thirst for happiness.

Bernard speaks of four degrees of love. First, man loves himself for his own sake. This is natural, since man is flesh. Second, man loves God, but for his own sake, not for God. Through a life of meditation, reading, prayer and obedience, man slowly arrives at the third degree, which is to love God for the sake of God. The fourth and final degree, which Bernard confesses appears to be impossible in this life, would be when a man loves himself only for the sake of God. This is perfect love for Bernard and can be achieved only at the final Resurrection.

Bernard's charm, intelligence and eloquence, along with his overwhelming energy, made him an influential person during his lifetime. His teaching was central to the monastic renewal in which he was involved. For several centuries after his death, Bernard's insights continued to play a role in the shaping of spiritual theology.

ON THE LOVE OF GOD

CHAPTER I

WHY AND HOW GOD SHOULD BE LOVED.

Y ou wish, therefore, to hear from me why and how God
should be loved? And I: the reason for loving God is
God Himself; the way is to love Him beyond measure.
Is this enough? It is, perchance, but only for one who is wise.
But if *to the unwise I am debtor*; where enough has been said to
the wise I must also, as usual, administer to the needs of others.
And so out of consideration for those who are slower to understand, I shall consider it no burden to repeat what I have said,
more fully rather than more profoundly. There is a twofold
reason, I should say, why God should be loved for His own sake:
because nothing can be more justly, nothing more profitably
loved. Indeed when the question is asked why God should be
loved it may have one of two meanings. For the question may
arise from the fact that a person does not clearly see what particularly constitutes the basis of his inquiry: whether it is God's
title to our love or our own advantage in loving Him. To be sure,
I would give the same answer to both of these questions: I find
no other worthy reason for loving Him except Himself. And first
let us examine the question of God's title to our love. A very
special title to it is He who gave Himself to us despite the fact
that we were so undeserving. For, what better than Himself could
even He have given? If, then, in asking the reason why we should
love God we seek to know His title to our love, it is chiefly
this: *because He hath first loved us.* He it is who is clearly deserving of being loved in return, especially if one considers who
He is that loved, who they are whom He loved and how much
He loved them. And who is He? Is He not the One to whom
every spirit bears witness: *Thou art my God, for Thou has no
need of my goods?* And the true love of this Sovereign One lies
in this, that it does not seek its own interests. But to whom is

such unmixed love shown? *When we were enemies, it is said, we were reconciled to God.* God, therefore, has loved His enemies and that, *gratis.* But how much? As much as Saint John says: *God so loved the world as to give his only begotten Son.* And Saint Paul adds: *He spared not even His own Son, but delivered him up for us all.* That very Son says of Himself: *Greater love than this no man hath, that a man lay down his life for his friends.* Thus has the Just deserved from the ungodly, the Greatest from the least, the All-powerful from the weak. But some one may say: Yes, thus has He deserved of mankind, but of the Angels, not so. That is true, because the Angels had no need of it. Moreover, He who succored men in so great a necessity preserved the Angels from it, and He who by his love for men brought it about that they should no longer remain such as they were, the Same with equal love bestowed upon the Angels the grace of never becoming such as men once were.

CHAPTER II

HOW GREATLY GOD DESERVES TO BE LOVED BY MAN BECAUSE OF HIS GIFTS OF BODY AND SOUL. HOW THESE ARE TO BE KNOWN AND KEPT WITHOUT WRONG TO HIM WHO GAVE THEM.

Those to whom what I have said is plain will also, I think, plainly see why God should be loved: that is, whence he deserves to be loved. But if unbelievers blind themselves to these truths God is still ready to confound their ingratitude with His numberless benefits conferred for man's advantage and manifest to human sense. Who else, forsooth, supplies food to everyone who eats, light to everyone who sees, breath to everyone who breathes? But it is foolish to strive to enumerate what I have just spoken of as innumerable. It is enough, by way of example, to have mentioned the chief ones—bread, sun and air. The chief ones, I mean, not because they are superior but because they are more necessary since they pertain to the body. Let man seek his higher goods—dignity, knowledge and virtue—in that higher part of him which excels self, that is, in the soul. By man's dignity I mean his free will in which it is surely given him not only to excel other creatures but also to rule over all other [visible] living things. By knowledge I mean that which he recognizes that his dignity is within himself but not from himself. By virtue I mean that by which he ardently seeks Him from whom he has his being and valiantly holds fast to Him when found.

Thus every one of these three goods presents a twofold aspect. Accordingly, human dignity appears not only as the prerogative of man naturally considered, but as the basis of his [moral] power of dominion which determines the fear which he commands in every other living creature on the face of the earth. Knowledge will likewise be of a double nature if we perceive that this same dignity as well as any other good that is in us dwells within us but is not from ourselves. Lastly, virtue, too, will be recognized as twofold if it leads us to seek after Him to whom we owe our existence and when we have found Him, makes us cling to Him so that we shall never again be separated from Him. And so dignity without knowledge is of no avail; nay, it is even a hindrance if virtue be lacking, as the reasoning that follows makes clear. What glory can one have in possessing what he does not know that he possesses? Furthermore, to know what you have while not knowing that it does not come from yourself, begets glory but not in the sight of God. And to him who glories in himself the Apostle says: *What hast thou that thou hast not received? And if thou hast received, why dost thou glory as if thou hadst not received it?* He does not say simply, *Why dost thou glory?* but he adds, *as if thou hadst not received it,* as if to declare that not he is blameworthy who glories in what he has, but he who glories in it as though he had not received it. Not without reason *vain* glory is the name given to glory of this sort for it lacks the solid foundation of truth [i.e., is not in accordance with the facts of the case]. Indeed the Apostle draws a distinction between this and true glory when he says: *He that glorieth, may glory in the Lord.* That is, in truth. For the Lord is truth.

It is necessary, therefore, that you know both what you are, and that you are not such of yourself, lest you be altogether boastful [i.e. without any limitation], or vainly so [i.e. without any foundation in truth]. Finally it is said: *If thou know not thyself, . . . go forth and follow after the steps of the flocks . . . of thy companions.* This is in truth what happens. When man fashioned in honor does not perceive the honor that is his, he is, by reason of such ignorance justly likened to the beasts of the field that share his present corruption and mortality. It happens, therefore, that a creature distinguished by the gift of reason, through not knowing itself begins to be herded with the droves of unthinking beasts. While ignorant of his own peculiar glory which is from within he is carried away by his own curiosity, determined upon fashioning himself conformably to things purely sensible and becomes one with the rest of visible creatures because he thinks that he has received nothing beyond the rest of them. And so we must be especially on our guard against this ignorance by which, perchance, we think of ourselves as being less than we really are. But no less, indeed much more, must we avoid that other ignorance by which we attribute to ourselves more than we possess. This is what happens when we deceive ourselves into thinking that any good whatever that we have comes from ourselves. But besides both these kinds of ignorance you must shun and abhor that sort of presumption by which knowingly and of set purpose you may, perchance, dare to seek your own glory in goods that are not yours. Thus you would not fear to rob Another of the honor which comes from a good which you well know is in no way attributable to yourself. The former ignorance has no glory at all: the latter has, but not in God's sight. But this third evil, because it is now knowingly committed, usurps what belongs to God Himself. By comparison with that latter ignorance, this presumption is clearly more grievous and more dangerous in this, that in ignorance God is not known but in presumption He is contemned. It is worse and more detestable than the former because while the former puts us in a class with the beasts of the field, this latter makes us the fellows of demons. Assuredly it is pride and the greatest offence of all to use the gifts we have received as if they were part of our very selves, and after having accepted favors to usurp the glory of the Bestower.

Thus it is that with these two, dignity and knowledge, there is also need of virtue which is the fruit of both. For it is through virtue that He is sought after and retained who, as Author and Giver of all things, is deservedly glorified in everything. Otherwise, knowing and not doing what is worthy of him, a man *shall be beaten with many stripes*. Why? Because *he would not understand that he might do well*, rather, *he hath desired iniquity on his bed*, while as a wicked servant he strives to arrogate to himself, nay, even to destroy the glory due his gracious Lord from those goods which, by the gift of intelligence, he knows for certain he has not of himself. It is evident, therefore, that dignity is altogether useless without knowledge, and knowledge without virtue is sinful. But the man of virtue to whom neither knowledge can be sinful nor dignity unfruitful, lifts up his voice to God and frankly confesses: *Not to us, O Lord, not to us; but to Thy name give glory*. That is: We attribute to ourselves, O Lord, neither any knowledge nor any dignity; but to Thy name from whom all proceeds do we impute all.

But we have wandered rather far from our purpose while engaged in showing that those also who do not know Christ are sufficiently admonished by the natural law through the goods of body and soul which they perceive are theirs; how much they, too, should love God for God's own sake. For, to repeat briefly what has been said on this point, what infidel does not know that the necessities to which allusion has already been made—whence he derives life, whereby he sees, whereby he breathes—are administered to his body in this mortal life by no other than by Him *who giveth food to all flesh, who maketh his sun to rise upon the good and the bad, and raineth upon the just and the unjust?* What man is there, even though he be ungodly, who can think that the human dignity with which his soul is resplendent is attributable to any other than to Him who says in Genesis: *Let us make man to our image and likeness?* Who can deem any other the Bestower of knowledge save him *that teacheth man knowledge?* Who, again, can think that the gift of virtue has been bestowed in the past or hope for it to be given in the future, save from the hand, likewise, of the Lord of Hosts? God, then, deserves to be loved for His own sake even by the infidel who, although he knows not Christ, yet knows himself. Hence there is no excuse for any infidel, even, if he does not love the Lord his God with his whole heart, with his whole soul, and with all his strength. For, that innate sense of justice which reason is not ignorant of, cries out to him from within that he is bound with his whole self to love Him to whom, he is not unaware, he owes all that he is. But it is difficult, nay impossible, for anyone with his powers of free will to render wholly to God's will the things he once received from God, and not rather to twist them according to his own will and retain them as his own, according as it is written: *all seek the things that are their own;* and again: *the imagination and thought of man's heart are prone to evil.*

CHAPTER III

HOW MANY INCENTIVES CHRISTIANS HAVE, MORE THAN INFIDELS, FOR LOVING GOD.

The faithful, on the other hand, know well how complete is their need of Jesus and of Him crucified. While embracing in wonder *the charity* revealed in Him *which surpasseth all knowledge,* they are filled with shame at not paying back even the very little which they are themselves, in return for love and condescension so great. Easily, therefore, do they grow in love who know that they themselves are more loved: for he to whom less has been given loves less. The Jew or the Pagan, to be sure, can never be urged on by such spurs of love as the Church feels who says: I am wounded with charity; and again: *Stay me up with flowers; compass me about with apples: because I languish with love.* She sees *King Solomon in the diadem wherewith his mother crowned him;* she sees the Only-begotten of the Father *bearing his own cross;* she sees the Lord of Majesty struck and spat upon; she sees the Author of life and glory held fast with nails, pierced with a lance, overwhelmed with reproaches, finally laying down that precious life of His for His friends. She sees all this and the sword of love pierces her soul the more and she says: *Stay me up with flowers, compass me about with apples, for I languish with love.* These *apples,* to be sure, are the pomegranates which the bride led into the garden of her Beloved, plucks from the tree of life; they have borrowed their own peculiar savour from the Bread of Heaven, their color from the Blood of Christ. She [the Church] then sees death itself struck dead and the Author of death led in triumph. She sees captivity led captive from hell [limbo] to earth, from earth to heaven, *that in the name of Jesus every knee should bow of those that are in heaven, on earth and under the earth.* She per-

ceives that the earth which under the ancient curse had brought
forth thorns and thistles, has sprung into blossom again at the
grace of a new benediction. And in all this recalling that verse:
*And my flesh hath flourished again, and with my will I will
give praise to him,* she longs to add to the fruits of the Passion
which she has plucked from the tree of the cross, some of the
flowers of the resurrection whose fragrance especially allures
the Beloved to visit her again and again.

At last she exclaims: *Behold thou art fair, my beloved, and
comely; our bed is decked with flowers.* In showing Him the
bridal-couch she frankly makes known what she desires; and
when she speaks of it as *decked with flowers,* she reveals whence
she presumes to obtain the gratification of her desires. For it is
not from her own merits but from the flowers gathered in a
field which God has blessed. Christ who willed to be conceived
and reared in Nazareth finds his delight in flowers. The heavenly
Bridegroom rejoices in such fragrance and freely enters often
into the bridal-chamber of the heart which He has found filled
with fruits of this sort and strewn with flowers. For where He
perceives that the grace of His Passion or the glory of His resurrection is pondered as the subject of diligent meditation, there
straightway He is present with eagerness and joy. Know well
that the memorials of the Passion are as the fruits of the past
year and of all times past under the domination of sin and death,
now at last in the fulness of time beginning to appear. But the
signs of the Resurrection, mark you, are the new flowers of the
season that follows and blooms forth, a new summer, under
the influence of grace. Of these flowers the general resurrection
which is to come will in the end of time bring forth the fruit
which will remain forever. *For,* it is said, *winter is now past;
the rain is over and gone. The flowers have appeared in our
land;* which means that summer has returned with Him who,
released from the coldness of death, was restored to the mild
Spring of a new life. *Behold,* he says, *I make all things new.* He
whose flesh was sown in death, bursts into blossom again in the
resurrection, at the sweet odor whereof in the field of our
valley, withered things straightway grow green once more,
things that were cold grow warm again, and the dead pulse
anew with life.

Because of the freshness of these flowers and fruits and because of the beauty of the field giving forth the sweetest fragrance, the Father Himself so delights in the Son that he says: *Behold the smell of my son is as the smell of a plentiful field which the Lord hath blessed.* Plentiful indeed, *of whose fulness we all have received.* But the Bride, on terms of greater intimacy, gathers flowers and plucks fruit therefrom, with which to deck the innermost chamber of her own conscience so that the little bed of her heart may give forth sweet odors to the Bridegroom at His coming. For if we wish to have Christ as a frequent guest, we must ever have our hearts fortified with unfailing testimonies both of His mercy in dying and of His power in rising from the dead. This is what David meant when he said: *these two things have I heard, that power belongeth to God, and mercy to thee, O Lord.* The testimonies concerning both of these truths have become credible in the highest degree, for Christ died for our sins and rose from the dead for our justification and ascended [into Heaven] for our protection and sent the [Holy] Spirit for our consolation and will one day return for the consummation [of our souls' salvation]. Surely in death He showed mercy; power, in rising from the dead; and both in all the rest [of His life's mysteries].

These are the apples, these the flowers with which the Bride prays that meanwhile she may be encompassed and sustained; feeling, I believe, that the power of love within her can in a measure become lukewarm and languid if it be not continually fostered by such helps, until, brought at last into the bridal-chamber she is caught in the long-desired embrace and exclaims: *His left hand is under my head, and his right hand shall embrace me.* Then she will feel and judge how all the evidences of love which at His former coming she had received as if from the left hand of the Beloved are to be disdained in comparison with the surpassing sweetness of the right hand's embrace, and in time to come to be regarded as of a lower degree. She will feel what she has heard: *It is the spirit that quickeneth: the flesh profiteth nothing.* She will know from experience what she had known from hearsay: *my spirit is sweet above honey, and my inheritance above honey and honeycomb.* In regard to what follows: *My memory is unto everlasting generations;* this means that as long as the present age is seen to abide, in which a generation comes and a generation goes, the consolation which flows from the memory will not be lacking to the elect to whom, as yet, the full satisfaction of the presence [of the Bridegroom] is not granted. Hence it is written: *They shall publish the memory of the abundance of thy sweetness.* There can be no doubt that *they* are those of whom it had been said a little before: *Generation and generation shall praise thy works.* Memory, therefore, in a generation of time; presence in the kingdom of heaven. By this latter the company of the elect already taken up into heaven is glorified: by the former, meanwhile, the generation of wayfarers is consoled.

CHAPTER IV

WHO THEY ARE WHO FIND CONSOLATION IN THE REMEMBRANCE OF GOD; AND WHO ARE MORE CAPABLE OF LOVING HIM.

But it is important to consider what generation it is that finds comfort in the remembrance of God. Not *a perverse and exasperating generation*, to which it is said: *Woe to you that are rich: for you have your consolation*; but such as can say with truth: *My soul refused to be comforted.* It is indeed right that those who do not find their delight in things present should here rejoice in the remembrance of things to come, and the remembrance of eternity should prove a source of delight to those who disdain to derive consolation from any of the things that pass away. And this is the generation of those who seek the Lord, seeking not *the things that are their own*, but *the face of the God of Jacob.* To those, therefore, who seek and sigh for the vision of God there is present, meanwhile, a sweet remembrance which, however, does not afford them complete satisfaction but makes them hunger the more for that which will satisfy them fully. To this, indeed, He who is their Food bears witness in His own regard when He speaks thus: *They that eat me, shall yet hunger*; and he who is fed says, *I shall be satisfied when thy glory shall appear.* Yet, *blessed are they*, even now, *that hunger and thirst after justice, for*, one day, *they* and not others, *shall have their fill.* Woe to thee, *a wicked and perverse generation!* Woe to thee, a people foolish and unwise who both loathes the remembrance of Him, and is terrified at the thought of His coming! Deservedly indeed, for neither now [on earth] would you be delivered *from the snare of the hunters*, since *they that will become rich* in this world *fall into . . . the snare of the devil*; nor will you then [at the Last Judgment] be able to be *delivered . . . from the sharp word*. O sharp word, O hard saying! *Depart from me ye cursed into everlasting fire*. Much harder, indeed, and sharper than that word which in the Church is repeated every day [at Mass] in remembrance of the Passion: *He that eateth my flesh and drinketh my blood, hath everlasting life*. That is, he who recalls to mind My death and after My example mortifies his *members which are upon the earth*, shall have life everlasting; that is, if you suffer with Him now you shall reign with Him hereafter. And nevertheless, a very great number in these days also [as of old], recoiling from His voice, going back and walking no more with Him, answers not by word but by deed: *This saying is hard, and who can hear it*? And so, *A generation that set not their heart aright: and whose spirit was not faithful to God*, but rather trusting *in the uncertainty of riches*, is weighed down at hearing even *the word of the cross*, and looks upon any reminder of the Passion as burdensome. But in [His] presence how will [that generation] ever bear the weight of that [other] word: *Depart from me, you cursed, into everlasting fire which was prepared for the devil and his angels*. Assuredly *on whomsoever* this stone *shall fall, it shall grind him to powder*. But *the generation of the righteous shall be blessed*: they who with the Apostle, *whether absent or present*, labor to please God. In the end they shall hear: *Come, ye blessed of my Father, possess you the kingdom prepared for you from the foundation of the world*. Then that *generation that set not their heart aright*, will too late, alas, come to know how sweet was the yoke of Christ, in comparison with their anguish, and how light was His burden from which, in pride, they withdrew their stiff necks as from a weight bitter and crushing. You cannot, O wretched slaves of Mammon, you cannot at the same time glory *in the cross of Our Lord Jesus Christ*, and place your trust in great hoards of money. To go after gold is to prove how sweet is the Lord. Hence He whom you do not know in remembrance, as sweet, will prove bitter, no doubt, in His [actual] presence.

St. Bernard of Clairvaux

The faithful soul, on the other hand, longs eagerly for the presence [of God] and reposes sweetly in the remembrance [of Him], and until she is capable of *beholding the glory of the Lord with open face,* she glories in the ignominy of the Cross. Thus, truly, thus the bride and dove of Christ finds rest meanwhile and sleeps *among the midst of lots,* having chosen for the present in remembrance of the abundance of Thy sweetness, Lord Jesus, *wings . . . covered with silver,* that is, the whiteness of innocence and purity; and hoping, besides, to be filled with joy at Thy countenance where, also, *the hinder parts of her back* will be covered *with the paleness of gold.* When with joy she has been brought into *the brightness of the saints,* she will be more completely illumined by the light of Wisdom. With good reason, therefore, does she glory even now and say: *His left hand is under my head, and his right hand shall embrace me;* reflecting that in His left hand is the remembrance of that love than which there is no greater, by which He laid down His life for His friends; but in His right hand is the Beatific Vision which He has promised his friends and the joy [that flows] from the presence of Majesty itself. Justly is that vision of God, that vision that makes us like unto God, that inconceivable delight of the Divine presence, justly is it ascribed to the right hand concerning which it is joyously sung: *at thy right hand are delights even to the end.* Justly is it the left hand in which is placed that wonderful love which we have recalled to mind and which is ever to be remembered, for, *until iniquity pass away,* it is upon this hand that the bride shall lay her head and rest.

Justly, therefore, is the left hand of the Bridegroom under the head of the bride. Leaning back, it is upon it that she rests her head, that is, the intention of her mind, lest it should be inclined and bent toward fleshly and worldly desires; *For the corruptible body is a load upon the soul, and the earthly habitation presseth down the mind that museth upon many things.* For when we come to consider it, what else is effected by compassion so great and so undeserved, by love so gratuitous and hence so amply proved, by esteem so unexpected, by meekness so invincible, by sweetness so wonderful? What, I ask, will all these effect when they are diligently pondered save that they will marvelously draw to themselves the soul of him who ponders them freed from every unworthy love; they will powerfully affect that soul and make it despise, as compared with themselves, whatever one cannot make the object of his desire save by contemning them [the aforesaid higher enjoyments]? Surely, then, the bride runs eagerly to the odor of their ointments, loves ardently; and so loves, she seems to herself to love very little even when she has wholly bound herself first in love. Not without cause. For, what that is great can recompense a love so great shown by One who is Himself great; if a grain of dust will have brought together its whole self to return the love of another, and that other--Majesty itself, forsooth—outstripping it in love, is seen wholly bent upon its salvation? Finally, *God so loved the world, as to give his only begotten Son.* This, beyond doubt, is said of the Father. Again: *he hath delivered his soul unto death;* nor is there any doubt that this is spoken of the Son. And it is said of the Holy Ghost: *But the Paraclete, the Holy Ghost, whom the Father will send in my name, he will teach you all things, and bring all things to your mind, whatsoever I shall have said to you.* God therefore loves and loves with His whole Self because the whole Trinity loves, if, indeed, *the whole* can be said of the Infinite and Incomprehensible, or of what is simply One.

CHAPTER V

TO WHAT DEGREE THE OBLIGATION OF LOVE IS BINDING, ESPECIALLY UPON CHRISTIANS.

One who knows these truths, I believe, realizes fully why God should be loved, that is by what title he deserves to be loved. But the infidel not having the Son, consequently has neither the Father nor the Holy Ghost. For *He who honoreth not the Son, honoreth not the Father who hath sent him,* nor the Holy Ghost whom He sent. It is therefore no wonder if he has less love for Him whom he knows less. Nevertheless even he [the infidel] is not unaware of the fact that he owes all that he is to Him whom he recognizes as the Author of his whole being. What of me, then?—I who hold my God not only as the gratuitous Bestower of my life, most bountiful in His providence, a devoted Consoler, a solicitous Ruler, but a most abundant Redeemer as well, an eternal Conserver, One who enriches, One who gives glory. As it is written: *with him (there is) plentiful redemption;* and again: *(Christ) entered once into the holies, having obtained eternal redemption.* Concerning His providence: *(The Lord) will not forsake his saints: they shall be preserved forever;* and concerning His enriching [of us]: *good measure and pressed down and shaken together and running over shall they give into your bosom.* And again: *eye hath not seen, nor ear heard, neither hath it entered into the heart of man, what things God hath prepared for them that love Him.* And concerning His giving of glory: *we look for the Saviour, our Lord Jesus Christ, Who will reform the body of our lowness, made like to the body of his glory;* and this: *the sufferings of this time are not worthy to be compared with the glory to come, that shall be revealed in us;* and again: *For that which is at present momentary and light of our tribulation worketh for us above measure exceedingly an eternal weight of glory, while we look not at the things which are seen, but at the things which are not seen.*

What shall I render to the Lord for all these things? Reason as well as natural justice impels that other [the infidel] to surrender his whole self to Him from Whom he has received all that he is, and reminds him that he is bound to love Him with his whole self. To me [a Christian], to be sure, faith reveals that He should be loved the more and to the degree that I understand He is to be esteemed above myself; I, forsooth, who hold that He is the Bestower not only of myself but even of His very Self as well. Finally (when the Psalmist asked, *what shall I render,* etc.) the time of [Christian] faith had not yet come, God had not yet become known in the Flesh, died upon the cross, come forth from the tomb, returned to the Father. Not as yet, I say, had He commended His great charity towards us—that charity concerning which we have already spoken much—at the time when it was already commanded man to love the Lord his God with his whole heart, with his whole soul, with his whole strength, that is with all that he is, with all that he knows, and with every power that he has. Nor is God unjust in claiming as His own the work of His hands and His gifts. For why should not a thing which has been made, love its Maker since it has the power of doing so? And why should it not do so as much as it can, since it has no power at all except as a gift from Him? In addition to

this, the fact that it was made out of nothing, and that, gratu-
itously and in this present state of dignity, this fact makes the
debt of love clearer and makes what is demanded of it appear
more just. Moreover, how great do we consider that increase of
His benefaction when He preserved *men and beasts,* whereby
God has multiplied His mercy! We, I say, who *changed* our *glory
into the likeness of a calf that eateth grass,* were by sinning *compared to senseless beasts.* If I owe my whole self for being made,
what more shall I give now in return for being re-made and re-
made in such wise? For I was not re-made as easily as I was made,
if, indeed, it is written not only of me but of every thing that
was made: *he spoke, and they were made.* But, in truth He who
made me so great, and that, by speaking once only, in re-making
me, to be sure, spoke many times and worked wonders and
endured hardships; not only hardships but things unworthy, even.
*What shall I render to the Lord, for all the things that he hath
rendered to me?* In the first work He gave me myself; in the
second, Himself: and when He gave me Himself, He restored me
to myself again. Given, therefore, and restored, I owe myself in
return for myself and I owe it as a twofold debt. What shall I
render to God in return for Himself? For even if I were able to
give myself back a thousand times, whom am I in God's sight?

CHAPTER VI

A BRIEF RECAPITULATION AND SUMMARY OF WHAT HAS BEEN SAID.

Here first see in what measure, yes, how beyond measure
God has deserved to be loved by us; He who (if I may repeat in
a few words what has been said) first loved us Himself—He so
great, yet He loved us greatly and *gratis;* we, so small and [sin-
ners] such as we are. Notice! I remember what I said in the
beginning, that the way to love God is to love Him beyond
measure. And since love which has God as its object, has as its
object the Immeasurable and Infinite (for God is both Immeasurable and Infinite), what, I ask, ought to be the end or method
of our love? What of the fact that our love itself is not given as
a free gift but as the payment of a debt? Immeasurableness, therefore, loves, Eternity loves, *the charity . . . which surpasseth all
knowledge* loves. God loves of Whose *greatness there is no end,*

of Whose wisdom there is no measure, Whose *peace* ... *surpasseth all understanding;* and do we love Him in turn so much and no more? *I will love thee, O Lord, my strength* ... *my firmament, my refuge, and my deliverere;* and finally, [He is] whatever of mine that can be said to be the object of my desires and of my love. My God, my Help, I shall love Thee according to Your gift to me. And [this I shall do] after my own manner —which is less, to be sure, than justice demands but clearly not less than I am able to give; I, who although I cannot [give] as much as I owe, cannot, however, [give] beyond what I am able. I shall be able [to give] more when You deign to give me more: but never according to Your worth. *Thy eyes did see my imperfect being;* but nevertheless, *in thy book all shall be written*—they who do what they are able to do, although they are not able to do what [in strict justice] they ought to do. It is clear enough, as far as I can judge, both how God should be loved and by what desert of his own. By *what* desert of His, I say, for to whom can its *greatness* be clearly manifest? Who can say? Who can know?

CHAPTER VII

NOT WITHOUT FRUIT AND REWARD, IS GOD LOVED, AND EARTHLY THINGS CANNOT SATISFY THE LONGING OF THE HUMAN HEART.

Now let us see with what advantage to ourselves God is to be loved. But how little is our insight into this compared with what it really is! Nevertheless one ought not to remain silent about what is seen, even though it is not seen entirely as it is. Above, when it was asked why and how God should be loved, I said that the question *why* can be understood in two ways, so that it seems equally to ask, either by what desert of His or for what advantage of ours God should be loved. Then something having been said on the subject of God's desert—not in a manner worthy of Him but according to the power given me [i.e. to the best of my ability] —it remains that I should speak on the subject of reward in like manner, according as it is given me. For not without reward is God loved although He should be loved without thought of the reward. True charity cannot be unprofitable nor is it, however, mercenary; certainly it *seeketh not its own.* It is a matter of affection, not a contract: it neither gains nor is

211

gained by a compact. It exerts its influence freely and makes
one free. True love finds satisfaction in itself [i.e. is its own satis-
faction]. It has its reward but it is [the possession] the object it
loves. For whatever you seem to love because of something else,
you clearly love that to which the end of love ultimately attains
and not that [the means] by which it attains it. Paul does not
preach the Gospel in order that he may eat but he eats in order
that he may preach the Gospel: because he loves, not food, but
the Gospel. True love asks no reward but deserves one. It is when
a man has not yet learned to love that a reward is set before him;
it is due one who loves; it is awarded to him who preseveres.
Finally in appealing [to a man] in matters of a lower order, it is
the unwilling that we urge on with promises or rewards, but not
the willing. For who is there who thinks that a man should be
rewarded in order that he may do what he freely desires. No
one, for instance, pays a hungry man to eat, or a thirsty man to
drink, or a mother to give milk to the child of her womb. Or
who thinks that a man ought to be induced by a price or an
entreaty to fence in his own vine, to dig about his own tree, or
to erect the structure of his own home? How much less does the
soul that loves God seek anything besides God as the reward of
her love? If she seeks anything else, it is clearly something else
and not God that she loves.

It is natural to everyone who uses his reason, to desire
always according to his judgment and intention, what is more
capable of satisfying him and to be content with nothing which
is wanting in what he considers preferable. For he who has a
good-looking wife, for instance, gazes with wanton eye and mind
upon one more beautiful, and he who is dressed in costly attire
desires something more costly, and one possessing much wealth
envies the man who is wealthier. You may see those already
abounding in farms and property, still, day by day, adding field
to field and with unlimited avarice extending their boundaries.
You may see those, too, who dwell in the houses of kings and in
spacious palaces, nevertheless joining house to house and with
restless curiosity building up, tearing down, making the square
round [i.e. turning everything upside down]. What do we see if
not men elevated by honors? What do we see such men doing if
not, with insatiable ambition straining more and more with all

their might, toward higher things? And of all these there is no
end because there is nothing found in these things that is absolutely the highest or best. And what wonder is it if that which is
not able [by its very nature] to find rest anywhere short of the
highest or best should not be really satisfied by things lower and
worse? But this is foolish and [a sign] of utter madness always
to be striving after those things which never, I do not say satisfy,
but do not even moderate one's appetite, while whatever of
such things you may chance to have, you none the less long for
what you have not and ever restless pant after whatever may be
wanting. Thus it happens that a vagabond mind running hither
and thither among the varying and false delights of the world is
tired out, not satisfied, by its vain exertion; while, starved, it
counts as little whatever it gormandizes upon compared with
what remains to be devoured and ever it craves the things removed from it, not less anxiously than it joyfully has and holds
those that are at hand. For who is there who can gain the whole
world? And although a man can never be certain when, with
anguish, he may lose even the little which he has gained with
toil, he is certain, nevertheless, that some time or other he will
lose it. Thus a perverted will strains eagerly after a direct short-
cut to the "best" and hurries on to that whereby it may be filled.
Yea, in truth, by such tortuous routes as these does vanity amuse
itself, does iniquity deceive itself. So if you would attain to the
fulfilment of what you wish for, that is if you would lay hold
upon that which, once grasped, leaves no more to be desired—
what is the necessity of putting the rest to the test? You run
along by-paths and you will die long before you attain the
object of your desires along this circuitous route.

Thus, then, *the wicked walk round about,* desiring in a
natural way that whereby they may put an end to desire, and
foolishly rejecting the means by which they might approach
their [true] end [i.e. God]: by *the end* I mean not "consump-
tion" but consummation. Wherefore they make haste not to be
consummated in a blessed end but to be consumed with empty
toil—they who find their delight in the [external] appearance of
things rather than in the Author of them, they who would run
through everything to find out by experience concerning every
individual thing before they trouble themselves about attaining

to the Lord of the universe Himself. And indeed, they might reach their goal if at some time or other they might be made possessors of what they wish for, to wit, that one might possess everything except the Source of all things. For by the very law of his own cupidity, according to which in all other matters he is accustomed to hunger for what he has not rather than for what he has, and to loathe what he has because of what he has not; presently having obtained and having disdained everything in heaven and upon the earth, man would beyond the shadow of a doubt run at last to Him who alone is lacking to him, the God of all. There henceforth, he would find rest; for as no rest restrains him, on one side; so now, no unrest moves him, on the other. He would for certain say: *it is good for me to adhere to my God.* He would say: *For what have I in heaven? and besides thee what do I desire upon earth?* And in similar strain: *thou art the God of my heart, and the God that is my portion forever.* Thus therefore (as has been said) a greedy man might ultimately attain to what is best if he could really attain the object of his desires [a false "best] before he reached *the Best.*

Truly, since this is made absolutely impossible because life is too short, [man's] powers too weak, the number of his fellows too vast; they, assuredly, sweat along an endless road with futile toil who while they wish to get whatever they want refuse to attain to the end of all that is to be desired. And would that they wish to attain to an intellectual grasp of all things and not to an experimental knowledge of them! This, indeed, they could easily do and not in vain. For, the mind, as much quicker than bodily sense as it is more penetrating, has been given for this, that in all things it should anticipate sense, and that there is nothing that sense may dare to touch with the mind, preceding it, has not first proved useful. Hence I believe, the saying: *prove all things; hold fast that which is good;* to the end, that is to say, that the former [the mind] may so provide for the latter [sense] may not attain its desire save only in accordance with the judgment of the former [mind]. Otherwise you shall not *ascend into the mountain of the Lord,* nor *stand in his holy place,* because you have taken your soul in vain, that is, your rational soul, while like the beasts of the field you follow sense, your reason unconcerned and offering no resistance in anything. Those therefore whose steps reason does not anticipate, run, but off the path, and thus despising the counsel of the Apostle, *so run not that they may obtain.* For when will they obtain Him whom they refused to obtain save after all things else? It is a crooked road and an endless maze, to wish to attain all things first [i.e. before attaining God].

But not so the just man. Hearing, of course, the blame of the many tarrying in the maze (for many there are who eagerly pursue the broad way that leads to death), he chooses for himself the king's highway, neither turning to the right hand nor to the left. Finally the prophet bears witness to this: *The way of the just is right, the path of the just is right to walk in.* These are they who by a salutary short way are careful to avoid the round-about way, dangerous and fruitless and choose the shortened and shortening world, not to desire everything they see but rather to *see what thou hast, and give to the poor.* [Rev. Mr. Williams suggests that the *shortened word* may be: *One thing is wanting unto thee.*] Clearly, *Blessed are the poor in spirit: for theirs is the kingdom of heaven.* All indeed run: but there is a distinction made among the runners. *For the Lord knoweth the way of the just: and the way of the wicked shall perish.* Therefore, *Better is a little to the just, than the great riches of the wicked,* since indeed, as the wise man says and the fool finds out from experience, *A covetous man shall not be satisfied with money;* but *they that hunger and thirst after justice . . . shall have their fill.* If indeed justice is the life-giving and natural food of the spirit that makes use of reason, money to be sure, no more lessens the hunger of the mind than air does that of the body. If then you should happen to see a starved man with mouth opened in the wind drinking in the air with puffed-out cheeks as if to satisfy his hunger thereby, would you not believe him mad? Thus it is not less madness if you think that a rational spirit is not more puffed up than satisfied by any bodily things whatever. For, what have bodies to do with spirits? Neither can bodies, surely, find refreshment in things spiritual nor can spirits find refreshment in bodily things. *Bless the Lord, O my soul . . . who satisfieth thy desire with good things.* He satisfies us with good things, He incites us to good [*gratia praeveniente*] He preserves us in good [*gratia efficaci*], He prevents, He sustains, He fulfils. It is He who makes you desire; He is what you desire.

I said above: The cause of loving God is God. I spoke the truth, for He is both the efficient and final Cause. It is He who gives the occasion, it is He who creates the affection, He consummates the desire. It is He who wrought, or rather, was "made" [i.e. is what He is] in order that He might be loved; He it is hoped, will be so fruitfully loved as not to be loved in vain. His love makes our love ready and rewards it. He goes before more graciously [than any other], He is repaid more justly, He is awaited more sweetly. He *is rich unto all who call upon him;* still He has nothing better than Himself [to give]. He gave Himself to merit for us, He retains Himself to be our reward, He offers Himself as the food of saintly souls, He gives Himself as the price of the redemption of those [i.e. of every individual soul] in captivity. You are *good,* O Lord, *to the soul that seeketh thee:* what, then to one who finds? But in this is the wonder that no one can seek Thee save him who first has found thee. Therefore You wish to be found in order that You may be sought, to be sought in order that You may be found. You can, indeed, be sought and found but not prevented. For although we say, *in the morning my prayer shall prevent thee;* there can be no doubt, however, that every prayer is lukewarm which inspiration has not prevented. We must now state whence our love has its beginning, since we have already told where it has its consummation.

CHAPTER VIII

THE FIRST DEGREE OF LOVE, WHEREBY A MAN LOVES HIMSELF FOR HIS OWN SAKE.

Love is a natural affection, one of four. They are well known; there is no need of mentioning them by name. [They are love, fear, joy and sorrow.] It would therefore be just that what is natural should serve its own Author before all others. Hence the first commandment is called the greatest: *Thou shalt love the Lord thy God, etc.* But since nature is rather weak and feeble, it is impelled at the bidding of necessity to serve itself first. And there is carnal love by which before all other things

216

man loves himself for his own sake, as it is written: *first . . . that which is natural; afterwards that which is spiritual.* And it is not imposed by a command but implanted in nature; for *who ever hated his own flesh?* But truly if this love, as is its wont, begins to be too precipitate or too lavish and is not at all satisfied with the river-bed of necessity, overflowing rather widely it will be seen to invade the fields of pleaure. At once its overflow is held in check by the commandment that opposes itself to it: *Thou shalt love thy neighbor as thyself.* It happens, very justly indeed, that the sharer in nature should not be excluded from a part in grace as well, especially in that grace which is inborn in nature itself. If man finds it a burden, I do not say to relieve his brother in matters of necessity but to administer to his pleasures, let him restrain his own unless he wishes to be a transgressor of the law. Let him be as indulgent as he likes to himself, so long as he is mindful to show the same degree of indulgence to his neighbor. The bridle of temperance is put upon you, O man, out of the law of life and of discipline lest you should go after your concupiscences and perish; lest in the goods of nature you become a slave to your soul's enemy, that is, to lust. How much more justly and honorably do you give such things to your fellow-sharer, that is, your neighbor rather than to your enemy! And if indeed, according to the advice of the wise man, you turn away from your own pleasures, and according to the teaching of the Apostle, content with food and raiment, you find it no burden to withhold your love for a little while *from carnal desires which war against the soul;* surely, I think, what you take away from your soul's enemy you will find no burden to bestow upon the sharer of your nature. Your love will then be both temperate and just if what is taken from your own pleasures is not denied to your brother's needs. Thus carnal love is made to belong to our neighbor when it is extended to the common good.

But if, while you are sharing what you have with your neighbor, even the necessities of life should, perchance, be lacking to you, what will you do? What indeed, unless with all confidence you should *ask of* Him *who giveth to all men abundantly, and upbraideth not; who openest thy hand, and fillest with blessing every living creature?* There is no doubt, surely, that He who is not absent in the midst of plenty will gladly be present in the time of need. He says, at length: *seek ye first the kingdom of God and his justice, and all these things shall be added to you.* He promises that He will of His own accord give whatever is necessary to him who restricts himself in superfluities and loves his neighbor. This surely, is to seek first the kingdom of God and to implore help against the tyranny of sin, that you prefer to bear the yoke of modesty and restraint rather than endure that sin should reign in your mortal body. But this, too, is part of the righteousness in question, not to possess the gift of nature independently of him whose common nature you share.

Nevertheless, in order that it may be perfect justice to love one's neighbor, it is imperative that it be referred to God as its cause. Otherwise how can he love his neighbor without alloy who does not love him in God? He surely cannot love in God who does not love God. God must be loved first, in order that one's neighbor, too, may be loved in God. God, therefore, who makes all else that is good, makes Himself to be loved. And He does it as follows. He who fashioned nature, it is He who shields it from harm as well. For it was so fashioned that it should have as a necessary Protector, Him whom it had as Maker, in order that what could not have come into being save through Him, should not be able to subsist at all without Him. And lest the creature might not know this about itself and consequently (which God forbid) in its pride arrogate to itself the benefits it had received from its Creator, the same Maker, in His high and salutary counsel wills that man should be harrassed with troubles; so that when man has failed and God has come to his assistance, while man is being delivered by God, God, as is fitting, may be honored by man. For this is what He says: *call upon me in the day of trouble: I will deliver thee, and thou shalt glorify me.* Thus it comes to pass in this wise that a man, an animal and carnal by nature, who knew how to love no one except himself may begin even for his own sake, to love God too, because in Him beyond a shadow of doubt, as he has often learned from experience, he can do all things—those, to be sure, which it is good to be able to do—and without Him he can do nothing.

CHAPTER IX

THE SECOND AND THIRD DEGREES OF LOVE.

A man, therefore, loves God but still for a while for his own sake, not for Himself. It is, however, a sort of prudence to know what you are able to do by yourself, what with God's help, and to preserve yourself guiltless for Him who keeps you unharmed. But if tribulation assails you again and again, and on this account there occurs an off-repeated turning towards God; and as often, there follows deliverance obtained from God, is it not true that even though the breast were of steel or the heart of stone in one so many times rescued, it must of necessity be softened at the grace of the Rescuer so that man might love God not merely for his own sake but for God Himself. From the occasion that arises from frequent needs it is necessary that man should frequently, in repeated intercourse, go to God who in such intercourse is tasted, and it is by tasting that it is proved how sweet is the Lord. Thus it happens that when once His sweetness has been tasted, it draws us to the pure love of God more than our need impels. Just as in the case of the Samaritans who said, speaking to the woman who had announced that the Lord was come: *We now believe, not for thy saying: for we ourselves have heard him, and know that this is indeed the Savior of the world,* similarly I say, we too, following their example, speaking to our flesh may justly say: We now love God, not for your necessity; for we ourselves have tasted and know how sweet is the Lord. For it is true that a need of the flesh is a sort of speech, and the benefits which it knows from experience it proclaims in transports of joy. And so for one who feels thus, it will not now be hard to fulfil the commandment in regard to loving his neighbor. For he truly loves God and in this way also loves the things which are God's. He loves purely and it is no burden for the pure to be obedient to a command; rather, *purifying* his heart, as it is written, *in* the obedience of *charity*. He loves justly and gladly embraces a just command. This love is deservedly acceptable because it is disinterested [i.e. not offered with a view to obtaining future favors]. It is pure because it is paid neither by word nor tongue, but by deed and truth. It is just, since it is paid back as it is received. For he who loves thus, to be sure, loves in no other wise than he is loved; seeking, in his turn, not the things that are his own but the things that are Jesus Christ's, just as He sought the things that are ours, or rather ourselves and not His own. It is thus He loves who says: *Give praise to the Lord, for He is good.* He who gives praise to the Lord not because He is good to him but because He is good, he truly loves God for God and not for his own sake. It is not thus that he loves of whom it is said: *he will praise thee when thou shalt do well to him.* This is the third degree of love by which God is now loved for His very self.

CHAPTER X

THE FOURTH DEGREE OF LOVE, WHEN A MAN DOES NOT LOVE EVEN HIMSELF EXCEPT FOR THE SAKE OF GOD.

Happy is he who has deserved to attain as high as the fourth degree where a man does not love even himself except for the sake of God. *Thy justice, (O Lord) is as the mountains of God.* This love is a mountain and the high mountain of God. In truth, *a curdled mountain, a fat mountain. Who shall ascend into the mountain of the Lord? Who will give me wings like a dove, and I will fly and be at rest?* This *place is in peace: and this abode in Sion. Woe is me, that my sojourning is prolonged.* Flesh and blood, vessel of clay, when will your earthly dwelling-place compass this? When will the mind experience such an affection as this so that inebriated with divine love, forgetful of self, and become in its own eyes *like a vessel that is destroyed,* the whole of it may continue on to God and being joined to God, become one spirit with Him, and say: *For thee my flesh and my heart hath fainted away: thou art the God of my heart, and the God that is my portion forever?* Blessed and holy, I would say, is he to whom it has been given to experience such a thing in this mortal life at rare intervals or even once, and this suddenly and scarcely for the space of a single moment. In a certain manner to lose yourself as though you were not, and to be uttery unconscious of yourself and to be emptied of yourself and, as it were, brought to nothing, this pertains to heavenly intercourse, not to human affection. And if indeed, anyone among mortals is suddenly, from time to time (as has been said) even for the space of a moment admitted to this, straightway the wicked world grows envious, the evil of the day throws everything into confusion, the body of death becomes a burden, the necessity of the flesh causes unrest, the fainting away of corruption offers no support, and what is more vehement than these, fraternal charity [i.e. obligations to one's neighbor] recalls one [from the state of contemplation]. Alas! he is forced to return to himself, to fall back upon his own, and in his wretchedness to cry out: *Lord, I suffer violence, answer thou for me;* and this: *Unhappy man that I am, who shall deliver me from the body of this death?*

Since however, Scripture says God *hath made all things for himself;* it will certainly come to pass that the creature will at one time or other conform itself to its Author and be of one mind with Him. We ought therefore be transformed into this same disposition of soul, so that as God has willed that everything should be for Himself, so we too may deliberately desire neither ourselves nor any other thing to have been in the past, or to be in the future, unless it be equally for His sake, to wit, for His sole will, not for our own pleasure. A need satisfied [calmed by satisfaction], or good fortune received will not delight us so much as that His will is seen perfectly fulfilled in us and by us; which, too, is what we daily ask in prayer when we say: *Thy will be done on earth as it is in heaven.* O love, holy and chaste! O sweet and pleasing affection! O pure and undefiled intention of the will! the more surely undefiled and purer, as there is mixed with it, now, nothing of its own; so much the sweeter and more pleasing, as its every feeling is wholly divine. To be thus affected is to become one with God. Just as a little drop of water mixed with a lot of wine seems entirely to lose its own identity, while it takes on the taste of wine and its color; just as iron, heated and glowing, looks very much like fire, having divested itself of its original and characteristic appearance; and just as air flooded with the light of the sun is transformed into the same splendor of light so that it appears not so much lighted up as to be light itself; so it will inevitably happen that in saints every human affection will then, in some ineffable manner melt away from self and be entirely transfused into the will of God. Otherwise how will *God . . . be all in all,* if in man there is left anything at all of man himself. The substance, indeed, will remain, but in another "form," another glory, and another power [i.e. a man's human nature and individual identity will remain, transfigured]. When will this be? Who will see this? Who will possess it? *When shall I come and appear before the face of God?* O Lord, my God, *My heart hath said to thee: my face hath sought thee: thy face, O Lord, will I still seek.* Will I, do you think, see Thy holy temple?

As for me, I think that it will not have come to pass with perfect fulfilment that: *Thou shalt love the Lord thy God with thy whole heart, and with thy whole soul, and with thy whole strength,* until the heart itself is no longer compelled to think about the body, and the soul ceases to have to attend to quickening the body and to providing it with sense-preception, and the body's strength freed from vexations is made strong in the power that is of God. For it is impossible wholly to concentrate all these [the heart, mind and virtue] upon God and to hold them fixed upon the Divine Countenance so long as it is necessary for them, absorbed and dissipated, to be subject to this frail and wretched body. And so, in a spiritual and immortal body, in a body perfect, calm and acceptable, and in all things subject to the spirit, let the soul hope to *apprehend* the fourth degree of love, or, rather, to be *apprehended in it;* for, in truth, it is within the power of God to give it to whomsoever He wishes, not for human diligence to procure by its own efforts. Then, I say, she will easily come into the possession of the highest degree, when, without the slightest delay, as she hastens most eagerly into the joy of her Lord, no allurement of the flesh will now retard her progress, no vexation destroy her peace. Do we think, however, that the holy martyrs actually attained to this grace, even in part, while still detained in those victorious bodies of theirs? Great power of love, certainly, had caught up their souls, within, and thus they had strength so to expose their bodies, without, and contemn their tortures. But, assuredly, the sense of most bitter pain could not but disturb their calm, although it had no power to destroy their peace.

CHAPTER XI

THIS PERFECTION OF LOVE IS NOT POSSIBLE OF ATTAINMENT EVEN BY
THE SOULS OF THE BLESSED SEPARATED FROM THEIR BODIES,
BEFORE THE RESURRECTION.

But what, now, of souls separated from their bodies? We
believe that they are completely immersed in that sea of eternal
light and of eternity overflowing with light. But if (as is not
denied) they would fain have received their bodies or, certainly long and hope to receive them; it is clear beyond a shadow of
doubt that they are not yet completely changed from their
former selves, for admittedly there is still something which they
regard as their own, to which at least in small measure their
attention returns. Therefore, until *death is swallowed up in
victory,* and until the very moment when perpetual light invades
the boundaries of night on every side and holds them, until the
heavenly glory shines forth even in bodies, until that moment
souls cannot altogether set themselves aside as of no account
and completely transformed pass over into God, since even
then they are surely bound to their bodies, if not by life or
sense, certainly by a natural affection [i.e. disembodied souls
depend upon their bodies neither for life nor perception, yet
they have a natural longing which will not be satisfied until
they are again united with their bodies], so that without them
they have neither the desire nor the power to attain their
[ultimate] consummation. And so, before the restoration of
their bodies there will not be that complete absorption of
souls in God [i.e. that fainting away, into God], which is their
perfect and highest state; nor would the spirit now seek again
for the fellowship of the flesh if it could attain to its perfect
consummation without it. In truth, not without progress for
the soul is the body laid down or taken up again. *Precious,*
indeed, *in the sight of the Lord is the death of his saints.* But
if death is precious, what is life, and *that* life? Nor is it any
wonder if the body, now glorified, seems to confer something
upon the spirit, since even when weak and mortal it is manifest
that it was of no little help to it. O how truly did he speak who
said: *to them that love God, all things work together unto
good.* To the soul that loves God the body avails in its weak-

ness, it avails in its death, it avails in its restoration: in the first instance, forsooth, for the fruit of penitence; in the second, for rest; in the last, for consummation. Rightly she does not wish to be made perfect without that which she feels helps her to what is good for her in every state.

Clearly a good and faithful companion to a good spirit is the flesh which if it is a burden, is a source of delight; or, certainly is a source of delight and hardly a burden at all. The first state is full of toil but abounding in fruit; the second is one of complete repose but in no wise wearisome; the third abounds in glory, as well. Listen to the Bridegroom in the Canticle inviting to this three-fold progress: *Eat, he says, O friends, and drink, and be inebriated, my dearly beloved.* Those still toiling in the body He calls to food; those who have laid down the body and are enjoying complete repose. He invites to drink; those who again take their bodies up He urges even to inebriation, and these he calls His most beloved ones because they most abound in charity. For, in the case of all others whom He calls not *most beloved,* but *friends,* there is a difference. As a result, those, to be sure, who groan, still weighed down in the flesh, are held dear in return for the love that they have. But those who are already freed from the fetters of the flesh are dearer according as they are made more ready and become less incumbered for loving. Rightly, then, beyond both others are they called *most beloved* and are so, who having now received a second garment in bodies which they have resumed with glory, are borne along in the love of God more freely and more swiftly according as there is nothing of their own left in them to cause them the slightest anxiety or to retard their progress. This distinction neither of the other states can claim since in the first the body is carried along with labor; and in the second it is awaited not without a certain peculiar quality of desire for something that is absent.

First, then, the faithful soul eats her bread but alas! in the sweat of her brow. Still, in fact, remaining in the flesh she still walks by faith, which, to be sure, must be reduced to action through love because if it be not expressed in works it is dead. This very work itself is food, as the Lord says: *My meat is to do the will of my Father.* Henceforth, having divested herself of the flesh she no longer eats the bread of sorrow but it is allowed her to drink more abundantly, as if after meat, of the wine of love not unmixed however, but as is read in the Canticle as spoken by the Bridegroom: *I have drunk my wine with my milk.* For the soul even then, mixes with the wine of divine love the sweetness of natural affection with which she longs to resume her body and that, glorified. She glows [with love], therefore, having already drunk of the wine of holy charity but clearly not as yet to the point of inebriation; for, in the meanwhile, the admixture of this milk tempers that ardor. Finally, inebriation is wont to upset the mind and to render it altogether forgetful of itself. But she has not entirely forgotten self who still dwells upon her own body that is to be raised from the dead. But when this has been attained which alone was lacking, what is there now that hinders her from leaving self, in a way, wholly to go to God to become completely unlike herself [as she was before assuming her glorified body], to the degree in which it is granted her to be made most like unto God? Then, at last, admitted to the cup of wisdom concerning which it is read: *my chalice which inebriateth me, how goodly it is!*—what wonder is it if now she becomes inebriated with the plenty of the house of God, when, vexed with no anxiety for what is her own and free from care she drinks that wine pure and new, with Christ in the kingdom of His Father.

Wisdom, in truth, gives a triple banquet and from a single love [her own] she supplies the fare,—she herself feeding those who labor, she herself giving drink to those who rest, she herself inebriating those who reign as kings. But just as in a banquet for the body food is served before drink, since nature prescribes such an order, so too here. First, indeed, before death *we eat the labors of* our *hands,* with labor masticating what is to be swallowed. But after death, in the spiritual life, we drink, clarifying what is perceived by a very pleasing sort of facility. Finally, our bodies living once again in immortal life, we become inebriated, abounding in wondrous plenty. This is the meaning of what the Spouse says in the Canticle: *eat, O friends, and drink, and be inebriated, my dearly beloved.* Eat before death, drink after death, become inebriated after the resurrection. Justly now are they *most beloved* who are inebriated with love, and justly are they inebriated who have deserved to be brought into the wedding-feast of the Lamb, eating and drinking at His table in His kingdom, when He now *presents to himself a glorious church, not having spot or wrinkle, or any such thing.* Then straightway He inebriates His most beloved, then does He *make them drink of the torrent of* His *pleasures:* since, indeed, in that close and pure embrace of Bridegroom and bride, *the stream of the river maketh the city of God joyful.* This I think is nothing else than the Son of God who *passing will minister unto them as* He Himself promised, so that from this source *the just feast and rejoice before God: and be delighted with gladness.* Hence that satiety without weariness; hence that insatiable desire of knowledge, without restlessness; hence that longing never satisfied [*inexplebile*] yet never knowing want; hence, finally, that inebriation without drunkenness, filled with truth, not with strong drink, not drenched with wine, but on fire with God. Thus that fourth degree of love is now possessed forever when God alone is loved in the highest possible degree; because, now, we do not even love ourselves save for His sake, so that He Himself is the reward of those who love Him, the reward eternal of those who love for all eternity.

CHAPTER XII

CHARITY, AS TREATED IN A LETTER TO THE CARTHUSIANS.

I remember well that, a while ago I wrote a letter to the holy Carthusian brethren and in it, among other matters, I discussed these very grades of love. But, perchance, I there said other things though not foreign to the matter, on the subject of charity, and for this reason certain of those remarks I do not consider it useless to add to this discourse as well, especially since it is easier to transcribe what has already been written than to write something new. That, I say, is true and genuine charity and must be admitted as proceeding entirely from a pure heart, a good conscience and a faith unfeigned, by which we love the good of our neighbor as well as our own. For he who loves only what is his, or loves it more, stands convicted of loving good unchastely, since he loves for his own and not for His sake. And such a one cannot obey the prophet who says: *Give praise to the Lord for he is good.* He gives praise, to be sure, because, perhaps, He is good to him but not because He is good in himself. Therefore let him understand that it is against him that that reproach was directed by the same prophet: *he will praise thee when thou shalt do well to him.* There is a man who gives praise to the Lord because He is powerful, and there is a man who gives praise to Him because He is good to him, and, again, there is a man who gives praise to Him because He is simply good. The first is a servant and fears for himself; the second, a hireling, desires things for his own sake; the third, a son, gives honor to the Father. And so he who is afraid and he who desires things for his own sake, both act for themselves. Only the charity which is found in a son, *seeketh not her own.* For this reason I think that it was of charity that it was said: *The law of the Lord is unspotted, converting souls;* for it is she [Charity] alone which is strong enough to *convert* a soul from love of self and of the world, and direct it to God. For, neither fear nor love of one's self converts the soul. At times they change an expression of countenance or an external act, but an affection, never. Even a servant, to be sure, sometimes does the work of God but because he does not do it freely he is known still to remain in his hardness. Even the hireling does the work of God but because he does not do it without recompense he is convicted of being carried along by his own cupidity. Truly, where there is something of one's own there is a distinction between one person and another; where there is a distinction between one person and another there is a corner [reserved for one's self] ; and where, to be sure, there is a corner there without doubt there is dirt and mouldiness. And so, may that very fear by which he is restrained be his law for the servant; may his cupidity by which he, too, is circumscribed be the hireling's law, since by it he *is tempted . . . being drawn away and allured.* But neither one of these two can be unspotted, or can convert souls. But charity converts souls whom she makes free agents.

Again, I would call her unspotted because she has accustomed herself to retain for herself nothing of her own. Certainly, in the case of one who has nothing of his own, all that he has is assuredly God's, but what is God's cannot be unclean. Therefore the unspotted law of the Lord is charity, which seeks not what is useful for itself but what is of use to many. For it is called the law of the Lord either because He Himself lives by it or because no one possesses it except as a gift from Him. Nor let it seem absurd that I have said that even God lives by law, since I said by no other law save charity. What in that supreme and blessed Trinity preserves that supreme and unspeakable unity, save charity? It is law, then, and charity the law of the Lord which in a certain way holds the Trinity together in unity and binds it *in the bond of peace*. Let no one think, however, that I am here taking charity as a quality or as a sort of accident (otherwise I should be saying, which Heaven forbid, that there is in God something which is not God), but as that divine substance which, surely, is neither new or unusual because John says: *God is charity*. Therefore charity is rightly called both God and the gift of God. And so charity gives charity, the substantial gives what is an accident. Where it means the Giver it is the name of substance, where it means the gift it is the name of a quality. This is the eternal law, the Creator and Ruler of the universe. Indeed, *all things* have been made by *her in measure, and number and weight,* and nothing is left without a law, since even the very law of all [charity] is not without a law, not however any other than itself, by which, although it did not create itself nevertheless it is its own rule.

CHAPTER XIII

THE LAW OF SELF-WILL AND CUPIDITY: THE LAW OF SERVANTS AND HIRELINGS.

But the servant and the hireling have a law, not from the Lord, but which they themselves have made for themselves:— the former by not loving God; the latter by loving something else, more. They have, I say, a law; not the Lord's but their own; nevertheless it is subject to the law which is the Lord's. And indeed each one of them could make a law for himself, but he could not withdraw it from [subjection to] the unchangeable order of the law eternal. Then, I should say, each one made a law unto himself when he preferred his own will to the universal and eternal law, perversely, to be sure, wishing to imitate the Creator, so that just as He is a law unto Himself and this of His own right, so, Man also would rule himself and make his own will his own law. Heavy and insupportable yoke upon all the children of Adam alas! bending down our necks and bowing [our heads], so that our *life hath drawn nigh to hell. Unhappy man that I am, who shall deliver me from the body of this death?* by which, surely, I am pressed down and almost crushed so that *unless the Lord had been my helper, my soul had almost dwelt in hell.* Weighed down under this burden was he groaning who said: *Why hast thou set me opposite to thee, and I am become burdensome to myself?* Where he said, *I am become burdensome to myself,* he shows that he himself was a law unto himself and that no other had done this [i.e. made this law] save himself for himself. But what, speaking to God, he first said,—thou hast *set me opposite to thee,—* indicated, nevertheless, that he had not escaped the law of God. This, to be sure, pertained to the eternal and just law of God, that he who would refuse to be ruled sweetly by God should be ruled by himself as a criminal, and he who of his own accord cast off the sweet yoke and light burden of charity should unwillingly carry the insupportable burden of his own will. Thus in a wonderful and just way the eternal law both set its fugitive opposite to Himself and kept him subject, for while he did not elude the law of justice which judges according to every man's deserts, he did not, however, remain with God in His light, in His rest, in His glory, but was subject to His *power* and excluded from His felicity. O Lord my God, *why dost thou not remove my sin, and why dost thou not take away my iniquity?* so that having cast away the heavy load of my own will I may breathe under the light burden of charity, that now I may not be encompassed with servile fear nor seduced by mercenary cupidity, but that I may be led by Thy spirit, the spirit of liberty by which Thy sons are led and may it give testimony to my spirit that I am one of Thy sons since the same law is mine as is Thine, and as Thou art so may I also be in this world. These, indeed, are they who do what the Apostle says: *Owe no man anything, but love one another;* without any doubt as God is, so too are they in this world. They are neither servants nor hirelings, but sons.

CHAPTER XIV

THE LAW GOVERNING THE CHARITY OF SONS.

Thus neither are sons without law unless perchance someone should think otherwise because of this which has been written: *the law is not made for the just.* But it ought to be known that the law promulgated in fear by a spirit of servitude is one thing; it is quite another, given in sweetness by a spirit of liberty. Sons are neither constrained to be under the former, nor do they suffer themselves to be without the latter. Do you wish to hear why the law is not made for the just? *You have not received,* he says, *the spirit of bondage again in fear.* Do you wish to hear how, nevertheless, they are not without the law of charity? *But you have received,* he adds, *the spirit of adoption of sons.* Then, hear the just man confessing how he is not under the law nor yet without law. *I became,* he says, . . . *to them that are under the law, as if I were under the law (whereas myself was not under the law), . . . To them that were without the law, as if I were without the law, (whereas I was not without the law of God, but was in the law of Christ).* Hence it is not rightly said that the just have no law, or that the just are without the law, but *the law is not made for the just;* that is, it is not imposed upon them as upon unwilling subjects but it is given them as to willing subjects, with a freedom equal to the sweetness with which it is breathed into them. Hence, also, the Lord says beautifully: *Take up my yoke upon you;* as if he would say: I do not place it upon the unwilling, but you, if you are willing, take it up; otherwise you will find not rest but labor for your souls.

The law of charity, therefore, is good and sweet. It is not only lightly and sweetly borne but renders the laws even of servants and hirelings bearable and light. It does not destroy these laws, to be sure, but it brings about their fulfilment in accordance with Our Lord's words when He said: *I am not come to destroy (the law) but to fulfill it.* It modifies the one, it puts order into the other, and it lightens both of them. Never will charity be without fear, but chaste fear; never will it be without its desire of personal gratification, but kept within bounds. Charity, therefore, perfects the law of the servant when it imparts devotion, and that of the hireling when it directs aright his desire of reward. Surely devotion mingled with fear does not annihilate those last but purifies them. Dread of punishment, only, is taken away, without which fear can not exist so long as it is servile; and this fear is pure and filial, *enduring for ever and ever.* For, the text which reads, *perfect charity casteth out fear,* is to be understood of a dread of punishment which (as we have said) is never wanting to servile fear. This (we said) making use of that sort of speech in which, often, the cause is put for the effect. As for a desire for personal gratification, it is then kept within bounds by the charity which is joined to it, when evil is completely rejected, better things are preferred to the good, nor are good things desired save on account of those which are better. When the complete fulfilment of this will have been attained through God's grace, the body and every good that pertains to the body will be loved only for the sake of the soul; the soul for the sake of God; but God for His own sake.

CHAPTER XV

THE FOUR DEGREES OF LOVE, AND THE HAPPY STATE OF THE HEAVENLY
  COUNTRY.

Nevertheless, because we are carnal and are born of the concupiscence of the flesh, it follows as a necessary consequence that our desire for personal gratification, or our love should have its source in the flesh. But if it is directed according to the right order of things, advancing by its several degrees under the guidance of grace, it will at last be consummated by the spirit: because *that was not first which is spiritual, but that which is natural; afterwards that which is spiritual.* First, therefore, man loves himself for his own sake; for, he is flesh and he can have no taste for anything except in relation to himself. And when he sees that he cannot subsist of himself he begins to seek God through faith as something, as it were, necessary for him, and to love Him. Thus he loves God according to the second degree, but for his own sake, not for Himself. But when, in truth, on account of his own necessity he has begun to worship and come to Him again and again by meditating, by reading, by prayer and by being obedient, little by little God becomes known to him through experience, in a sort of familiarity, and consequently He grows sweet; and thus by tasting how sweet is the Lord he passes to the third degree so that he loves God now, not for his own sake but for Himself. Yes, in this degree he stands still for a very long time and I know not if the fourth degree is attained in its perfection by any man in this life so that forsooth, a man loves himself only for the sake of God. If there are any who have experience of this let them declare it; to me, I confess, it seems impossible. But it will be so, beyond a doubt, when the good and faithful servant has been brought into the joy of his Lord and inebriated with the plenty of God's house. For, forgetful of himself in a wonderful way, as it were, and as if entirely freed of self he will continue on, wholly, into God, and thereafter being joined to Him he will be one spirit with Him. I am of the opinion that this is what the prophet meant when he said: *I will enter into the powers of the Lord: O Lord I will be mindful of they justice alone.* He felt, certainly, that when he entered into the spiritual powers of the Lord he would have laid aside self in all that concerns the infirmities of the flesh, so that he would have to give no thought to the flesh, but his whole being would in the spirit, be mindful of the justice of the Lord alone.

Then, for certain, the several individual members of Christ will be able to say, everyone concerning himself, what Paul said of the Head: *And if we have known Christ according to the flesh; but now we know him no longer.* No one, there, will know himself according to the flesh because flesh and blood shall not possess the kingdom of God. Not that the substance of flesh will not be there, but that every carnal necessity will be wanting and the love of the flesh will be absorbed in the love of the spirit, and human affections, weak as they now are, shall be changed into those which are divine. Then the net of charity which now, drawn through this great and vast sea does not cease to gather together fish of every kind, when brought at last to the shore, casting forth the bad, will retain only the good. Indeed in this life the net of charity includes fish of every kind within its vast folds, where, fashioning itself to suit all according to the time and taking over the good and evil fortunes of all and, in a sense, making them its own, it is wont not only to *rejoice with them that rejoice,* but also to *weep with them that weep.* But when it shall have reached the shore [eternity] casting away as bad fishes everything that it suffered in sadness, it will retain those only which can give it pleasure and be to it a source of gladness. For can it be that Paul, for instance, will then be weak with the weak or be on fire for those who are scandalized, where scandals and weakness will be so far away? Or will he, surely, mourn for those who have done penance, where it is certain there will be no one either sinning or doing penance? Far be it from us to think that he will lament and weep over those who are to be condemned to everlasting fire together with the devil and his angels, in that *city [of God] which the stream of the river maketh . . . joyful,* and whose gates *the Lord loveth . . . above all the tabernacles of Jacob;* because in the tabernacles although the joy of victory is sometimes felt, there is, nevertheless, the anxiety of combat and often danger to life itself, but in that native land no suffering or sadness will be allowed to enter in, even as it is sung thereof: *The dwelling in thee is as it were of all rejoicing;* and again: *everlasting joy shall be unto them.* Finally, how shall one be mindful of mercy where the justice of God alone will be remembered. Just so, where now there will be no place for misery or occasion for pity, surely there can be no feeling of compassion.

Richard of St. Victor
d. 1173

"I am wounded by love. Love urges me to speak of love." With these dramatic words, the quiet monk, Richard of St. Victor, begins his brief reflection on love, Of the Four Degrees of Passionate Love.

Very little is known of Richard's life. He was a Scot who went to Paris, probably around 1140. Attracted to the Abbey of St. Victor because of its reputation for serious study and piety, he decided to join the community. From 1162 to 1173, Richard served as prior of the abbey.

Richard's writings reveal a talented, studious and dedicated man. He was familiar with and influenced by the teachings of Augustine, Gregory the Great, Jerome, Bede and Hugh of St. Victor. Though he borrowed generously from the sources, he reworked their insights into a new theological statement that was truly his. In the face of the two major tendencies of the twelfth century, viz., the overemphasis on reason and dialectic as exemplified in Abelard, and the concurrent overemphasis on faith as stressed by Bernard, Richard strove to find a middle way. He took no sides in his search for truth. He clearly gives a significant role to reason, for he considers it to be the highest natural gift possessed by man. Yet he was aware that it must be transcended by a life of faith.

What seems to color Richard's writings more than anything else is his fascination with the human psyche. He observed the human with wonder, admiration, gratitude and joy. He was keenly aware of the almost limitless capacity of the human for growth, life, love. Man, for Richard, is a single being. While admitting that the human, by its own power, is not capable of the direct vision of God, he was convinced that this same human could be transformed, in ecstasy, into a being directly beholding God. At this point, knowledge is love.

Of the Four Degrees of Passionate Love *attempts to analyze the nature of love. Richard explores various aspects of human love in an effort to understand the dynamic of love in relation to God. Passionate love wounds, binds, makes one languish, faint. Love is insuperable, inseparable, singular, insatiable. Driven by love, the soul thirsts for God (meditation), thirsts to go to God (contemplation), thirsts to be in God (jubilation), thirsts in God's way (compassion). By love, the soul ascends to itself, transcends itself, is conformed to the glory of Christ, is conformed to the humility of Christ.*

Richard's insights challenge the reader to take a chance on love. His language is exciting, energetic, hurried. At times he pushes his terminology to the limits and almost speaks in contradictions, for he sees the soul caught up in love as simultaneously active and passive. He wants the human to burst out of time and space but he realizes that to do so would destroy the human. It is interesting to note where love, at its fullest, richest, most glorious moment of madness is perfected—not in a cloud, not in beatific vision, but in the humility of Christ by which one places oneself at the service of the neighbor.

Within the tradition of Christian spiritual writers, Richard deserves a place of honor. He is one of the twelfth century authors who pulled together the major currents of mystical theology as developed in Augustine, Gregory the Great and Pseudo-Denis. He allowed his deep respect for the power of human reason to color his understanding of these traditions. Richard thus helped prepare the way for the great discoveries in mystical theology of the thirteenth, fourteenth and fifteenth centuries.

OF THE FOUR DEGREES
OF PASSIONATE LOVE

I am wounded by love. Love urges me to speak of love. Gladly do I give myself up to the service of love and it is sweet and altogether lovely to speak about love. This is a joyful subject and very fruitful; one that will not weary the writer or fatigue the reader. For that which savours of charity pleases the heart's taste beyond measure. 'If a man would give all the substance of his house for love, it would utterly be condemned.' Great is the power of love, wonderful the virtue of charity. It has many degrees and the difference between them is great. And who shall worthily distinguish between them, or be able to number them? For there is affection for mankind, for the group, for kindred and family, and the brotherhood and so forth and many more kinds in this world. But above all these degrees there is that ardent and burning love which penetrates the heart, inflames the affection and transfixes the soul itself to the very core, so that she may truly say: 'I am wounded by love.' Let us consider what this surpassing quality of Christ's love is, which transcends and extinguishes affection for parents, or love of children and wife and beyond all that converts a man to the hating of his own soul. O vehemence of love! O thou violence of charity! O thou excellent and surpassing charity of Christ! Brethren, this is what we purpose, this is what we wish to speak about, namely the passion of charity, the supremacy of perfect zeal. You know already that it is one thing to speak of this charity another of its fulfilment. One to speak about it, another to make known its passion. I consider the works of passionate love and I find out what the power of perfect zeal is. Behold! I see some men wounded, others bound, languishing, fainting, and all for love. Charity wounds, charity binds, makes a man sick, causes him to faint. Which of these is not powerful, not passionate? These are the four steps of passionate love which we are soon to consider. You must attend earnestly, brethren, to that charity which you so greatly desire to have, learn from her, long for her whom you seek so passionately. Would you hear about passionate charity? 'Thou hast wounded my heart with one of thy eyes, with one hair of thy neck.' Would you hear of binding love? 'I will draw them with the cords of Adam, with the bands of love.' And of languishing love? 'Daughters of Jerusalem, if you find my beloved, tell him that I am sick with love.' Would ye hear of the swoon of love and that which causes it? 'My soul fainted for thy salvation but I have greatly hoped in thy word!' For love causes swooning and sickness: love has its chains and love wounds.

But what are these cords of Adam our first parent but the gifts of God? What, I say, are these chains of charity but the blessings of God? Blessings of nature, of grace and of glory. By these bonds He puts Adam under obligation for kindness, and makes him debtor to goodwill. He founded nature, conferred grace and promised glory. Here is the triple cord: the gifts of creation, the blessings of redemption, the rewards of glory. And we know that a threefold cord is hard to break—yet it was broken! From everlasting man has broken the yoke and burst the chains. Nevertheless the Lord with a strong hand multiplied his bonds of love upon us to fasten us more tightly to himself, to entangle us further. He granted us his benefits, he bore our ills for us, that he might make us debtors for both, for the good things he gave us, for the bad things he bore for us. By the cords of this kind of charity he took captivity captive, and generously gave gifts unto men and willingly suffered evil things for men. O how far from strong is he who cannot be held back by such bonds of charity. O how far from free is he whom the laws of this captivity cannot restrain!

But let us return to that degree of love which we first mentioned and called 'wounded love'. Do you not feel as if sometimes you were shot through the heart when the fiery dart of this love penetrates the inmost mind of man, pierces his affections so that he can in no way contain or hide the burning of his desire. He burns with desire, his affections are stirred, he is in fever and gasps, sighing deeply and drawing long breaths.

These are certain signs of a wounded soul, groans and sighs, a pale and averted face. But this degree sometimes affords some respite and allows for the cares and anxieties of necessary business. After the manner of feverish men who are troubled by this illness, sometimes they burn more fiercely, then by attending to their affairs they feel some relief. But after a short interval they burn again, greater heat supervenes and the broken spirit is once more set on fire and burns more fiercely. Thus the fever of love often waning but always returning more acutely, gradually weakens the spirit, wears down and exhausts the strength until it completely conquers the soul and lays it low. It occupies the soul wholly with thoughts about itself, engrosses and controls it wholly so that it cannot tear itself away or consider anything else and so it passes from the first to the second degree.

For we said the first degree was wounding love and the second binding love. For the soul is surely and undoubtedly bound when it cannot forget this one thing or think about anything else. Whatever it does or says it is always turning this over in its mind and keeping it continually in memory. It dreams of love when sleeping and waking it thinks of it all the time. It is easy, I think, to understand how this degree which does not allow man's mind to be quiet even for an hour, surpasses the former. For often wounding is less than binding. Everyone knows how often it happens that a soldier hit and wounded in battle, flees from the hand of the pursuer and escapes, though wounded. But afterwards, in the thick of the fighting, the wounded soldier falls and having fallen is taken prisoner, as a prisoner he is brought to trial, imprisoned, chained and bound and so held captive in everyway. Which of these is the worse and more troublesome fate, I ask? Is it not more tolerable to escape though wounded rather than to be held captive?

But this degree unlike the first is not subject to intermittent relief, but burns up the soul with continual heat as in a state of acute fever. Continually the soul is kindled with the fire of its desires and prevented from resting, day or night. And so like one who lies in his bed, or is bound by a chain and cannot move away from the place where he has been fastened, so he who is absorbed by this second degree of passionate love, whatever he does, wherever he turns, he cannot tear himself away from this one deep preoccupation with the object of his anxiety. Therefore we are able and we ought to repel the urge towards evil desires in the first degree, not so much by resistance as by turning away, not reluctantly, but by flight. If we are careful always to busy ourselves with useful and sober occupations and meditations, with foresight, this is flight and we fulfil what is written: 'Flee from fornication.' In the first degree the passion may be avoided, it cannot be overcome; in the second it cannot in any way be overcome either by opposition or by flight. Hearken to the captive who moans and despairs of flight: 'Flight hath failed me and there is no one that hath regard unto my soul.' But we often see those who cannot take flight but are able to ransom themselves. When we are unable to resist temptation either by virtue or to turn it away by foresight, we should ransom ourselves by works of mercy and obedience and tear ourselves free from this yoke of bondage. These are the true and personal riches, of which it is written: 'The ransom of a man's life are his riches.' But when love has grown beyond this second degree of strength, to what further point can it reach? How can this passion become more passionate if it cannot be avoided nor turned back? If it cannot be overcome by any other feeling, it is supreme and if it abides inseparably, it is everlasting. And what passion can be more violent if it is at its height and last forever? But it is one thing to be supreme and another to be the only one: just as it is one thing to be the first and another to admit no fellowship. We may be first and have many companions with us and yet take the highest place among them. Behold then what great opportunities remain for love to grow so that when it is highest it may also be unique.

Love rises up to the third degree of passion when it excludes every other love, when it loves nothing but the one, for the sake of the one. In this third degree of passionate love nothing can give any satisfaction but the one thing and nothing is known but the one. The soul loves one and is devoted to one, it thirsts for and desires the one, it clings to one, sighs for him, is kindled by him, rests in him. In him alone it is re-created and satisfied. There is no sweetness nor taste except for him only. Whatever offers itself beyond this, whatever may by chance present itself, is quickly rejected and immediately despised, if it does not foster this love nor serve this desire. Who can worthily describe the tyranny of this state? How it extinguishes every desire and excludes every activity, how violently it represses every effort which does not appear to further its desires! Whatever a man does or suffers seems altogether useless and intolerable, unless it concurs with or leads to the one end of his desire. When he can enjoy what he loves he thinks he has everything. Without it he is disgusted by everything and all things are foul. If he cannot enjoy it he grows weak in body and faint at heart. He does not accept advice nor acknowledge reason, he will not take to himself any form of consolation.

In the second degree a man can attend to outward business in action but not in thought, for he cannot in any way forget what he loves. In this degree the mind is wasting away and sick with excessive love and as it cannot meditate on anything else, so it cannot work on outward things. The first degree involved the thoughts, the second destroys action. The first restricts thinking, the latter weakens activity. In the former our hands and feet are still free, and like a feverish patient, we can stretch and throw them about hither and thither, for we can and must move them according to the dictates of discretion, and exercise them in good deeds. But in this degree, excess of love makes hands and feet nerveless as in illness, so that henceforth the mind can scarcely act with any freedom. In this state the mind remains almost motionless and never exerts itself to think or do anything unless it is drawn by its desire or impelled by its affection. In the first degree, as we have said, when stirred by evil desires it can escape by the exercise of caution, in the second degree, when flight is altogether impossible, it may still ransom itself by good works. But in this degree what help can there be, what kind of remedy is possible for those who cannot reflect on what is necessary, nor do what might be useful? Listen to him who is sick in body and soul; to him who is weak in body and troubled at heart: 'My heart is troubled, my strength has left me.' I can find no other remedy in this state of misery but to look to the divine clemency and implore His mercy. If you are sick, if your hands and feet are not free, you still have a tongue and can move your lips. If there is no way of escape left which you can actively pursue, call upon Him who is able to do

241

all things. You will see I think, how that power of love increases when by exercise it grows to the vehemence of this third degree; indeed it is strange that anything remains by which it can still grow. In the first degree love pierces the affections, in the second it binds the thoughts, in the third it destroys action. The whole of man is in these and what can he have beyond this? If therefore every thing which belongs to a man is made captive what more can be done to him? If this power of love possess everything, if the greatness of love absorbs everything how can it increase still more? If it has obtained everything there is nothing left to be claimed. But what shall we say when everything is obtained and that is still not enough to satisfy love? What, I ask, what shall we say if everything is in its power and yet that is not enough to satisfy its desire? Truly the things that are impossible to man are incomparably more than those which are possible. Both things therefore may be desired, what man can do and what he cannot. See therefore how infinitely he is able to extend his desire in himself, even after he has reached the third degree.

Therefore the fourth degree of passionate love is that in which nothing at all can satisfy the desire of the passionate soul. This degree in that it has once passed beyond the bounds of human power, is, unlike others, unlimited in its expansion, for it always finds something which it can still desire. Whatever it may do or whatever may be done to it, does not satisfy the desire of the ardent soul. It thirsts and drinks but the draught does not quench the thirst and the more it drinks the more it thirsts. When the thirst and hunger of a greedy or an insatiable soul is indulged wilfully and at will, it is not slaked but stimulated. In this state the eye is not satisfied by seeing nor the ear filled by hearing, whether the soul speaks to one not seen or looks upon one not present. But who is able to explain this highest degree of passion worthily and who can even adequately conceive its surpassing greatness. What is there, I ask, that could penetrate a man's heart more deeply, crucify it more cruelly, agitate it more wildly? What could be more troublesome, more bitter to a man than not to be able to lessen his thirst by restraint nor extinguish it by drunkenness? A wondrous, a miserable gluttony which cannot be reduced by any means nor stilled by any satisfaction. An incurable and wholly desperate sickness, in which a remedy is for ever being sought and never found, in which indeed, whatever is considered remedial to health turns into an increase of the raging sickness. This is the degree which brings about complete decline and despair of recovery. And the patient is like a man desperately ill who lies with his limbs as it were half dead and there is nothing more that he can do, or hope for from the help of another. All the care of doctors has been withdrawn from him, he is left altogether to himself, his breath comes in gasps and he draws nearer to death at every moment. Now he draws his last breath and neither heeds nor is aware of what is going on around him or is being done to him. So it is indeed with him who suffocates with the heat of his burning desire: whatever happens to him he can find no remedy nor receive any consolation. When therefore any kind of comfort is offered to him it does not touch his soul, which like one already dead feels nothing of what is going on around. When it is a case of evil desires, and the mind is violently drawn into such a state, nothing can be done except that others should pray for him, so that the Lord, seeing their faith, may perhaps restore his life and give him back to his mother. For the Lord is able to raise up sons to Abraham from stones and whenever He wills He brings men down into hell and raises them up again. In this state, love often turns into a kind of madness unless its impetus is restrained by great prudence and an equally great steadiness. There are often outbursts of temper between lovers in this state, they work up quarrels and when there are no causes for enmity they seek false and often quite unlikely ones. In this state, love often turns into hatred since nothing can satisfy the lovers' mutual desire. Hence arises what we have often seen in some people, namely that the more ardently they seem to love one another at first, the more they persecute each other afterwards with passionate hatred. Indeed, and this is even more astounding, at one and the same time they hate and yet do not cease to burn with desire for each other, and love in such a way that they do not desist from persecuting each other by hatred. Loving thus they hate, and hating they love and strange to tell, hatred grows miserably by desire and desire by hatred. They endure fire and hail at the same time, since neither the heat of desire can dissolve the ice of hatred, nor can the hail of dislike extinguish the fire of passionate desire. Beyond measure, indeed contrary to nature, this fire burns more fiercely in water, for the conflagration of love flares up more strongly by the mutual conflict of opposites than it could by mutual peace.

So now we have four degrees of violence in the passion of love, and we have discussed them above. The first degree of violence is when the mind cannot resist its desires; the second when it cannot forget them; and third is when nothing else pleases it; the fourth and last when even this love cannot satisfy it. In the first love is insuperable, in the second inseparable, in the third singular, in the fourth insatiable. Love is insuperable when it will not yield to any other feeling; inseparable when it never leaves the memory; singular when it will have no companion; insatiable when it cannot be satisfied. And though different things may be noticed about each degree, we should more especially note the excellence of love in the first degree, its passion in the second, its violence in the third, its surpassing greatness in the fourth. For how excellent is that love that exceeds all other affection. How great is the vehemence of love that will not allow the mind to be still. How violent that love which expels every other affection violently. How surpassing the zeal that is not satisfied by anything. . . . These four degrees of love are not grouped in divine love as they are in human love, and the degrees of spiritual desires are altogether different from those of the desires of the flesh. In spiritual desires the greater the degree of love, the better; in fleshly desires the greater, the worse. In love of God the highest is supreme, in human affections that which is highest in degree, is worst of all. Indeed in human affections the first degree may be good but the second is certainly bad, the third worse, the fourth worst of all. We know that among human affections conjugal love must take the first place and therefore in wedded life, that degree of love which generally dominates all other affections seems to be good. For the mutual affection of intimate love draws closer the bonds of peace between those who are pledged to each other, and makes that indissoluble, life-long association, pleasant and happy. Therefore, the first degree in human affections is good but the second is certainly bad. For when it fastens the mind indissolubly by not allowing it to move over to other concerns it

often takes away a man's attention and his foresight from providing and disposing things suitably. But the third degree of love
which excludes every other affection is not only bad, but begins
to be bitter, when it is impossible to enjoy one's desire according
to one's desire and one cannot be consoled by any other thing.
And the fourth degree is worst of all, as we have said. What
can be worse than that which makes a soul not only bad but
miserable also? And what is more miserable than always to
be plagued by desire for a thing, the fruit of which can never
satisfy? We showed above how in this degree the mind burns
constantly with heat and frost and the hatred cannot be extinguished by desire, nor the desire by hatred. And what else can
this be but a symbol of future damnation, where one passes
forever from the heat of the fires to the cold of snow and from
the cold of snow to the heat of fires. So this last degree of love
belonging to human desires is worst of all but in spiritual affections it is highest of all. For in the former whatever may be
done to the human soul cannot satisfy it, but in the latter whatever the soul can do for God cannot satisfy its desire. In the
first the mind is always anxious about what will happen to itself,
not what it may do. In the second the mind feels greater anxiety
about what it will do than about what can be done to it. Therefore in the realm of heavenly desires the greater the affection
and the higher the degree, so much the better and the more
precious is the love. O how precious is that first degree of the
love of God when it is insuperable. More precious still the second
when the ardent affection begins to be inseparable. But much
better again when the soul cannot be pleased by any other thing
but God. . . .

In the first degree God is loved with the heart, the soul and
the mind but not wholly by any one of these. In the second He
is loved with all the heart; in the third with all the soul; in the
fourth with all the strength. Love of the heart is a love arising
from deliberate consideration; love of the soul is love arising
from the affection; deliberation belongs to the heart but desire
belongs to the soul. . . . To love with the heart is to love by
judgement and deliberation, to love with the soul is to love
because of desire and affection. The first is with effort, the
second according to desire. To love with one's whole heart, soul

and all one's strength is to concentrate all one's efforts, desires and powers upon this one thing.

We often are drawn to love a thing through our affection and yet we renounce it because of reason. And we often love many things through considered opinion, which we care very little for in the realm of feeling. Therefore where fleshly desires are concerned we often love first with the soul, rather than the heart. In spiritual things, however, we always love first by deliberation rather than affection. We never love spiritual things through the desires, unless with much labour, our hearts are kindled with good feelings for them. If therefore we want to love God with all our soul, we must first try to love Him with all our heart. If we wish to love with all our desire, let all our thoughts be on this, all our deliberation and all our meditation. But because we never love with all our soul unless we first love with all our heart, so also we never love with all our strength unless we first love with all our soul. But if we have an affection for something which we do not love for God's sake, the adulterous affection immediately breaks the constancy of the highest charity and diminishes its strength in proportion as it draws or drives the soul to extraneous desires. . . .

Let us go deeper and speak more openly. In the first degree the soul thirsts for God, in the second she thirsts to go to God, in the third she thirsts to be in God, in the fourth she thirsts in God's way. She thirsts for God when she desires to experience what that inward sweetness is that inebriates the mind of man, when he begins to taste and see how sweet the Lord is. She thirsts for God when she desires to be raised above herself by the grace of contemplation and to see the Lord in all His beauty, that she may truly say: 'For I have seen the Lord face to face, and my life is preserved.' She thirsts in God, when in ecstasy she desires to pass over into God altogether, so that having wholly forgotten herself she may truly say: 'Whether in the body or out of the body I cannot tell.' She thirsts in God's way when, by her own will I do not mean in temporal matters only but also in spiritual things, the soul reserves nothing for her own will but commits all things to God, never thinking about herself but about the things of Jesus Christ, so that she may say: 'I came not to do my own will but the will of the Father which is in heaven.' In the first degree, God enters into the soul and she turns inward into herself. In the second, she ascends above herself and is lifted up to God. In the third the soul, lifted up to God passes over altogether into Him. In the fourth the soul goes forth on God's behalf and descends below herself. In the first she enters into herself, in the second she goes forth from herself. In the first she reaches her own life, in the third she reaches God. In the first she goes forth on her own behalf, in the fourth she goes forth because of her neighbour. In the first she enters in by meditation, in the second she ascends by contemplation, in the third she is led into jubilation, in the fourth she goes out by compassion. In the first degree a spiritual feeling sweeter than honey enters into her soul and inebriates her with its sweetness, so that she has honey and milk on her tongue and her lips distil the honeycomb. Those who have felt this will give forth a memorial of abundant sweetness, for the mouth speaketh out of the abundance of the heart. This is the first consolation which they who renounce the world receive at first and it generally confirms them in their good intention. This is the heavenly food which is wont to refresh those who go forth from Egypt and feed them in the wilderness; this is the hidden manna which no man knoweth who hath not received it. This is that spiritual sweetness and inward delight which is the milk and food of those who are as newborn babes and which brings them gradually to the strength of full grown men.

In this same state the soul is led by God into the wilderness where it is fed with milk so that it may be inebriated with inward sweetness. Hearken what is said of this state when the Lord speaks by the prophet: 'Therefore', he saith, 'I will feed her with milk and will lead her into the wilderness and will speak to her heart.' But first we must leave Egypt behind, first we must cross the Red Sea. First the Egyptians must perish in the waves, first must we suffer famine in the land of Egypt before we can receive this spiritual nourishment and heavenly food. He who desires that food of heavenly solitude let him abandon Egypt both in body and heart, and altogether set aside the love of the world. Let him cross the Red Sea, let him try to drive all sadness and bitterness out of his heart, if he desires to be filled with inward sweetness. First the Egyptians must be

247

swallowed up. Let perverse ways perish lest the angelic citizens disdain an ignoble companion. First the foods of Egypt must fail, and carnal pleasures be held in abomination before we may experience the nature of those inner and eternal pleasures. Truly the more fully the love of God overcomes any other affection, the more often and more abundantly it refreshes the soul with inward gladness. In this state the mind sucks honey from the stone and oil from the hardest rock. In this state the mountain shall distil sweetness and the hills flow with milk and honey. In this state the Lord often visits the hungry and thirsty soul, often He fills her with inward delight and makes her drink with the sweetness of His Spirit. In this state the Lord often descends from heaven and visits him who sits in darkness and the shadow of death. Often the glory of the Lord abides over the tabernacle of the covenant. Nevertheless he reveals his presence but without showing his face. He infuses his sweetness but does not show his fair beauty. His loveliness is felt but his form is not discerned. Even now the clouds and darkness are round about him and his throne is in the pillar of the cloud. Gentle and soothing is that which is felt but altogether dark, what is seen. For he does not yet appear in the light and though he be seen in the fire, the fire is a burning rather than an illumination. For he kindles the affection but does not yet illuminate the intellect. He inflames the desire but does not yet enlighten the intelligence. In this state the soul can feel her beloved but she cannot see him. And if she does see him it is as one sees by night. She sees as it were in a cloud, she sees him at last in a mirror and darkly, not yet face to face. Hence it is written: 'Make thy face to shine upon thy servant.' And so it often happens that in the first degree, while the mind is being frequently visited, refreshed and inebriated, sometimes this is to give her greater courage. At times it begins to be more bold and to ask for higher things, so much so that it dares to say: 'If I have found grace in thine eyes show me now thyself.' Nevertheless it does not receive immediately what it asks, nor according to its desire, though it may ask with deep desire. We must indeed ask earnestly, seek diligently, knock loudly and continue perseveringly in all these things, if we would obtain what we desire. Do you not think that he who said: 'How long O Lord, wilt thou forget me unto the end?

How long dost thou turn away thy face from me?' must have laboured greatly and have been almost fainting and ready to give up hope? But knowing that he who asketh receiveth, who seeketh findeth, and that the door is opened to him that knocketh, again and again he is given confidence and his strength is renewed and he says: 'My face hath sought thee. Thy face O Lord, will I seek.' When the mind therefore goes forward to the grace of contemplation with great effort and ardent desire, it moves as it were into the second degree of love, where it deserves to look, by divine shewing, upon that which the eye cannot see nor the ear hear nor shall it enter the heart of man, so that it may truly say: 'But to us, God hath revealed them by his spirit.' Did not he who saw the angels ascending and descending and God leaning on the ladder, deserve to receive that grace? Whence it is written: 'I have seen the Lord face to face and my life is preserved.' He who received this grace almost habitually, said; 'Send forth thy light and thy truth: they have led me and brought me unto thy holy hill and to thy tabernacles.' . . . And another prophet says: 'They that wait upon the Lord shall renew their strength, they shall take wings as eagles, they shall fly and not faint.' In this degree of contemplation they are borne up above the clouds on the wings of their souls and they fly away to the heavens, not only the first heaven, but also to the second heaven; so that they may indeed say: 'Our conversation is in heaven.' . . .

Truly who can express worthily how great is the joy of this vision? When this joy has once been experienced and tasted it cannot become a weariness when present nor be forgotten when absent. When the soul comes down from this life and returns to herself she brings with her the remainder of her thoughts to refresh herself with, indeed she celebrates a holy day, as the Scripture saith: 'And the remainder of the thoughts shall keep holyday to thee.' Consider therefore how solemn the fullness of the vision must be if a feast can be made of what is left over. And what will the happiness of the vision be if there is such delight in remembering it? Therefore the shewing of the divine light in this state and the wonder of the revelation arising from it, together with the perennial memory thereof bind the soul indissolubly so that she is not able to forget the happiness of her experience. And as in the earlier degree, the delight which she has tasted satisfies the soul and transfixes the affections, so in this degree, the brightness she has looked upon binds the thoughts that she may neither forget it nor think about anything else. In the second degree, as has been said, in the heaven of heavens, that inaccessible light may be seen but not reached, for if it could be reached it would not be inaccessible, as the Apostle saith: 'The blessed and only Potentate, the King of kings, and Lord of lords, who only hath immortality, dwelling in the light which no man can approach unto.' It cannot be approached for it is inaccessible. Nevertheless the Apostle glories in that he was rapt away to that region of eternal light: I know a man in Christ, whether in the body or out of the body, I cannot tell: God knoweth; such an one caught up to the third heaven.'

Therefore the third degree of love is when the mind of man is ravished into the abyss of divine light so that the soul, having forgotten all outward things is altogether unaware of itself and passes out completely into its God and fulfills what is written, 'Yea those also who do not believe, shall dwell in the Lord God.' In this state it is wholly subdued, the host of carnal desires are deeply asleep and there is silence in heaven as it were for half an hour. And any suffering that is left is absorbed in glory. In this state, while the soul is abstracted from itself, ravished into that secret place of divine refuge, when it is surrounded on every side by the divine fire of love, pierced to the core, set alight all about, then it sheds its very self altogether and puts on that divine life, and being wholly conformed to the beauty it has seen, passes wholly into that glory.

Consider the difference between iron and iron: between cold and hot iron, such as the difference between souls, between the tepid soul and that kindled by divine fire. When the iron is first cast into the fire it certainly appears to be as dark as it is cold. But after having been a time in the flame of the fire it grows warm and gradually changes its dark colour. Visibly it begins to glow, and little by little draws the likeness of fire into itself until at last it liquefies entirely and ceases altogether to be itself, changing into another kind of thing. So also, the soul absorbed in the consuming fire in the furnace of the divine love, surrounded by the glowing body of eternal desires, first kindles then grows red hot, at last liquefies completely and is altogether changed from its first state. Would you hear of those glowing already in the fire and beginning to burn with the heat of inward desires? 'Did not our heart burn within us while he talked with us by the way, and while he opened the scriptures to us?' And are these souls not beginning to glow by the surrounding flame of divinity and the glory they have seen, and being conformed to the divine light they pass over into another glory, beholding the glory of the Lord openly and are transformed in the same image from glory to glory as by the Spirit of the Lord. Hear, now the soul enkindled and melted by the fire of the divine word! 'My soul melted when my beloved spake.' As soon as she is admitted to that inner secret of the divine mystery, through the greatness of her wonder and the abundance of joy, she is wholly dissolved in herself or rather into Him who speaks, when she begins to hear words that it is not lawful for man to utter and to understand the strange and hidden things of God. In this state she who cleaves to the Lord is one spirit with him. In this state, as we have said, the soul is altogether melted into him whom she loves and is herself fainting away. Hence she says: 'Stay me with flowers, compass me about with apples because I languish with love.' Just as we see that there is nothing hard or firm in liquids or liquefied solids, but they yield to all hard and rigid objects, so too we see that sick men have no personal strength or natural power and they depend on the will of others for assistance in everything. Similarly those who have reached the third degree of love, do nothing according to their own will, they leave nothing at their own desire, but commit all things to the providence of God. Every wish or desire of theirs hangs upon God's sign and awaits the divine good pleasure. And as the first degree wounds the affection and the second binds the thoughts, so the third hinders action, so that a man cannot be occupied about anything unless the power of the divine will draws or drives him. When in this way the soul has been reduced in the divine fire, softened to the very core and wholly melted, nothing is wanting except that she should be shown what is God's goodwill, all-pleasing and perfect, even the form of perfect virtue, to which she must be conformed. For just as the metal workers, when the metals are melted and the moulds set out, shape any form according to their will and produce any vessel according to the manner and mould that has been planned, so the soul applies herself in this degree, to be readily at the beck and call of the divine will, indeed she adapts herself with spontaneous desire to every demand of God and adjusts her own will, as the divine good pleasure requires. And as liquefied metal runs down easily wherever a passage is opened, so the soul humbles herself spontaneously to be obedient in this way, and freely bows herself in all acts of humility according to the order of divine providence. In this state the image of the will of Christ is set before the soul so that these words come to her: 'Let this mind be in you, which was also in Christ Jesus: who being in the form of God, thought it not robbery to be equal with God, but emptied himself, and took upon him the form of a servant and was made in the likeness of men and was found in the habit of man; he humbled himself and became obedient unto death, even the death of the cross.' This is the form of the humility of Christ to which every man must conform himself, who desires to attain to the highest degree of perfect charity. For greater love has no man than this, that a man lay down his life for his friends. Those who are able to lay down their lives for their friends have reached the highest peak of charity and are already placed in the fourth degree of charity. They can fulfil the Apostle's bidding: 'Be ye therefore followers of God, as dear children; and walk in love, as Christ also hath loved us, and hath given himself for an offering and a sacrifice to God for a sweet-smelling saviour.' Therefore in the third degree the soul is glorified, in the fourth she is humbled for God's sake. In the third she is conformed to the divine light, in the fourth she is conformed to the humility of Christ. And though in the third she is in a way almost in the likeness of God, nevertheless in the fourth she begins to empty herself, taking the form of a servant and begins to be found in fashion as a man. In the third degree she is as it were put to death in God, in the fourth she is raised in Christ. He that is in the fourth degree may say truly: 'I live yet not I, Christ liveth in me.' Such a man begins to live in newness of life and for the rest, 'to him to live is Christ and to die gain'. He is truly in a strait between two desires, to be dissolved and be with Christ which is far better, but to remain in the flesh is necessary for our sakes. The charity of Christ compels him. Such a man becomes a new creature, for old things are passed away and lo all things are made new. For in the third degree he is put to death, in the fourth as it were, he rises from the dead, now he dieth no more, death hath no more dominion over him, for in that he liveth he liveth unto God.

Therefore, in this fourth degree, the soul is made in some way immortal and impassible. How can it be mortal if it cannot die? and how can it die if it cannot be separated from Him who is life? We know who said this: 'I am the way, the truth and the life.' How then can a man die who cannot be separated from Him? 'For I am sure', he saith, 'that neither death nor life, nor angels nor principalities, nor powers, nor things present, nor thing to come, nor might nor height, nor depth, nor any other creature, shall be able to separate us from the love of God which is in Christ Jesus.' Besides, does a man not seem, in some degree, impassible, who does not feel the misfortunes that he bears, who rejoices in injuries, and whatever pain he suffers he counts it to be glory? according to the saying of the Apostle: 'Gladly therefore will I glory in my infirmities that the power of Christ may dwell in me.' He who takes pleasure in sufferings and contumely for Christ, also seems to be impassible. 'Therefore, I take pleasure in infirmities in reproaches, in necessities, in persecutions, in distresses for Christ's sake.' He who is in this degree can say confidently: 'I can do all things in him who strengtheneth me,' in that he knows how to be filled and how to be hungry to abound and to suffer poverty. In this degree of charity 'he beareth all things, believeth all things, hopeth all things, endureth all things.' In this degree charity is long suffering and is kind, is not ambitious, seeketh not her own, does not render evil for evil nor curse for a curse. But rather blesseth. He who ascends to this degree of charity is truly in the state of love that can say: 'I am made all things to all men that I might save all.' And such a man then desires to be made anathema from Christ for his brethren's sake. What shall we say then? In this degree of love the soul of man might seem to be mad, in that it will not suffer his zeal to be kept within bounds or measure. Is it not complete madness to reject true life, to accuse the highest wisdom, to resist omnipotence? And if a man desires to be separated from Christ for his brethren's sake, is that not a rejection of true life? as one who says: 'Either forgive them their sin or blot me out of the book that thou hast written!' He who says to the Lord: 'Far be it from thee to do this thing to slay the just with the wicked, and for the just to be in like case as the wicked: shall not the Judge of all the earth do right?' is he not accusing the Lord and trying to teach wisdom? . . . Did not this man attempt to resist the Almighty when after the judgement of God had gone forth, when the savage conflagration had begun to rage, man stood up to the roaring fire and placed himself as an intermediary between those who were afraid and those who were dying and compelled an end to the calamity. Consider to what boldness of presumption the perfection of charity can raise up the mind of man: behold how it induces him to presume beyond the power of a man! That which he hopes of God, what he does for God and in God and effects with God, is more than merely human. How utterly wondrous and amazing! The more he hopes from God the more he abases himself for God. The more he rises up in boldness, the more he descends in humility. Just as the goal to which he ascends by confidence is above man, so is the point to which he descends by patience, beyond man.

Therefore as we have said, in the first degree, the soul returns to itself; in the second it ascends to God; in the third it passes out into God; in the fourth it descends below itself. In the first and second it is raised; in the third and fourth it is transfigured. In the first it ascends to itself; in the second it transcends itself; in the third it is conformed to the glory of Christ; in the fourth it is conformed to the humility of Christ. Again, in the first it is led back; in the second it is transferred; in the third it is transformed; in the fourth it is resurrected.

St. Francis of Assisi
1182-1226

Few personalities in the history of Christianity have had the attractiveness and magnetism of Saint Francis of Assisi. His name evokes images of peacefulness and joy, of poverty, of oneness with nature. His impact on the centuries that have passed since his death in 1226 extends far beyond the religious orders that consider themselves his spiritual sons and daughters. Laypersons, Catholic and Protestant alike, easily identify with him, feel that they know him. He has captured the attention and imagination of countless writers, artists and poets and had been a source of inspiration for them.

Why? What was it about this ordinary man from Assisi who lived only 45 years or so? He was born into a comfortable family, lived the beautiful life and then went through a conversion process. Followers quickly gathered around the "new" Francis, who demanded of them only that they live the gospel of Jesus Christ. Perhaps it was the simplicity with which he understood and lived the gospel that made of him a man most rare. The message was in no way complicated; yet the living called for more than most humans are willing to give.

Poverty—a deliberate, responsible, symbolic renunciation of all possessions both material and immaterial; Joy—the endurance of rejection and abuse, and the acceptance of all suffering with love and gladness; Fraternal Love—the willing of the good of one's brothers and sisters (and all humans are brothers and sisters); Peace—the capacity to be totally at home with oneself, all creatures, the universe—such were the evangelical insights on which Francis built his life. Most all humans dream of such a life. Francis is proof that these basic teachings of Jesus can be realized in time.

Of course, as is often the case with great persons, Francis' life is more easily admired than imitated. For he purchased his poverty, joy, love and peace at no small cost. It required a lifetime of prayer, of negation, of renewal of spirit, of detachment.

The Little Flowers of St. Francis *appeared in the fourteenth century. They are most likely the written version of an oral tradition that developed among some of the followers of Francis shortly after his death. The fifty-three chapters that make them up are a collection of simple stories about Francis and his companions, St. Anthony of Padua, and second and third generations of Franciscan friars.* The Little Flowers *are clearly poetic and are designed to paint a very warm image of Francis. It is for this reason that they have enjoyed such great popularity, for Francis certainly comes across as a wonderful, kind, loving human being. They allow the reader to be at ease with this ordinary but unusual person who seems constantly to be reassuring mankind that Christian maturity and perfection is much more simple than one can imagine, that love, joy and peace actually can be one's way of life in time, that even poverty, suffering and rejection can be put to good use, that all one need do is live the gospel of Christ.*

THE LITTLE FLOWERS

CHAPTER V

HOW THE HOLY BROTHER BERNARD OF ASSISI WAS SENT BY S. FRANCIS TO BOLOGNA AND THERE FOUNDED A HOUSE

Seeing that S. Francis and his companions were called of God and elect to bear in their hearts and in their deeds and preach with their tongues the cross of Christ, they seemed to be and were in very sooth men crucified, so by reason of their habit as of their austere life and deeds and works: and therefore they desired the more to suffer shame and contumely for the love of Christ, rather than honour of the world and reverence and praise of men: in insults they rejoiced and at honours they grew sad; and so they passed through the world as strangers and pilgrims, bearing with them naught save Jesu Christ Crucified. And sith they were true branches of the true vine, that is Christ, they brought forth great and good fruit of souls, that they won for God. It happened in the beginning of the Order that S. Francis sent Brother Bernard to Bologna to the end that he might there, according to the grace that God had given him, bring forth fruit to God; and Brother Bernard making the sign of the most holy cross, for holy obedience departed and came unto Bologna. And the children seeing him in poor and threadbare habit, despitefully intreated and made much mock of him, as though he were a fool: but Brother Bernard with patience and with joy bore all things for the love of Christ; nay, of set purpose that he might the more be evilly intreated, betook him to the market-place of the city: whereby, he sitting there, many children and men came together about him, and some from behind, and others before, plucked at his hood; some pelted him with dust and some with stones; some pushed him this way and others that: and Brother Bernard continuing always after the same fashion and with the same patience, with a joyful countenance, neither complained nor changed at all, and for the space of many days returned to the same place, but for to suffer the like usage. And sith patience is a work of perfection and proof of virtue, a learned doctor of the law, beholding and musing on the great constancy and virtue of Brother Bernard, how for so many days nor taunt nor contumely could e'er disquiet him said thus within himself: "Of a surety this needs must be a holy man;" and coming near unto him, he asked: "Who art thou? and wherefore art thou come hither?" And Brother Bernard for reply put his hand into his bosom and drew forth the Rule of S. Francis, and gave it him that he might read, and when he had read it, musing on its most lofty state of perfection, with exceeding great marvel and amazement he turned him unto his companions and said: "Of a truth this is the highest state of religion whereof I have ever heard: wherefore this man and his companions are the holiest men in this world, and whoso does him wrong committeth a most grievous sin; most highly should we honour him, seeing that he is a true friend of God." And he said to Brother Bernard: "If 'tis your wish to found a House, wherein you may serve God conveniently, with right good will, for the salvation of my soul, will I give it you." Replied Brother Bernard: "Good sir, me-thinks our Lord Jesu Christ hath put this thought within your heart; and therefore for the honour of Christ I willingly accept your proffered gift." Then with great joy and love the said judge took Brother Bernard to his house; and gave him anon the promised House and made it all ready and at his own charges furnished it: and from that time forth became the father and special defender of Brother Bernard and his companions. And Brother Bernard, through his holy life, began to be much honoured of the people, in such sort that whoso might touch and see him, deemed himself blessed thereby; but he, like a true disciple of Christ and the humble Francis, fearing that the honour of the world might hinder the peace and salvation of his soul, on a day departed and returned unto S. Francis and spake thus unto him: "Father, the House is founded in the city of Bologna: send brothers thither to maintain it and abide therein: since I have no more profit therein, nay, rather for the too great honour done to me I fear me I have lost e'en more than I have gained." Thereat S. Francis, learning all things in order, how

God had worked through Brother Bernard, gave thanks to God, who thuswise was beginning to enlarge the poor little disciples of the Cross: and anon he sent of his companions to Bologna and into Lombardy, the which founded many Houses in diverse places.

CHAPTER VIII

HOW, AS S. FRANCIS AND BROTHER LEO WERE GOING BY THE WAY, HE SET FORTH UNTO HIM WHAT THINGS WERE PERFECT JOY

Whenas S. Francis was going one day from Perugia to S. Mary of the Angels with Brother Leo in the spring tide, and the very bitter cold grievously tormented him, he called to Brother Leo that was going on before and said thus: "Brother Leo, though the Brothers Minor throughout all the world were great ensamples of sanctity and true edifying, nathless write it down and take heed diligently that not therein is perfect joy." And going on a little further, S. Francis called a second time: "O Brother Leo, albeit the Brothers Minor should give sight to the blind, make straight the crooked, cast out devils, make the deaf to hear, the lame to walk, the dumb to speak, and (greater still) should raise them that have been dead a four days' space, write that not herein is perfect joy." And going on a little, he cried aloud: "O Brother Leo, if the Brother Minor should know all tongues and all sciences and all the Scriptures, so that he could prophesy and reveal not only things to come but also the secrets of consciences and souls, write that not therein is perfect joy." Going on yet a little further, S. Francis called aloud once more: "O Brother Leo, thou little sheep of God, albeit the Brother Minor should speak with the tongue of an angel, and know the courses of the stars and the virtues of herbs; and though all the treasures of the earth were revealed unto him and he understood the virtues of birds, and of fishes, and of all animals, and of men, and of trees, and of stones, and of roots, and of waters, write that not therein is perfect joy." And going on a little further, S. Francis cried aloud: "O Brother Leo, albeit the Brother Minor could preach so well as to turn all the infidels to the faith of Christ, write that not therein is perfect joy." And this manner of speech continuing for full two miles,

Brother Leo with much marvel besought him, saying: "Father, I pray thee in the name of God that thou tell me, wherein is perfect joy." And S. Francis thus made answer: "When we come to S. Mary of the Angels, all soaked as we are with rain and numbed with cold and besmirched with mud and tormented with hunger, and knock at the door of the house; and the porter comes in anger and says: 'Who are ye?' and we say: 'We be two of your brethren:' and he says, 'Ye be no true men; nay, ye be two rogues that gad about deceiving the world and robbing the alms of the poor; get ye gone:' and thereat he shuts to the door and makes us stand without in the snow and the rain, cold and a-hungered, till night-fall; if therewithal we patiently endure such wrong and such cruelty and such rebuffs without being disquieted and without murmuring against him; and with humbleness and charity bethink us that this porter knows us full well and that God makes him to speak against us; O Brother Leo, write that herein is perfect joy. And if we be instant in knocking and he come but full of wrath and drive us away as importunate knaves, with insults and buffetings, saying: 'Get ye gone hence, vilest of thieves, begone to the alms-house, for here ye shall find nor food nor lodging;' if we suffer this with patience and with gladness and with love, O Brother Leo, write that herein is perfect joy. And if we still constrained by hunger and cold and night, knock yet again and shout and with much weeping pray him for the love of God that he will but open and let us in; and he yet more enraged should say: 'These be importunate knaves, I will pay them well as they deserve,' and should rush out with a knotty stick and taking us by the hood, throw us upon the ground and send us rolling in the snow and beat us with all the knots of that stick: if with patience and with gladness we suffer all these things, thinking on the pains of the blessed Christ, the which we ought to suffer for the love of Him: O Brother Leo, write that here and herein is perfect joy: then hear the conclusion of the whole matter, Brother Leo: Above all graces and gifts of the Holy Spirit, that Christ granteth to His beloved, is to overcome oneself, and willingly for the love of Christ endure pains and insults and shame and want: inasmuch as in all other gifts of God we may not glory, sith they are not ours but God's; whence saith the Apostle: What hast thou that thou hast not received of God? And if thou hast received it of Him, wherefore boastest thou thyself as if thou hadst it of thyself? But in the cross of tribulation and affliction we may boast, sith this is ours; and therefore saith the Apostle, I would not that I should glory save in the cross of our Lord Jesu Christ."

CHAPTER XIII

HOW S. FRANCIS AND BROTHER MASSEO SET THE BREAD THAT THEY HAD BEGGED UPON A STONE HARD BY A FOUNTAIN, AND HOW S. FRANCIS PRAISED POVERTY EXCEEDINGLY. THEN BESOUGHT GOD AND S. PETER AND S. PAUL THAT HE WOULD SET IN HIS HEART THE LOVE OF HOLY POVERTY, AND HOW S. PETER AND S. PAUL APPEARED UNTO HIM

The wonderful servant and follower of Christ, to wit S. Francis, to the end that he might in all things conform himself perfectly unto Christ, who, as the Gospel saith, sent His disciples forth by two and two unto all the cities and places where He was Himself purposing to go; seeing that after the pattern of Christ he had gathered together twelve companions, sent them forth by two and two to preach throughout the world. And to give them an ensample of true obedience, he was himself the first to go, after the pattern of Christ who began to do before He taught. Wherefore having allotted to his companions the other parts of the world, he with Brother Masseo as his companion took the road that led to the land of France. And coming one day to a town sore hungered, they went, according to the rule, begging their bread for the love of God; and S. Francis went by one street, and Brother Masseo by another. But because S. Francis was mean to look upon and small of stature, and was deemed thereby a vile beggar by whoso knew him not, he got by his begging naught save a few mouthfuls and scraps of dry bread: but to Brother Masseo, in that he was tall and fair of form, were given good pieces, large and in plenty, and of fresh bread. When that they had done their begging, they met together to eat in a place without the city, where was a fair fountain and, hard by, a fine, broad stone; upon the which each set the alms that he had begged. And S. Francis, seeing that Brother Masseo's pieces of bread were more and finer and larger than his own, rejoiced with great joy, and said: "O Brother

Masseo, we are not worthy of such vast treasure:" and when he repeated many times these selfsame words, Brother Masseo made answer: "Father, how can one speak of treasure where is such poverty and lack of all things whereof there is need? Here is nor cloth, nor knife, nor plate, nor porringer, nor house, nor table, nor man-servant, nor maid-servant." Quoth S. Francis: "And this it is that I account vast treasure, wherein is no thing at all prepared by human hands, but whatsoe'er we have is given by God's own providence, as manifestly doth appear in the bread that we have begged, in the table of stone so fine, and in the fount so clear; wherefore I will that we pray unto God that He make us to love with all our heart the treasure of holy poverty which is so noble, that thereunto did God Himself become a servitor." And when he had said these words, and they had done their prayer, and for refreshment of the body had taken of those pieces and drunk of that water, they rose up to journey into France, and drawing nigh unto a church S. Francis said to his companion: "Let us go into the church to pray." And S. Francis gat him behind the altar and gave himself to prayer: and in that same prayer he received from the divine visitation fervour so exceeding great, the which inflamed his soul so mightily with the love of holy poverty that, by the colour of his face and the unwonted opening of his lips, it seemed as though he breathed forth flames of love. And coming thus enkindled to his companion, he bespake him thus: "Ah! ah! ah! Brother Masseo, give thyself to me;" and thus spake he three times; and at the third time S. Francis with his breath lifted Brother Masseo up into the air, and threw him a great spear's length in front of him; whereby exceeding great amazement took hold on Brother Masseo. Afterwards he recounted to his companions how that, when as he was uplifted and hurled along by the breath that S. Francis breathed on him, he tasted such sweetness of soul, and consolation of the Holy Spirit, that in all his life he ne'er had felt the like. And this done, S. Francis said: "My comrade, let us go to S. Peter and S. Paul and pray them to teach us and help us to possess the immeasurable treasure of most holy poverty; for it is a treasure so high excelling and so divine that we be not worthy to lay it up in our vile vessels; since this is that celestial virtue whereby all earthly things and fleeting are trodden under foot, and whereby all hindrances are lifted from the soul, so that freely she may join herself to God eternal. And this is the virtue that makes the soul, still tied to earth, hold converse with the angels in heaven, and this it is that hung with Christ upon the cross, with Christ was buried, with Christ rose up again, with Christ ascended into heaven; the which also in this life grants to the souls that love it an easier flight to heaven; in that it guards the arms of true humility and love. Wherefore let us pray the most holy apostles of Christ, the which were perfect lovers of this gospel pearl, that they may beg for us this grace from our Lord Jesu Christ, that of His most holy mercy He may make us worthy to become true lovers, followers, and humble disciples, of the most precious, most lovable, and gospel poverty." With such converse they so fared until they came unto Rome, and went into the church of S. Peter; and S. Francis set himself to pray in one corner of the church, and Brother Masseo in another; and as he continued a long time in prayer with much weeping and devotion, there appeared unto S. Francis the most holy apostles Peter and Paul in great splendour, and said: "Because thou hast asked and desired to observe that which Christ and His holy apostles observed, the Lord Jesu Christ hath sent us unto thee to announce that thy prayer is heard, and that God has granted to thee and to thy followers in uttermost perfection the treasure of most holy poverty. And further we tell thee in His name that whoso after thy pattern shall perfectly follow this desire, he is assured of the blessedness of life eternal: and blessed shalt thou and all thy followers be;" and with these words they were away, leaving S. Francis filled with consolation. And rising from prayer, he returned to his companion and asked him if God had revealed naught unto him; and he answered, "Naught." Then S. Francis told him how the holy apostles had appeared to him, and what they had revealed. Whereat they both being filled with joy resolved to return unto the valley of Spoleto, and leave their journeying into France.

CHAPTER XXX

OF THE BEAUTIFUL SERMON PREACHED IN ASSISI BY S. FRANCIS AND BROTHER RUFFINO

The aforesaid Brother Ruffino, through continual contemplation, was so absorbed in God, that he became as it were insensible and dumb, spake but seldom, and therewithal had neither the gift of preaching, nor boldness nor eloquence therein; nevertheless S. Francis on a time bade him go to Assisi and preach to the people whatsoever God might inspire him withal. Wherefore Brother Ruffino answered: "Reverend father, I pray thee pardon me and send me not; for, as thou wottest, I have not the gift of preaching, but am simple and ignorant." Then quoth S. Francis: "Seeing that thou hast not obeyed incontinent, I command thee by holy obedience that thou get thee to Assisi naked as thou wast born, save in thy breeches only, and enter into a church and preach unto the people." At this command, the said Brother Ruffino stripped himself and went to Assisi and entered into a church, and having done reverence to the altar went up into the pulpit and began to preach; for the which cause the children and the men began to laugh, and said: "Now look you how these fellows do so much penance that they become fools and are beside themselves." Meantime, S. Francis, bethinking him of the ready obedience of Brother Ruffino, the which was one of the most noble gentles of Assisi, and of the hard commandment he had laid upon him, began to chide himself, saying: "Whence comes to thee such boldness, thou son of Peter Bernardoni, vile wretch, to command Brother Ruffino, that is one of the most noble gentles of Assisi, to go and preach to the people like a madman? By God, thou shalt have proof in thine own self of what thou biddest others do." And straightway in fervour of spirit he stripped himself in like fashion, and set out for Assisi, and took with him Brother Leo to carry his habit and that of Brother Ruffino. And the folk of Assisi beholding him in the self-same guise, made mock of him, deeming that he and Brother Ruffino had grown mad through overmuch penance. S. Francis entered into the church where Brother Ruffino was preaching these words: "Dearly beloved, flee from the world and put away sin; render to others their due, if ye would escape from hell; follow the commandments of God, in loving God and your neighbour, if ye would go to heaven; do penance, if ye would possess the kingdom of heaven." Then S. Francis went up into the pulpit and began to preach so marvellously of the contempt of the world, of holy penitence, of voluntary poverty, and of the desire of the kingdom of heaven, and of the nakedness and shame of the passion of our Lord Jesu Christ, that all they that heard the preaching, men and women in great multitude, began to weep most bitterly with devout and contrite hearts; and not there alone, but in all Assisi was there that day such weeping for the passion of Christ, that never had there been the like. And the people being thuswise edified and comforted by this act of S. Francis and Brother Ruffino, S. Francis re-clad Brother Ruffino and himself; and so re-clad, they returned to the House of Portiuncula, praising and glorifying God, that had given them grace to overcome themselves, by the contempt of themselves, and to edify the little sheep of Christ by good example, and to show how greatly the world is to be despised. And on that day so much did the devotion of the people towards them increase, that he deemed himself blessed whoso could touch the hem of their garment.

OF THE MOST HOLY STIGMATA OF S. FRANCIS AND A REFLECTION THEREON

In this part we shall gaze with devout reflection on the first of the glorious and most holy Stigmata of our blessed Father S. Francis, the which he received of Christ on His holy mount of Alvernia. This reflection will be touching the manner in which S. Francis came to the holy mount of Alvernia.

* * * * *

As touching the first reflection, ye must needs know that S. Francis, being forty and three years of age, in the year 1224, being inspired of God, set out from the Vale of Spoleto for to go into Romagna with Brother Leo his companion; and as they went, they passed by the foot of the Castle of Montefeltro; in the which Castle there was at that time a great company of gentle folk, and much feasting, by reason of the knighting of one of the same Counts of Montefeltro. And S. Francis, hearing of the festivities that were holden there and how that many gentle folk of divers countries were there gathered together, spake unto Brother Leo: "Let us go up unto this feast, for with the help of God we may win some good fruit of souls." Among the other gentle folk from that country, that were of that knightly company, was a great and eke a wealthy gentleman of Tuscany, by name Orlando da Chiusi, of Casentino; who by reason of the marvellous things that he had heard of the sanctity and the miracles of S. Francis, bore him great devotion, and felt an exceeding strong desire to see him and to hear him preach. Coming to the castle, S. Francis entered in, and came to the courtyard where all that great company of gentle folk was gathered together, and in fervour of spirit stood up upon a parapet, and began to preach, taking as the text of his sermon these words in the vulgar tongue:

So great the joys I have in sight,
That every sorrow brings delight;

and upon this text, as the Holy Spirit gave him utterance, he preached so devoutly and sublimely, citing as proof thereof the divers pains and martyrdoms of the holy Apostles and the holy Martyrs, and the hard penances of the holy Confessors, and the many tribulations and temptations of the holy Virgins and the other saints, that all the folk stood with their eyes and their minds turned towards him, and gave such heed as though it were an angel of God speaking: among the which the said Orlando, touched in the heart by God through the marvellous preaching of S. Francis, set it in his heart to confer and to have speech with S. Francis, after the sermon, touching the state of his soul. Therefore, when the preaching was done, he drew S. Francis aside, and said unto him: "O father, I would confer with thee touching the salvation of my soul." Replied S. Francis: "It pleaseth me right well; but go this morning and do honour to thy friends, who have called thee to the feast, and dine with them; and after thou hast dined, we will speak together as much as thou wilt." So Orlando gat him to the dinner: and after that he had dined, he returned to S. Francis, and conferred with him, and set forth unto him fully the state of his soul. And at the end, this Orlando said to S. Francis: "I have in Tuscany a mountain, most proper for devotion, the which is called the Mount of Alvernia, and is very lonely and right well fitted for whoso may wish to do penance in a place remote from men, or whoso may desire to live a solitary life; if it should please thee, right willingly would I give it to thee and thy companions for the salvation of my soul." S. Francis hearing this liberal offer of the thing that he so much desired, rejoiced with exceeding great joy; and praising and giving thanks first to God and then to Orlando, he spake thus: "Orlando, when you have returned to your house, I will send unto you certain of my companions and you shall show them that mountain; and if it shall seem to them well fitted for prayer and penitence, I accept your loving offer even now." And this said, S. Francis departed: and when his journey was done, returned to S. Mary of the Angels: and likewise Orlando, when the festivities of that knightly company were over, returned to his castle, which was called Chiusi, the which was but a mile distant from Alvernia. Whenas S. Francis had returned to S. Mary of the Angels, he sent two of his companions to the said Orlando; who when they were come to him, were received of him with exceeding great joy and charity. And desiring to show them the mount of Alvernia, he sent with them full fifty men-at-arms to defend them from the wild beasts of the wood, and thus accompanied these brothers climbed up the mountain and searched diligently; and at last they came to a part of the mountain that was well fitted for devotion and contemplation; for in that part there was some level ground; and this place they chose out for them and for S. Francis to dwell therein; and with the help of the men-at-arms that bore them company, they made a little cell of branches of trees: and so they accepted in the name of God, and took possession of the mount of Alvernia and of the dwelling-place of the brothers on the mountain, and departed, and returned to S. Francis. And when they were come unto him, they told him how and in what manner they had taken a place on the mount of Alvernia most fitted for prayer and meditation. Hearing these tidings, S. Francis was right glad, and praising and giving thanks to God, he spake to those brothers with joyful countenance, and said: "My sons, our forty days' fast of S. Michael the Archangel draweth near: I firmly believe that it is the will of God that we keep this fast on the mount of Alvernia, which by divine decree hath been made ready for us, to the end that to the honour and glory of God and of His Mother, the glorious Virgin Mary, and of the holy Angels, we may, through penance, merit at the hands of Christ the consolation of consecrating this blessed mountain." And thus saying, S. Francis took with him Brother Masseo of Marignano by Assisi, the which was a man of great eloquence; and Brother Angelo Tancredi of Rieti, the which was a man of very gentle birth and in the world had been a knight; and Brother Leo, a man of exceeding great simplicity and purity, for the which cause S. Francis loved him much. And with these three brothers S. Francis set himself to pray, commended himself and his companions aforesaid to the prayers of the brothers that remained behind, and set out with those three in the name of Jesu Christ, the Crucified, for to go to the mount of Alvernia. And as he went, S. Francis called unto one of those three companions, to wit, Brother Masseo, and said unto him: "Thou, Brother Masseo, shalt be our guardian and our superior in this journey, to wit, so long as we be going and staying together, and we will observe our rule, to wit, that we be either saying the office, or speaking of God, or keeping silence, and that we take no thought beforehand, either of eating or drinking or sleeping: but when it is time to seek a lodging, we will beg a little bread, and stay and rest in the place that God may make ready for us." Then the three companions bowed their heads, and making the sign of the cross, went on their way: and on the first night they came to a house of the brothers and lodged there. On the second night, by reason of the bad weather and because they were tired, not being able to reach any house of the brothers or any castle or village, the night overtaking them, and bad weather, they took refuge in a deserted and dismantled church, and there laid them down to rest. And while his companions slept, S. Francis threw himself on his knees to pray; and behold in the first watch of the night there came a great multitude of demons, exceeding fierce, with a great noise and tumult, and began to do him grievous battle and annoy; whereby the one plucked him this way and the other that; one dragged him up and another down; one threatened him with one thing, and the other accused him of another; and thus in divers manners they sought to distract him from his prayer; but they could not, for that God was with him. Therefore whence S. Francis had endured these assaults of the demons, he began to cry in a loud voice: "O damned spirits, ye can do naught, save what the hand of God alloweth you: wherefore in the name of God Almighty I bid you do unto my body whatever is permitted you of God; for gladly shall I bear it sith I have no greater enemy than my body: and therefore if you avenge me of mine enemy, ye will do me good service." Then the demons with great fury and violence took hold of him, and began to drag him through the church, and to do him greater trouble and annoy than at first. Thereat S. Francis began to cry aloud, and said: "My Lord Jesu Christ, I give Thee thanks for the so great honour and charity that Thou showest me; for it is a token of great love when the Lord punishes His servant for all his faults in this world, so that he be not punished in the next. And I am ready gladly to endure every pain and adversity, that Thou, my God, dost will to send me for my sins." Then the demons, put to confusion and vanquished by his patience and endurance, were away. And S. Francis in fervour of spirit left the church and entered into a wood that was there hard by, and threw himself upon his knees in prayer; and with prayers and tears and beating of the breast he sought to find Jesu Christ, the spouse and the delight of his soul.

And at the last finding Him in the secret places of his soul, he now bespake him with reverence as his Lord: now made answer to Him as his judge; now besought Him as his father; now held converse with Him as with a friend. On that night within the wood, his companions, sith they were awake and were come to hear and mark what he did, saw and heard him, with tears and cries, devoutly beseeching God to have mercy upon sinners. Then was he seen and heard to weep with a loud voice over the Passion of Christ, as though he saw it with his own eyes. On that self same night they beheld him praying with his arms stretched out in the form of a cross, for a great space uplifted and floating above the earth, and surrounded by a cloud of glory. And so in such holy exercises he passed the whole night through without sleep. And thereafter in the morning, his companions, being ware that through the fatigues of the night, which he had passed without sleep, S. Francis was much weakened in body and could but ill go on his way afoot, went to a poor peasant of those parts, and begged him, for the love of God, to lend his ass for Brother Francis, their Father, that could not go afoot. Hearing them make mention of Brother Francis, he asked them: "Are ye of the brethren of that brother of Assisi, of whom so much good is spoken?" The brothers answered: "Yes," and that in very sooth it was for him that they asked for the sumpter beast. Then the good man, with great diligence and devotion, made ready the ass, and brought it to S. Francis, and with great reverence let mount him thereon, and they went on their way; and he with them, behind his ass. And when they had gone on a little way, the peasant said to S. Francis: "Tell me, art thou Brother Francis of Assisi?" Replied S. Francis, "Yes." "Try then," said the peasant, "to be as good as thou art of all folk held to be, seeing that many have great faith in thee; and therefore, I admonish thee that in thee there be naught save what men hope to find therein." Hearing these words, S. Francis thought no scorn to be admonished by a peasant, nor said within himself "What beast is this doth admonish me?" as many proud folk that wear the cowl would say now-a-days; but straightway he threw himself from off the ass upon the ground, and kneeled him down before him, and kissed his feet; and thus humbly thanked him for that he had deigned thus lovingly to admonish him. Then the peasant, together with the companions of S. Francis, with great devotion lifted him from the ground and set him on the ass again, and they went on their way. And when that they were come about half way up the mountain, as the head was very great and the ascent was weary, the peasant became very thirsty, in such sort that he began to cry aloud behind S. Francis, saying: "Woe is me, for I die of thirst: if I find not something to drink, I shall choke outright." Wherefore S. Francis got down off the ass and fell on his knees in prayer. Then said S. Francis to the peasant: "Run quickly to that rock, and there shalt thou find the living water, which Jesu Christ in this hour, of His mercy, hath made to come forth from out that rock." So he ran to the place that S. Francis had shown him, and found a fair spring that had been brought out of the hard rock by virtue of the prayer of S. Francis: and he drank his fill thereof and was comforted. And it doth well appear that this spring was brought out by God in miraculous fashion at the prayers of S. Francis, seeing that neither before nor after was there ever seen in that place a spring of water, nor say living water near to that place for a great space round. This done, S. Francis with his companions and the peasant gave thanks unto God for the miracle shown forth to them, and then went they on their way. And as they drew near to the foot of the rock of Alvernia itself, it pleased S. Francis to rest a little under the oak that was by the way, and is there to this day; and as he stood under it, S. Francis began to take note of the situation of the place and of the country round. And as he was thus gazing, lo! there came a great multitude of birds from divers parts, the which, with singing and flapping of their wings all showed joy and gladness exceeding great, and came about S. Francis in such fashion that some settled on his head, some on his shoulders, and some on his arms, some in his lap, and some round his feet. When his companions and the peasant marvelled, beholding this, S. Francis, all joyful in spirit, spake thus unto them: "I believe, brothers most dear, that it is pleasing unto our Lord Jesu Christ that we should dwell in this lonely mountain, seeing that our little sisters and brothers the birds show such joy at our coming." And said these words, they arose, and went on their way and came at last to the place that his companions had first chosen. And this is touching the first reflection, to wit, how S. Francis came to the holy mount of Alvernia.

St. Thomas Aquinas
1225-1274

Among the great thinkers and writers of the Christian theological tradition, St. Thomas Aquinas is one of the very few whose influence is too vast to measure. His philosophy and theology have been central to Catholic teaching for seven centuries. He was born in Italy in 1225. He was schooled as a child in the Benedictine Monastery of Montecassino, studied at the University of Naples and continued his studies in Paris and Cologne. From 1252 through to the end of his life, he was dedicated to teaching, though he also found time to preach. He was a member of the Dominican Order. He died at the age of 49.

Thomas lived during a period of tremendous intellectual ferment. The philosophies of Plato and Aristotle were being explored vigorously by the theologians of the thirteenth century. Thomas contributed his abilities generously. The result was the creation of a philosophico-theological structure which incorporated not only the best in Plato and Aristotle but the major elements of the Christian theological tradition as well.

No doubt, Thomas is best known for his Summa Theologiae, *though he wrote much more than that. The* Summa *is an exhaustive and systematic treatment of all the significant themes of theology, such as, God, creation, Man—his nature, purpose, knowledge, actions, habits, law, and grace.*

We have included here Thomas' treatment of the contemplative life. A few words of caution are in order. Thomas wrote in the style of the schoolmen of his time. He used the question—response methodology. It is a slow, steady, unusually logical method, designed to analyze the question at hand, to arrive at sound conclusions and to offer good reasons for the conclusions. The twentieth century reader may find this approach somewhat tedious. Further, in order to appreciate Thomas' insights for what they are worth, one must have some introduction to the technical terms used in philosophy and theology during the thirteenth century.

To the question, what did Thomas contribute to spirituality and spiritual writing, one can only respond that he revolutionized the entire theological structure that supports Christian spirituality. He expanded the meaning of all the basic terms in the Christian vocabulary. As a result, the generations of Christians since his time hear, speak and understand words such as God, man, Christ, sacrament, prayer, and perfection in an atmosphere colored by Thomas' theology. His influence is one that pervades the whole Christian interpretation of existence. Many of the spiritual writers in the centuries since Thomas drew their inspiration from him, for they recognized the depths to which his intellect penetrated in the search for truth and the heights to which one could climb who would build upon his insight.

SUMMA THEOLOGICA
ON THE CONTEMPLATIVE LIFE

QUESTION CLXXX

(In Eight Articles)

We must now consider the contemplative life, under which head there are eight points of inquiry: (1) Whether the contemplative life pertains to the intellect only, or also to the affections? (2) Whether the moral virtues pertain to the contemplative life? (3) Whether the contemplative life consists in one action or in several? (4) Whether the consideration of any truth whatever pertains to the contemplative life? (5) Whether the contemplative life of man in this state can arise to the vision of God? (6) Of the movements of contemplation assigned by Dionysius (*Div Nom.* iv.). (7) Of the pleasure of contemplation. (8) Of the duration of contemplation.

FIRST ARTICLE

WHETHER THE CONTEMPLATIVE LIFE HAS NOTHING TO DO WITH THE AFFECTIONS, AND PERTAINS WHOLLY TO THE INTELLECT?

We proceed thus to the First Article:—

Objection 1. It would seem that the contemplative life has nothing to do with the affections and pertains wholly to the intellect. For the Philosopher says (*Met.* ii., text. 3) that *the end of contemplation is truth.* Now truth pertains wholly to the intellect. Therefore it would seem that the contemplative life wholly regards the intellect.

Obj. 2. Further, Gregory says (*Moral.* vi. 37) that *Rachel, which is interpreted 'vision of the principle,' signifies the contemplative life.* Now the vision of a principle belongs properly to the intellect. Therefore the contemplative life belongs properly to the intellect.

Obj. 3. Further, Gregory says (*Hom.* xiv. *in Ezech.*) that it belongs to the contemplative life, *to rest from external action.* Now the affective or appetitive power inclines to external actions. Therefore it would seem that the contemplative life has nothing to do with the appetitive power.

On the contrary, Gregory says (*ibid.*) that *the contemplative life is to cling with our whole mind to the love of God and our neighbour, and to desire nothing beside our Creator.* Now desire and love pertain to the affective or appetitive power, as stated above (I.-II., Q. XXV., A. 2; Q. XXVI., A. 2). Therefore the contemplative life has also something to do with the affective or appetitive power.

I answer that, As stated above (Q. CLXXIX., A. 1) theirs is said to be the contemplative who are chiefly intent on the contemplation of truth. Now intention is an act of the will, as stated above (I.-II., Q. XII., A. 1), because intention is of the end which is the object of the will. Consequently the contemplative life, as regards the essence of the action, pertains to the intellect, but as regards the motive cause of the exercise of that action it belongs to the will, which moves all the other powers, even the intellect, to their actions, as stated above (Part I., Q. LXXXII., A. 4; I.-II., Q. IX., A. 1).

Now the appetitive power moves one to observe things either with the senses or with the intellect, sometimes for love of the things seen because, as it is written (Matth. vi. 21), *where thy treasure is, there is thy heart also,* sometimes for love of the very knowledge that one acquires by observation. Wherefore Gregory makes the contemplative life to consist in the *love of God,* inasmuch as through loving God we are aflame to gaze on His beauty. And since everyone delights when he obtains what he loves, it follows that the contemplative life terminates in delight, which is seated in the affective power, the result being that love also becomes more intense.

Reply Obj. 1. From the very fact that truth is the end of contemplation, it has the aspect of an appetible good, both lovable and delightful, and in this respect it pertains to the appetitive power.

Reply Obj. 2. We are urged to the vision of the first principle, namely God, by the love thereof; wherefore Gregory says (*Hom. xiv. in Ezech.*) that *the contemplative life tramples on all cares and longs to see the face of its creator.*

Reply Obj. 3. The appetitive power moves not only the bodily members to perform external actions, but also the intellect to practise the act of contemplation, as stated above.

SECOND ARTICLE

WHETHER THE MORAL VIRTUES PERTAIN TO THE CONTEMPLATIVE LIFE?

We proceed thus to the Second Article:—

Objection 1. It would seem that the moral virtues pertain to the contemplative life. For Gregory says (*Hom. xiv. in Ezech.*) that *the contemplative life is to cling to the love of God and our neighbour with the whole mind.* Now all the moral virtues, since their acts are prescribed by the precepts of the Law, are reducible to the love of God and of our neighbour, for *love . . . is the fulfilling of the Law* (Rom. xiii. 10). Therefore it would seem that the moral virtues belong to the contemplative life.

Obj. 2. Further, The contemplative life is chiefly directed to the contemplation of God; for Gregory says (*Hom. xiv. in Ezech.*) that *the mind tramples on all cares and longs to gaze on the face of its Creator.* Now no one can accomplish this without cleanness of heart, which is a result of moral virtue. For it is written (Matth. v. 8): *Blessed are the clean of heart, for they shall see God:* and (Heb. xii. 14): *Follow peace with all men, and holiness, without which no man shall see God.* Therefore it would seem that the moral virtues pertain to the contemplative life.

Obj. 3. Further, Gregory says (*Hom. xiv. in Ezech.*) that *the contemplative life gives beauty to the soul,* wherefore it is signified by Rachel, of whom it is said (Gen. xxix. 17) that she was *of a beautiful countenance.* Now the beauty of the soul consists in the moral virtues, especially temperance, as Ambrose says (*De Offic.* i. 43, 45, 46). Therefore it seems that the moral virtues pertain to the contemplative life.

On the contrary, The moral virtues are directed to external actions. Now Gregory says (*Moral.* vi.; *Hom. xiv. in Ezech.*) that it belongs to the contemplative life *to rest from external action.* Therefore the moral virtues do not pertain to the contemplative life.

I answer that, A thing may belong to the contemplative life in two ways, essentially or dispositively. The moral virtues do not belong to the contemplative life essentially, because the end of the contemplative life is the consideration of truth: and as the Philosopher states (*Ethic.* ii. 4), *knowledge,* which pertains to the consideration of truth, *has little influence on the moral virtues:* wherefore he declares (*Ethic.* x. 8) that the moral virtues pertain to active but not to contemplative happiness.

On the other hand, the moral virtues belong to the contemplative life dispositively. For the act of contemplation, wherein the contemplative life essentially consists, is hindered both by the impetuosity of the passions which withdraw the soul's intention from intelligible to sensible things, and by outward disturbances. Now the moral virtues curb the impetuosity of the passions, and quell the disturbance of outward occupations. Hence moral virtues belong dispositively to the contemplative life.

Reply Obj. 1. As stated above (A. 1), the contemplative life has its motive cause on the part of the affections, and in this respect the love of God and our neighbour is requisite to the contemplative life. Now motive causes do not enter into the essence of a thing, but dispose and perfect it. Wherefore it does not follow that the moral virtues belong essentially to the contemplative life.

Reply Obj. 2. Holiness or cleanness of heart is caused by the virtues that are concerned with the passions which hinder the purity of the reason; and peace is caused by justice which is about operations, according to Isa. xxxii. 17, *The work of justice shall be peace:* since he who refrains from wronging others lessens the occasions of quarrels and disturbances. Hence the moral virtues dispose one to the contemplative life by causing peace and cleanness of heart.

Reply Obj. 3. Beauty, as stated above (Q. CXLV., A. 2), consists in a certain clarity and due proportion. Now each of these is found radically in the reason; because both the light that makes beauty seen, and the establishing of due proportion among things belong to reason. Hence since the contemplative life consists in an act of the reason, there is beauty in it by its very nature and essence; wherefore it is written (Wis. viii. 2) of the contemplation of wisdom: *I became a lover of her beauty.*

On the other hand, beauty is in the moral virtues by participation, in so far as they participate the order of reason; and especially is it in temperance, which restrains the concupiscences which especially darken the light of reason. Hence it is that the virtue of chastity most of all makes man apt for contemplation, since venereal pleasures most of all weigh the mind down to sensible objects, as Augustine says (*Soliloq.* i. 10).

THIRD ARTICLE

WHETHER THERE ARE VARIOUS ACTIONS PERTAINING TO THE CONTEMPLATIVE LIFE?

We proceed thus to the Third Article:—

Objection 1. It would seem that there are various actions pertaining to the contemplative life. For Richard of S. Victor distinguishes between *contemplation, meditation,* and *cogitation.* Yet all these apparently pertain to contemplation. Therefore it would seem that there are various actions pertaining to the contemplative life.

Obj. 2. Further, The Apostle says (2. Cor. iii. 18): *But we . . . beholding (speculantes) the glory of the Lord with open face, are transformed into the same clarity.* Now this belongs to the contemplative life. Therefore in addition to the three aforesaid, vision (*speculatio*) belongs to the contemplative life.

Obj. 3. Further, Bernard says (*De Consid.* v. 14) that *the first and greatest contemplation is admiration of the Majesty.* Now according to Damascene (*De Fide Orthod.* ii. 15) admiration is a kind of fear. Therefore it would seem that several acts are requisite for the contemplative life.

Obj. 4. Further, *Prayer, reading,* and *meditation,* are said to belong to the contemplative life. Again, *hearing* belongs to the contemplative life: since it is stated that Mary (by whom the contemplative life is signified) *sitting . . . at the Lord's feet, heard His word* (Luke x. 39). Therefore it would seem that several acts are requisite for the contemplative life.

On the contrary, Life signifies here the operation on which a man is chiefly intent. Wherefore if there are several operations of the contemplative life, there will be, not one, but several contemplative lives.

I answer that, We are now speaking of the contemplative life as applicable to man. Now according to Dionysius (*Div. Nom.* vii.) between man and angel there is this difference, that an angel perceives the truth by simple apprehension, whereas man arrives at the perception of a simple truth by a process from several premises. Accordingly, then, the contemplative life has one act wherein it is finally completed, namely the contemplation of truth, and from this act it derives its unity. Yet it has many acts whereby it arrives at this final act. Some of these pertain to the reception of principles, from which it proceeds to the contemplation of truth; others are concerned with deducing from the principles, the truth the knowledge of which is sought; and the last and crowning act is the contemplation itself of the truth.

Reply Obj. 1. According to Richard of S. Victor *cogitation* would seem to regard the consideration of the many things from which a person intends to gather one simple truth. Hence cogitation may comprise not only the perceptions of the senses in taking cognizance of certain effects, but also the imaginations, and again the reason's discussion of the various signs or of anything that conduces to the truth in view: although according to Augustine (*De Trin.* xiv. 7), cogitation may signify any actual operation of the intellect.—*Meditation* would seem to be the process of reason from certain principles that lead to the contemplation of some truth: and *consideration* has the same meaning, according to Bernard (*De Consid.* ii. 2), although, according to the Philosopher (*De Anima*, ii. 1), every operation of the intellect may be called *consideration*.—But *contemplation* regards the simple act of gazing on the truth; wherefore Richard says again (*ibid.* 4) that *contemplation is the soul's clear and free dwelling upon the object of its gaze; meditation is the survey of the mind while occupied in searching for the truth: and cogitation is the mind's glance which is prone to wander.*

Reply Obj. 2. According to a gloss of Augustine on this passage, *beholding (speculatio)* denotes *seeing in a mirror (speculo), not from a watch-tower (specula).* Now to see a thing in a mirror is to see a cause in its effect wherein its likeness is reflected. Hence *beholding* would seem to be reducible to meditation.

Reply Obj. 3. *Admiration* is a kind of fear resulting from the apprehension of a thing that surpasses our faculties: hence it results from the contemplation of the sublime truth. For it was stated above (A. 1) that contemplation terminates in the affections.

Reply Obj. 4. Man reaches the knowledge of truth in two ways. First, by means of things received from another. In this way, as regards the things he receives from God, he needs *prayer,* according to Wis. vii. 7, *I called upon* God, *and the spirit of wisdom came upon me:* while as regards the things he receives from man, he needs *hearing,* in so far as he receives from the spoken word, and *reading,* in so far as he receives from the tradition of Holy Writ. Secondly, he needs to apply himself by his personal study, and thus he requires *mediation.*

FOURTH ARTICLE

WHETHER THE CONTEMPLATIVE LIFE CONSISTS IN THE MERE CONTEMPLATION OF GOD, OR ALSO IN THE CONSIDERATION OF ANY TRUTH WHATEVER?

We proceed thus to the Fourth Article:—

Objection 1. It would seem that the contemplative life consists not only in the contemplation of God, but also in the consideration of any truth. For it is written (Ps. cxxxviii. 14): *Wonderful are Thy works, and my soul knoweth right well.* Now the knowledge of God's works is effected by any contemplation of the truth. Therefore it would seem that it pertains to the contemplative life to contemplate not only the divine truth, but also any other.

Obj. 2. Further, Bernard says (*De Consid.* v. 14) that *contemplation consists in admiration first of God's majesty, secondly of His judgments, thirdly of His benefits, fourthly of His promises.* Now of these four the first alone regards the divine truth, and the other three pertain to His effects. Therefore the contemplative life consists not only in the contemplation of the divine truth, but also in the consideration of truth regarding the divine effects.

Obj. 3. Further, Richard of S. Victor distinguishes six species of contemplation. The first belongs to *the imagination alone,* and consists in thinking of corporeal things. The second is in *the imagination guided by reason,* and consists in considering the order and disposition of sensible objects. The third is in *the reason based on the imagination;* when, to wit, from the consideration of the visible we rise to the invisible. The fourth is in *the reason and conducted by the reason,* when the mind is intent on things invisible of which the imagination has no cognizance. The fifth is *above the reason,* but not contrary to reason, when by divine revelation we become cognizant of things that cannot be comprehended by the human reason. The sixth is *above reason and contrary to reason;* when, to wit, by the divine enlightening we know things that seem contrary to human reason, such as the doctrine of the mystery of the Trinity. Now only the last of these would seem to pertain to the divine truth. Therefore the contemplation of truth regards not only the divine truth, but also that which is considered in creatures.

Obj. 4. Further, In the contemplative life the contemplation of truth is sought as being the perfection of man. Now any truth is a perfection of the human intellect. Therefore the contemplative life consists in the contemplation of any truth.

On the contrary, Gregory says (*Moral.* vi. 37) that *in contemplation we seek the principle which is God.*

I answer that, As stated above (A. 2), a thing may belong to the contemplative life in two ways: principally, and secondarily or dispositively. That which belongs principally to the contemplative life is the contemplation of the divine truth, because this contemplation is the end of the whole human life. Hence Augustine says (*De Trin.* i. 8) that *the contemplation of God is promised us as being the goal of all our actions and the everlasting perfection of our joys.* This contemplation will be perfect in the life to come, when we shall see God face to face, wherefore it will make us perfectly happy: whereas now the contemplation of the divine truth is competent to us imperfectly, namely *through a glass* and *in a dark manner* (1 Cor. xiii. 12). Hence it bestows on us a certain inchoate beatitude, which begins now and will be continued in the life to come; wherefore the Philosopher (*Ethic.* x. 7) places man's ultimate happiness in the contemplation of the supreme intelligible good.

Since, however, God's effects show us the way to the contemplation of God Himself, according to Rom. i. 20, *The invisible things of God . . . are clearly seen, being understood by the things that are made,* it follows that the contemplation of the divine effects also belongs to the contemplative life, inasmuch as man is guided thereby to the knowledge of God. Hence Augustine says (*De Vera Relig.* xxix.) that *in the study of creatures we must not exercise an empty and futile curiosity, but should make them the stepping-stone to things unperishable and everlasting.*

Accordingly it is clear from what has been said (AA. 1, 2, 3) that four things pertain, in a certain order, to the contemplative life; first, the moral virtues; secondly, other acts exclusive of contemplation; thirdly, contemplation of the divine effects; fourthly, the complement of all which is the contemplation of the divine truth itself.

Reply Obj. 1. David sought the knowledge of God's works, so that he might be led by them to God; wherefore he says elsewhere (Ps. cxlii. 5, 6): *I meditated on all Thy works: I meditated upon the works of Thy hands: I stretched forth my hands to Thee.*

Reply Obj. 2. By considering the divine judgments man is guided to the consideration of the divine justice; and by considering the divine benefits and promises, man is led to the knowledge of God's mercy or goodness, as by effects already manifested or yet to be vouchsafed.

Reply Obj. 3. These six denote the steps whereby we ascend by means of creatures to the contemplation of God. For the first step consists in the mere consideration of sensible objects; the second step consists in going forward from sensible to intelligible objects; the third step is to judge of sensible objects according to intelligible things; the fourth is the absolute consideration of the intelligible objects to which one has attained by means of sensibles; the fifth is the contemplation of those intelligible objects that are unattainable by means of sensibles, but which the reason is able to grasp; the sixth step is the consideration of such intelligible things as the reason can neither discover nor grasp, which pertain to the sublime contemplation of divine truth, wherein contemplation is ultimately perfected.

Reply Obj. 4. The ultimate perfection of the human intellect is the divine truth: and other truths perfect the intellect in relation to the divine truth.

FIFTH ARTICLE

WHETHER IN THE PRESENT STATE OF LIFE THE CONTEMPLATIVE LIFE CAN REACH TO THE VISION OF THE DIVINE ESSENCE?

We proceed thus to the Fifth Article:—

Objection 1. It would seem that in the present state of life the contemplative life can reach to the vision of the Divine essence. For, as stated in Gen. xxxii. 30, Jacob said: *I have seen God face to face, and my soul has been saved.* Now the vision of God's face is the vision of the Divine essence. Therefore it would seem that in the present life one may come, by means of contemplation, to see God in His essence.

Obj. 2. Further, Gregory says (*Moral.* vi. 37) that *contemplative men withdraw within themselves in order to explore spiritual things, nor do they ever carry with them the shadows of things corporeal, or if these follow them they prudently drive them away: but being desirous of seeing the incomprehensible light, they suppress all the images of their limited comprehension, and through longing to reach what is above them, they overcome that which they are.* Now man is not hindered from seeing the Divine essence, which is the incomprehensible light, save by the necessity of turning to corporeal phantasms. Therefore it would seem that the contemplation of the present life can extend to the vision of the incomprehensible light in its essence.

Obj. 3. Further, Gregory says (*Dial.* ii. 35): *All creatures are small to the soul that sees its Creator: wherefore when the man of God,* the blessed Benedict, to wit, *saw a fiery globe in the tower and angels returning to heaven, without doubt he could only see such things by the light of God.* Now the blessed

Benedict was still in this life. Therefore the contemplation of the present life can extend to the vision of the essence of God.

On the contrary, Gregory says (*Hom.* xiv. *in Ezech.*): *As long as we live in this mortal flesh, no one reaches such a height of contemplation as to fix the eyes of his mind on the ray itself of incomprehensible light.*

I answer that, As Augustine says (*Gen. ad Lit.* xii. 27), *no one seeing God lives this mortal life wherein the bodily senses have their play: and unless in some way he depart this life, whether by going altogether out of his body, or by withdrawing from his carnal senses, he is not caught up into that vision.* This has been carefully discussed above (Q. CLXXV., AA. 4, 5), where we spoke of rapture, and in the First Part (Q. XII., A. 2), where we treated of the vision of God.

Accordingly we must state that one may be in this life in two ways. First, with regard to act, that is to say by actually making use of the bodily senses, and thus contemplation in the present life can nowise attain to the vision of God's essence. Secondly, one may be in this life potentially and not with regard to act, that is to say, when the soul is united to the mortal body as its form, yet so as to make use neither of the bodily senses, nor even of the imagination, as happens in rapture; and in this way the contemplation of the present life can attain to the vision of the Divine essence. Consequently the highest degree of contemplation in the present life is that which Paul had in rapture, whereby he was in a middle state between the present life and the life to come.

Reply Obj. 1. As Dionysius says (*Ep.* i. *ad Caium. Monach.*), *if anyone seeing God, understood what he saw, he saw not God Himself, but something belonging to God.* And Gregory says (*Hom.* xiv. *in Ezech.*): *By no means is God seen now in His glory; but the soul sees something of lower degree, and is thereby refreshed so that afterwards it may attain to the glory of vision.* Accordingly the words of Jacob, *I saw God face to face* do not imply that he saw God's essence, but that he saw some shape, imaginary of course, wherein God spoke to him.— Or, *since we know a man by his face, by the face of God he signified his knowledge of Him,* according to a gloss of Gregory on the same passage.

Reply Obj. 2. In the present state of life human contemplation is impossible without phantasms, because it is connatural to man to see the intelligible species in the phantasms, as the Philosopher states (*De Anima*, iii. 7). Yet intellectual knowledge does not consist in the phantasms themselves, but in our contemplating in them the purity of the intelligible truth: and this not only in natural knowledge, but also in that which we obtain by revelation. For Dionysius says (*Cœl. Hier.* i.) that *the Divine glory shows us the angelic hierarchies under certain symbolic figures, and by its power we are brought back to the single ray of light,* i.e. to the simple knowledge of the intelligible truth. It is in this sense that we must understand the statement of Gregory that *contemplatives do not carry along with them the shadows of things corporeal,* since their contemplation is not fixed on them, but on the consideration of the intelligible truth.

Reply Obj. 3. By these words Gregory does not imply that the blessed Benedict, in that vision, saw God in His essence, but he wishes to show that because *all creatures are small to him that sees God,* it follows that all things can easily be seen through the enlightenment of the Divine light. Wherefore he adds: *For however little he may see of the Creator's light, all created things become petty to him.*

SIXTH ARTICLE

WHETHER THE OPERATION OF CONTEMPLATION IS FITTINGLY
DIVIDED INTO A THREEFOLD MOVEMENT, CIRCULAR,
STRAIGHT, AND OBLIQUE?

We proceed thus to the Sixth Article:—

Objection 1. It would seem that the operation of contemplation is unfittingly divided into a threefold movement, *circular, straight,* and *oblique* (*Div. Nom.* iv.). For contemplation pertains exclusively to rest, according to Wis. viii. 16, *When I go into my house; I shall repose myself with her.* Now movement is opposed to rest. Therefore the operations of the contemplative life should not be described as movements.

Obj. 2. Further, The action of the contemplative life pertains to the intellect, whereby man is like the angels. Now

286

Dionysius describes these movements as being different in the angels from what they are in the soul. For he says (*loc. cit.*) that the *circular* movement in the angel is *according to his enlightenment by the beautiful and the good.* On the other hand, he assigns the circular movement of the soul to several things: the first of which is the *withdrawal of the soul into itself from externals;* the second is *a certain concentration of its powers, whereby it is rendered free of error and of outward occupation;* and the third is *union with those things that are above it.*—Again, he describes differently their respective straight movements. For he says that the straight movement of the angel is that by which he proceeds to the care of those things that are beneath him. On the other hand, he describes the straight movement of the soul as being twofold: first, *its uplifting from external things to simple contemplation.*—Further, he assigns a different oblique movement to each. For he assigns the oblique movement of the angels to the fact that *while providing for those who have less they remain unchanged in relation to God:* whereas he assigns the oblique movement of the soul to the fact that *the soul is enlightened in Divine knowledge by reasoning and discoursing.*—Therefore it would seem that the operations of contemplation are unfittingly assigned according to the ways mentioned above.

Obj. 3. Further, Richard of S. Victor (*De Contempl.* i. 5) mentions many other different movements in likeness to the birds of the air. *For some of these rise at one time to a great height, at another swoop down to earth, and they do so repeatedly; others fly now to the right, now to the left again and again; others go forwards or lag behind many times; others fly in a circle now more now less extended; and others remain suspended almost immovably in one place.* Therefore it would seem that there are only three movements of contemplation.

On the contrary, stands the authority of Dionysius (*loc. cit.*)

I answer that, As stated above (Q. CLXXIX., A. 1, *ad* 3), the operation of the intellect, wherein contemplation essentially consists, is called a movement, in so far as movement is the act of a perfect thing, according to the Philosopher (*De Anima,* iii. 7). Since, however, it is through sensible objects that we come to the knowledge of intelligible things, and since sensible operations do not take place without movement, the result is that even intelligible operations are described as movements, and are differentiated in likeness to various movements. Now of bodily movements, local movements are the most perfect and come first, as proved in *Phys.* viii. 7; wherefore the foremost among intelligible operations are described by being likened to them. These movements are of three kinds; for there is the *circular* movement, by which a thing moves uniformly round one point as centre, another is the *straight* movement, by which a thing goes from one point to another; the third is *oblique,* being composed as it were of both the others. Consequently, in intelligible operations, that which is simply uniform is compared to circular movement; the intelligible operation by which one proceeds from one point to another is compared to the straight movement; while the intelligible operation which unites something of uniformity with progress to various points is compared to the oblique movement.

Reply Obj. 1. External bodily movements are opposed to the quiet of contemplation, which consists in rest from outward occupations: but the movements of intellectual operations belong to the quiet of contemplation.

Reply Obj. 2. Man is like the angels in intellect generically, but the intellective power is much higher in the angel than in man. Consequently these movements must be ascribed to souls and angels in different ways, according as they are differently related to uniformity. For the angelic intellect has uniform knowledge in two respects. First, because it does not acquire intelligible truth from the variety of composite objects; secondly, because it understands the truth of intelligible objects not discursively, but by simple intuition. On the other hand, the intellect of the soul acquires intelligible truth from sensible objects, and understands it by a certain discoursing of the reason.

Wherefore Dionysius assigns the *circular* movement of the angels to the fact that their intuition of God is uniform and unceasing, having neither beginning nor end: even as a circular movement having neither beginning nor end is uniformly around the one same centre. But on the part of the soul, ere it arrive at this uniformity, its twofold lack of uniformity needs to be removed. First, that which arises from the variety of external things: this is removed by the soul withdrawing from externals, and so the first thing he mentions regarding the circular movement of the soul is *the soul's withdrawal into itself from external objects.*—Secondly, another lack of uniformity requires to be removed from the soul, and this is owing to the discoursing of reason. This is done by directing all the soul's operations to the simple contemplation of the intelligible truth, and this is indicated by his saying in the second place that *the soul's intellectual powers must be uniformly concentrated,* in other words that discoursing must be laid aside and the soul's gaze fixed on the contemplation of the one simple truth. In this operation of the soul there is no error, even as there is clearly no error in the understanding of first principles which we know by simple intuition. Afterwards these two things being done, he mentions thirdly the uniformity which is like that of the angels, for then all things being laid aside, the soul continues in the contemplation of God alone. This he expresses by saying: *Then being thus made uniform unitedly,* i.e. conformably, *by the union of its powers, it is conducted to the good and the beautiful.* The *straight* movement of the angel cannot apply to his proceeding from one thing to another by considering them, but only to the order of his providence, namely to the fact that the higher angel enlightens the lower angels through the angels that are intermediate. He indicates this when he says: *The angel's movement takes a straight line when he proceeds to the care of things subject to him, taking in his course whatever things are direct,* i.e. in keeping with the dispositions of the direct order. Whereas he ascribes the *straight* movement in the soul to the soul's proceeding from exterior sensibles to the knowledge of intelligible objects. The *oblique* movement in the angels he describes as being composed of the straight and circular movements, inasmuch as their care for those beneath them is in accordance with their contemplation of God: while the *oblique* movement in the soul he also declares to be partly straight and partly circular, in so far as in reasoning it makes use of the light received from God.

Reply Obj. 3. These varieties of movement that are taken from the distinction between above and below, right and left, forwards and backwards, and from varying circles, are all comprised under either straight and oblique movement, because they all denote discursions of reason. For if the reason pass from the genus to the species, or from the part to the whole, it will be, as he explains, from above to below: if from one opposite to another, it will be from right to left; if from the cause to the effect, it will be backwards and forwards; if it be about accidents that surround a thing near at hand or far remote, the movement will be circular. The discoursing of reason from sensible to intelligible objects, if it be according to the order of natural reason, belongs to the straight movement; but if it be according to the Divine enlightenment, it will belong to the oblique movement as explained above (*ad* 2). That alone which he describes as immobility belongs to the circular movement.

Wherefore it is evident that Dionysius describes the movement of contemplation with much greater fulness and depth.

SEVENTH ARTICLE

WHETHER THERE IS DELIGHT IN CONTEMPLATION?

We proceed thus to the Seventh Article:—

Objection 1. It would seem that there is no delight in contemplation. For delight belongs to the appetitive power; whereas contemplation resides chiefly in the intellect. Therefore it would seem that there is no delight in contemplation.

Obj. 2. Further, All strife and struggle is a hindrance to delight. Now there is strife and struggle in contemplation. For Gregory says (*Hom.* xiv. *in Ezech.*) that *when the soul strives to contemplate God, it is in a state of struggle; at one time it almost overcomes, because by understanding and feeling it tastes something of the incomprehensible light, and at another time it almost succumbs, because even while tasting it fails.* Therefore there is no delight in contemplation.

Obj. 3 Further, Delight is the result of a perfect operation, as stated in *Ethic.* x. 4. Now the contemplation of wayfarers is imperfect, according to 1 Cor. xiii. 12, *We see now through a glass in a dark manner.* Therefore seemingly there is no delight in the contemplative life.

Obj. 4. Further, A lesion of the body is an obstacle to delight. Now contemplation causes a lesion of the body; wherefore it is stated (*Gen.* xxxii.) that after Jacob had said (*verse* 30) *'I have seen God face to face'* ... *he halted on his foot (31)* ... *because he touched the sinew of his thigh and it shrank (32).* Therefore seemingly there is no delight in contemplation.

On the contrary, It is written of the contemplation of wisdom (Wis. viii. 16): *Her conversation hath no bitterness, nor her company any tediousness, but joy and gladness:* and Gregory says (*Hom.* xiv. *in Ezech.*) that *the contemplative life is sweetness exceedingly lovable.*

I answer that, There may be delight in any particular contemplation in two ways. First by reason of the operation itself, because each individual delights in the operation which befits him according to his own nature or habit. Now contemplation of the truth befits a man according to his nature as a rational animal: the result being that *all men naturally desire to know,* so that consequently they delight in the knowledge of truth. And more delightful still does this become to one who has the habit of wisdom and knowledge, the result of which is that he contemplates without difficulty. Secondly, contemplation may be delightful on the part of its object, in so far as one contemplates that which one loves; even as bodily vision gives pleasure, not only because to see is pleasurable in itself, but because one sees a person whom one loves. Since, then, the contemplative life consists chiefly in the contemplation of God, of which charity is the motive, as stated above (AA. 1, 2, *ad* 1), it follows that there is delight in the contemplative life, not only by reason of the contemplation itself, but also by reason of the Divine love.

In both respects the delight thereof surpasses all human delight, both because spiritual delight is greater than carnal pleasure, as stated above (I.-II., Q. XXXI., A. 5), when we were treating of the passions, and because the love whereby God is loved out of charity surpasses all love. Hence it is written (Ps. xxxiii. 9): *O taste and see that the Lord is sweet.*

Reply Obj. 1. Although the contemplative life consists chiefly in an act of the intellect, it has its beginning in the appetite, since it is through charity that one is urged to the contemplation of God. And since the end corresponds to the beginning, it follows that the term also and the end of the contemplative life has its being in the appetite, since one delights in seeing the object loved, and the very delight in the object seen arouses a yet greater love. Wherefore Gregory says (*Hom.* xiv. *in Ezech.*) that *when we see one whom we love, we are so aflame as to love him more.* And this is the ultimate perfection of the contemplative life, namely that the Divine truth be not only seen but also loved.

Reply Obj. 2. Strife or struggle arising from the opposition of an external thing, hinders delight in that thing. For a man delights not in a thing against which he strives: but in that for which he strives; when he has obtained it, other things being equal, he delights yet more: wherefore Augustine says (*Conf.* viii. 3) that *the more peril there was in the battle, the greater the joy in the triumph.* But there is no strife or struggle in contemplation on the part of the truth which we contemplate, though there is on the part of our defective understanding and our corruptible body which drags us down to lower things, according to Wis. ix. 15, *The corruptible body is a load upon the soul, and the earthly habitation presseth down the mind that museth upon many things.* Hence it is that when man attains to the contemplation of truth, he loves it yet more, while he hates the more his own deficiency and the weight of his corruptible body, so as to say with the Apostle (Rom. vii. 24): *Unhappy man that I am, who shall deliver me from the body of this death?* Wherefore Gregory says (*Hom.* xiv. *in Ezech.*): *When God is once known by desire and understanding, He withers all carnal pleasure in us.*

Reply Obj. 3. The contemplation of God in this life is imperfect in comparison with the contemplation in heaven; and in like manner the delight of the wayfarer's contemplation is imperfect as compared with the delight of contemplation in heaven, of which it is written (Ps. xxxv. 9): *Thou shalt make them drink of the torrent of Thy pleasure.* Yet, though the contemplation of Divine things which is to be had by wayfarers is imperfect, it is more delightful than all other contemplation however perfect, on account of the excellence of that which is contemplated. Hence the Philosopher says (*De Part. Animal.* i. 5): *We may happen to have our own little theories about those sublime beings and godlike substances, and though we grasp them but feebly, nevertheless so elevating is the knowledge that they give us more delight than any of those things that are round about us:* and Gregory says in the same sense (*loc. cit.*): *The contemplative life is sweetness exceedingly lovable; for it carries the soul away above itself, it opens heaven and discovers the spiritual world to the eyes of the mind.*

Reply Obj. 4. After contemplation Jacob halted with one foot, *because we need to grow weak in the love of the world ere we wax strong in the love of God,* as Gregory says (*loc. cit.*). *Thus when we have known the sweetness of God, we have one foot sound while the other halts; since every one who halts on one foot leans only on that foot which is sound.*

EIGHTH ARTICLE

WHETHER THE CONTEMPLATIVE LIFE IS CONTINUOUS?

We proceed thus to the Eighth Article:—

Objection 1. It would seem that the contemplative life is not continuous. For the contemplative life consists essentially in things pertaining to the intellect. Now all the intellectual perfections of this life will be made void, according to 1 Cor. xiii. 8, *Whether prophecies shall be made void, or tongues shall cease, or knowledge shall be destroyed.* Therefore the contemplative life is made void.

Obj. 2. Further, A man tastes the sweetness of contemplation by snatches and for a short time only: wherefore Augustine says (*Conf.* x. 40), *Thou admittest me to a most unwonted affection in my inmost soul, to a strange sweetness, . . . yet through my grievous weight I sink down again.* Again, Gregory commenting on the words of Job iv. 15, *When a spirit passed before me,* says (*Moral.* v. 33): *The mind does not remain long at rest in the sweetness of inward contemplation, for it is recalled to itself and beaten back by the very immensity of the light.* Therefore the contemplative life is not continuous.

Obj. 3. Further, That which is not connatural to man cannot be continuous. Now the contemplative life, according to the Philosopher (*Ethic.* x. 7), *is better than the life which is according to man.* Therefore seemingly the contemplative life is not continuous.

On the contrary, Our Lord said (Luke x. 42): *Mary hath chosen the best part, which shall not be taken away from her,* since as Gregory says (*Hom.* xiv. *in Ezech.*), *the contemplative life begins here so as it may be perfected in our heavenly home.*

I answer that, A thing may be described as continuous in two ways: first, in regard to its nature; secondly, in regard to us. It is evident that in regard to itself contemplative life is continuous for two reasons: first, because it is about incorruptible and unchangeable things; secondly, because it has no contrary, for there is nothing contrary to the pleasure of contemplation, as stated in *Top.* i. 13. But even in our regard contemplative life is continuous,—both because it is competent to us in respect of the incorruptible part of the soul, namely the intellect, wherefore it can endure after this life,—and because in the works of the contemplative life we work not with our bodies, so that we are the more able to persevere in the works thereof, as the Philosopher observes (*Ethic.* x. 7).

Reply Obj. 1. The manner of contemplation is not the same here as in heaven: yet the contemplative life is said to remain by reason of charity, wherein it has both its beginning and its end. Gregory speaks in this sense (*Hom.* xiv. *in Ezech.*): *The contemplative life begins here, so as to be perfected in our heavenly home, because the fire of love which begins to burn here is aflame with a yet greater love when we see Him Whom we love.*

Reply Obj. 2. No action can last long at its highest pitch. Now the highest point of contemplation is to reach the uniformity of Divine contemplation, according to Dionysius, and as we have stated above (A. 6, *ad* 2). Hence although contemplation cannot last long in this respect, it can be of long duration as regards the other contemplative acts.

Reply Obj. 3. The Philosopher declares the contemplative life to be above man, because it befits us *so far as there is in us something divine (loc. cit.),* namely the intellect, which is incorruptible and impassible in itself, wherefore its act can endure longer.

Meister Eckhart
1260-1327

Pain and suffering are built into the structures of the human condition. One of the traditional efforts of spiritual writers is to reflect on this phenomenon and to give it an interpretation that in some way enriches the human who suffers. The following selection, taken from the treatises of Meister Eckhart, is entitled The Book of Divine Consolation. *In it, Eckhart presents an approach to suffering that is designed to comfort any man, no matter what his sorrow or pain may be. It reveals a highly intellectual treatment of human suffering. Eckhart establishes certain basic theses and is convinced that the person who understands the theses can accept suffering positively and joyously. Thus, God's will for mankind is the primary explanation of all pain and sorrow. Even sin, in some way, is willed by God. The just and good man knows this and therefore rejoices in his misfortune. He wills what God wills and finds his comfort in God alone. No matter what the particular type of suffering, be it poor health, loss of friend, family, reputation or fortune, there is always a way to see that whatever happened must be God's will.*

The ultimate reason why one suffers is the pure and simple fact that one is far from God and not free from creatures; one is unlike God and cold in divine love. The corrective for this is the way of negation (a person must empty out all earthly and human desires) which leads to the filling up of one's soul with true, heavenly desires. One must learn to detest created goods, for the fact that everything has been bestowed on man as a loan. One must remember this always and never grow attached to things other than the divine.

There is something cold about this particular approach to the spiritual life. Even when he speaks of love and fervor, Eckhart does so in such a logical manner that they take on the appearance of the "other-than-human." Though it may have a certain appeal for the person with an intellectual bent, one wonders how rich an approach to spirituality it ultimately can be.

Meister Eckhart was born in Thuringia around 1260. He was a member of the Dominican Order. He studied at Paris and Cologne, two important centers of learning in his day. His life was divided between administration and teaching. The major influences on his thinking were Thomas Aquinas and the neo-platonist philosophy available at the time. Eckhart is considered to be a good example of the school of spirituality that developed in the Rhineland during the late thirteenth and fourteenth centuries. The writers from this school were particularly concerned with the theme of union with God by way of contemplation and abnegation. They stressed divine transcendence yet contended that the infinite being of God was at the center of all creatures, especially the human. At its most profound level, the soul is one with God. However, man is free to choose not to live this union. Perfect union consists in returning to God by way of contemplation and by going beyond all creatures to the one true Being.

Toward the end of his life his own concept of suffering was put to the test. In 1326, the Archbishop of Cologne designated two inquisitors to examine his teaching. In spite of his efforts to justify himself, the list of questionable propositions was forwarded to the Holy See. He died before his case was decided. Though portions of his teachings were condemned in 1329, the greater part of his doctrine was judged to be acceptable to church authorities. Eckhart had an influence on the development of German spirituality from the fourteenth to the sixteenth centuries.

THE BOOK OF
DIVINE CONSOLATION

The noble Apostle St. Paul says these words: 'Blessed be God and the Father of our Lord Jesus Christ, the Father of all mercies and God of all comfort, who comforteth us in all our tribulation.' There are three kinds of tribulations or troubles that affect men and afflict them in this world. The first is due to the loss of outward possessions and the second to the losses of his relations or his friends. The third affects himself, in dishonour, in distress, in pain of the body and sorrow of the heart.

Hence I intend to impart in this book some instruction by which a man may be comforted in all his distress, trouble and pain. This book has three parts. In the first one will find some truths out of which and from which something may be derived that can and will rightly and indeed fully comfort a man in all his trouble. After this one will find some thirty sections and instructive observations, in each of which one can be well and fully comforted. Afterwards, in the third part of this book, there are examples taken from the works and words that wise people have done and said when they were in trouble.

I

First, one should know that the wise man and wisdom, the truthful man and truth, the just man and justice, the good man and goodness concern each other and are related to each other in the following way: goodness is neither created nor made nor born, but it bears and brings forth the good man; and the good man, in so far as he is good, is not made and uncreated, and yet born as the child and son of goodness. Goodness gives birth to itself, and to everything that it is, in the good man. It pours being, knowledge, love and activity all together into the good man, and the good man receives all his being, knowledge, love and activity from the heart and the inmost depths of goodness

and from her alone. The Good and goodness are but one goodness, entirely one in all things, apart from bearing and being born.
Yet the bearing of goodness and the being born in the good man
are all one being and one life. All that belongs to the good man
he receives both from goodness and in goodness. There he is and
lives and dwells. There he knows himself and everything that he
knows, and loves everything that he loves, and he works with
goodness in goodness, and goodness works all her works with
him and in him, as the Son says in the Scriptures: 'The Father
dwelleth in Me and doeth the works', 'The Father worketh hitherto and I work', 'All that is the Father's is Mine and all that is
Mine and of My own is My Father's.' It is His giving and my
receiving.

Further, one should know that, when we say 'good', this
word signifies and includes in itself nothing but pure and un-
adulterated goodness, neither more nor less; yet it gives itself.
When we say 'good', we imply that man's goodness is given to
him, poured in and begotten by the unbegotten Goodness. Therefore the Gospel says: 'As the Father hath life in Himself, so hath
He given to the Son, that He also may have life in Himself.' He
says 'in Himself', not 'from Himself', for the Father gave it to
Him.

Everything that I have now said of the good man and of
goodness is equally true of the truthful man and truth, of the
just man and justice, of the wise man and wisdom, of the Son of
God and God the Father, of everything that is born of God and
that has no father on earth, in which nothing that is created is
born, nor anything that is not God, in which there is no image
save God alone, purely and simply. For St. John says in his Gospel: 'To all those is given the power to become sons of God who
were born, not of the blood or the will of the flesh or the will
of man, but of and from God alone.'

By the blood he means everything in man that is not subject to man's will. By the will of the flesh he means everything
in man that is subject to his will, yet with opposition and with a
struggle. It tends towards the desires of the flesh and is common
to the soul and the body and is not really in the soul alone, and
hence these powers become tired, weak and old. By the will of
man St. John means the highest powers of the soul, whose nature

and work are unmixed with the flesh, but which stand in the purity of the soul, separated from time and place and from everything that is in any way related to, or savours of, time and place, which have nothing in common with anything. In them man is created in the image of God; in them he is of God's lineage and His family. And yet, since they themselves are not God, but were created in the soul and with the soul, they must be stripped of themselves and transformed into God alone, and born in God and from God, so that God alone may be their father, for in this way they are also sons of God and the only-begotten son of God. For I am the son of everything which forms me and gives birth to me in its image and likeness. A man so fashioned, God's son, being good as the son of goodness, just as the son of justice, in so far as he is her son alone, then she is unborn and yet bearing, and the son to whom she gives birth has the self-same being as justice has and is, and he enters into all the properties of justice and truth.

From all this instruction, which is written in the holy Gospels and recognized as certain in the natural light of the rational soul, man finds true comfort in all his sufferings.

St. Augustine says: 'God is neither far away nor long.' If you want nothing to be far away and long, submit to God, for with Him a thousand years are but as today. Thus, I say, in God there is no sadness, nor pain, nor suffering. If you would be free from all suffering and pain, cleave to God and turn whole-heartedly to Him alone. Assuredly all pain only comes from the fact that you do not turn to God and towards God alone. If you stood formed in justice alone and born in her, then indeed nothing could harm you, just as little as justice could harm God Himself. Solomon says: 'The just will not be troubled by anything that can happen to them.' He does not say 'the just man', nor 'the just angel', nor this nor that. He says 'the just'. Whatever belongs in any way to the just, in particular, what is their justice, and the fact that they are just, all that is a son, and has a father on earth and is a creature, and is made and created, for its father is a creature, made or created. But since pure justice has not a created father, and as God and justice are completely one, and justice alone is its father, therefore pain and suffering can no more affect the just than they can affect God. Justice cannot harm them, for all joy, pleasure and happiness are justice, and moreover, if justice made the just suffer, she would herself suffer also. Unlikeness and injustice could not make the just suffer, nor could anything made or created, for everything that is created is far beneath them, as far as it is beneath God, and it has no impress or influence on the just, nor is it born in them, whose father is God alone.

Hence man should diligently strive to strip himself of himself and of all creature, and to know no father, save only God. Then nothing can cause him pain or trouble him, neither God nor creature, neither created nor uncreated things, and all his being, living, knowing and loving is from God and in God, and it is God.

There is a second thing that one should know, which also comforts man in all his distress. This is that the just and good man certainly rejoices unequally; indeed he rejoices inexpressibly more in the work of justice than he, or even the highest angel, has joy and happiness in his natural being or life. And for this reason the saints gladly gave their lives for the sake of justice.

Now I will say that when the good and just man suffers eternal injury, provided that he remains in a state of equanimity and in peace of mind, then it is true, as I have said, that the just man is not troubled by anything that befalls him. If, however, he is troubled by the external injury, then indeed it is right and fitting that God should have decreed that the injury should befall the man who wished and believed himself to be just, although such small matters were able to trouble him. If it is then God's law, indeed he should not be troubled by it, but he should be glad of it, much more than of his own life, of which nevertheless every man is more glad and which he values more highly than the whole of this world. For what would the whole of this world avail a man if he did not exist?

The third fact that one may and should know is that in natural truth God alone is the one spring and artery of all goodness, of essential truth and comfort. Everything that is not God has of itself natural bitterness and despair and pain, and adds nothing at all to goodness, which is from God and is God. On the contrary, it diminishes and conceals and hides the sweetness, joy and comfort which God gives.

302

Now I will say further that all pain comes from the love of those things of which loss has robbed me. If then the loss of external things causes me sorrow, that is a true sign that I love external things, and that thus I really love sorrow and despair. What wonder is it that I suffer when I love and seek sorrow and despair? My heart and my love give to the creatures that goodness which is God's property. I turn to the creatures, from which despair comes by nature, and turn away from God, from whom all comfort flows forth. What wonder is it then that I suffer and am sad? Truly, it is indeed impossible with God and the whole world that the man who seeks comfort in the creatures should find true comfort. But he who loved God alone in the creature and the creatures in God alone, would find true, rightful and unvarying comfort in all directions. Let this suffice for the first part of this book.

II

There now follow in the Second Part some thirty sections, each one of which alone should fittingly comfort a rational man in his grief.

The first thing is this: that there is no suffering or loss without some comfort, neither is there any loss that is sheer loss. Hence St. Paul says that God's faithfulness and goodness do not allow any trial or trouble to be unbearable. He creates and bestows at all times some comfort of which one can avail oneself, for the sacred and the pagan masters also say that God and nature do not allow pure evil or pain to exist.

Now suppose that a man has a hundred marks. He loses forty and keeps sixty. If this man thinks continually of the forty that he has lost, he will remain in despair and grief. How could he be comforted and free from sorrow if he turns to his loss and his pain and pictures it to himself and himself in it, and looks at it, and it looks at him again and talks to him? He speaks to his loss and the loss talks to him again, and they see each other face to face. But if he were to turn his attention to the sixty marks that he still has and if he turned his back on the forty that are lost, concentrating on the sixty and looking at them face to face and talking to them, he would certainly be comforted. That which is something and is good, has the power to comfort,

303

but what is nothing and is not good, what is not mine and is lost to me, must necessarily give despair and pain and distress. Hence Solomon says: 'In the days of pain forget not the days of goodness.' That means, when you are in pain and suffering, remember the good and the comfort that you still have and retain. It should also comfort a man if he were to remember how many thousand persons there are who, if they had the sixty marks that you still possess, would think they were lords and ladies and feel very wealthy and truly happy.

Then there is a second point that should comfort a man. If he is sick and in great bodily pain, he still has his house and what he needs as to food and drink, the physicians' attendance and domestic service. He has the sympathy and the presents of his friends. What ought he to do? What do poor people do who endure the same or more severe illness and suffering, and have no one even to give them water? They must seek their very bread in rain, cold and snow from house to house. Therefore, if you would be comforted, forget those who are better placed and remember only those who are less fortunate.

I will go further. All suffering comes from love and affection. Therefore, if I suffer because of transient things, I still have, and my heart still has, love and affection for transient things, and I do not love God with all my heart, and I do not yet love what God would have me love, and join with Him in loving it. What wonder is it that God should decree that I should quite rightly suffer loss and pain?

St. Augustine says: 'Lord, I did not wish to lose Thee, but in my avarice I wanted to possess the creatures besides Thee, and therefore I lost Thee, because it is repugnant to Thee that one should possess the falsehood and deception of the creatures together with Thee, the Truth.' He also says elsewhere that 'he is far too avaricious who is not satisfied with God alone'. And in another place he says: 'How could he be satisfied with God's gifts to the creatures who is not satisfied with God Himself?' For a good man everything that is alien to God and unlike Him, and that is not God Himself alone, should be pain, not comfort. He should say at all times: 'Lord God, my consolation, if Thou turnest me away from Thee, then give me another Thee, that I may go from Thee to Thee, because I do not want anything but

Thee.' When our Lord promised Moses everything good and sent him into the Holy Land, which means heaven, Moses said: 'Lord, send me nowhere, unless Thou Thyself comest with me.'

All inclination, pleasure and love come from that which is similar, because all things are inclined to and love what is like them. The pure man loves all purity, the just man loves justice and inclines toward it. The mouth of man speaks of that which is within him, as our Lord says: 'Of the abundance of the heart his mouth speaketh.' And Solomon says that 'The labour of man is in his mouth'. Hence this is a true sign that not God, but the creatures, are in the heart of the man who still finds affection and comfort outside.

For this reason a good man should be very much ashamed before God and in his own eyes if he is still aware that God is not in him, and God the Father does not perform the works in him, but the evil creature still lives in him and influences him and does its works in him. Hence King David speaks and complains in the Psalter: 'Tears have been my comfort day and night, as long as they said unto me, Where is thy God?' For to be inclined to external things, to find consolation in despair, to speak of these things gladly and with pleasure and frequently, all this is a true sign that God does not show Himself in me, nor watch, nor work in me. Further, he should also be ashamed in the presence of good people, because they notice these things in him. A good man should never complain of loss or suffering; he should complain only because he complains and because he becomes aware of complaint and suffering in himself.

The masters say that immediately below the sky there is fire stretching far and wide and powerful in its heat, and yet the sky is not in the least affected by it. Now a writer says that the lowest part of the soul is higher than the highest part of the heavens. How then can man boast that he is a heavenly man and that his heart is in heaven, if he is still troubled and saddened by such small matters?

Now I will say something else. There cannot be a good man who does not want what God wants in particular cases, for it is impossible that God should will anything but good; and especially in and from the fact that God wills it, it is, and must needs be good and also the very best. And therefore our Lord taught the Apostles and us through them, and we pray every day that God's will may be done. And yet, when God's will comes and is done, we complain.

Seneca, a heathen master, asked: 'What is the best comfort in suffering and pain?' And he answered. 'It is that a man should take all things as if he had wished for them and prayed for them. For you would indeed have wished for them if you had known that all things happen because of, with and in God's will'. A pagan master says: 'King and supreme Father and Lord of high heaven, I am prepared for everything that Thou willest. Give me the will to will according to Thy will.'

A good man should trust God, believe Him and be assured and should know God to be so good that it would be impossible for God and His goodness and love to allow any pain or suffering to come to man, unless He wished either to take away greater pain from man, or to comfort him more abundantly on earth, or to make something better from it and out of it, by which God's glory would be more widely and more highly manifested. But however that may be, simply for that reason that it is God's will that it should happen, the will of a good man ought also to be so completely one with God's will and united to it that man wills the same thing as God, although it should lead to his loss and even to his damnation. Hence St. Paul wished that he might be separated from God for the sake of God and for Him and for His glory. For a truly perfect man should be accustomed to be dead to himself, stripped of himself in God, and so conformed to God's will that his whole happiness consists in not knowing himself or anything but God alone, to will nothing nor to know anything but God's will and to wish to know God as God knows me, as St. Paul says. God knows everything that he knows and loves. God wills everything that he loves and wills in himself, in his own will. Our Lord says Himself: 'Eternal life is to know God alone.'

Hence the masters say that the blessed in heaven know the creatures without any images of the creatures; they know them in the one image that is God, in which God knows Himself and all things, and loves and wills them. And God himself teaches us to pray for and to ask for this when we say 'Our Father . . . hallowed be Thy name', that is, to know Thee alone and Thee only; 'Thy kingdom come', that I may have nothing that I consider rich and know nothing but Thy riches. Hence the Gospel says: 'Blessed are the poor in spirit', that is, in the will; and we pray to God that His 'will be done on earth', that is, in us, 'as in heaven', that is, in God Himself.

Such a man is so one-willed with God that he wills everything that God wills and in the same way as God wills it. And therefore, since in a certain sense God wills that I should have sinned, I should not want not to have done it, for thus God's will is done on earth, that is, in sin, as in heaven, that is, in virtue. In this way man will renounce God for the sake of God and be separated from God for God's sake, and that alone is true repentance for my sins. Then my sin gives me pain without pain, as God is pained by all wickedness without pain. I have pain, and indeed the greatest possible pain, for sin, because I would not commit a sin for the sake of anything created or creatable, even if a thousand worlds could exist eternally, but without pain. And I take and receive the pain in God's will and from God's will. Such pain alone is perfectly painful, for it comes and originates in the pure love of the goodness and joy of God. Thus it becomes true and one becomes aware, as I have said in this little book, that a good man, in so far as he is good, enters into all the properties of goodness itself, which is God in Himself.

Now notice, what a wonderful and happy life this man has on earth, as in heaven, in God Himself! Discomfort serves as comfort to him, grief is the same as joy, and yet notice that in all this there is a special consolation. If I have the grace and the goodness of which I have just spoken, I am at all times and in all respects equally well comforted and cheerful. If I have nothing of it I should do without it for the sake of God and in pursuance of His will. If God will give what I desire, then I have it and am joyful. If God will not give it, then I receive it in its absence in God's will, in which He does not will it, and thus I receive it by renouncing it and not by receiving it. What then do I lack? And certainly one receives God more truly by renouncing than by receiving, for when a man receives, the gift has in itself the reason why he is joyful and comforted. But if one does not receive, one has nothing and knows nothing to rejoice in but God and God's will alone.

But there is also another consolation. If a man has lost external goods, or his friend, or his relative, an eye, a hand, or whatever it may be, he should be certain that if he suffers it patiently for the sake of God, then he has at least all that to his credit with God, for the sake of which he did not wish to suffer the loss. If a man loses an eye: if he would not have been without the eye for a thousand or for six thousand marks or more, then he has before God and in God certainly retained everything in exchange for which he would not have suffered the loss or the pain. And perhaps this explains the words spoken by our Lord: 'It is better to enter into eternal life with one eye than to go to perdition with two eyes.' The same meaning was perhaps also expressed by God when He said: 'He who forsaketh father and mother, sister and brother, farm or field, or whatever it may be, shall receive an hundredfold and eternal life.' Certainly, I make bold to say in God's truth and by my hopes of salvation, that if anyone for the sake of God and of goodness forsakes father and mother, brother and sister, or whatever it may be, he receives a hundredfold in two ways. The first is that his father, mother, brother and sister will become a hundred times dearer than they now are. The second is that not just a hundred, but all people, as far as they are people and human beings, will become incomparably dearer to him than now his father, mother or brother are dear by nature. If a man is not aware of this, it is due entirely to the fact that he has not yet purely, for the sake of God and goodness alone, and entirely, forsaken father and mother, sister and brother and all things.

In what sense has such a man forsaken father and mother, sister and brother for God's sake, if he still finds them on earth in his heart, if he is still troubled and remembers and considers what is not God? How has a man forsaken all things for God's sake if he still regards and considers this or that good? St. Augustine says: 'Take this away and that good, and there remains pure goodness, hovering in itself in its simple extent, that is God.' For, as I said above, this and that good add nothing at all to goodness, but they conceal and hide the goodness in us. If anyone sees that and beholds it in the truth he knows this and is aware of it, for it is true in the truth, and therefore one must be aware of it there and nowhere else.

Yet one should know that there is a gulf between having virtue and being willing to suffer, as we also see in nature: one man is superior to another in appearance, in knowledge and in skill. Hence I also say that a good man may quite well be a good man and yet be affected and made irresolute by the natural love of father, mother, sister and brother, more or less, and yet without deserting God or goodness. Still, he becomes good and even better according as he is more or less comforted and affected and becomes aware of the natural love and affection to father and mother, sister and brother and to himself.

Nevertheless, as I wrote above, if a man could accept it in God's will, in so far as it is God's will, that human nature has this particular defect as a result of God's justice, becuse of the sin of the first man, and also if he would willingly do without it in God's will, if it were not so, then it would be well with him and he would certainly be comforted in his suffering. This is the meaning of St. John's words that the true 'light shineth in the darkness', and St. Paul says that 'virtue is made perfect in infirmity'. If a thief could truly, fully, purely, gladly, willingly and cheerfully suffer death for the love of Divine justice, in which and from which God and His justice will that the evil-doer should be killed, he would certainly be saved and blessed.

But another consolation is this: one does not easily find anyone who does not love someone alive so dearly that he would not gladly do without an eye or be blind for a year, provided that he could have his eye afterwards, and if in this way he could save his friend from death. If then a man would do without his eye for a year for the sake of saving the life of a man who must die in a few years in any case, then he should much more fittingly and gladly renounce the ten or twenty years which he perhaps might live, in order to save himself for all eternity and to see God eternally in His Divine light, and in God to see himself and all creatures.

But there is another consolation: a good man, in so far as he is good and born of goodness itself and in the image of goodness, detests everything that is created and this or that, and it is bitter pain and shame to him. To lose all this means therefore to lose and be rid of pain and suffering and loss. Indeed, to lose pain is true consolation. Therefore man should never complain

of an injury. He should rather complain that consolation is unknown to him, that consolation cannot console him, as sweet
wine does not taste good to a sick man. He should complain, as
I have already written, because he is not completely stripped of
the creatures and is not transformed into goodness with all that
is his.

Man should also remember in his pain that God speaks the
truth and promises by Himself, the Truth. If God were to be
false to His word, His Truth, He would be false to His Divinity,
and then He would not be God. It is His promise that our pain
shall be changed into joy. Certainly, if I knew as a fact that all
my stones were to be transformed into gold, then the more stones
I had and the larger they were, the more pleased I should be. In
fact, I should beg for stones and obtain some if I could, large
ones and many of them. The more there were, and the larger
they were, the more I should like them. In this way man would
indeed be powerfully comforted in all his sufferings.

Moreover, there is another similar thought: no cask can
have two kinds of wine in it. If it is to contain wine, one must
necessarily pour out the water; the cask must be bare and empty.
Therefore, if you would receive Divine joy and God, it is necessary for you to pour out the creatures. St. Augustine says: 'Pour
out, that you may be filled. Learn not to love, in order that you
may love. Turn away, in order that you may be turned.' In short,
everything that is to receive and to be receptive must and should
be empty. The masters say: If the soul had any colour in it when
it observes, it would recognize neither the colour it had nor that
which it had not. Since, however, it is empty of all colour, it
recognizes all colour.

The wall has colour in itself, and hence it recognizes neither
its own nor any other colour and it has no pleasure in colour,
no more pleasure in that of gold or lapis lazuli than in charcoal.
The eye has no colour and yet it really has it, because it recognizes colour with pleasure and happiness and joy. And according
as the powers of the soul are more perfect and more pure, they
receive more perfectly and extensively all that they do receive,
and accept more extensively and have greater joy, and become
more fully one with that which they do receive, to such an
extent that the highest power of the soul, which is denuded of

all things and has nothing in common with anything, receives nothing less than God Himself in the breadth and fullness of being. And the masters prove that no other pleasure and joy can be compared with this union and this break-through and this joy.

Therefore our Lord speaks very clearly: 'Blessed are the poor in spirit.' He who has nothing is poor. 'Poor in spirit' means that, as the eye is poor and bare of colour and yet receptive of all colours, in the same way the man who is poor in spirit is receptive of all spirit, and the spirit of all spirits is God. The fruits of the spirit are love, joy and peace. To be bare, poor, having nothing, being empty, transform nature. Emptiness makes water flow uphill and many other miracles, of which we do not intend to speak at present.

Therefore, if you would have and find complete joy and consolation in God, then see to it that you are stripped of all creatures and of all comfort from the creatures. For indeed, as long as the creatures can and do comfort you, you will never find true consolation. When, however, nothing but God can comfort you, then indeed God, and with Him and in Him everything that is joy, will comfort you. If you are comforted by that which is not God, you will have comfort neither here nor hereafter. But if the creatures do not corrupt you and do not give you pleasure, you will find comfort both here and hereafter.

If a man was able and knew how to make a cup completely empty and keep it empty of everything that could fill it, even air, the cup would doubtless lose and forget its whole nature, and its emptiness would carry it up to the sky. In the same way, emptiness, poverty and absence of all creatures bear the soul up to God. Also similarity and fervour draw it up aloft. One ascribes equality to the Son in the Deity, fervour and love to the Holy Spirit. Similarity in all respects, especially however and first in the Divine nature, is the begetting of the One and similarity with the Other. In One and with One is the beginning and origin of blossoming, fervent love. One is the beginning without any beginning. Similarity is the beginning from the One alone, and it receives what it is, and the fact that it is a beginning, from and in the One. Love has the property of flowing and springing from

Two as One. One as unity does not give love; two as duality does not produce love; two as one naturally gives willing, fervent love.

Solomon says that all waters, that is, all creatures flow and return to their source. Therefore it is necessarily true, as I have said, that similarity and fervent love draw up and lead and bring the soul into the first source of the One, who is the Father of all in heaven and on earth. So I say then that similarity, begotten of the One, draws the soul into God, as He is one in His hidden unity, for that is the meaning of 'one'. We have a clear illustration of this: when the physical fire kindles the wood one spark receives the nature of the fire and becomes like the pure fire, which without any medium clings to the lower heavens. Immediately it forgets and deserts father and mother, brother and sister on this earth, and it darts up to the heavenly father. Here below, the father of the spark is the fire, its mother the wood, its brothers and sisters are the other sparks. The first little spark does not wait for them. It darts up swiftly to its true father, which is the sky. For, whoever knows the truth is well aware that the fire, is not the true, real father of the spark. The true, real father of the spark and of everything fiery is the sky. In addition, it is to be carefully noted that this small spark not only forsakes and forgets father and mother, brother and sister on earth, but it leaves, forsakes and denies itself also, being drawn by love to its real father, the sky, for it must necessarily be extinguished in the cold air. Yet it wishes to show the natural affection that it has for its true heavenly father.

And, as has been said above of emptiness or bareness, according as the soul is more pure, denuded and poor, and the less she has of the creatures and the more she is empty of all things which are not God, the more purely she receives God, the more she is in God and the more she becomes one with God. And she looks at God and God looks at her from face to face, as transformed into one image, as St. Paul says. In the same way I speak of similarity and of the ardour of love; for according as anything is more like something else, it pursues it more and more and it is swifter and its course is sweeter and more joyful. And the farther away it goes from itself and from everything that is not the other thing which it pursues, the more unlike itself (it becomes) and the more unlike everything that is not the other thing, while it becomes more and more like the thing it pursues. And since similarity flows from the One and draws and attracts by the power and in the power of the One, therefore nothing can calm or satisfy that which draws, nor that which is drawn, until they are united in the One.

Hence our Lord spoke through the prophet Isaiah and said: 'No high likeness and no peace of love will satisfy me until I myself am kindled and inflamed in the love of the Holy Spirit.' And our Lord prayed to His Father that we might become one with Him and in Him and not just united. We have a clear example and proof of this in nature, even externally. Whenever the fire burns and it lights and kindles the wood, the fire makes the wood so fine and unlike itself and takes away from it its coarseness, coldness, heaviness and dampness and makes the wood more and more like itself, the fire. Yet neither warmth nor heat nor similarity will ever calm or silence or satisfy the fire or the wood, until the fire begets itself in the wood and gives the latter its own nature and its own being, so that it is all one fire, equally shared and undivided, neither more nor less. And therefore, before this is achieved there is always smoke, fighting and crackling, struggling and strife between the fire and the wood. But when all unlikeness has been taken away and cast out, the fire abates and the wood is silent. And I will indeed go further, and say truly that the secret power of nature hates a secret similarity so far as it carries in itself a difference and duality. It seeks in this similarity that oneness which it loves in this and only for the sake of this, just as the mouth seeks and loves in the wine the taste of sweetness. If water had the taste that wine has, the mouth would not love wine more than water.

And hence I said that the soul in similarity hates similarity and does not love it in itself and for its own sake; but she loves it because of the One who is hidden in her and is the true Father, the beginning without any beginning of all things in heaven and on earth. And therefore I say: as long as [mere] similarity is found and appears between fire and wood, there is never true pleasure, nor silence, nor rest, nor satisfaction. And therefore the masters say: The coming of the fire is accompanied with strife, with pain and unrest and it takes place in time. But the birth of the fire and the joy are beyond time and beyond distance. Pleasure and joy do not seem long or far away to anyone.

All that I have just said was meant by our Lord when He said: 'When a woman gives birth to a child, she has suffering and pain and sorrow; but when the child is born she forgets the suffering and pain.' Hence also God says and exhorts us in the Gospel that we should ask our heavenly Father that our joy may be perfect, and St. Philip said: 'Lord, show us the Father and it sufficeth us' for 'Father' implies begetting and not similarity and denotes the One in whom similarity is mute, and everything that has desire for being is silenced.

Now a man can know clearly why and in what respect he remains unconsoled in all his pain, suffering and loss. It is entirely and solely due to the fact that he is far from God and not free from the creatures; he is unlike God and cold in divine love.

But there is still another reason. If one were to take heed of it and recognize it, one would be rightly consoled in case of external loss and pain.

As a man goes on his way, or does his work, or fails to do some other work, he may have an accident: he breaks his leg or his arm, he loses an eye, or he falls ill. If he then continually thinks: 'If I had only gone another way or done another piece of work, this would not have happened to me', he will remain unconsoled and will necessarily suffer. And therefore he ought to think: 'If I had gone another way, or done another piece of work, or left it undone, then perhaps a much greater injury and pain would have befallen me.' If he did so, then he would be rightly comforted.

I will make another supposition: if, let us say, you have lost a thousand marks; you should not complain about the thousand marks that are lost. You should thank God, who gave you a thousand marks that you were in a position to lose, and who allows you, by the exercise of the virtue of patience, to gain eternal life, which many thousand men will not possess.

There is another thing that may comfort a man. Let us suppose that a man has had honour and well-being for many years and now he loses it by God's decree. In this event he should be wise and thank God. When he becomes aware of the loss and the pain which he now suffers, he then knows for the first time what advantages and well-being he had before, and he should thank God for the well-being that he had enjoyed for so many years, although he never realized how fortunate he was, but he should not be angry. He should remember that, according to natural truth, man has nothing of himself but evil and sin.

Everything that is good and goodness itself was lent to him by God and not given. For, if anyone knows the truth, he is aware that God, the heavenly Father, gives the Son and the Holy Spirit everything that is good; nevertheless, He gives no good to the creature, but bestows it on him as a loan. The sun gives the air heat, but lends light to it; and therefore, as soon as the sun sets, the air loses the light, but the heat remains, because this is given to the air as its own. And therefore the masters say that God, the heavenly Father, is the Father of the Son and not His Lord, nor the Lord of the Holy Spirit. But God, Father, Son and Holy Spirit is one Lord and the Lord of the creatures, and we say that God has eternally been the Father, but from the time when He created the creatures He has been Lord.

Now I say: since everything that is good or consoling or temporal has been bestowed upon man as a loan, what right has he to complain if He who bestowed it wishes to take it back again? He should thank God who has lent it to him for so long. He should also thank Him because He does not take back entirely what He has bestowed on him. For it would be only reasonable for God to take back again from a man everything that He has lent him, if this man is angry because He takes back again part of that which has never belonged to the man, and of which he has never been the owner. And hence Jeremiah the prophet said very aptly, when he was in great suffering and lamentations: 'Manifold are the mercies of God that we are not altogether consumed.' If anyone had lent me his jacket, fur-coat and cloak, and he took back his cloak and left me the jacket and fur-coat in frosty weather, I should very properly thank him and be glad. And one should particularly notice how greatly I am in the wrong if I am angry and complain whenever I lose something. For if I wish that the property I have should be given to me and not lent, I want to be the master and I want to be God's son by nature and perfectly, although I am not yet God's son by grace, for it is the property of God's Son and of the Holy Spirit to be equable in all things.

Also, one should know that without any doubt even natural human virtue is so noble and so powerful that no outer work is too difficult for it nor adequate to be manifested by it and to be reproduced in it. And therefore there is an inner work which neither time nor place can enclose or grasp. In this work is contained what is divine and like God, whom neither time nor place encloses, since He is everywhere and always equally omnipresent. This work is also like God in this respect, that no creature can fully receive Him, nor can a creature reproduce God's goodness in itself. Therefore there must be something more inward and higher and uncreated, without size or shape, in which the heavenly Father can completely imprint Himself, pour Himself out and reveal Himself, that is, the Son and the Holy Spirit. Moreover, the inward work of virtue cannot be impeded by anyone, just as no one can impede God. The work glows and shines day and night.

It praises God and sings His praise and a new song, as David says: 'Sing unto God a new song.' God does not love the work whose praise is of the earth, and which is external and includes time and place, which is narrow and can be impeded and overwhelmed, which becomes tired and old as a result of time and wear. The other work consists in loving God, willing the good and goodness. In this work all that man wills and would like to do, with a pure, undivided will in all good works, is already done, in which respect also he is like God, of whom David wrote: 'Whatsoever He pleased, that He has now done and wrought.'

We have a clear illustration of this doctrine in a stone, of which the outer work consists of falling down and lying on the ground. This work may be impeded, and the stone does not fall the whole time without intermission. Another activity is more inward to the stone, namely the downward inclination, and this is inborn in it. Neither God, nor creature, nor anyone else can deprive it of this. The stone does this work without intermission, day and night. Even if it lay up above for a thousand years, it would incline downwards neither more nor less than on the first day.

In just the same way I say of virtue that she has an inner work: to will and to be inclined to all that is good, and to hasten away from and to resist all that is wicked and evil, or unlike goodness and God. The more wicked the work is and the more unlike God, the greater the resistance. The greater the work is and the more like God, the easier, more willing and joyful it will be to virtue. And all her complaint and grief, if grief could befall her, would be that this suffering for the sake of God is too slight and all outer works are too slight in time so that she cannot fully reveal herself or completely demonstrate herself or reproduce her image in it. She becomes powerful by practice and through generosity she becomes rich. She would not like to have suffered nor to have undergone pain and suffering. She wishes and has always wished without intermission to suffer for the sake of God and for the sake of doing good. All her happiness is [present] suffering, not past suffering for the sake of God. Hence our Lord says these memorable words: 'Blessed are they who suffer for the sake of justice.' He does not say 'who have suffered'. Such a man hates past suffering because past suffering is not the present suffering that he loves; it is a transcending and loss of the suffering for the sake of God, which He alone loves. Therefore I say that such a man also hates future suffering, because that is not present suffering either. Yet he hates future suffering less than past suffering, for past suffering is further away and less like suffering, because it is altogether past. The fact that someone has to suffer in the future does not altogether eliminate the suffering that he loves.

St. Paul says that he would like to renounce God for the sake of God, in order that the glory of God might be extended. We are told that St. Paul said this at a time when he was not yet perfect. I think, however, that these words came from a perfect heart. It is also said that he meant he would like to be separated from God for a time. I say that a perfect man would be as unwilling to be separated from God for an hour as for a thousand years. Yet, if it were God's will and for His glory that he should renounce God, it would be just as easy to do so for a thousand years, or even for eternity, as for a day, or an hour.

Also the inward work is godlike and godly, and it suggests the Divine attributes in this respect: in the same way as all the creatures—even if there were a thousand worlds—are not a hair-breadth better than God alone, I say, as I have said before, that this outward work, its quality and its size, its length and its breadth do not in the least increase the goodness of the inward work: it has its goodness in itself.

Hence the outward work can never be small if the inward one is great, and the outward can never be great or good if the inward is small or of little worth. The inward work always includes in itself all size, all breadth and length. The inward work receives and draws all its being from nowhere else but from and in the heart of God. It receives the Son and is begotten as a son in the bosom of the heavenly Father. The outward work does not, but it receives its divine goodness by means of the inward work, borne out and poured out in an emanation of the Deity, who is veiled by differentiation, by quantity and parts, all of which and everything like it, and also similarity itself, is foreign and alien to God. They cling and adhere and become calm in that which is good, which is illumined, which is a creature, blind altogether as to goodness and light in themselves and as to the One, in whom God begets His only begotten Son and in Him all those who are God's children and born as sons. In Him is the outflow and source of the Holy Spirit, from whom alone, since He is God's Spirit, and God Himself is spirit, the Son comes into being in us. In Him also is the origin of all those who are the sons of God, according as they are more or less purely born of God alone, transformed in God's image and in Him, and estranged from all number, which one nevertheless still finds even in the highest angels, according to their nature, yet, if one will rightly recognize it, estranged from goodness, from truth and everything which—even in thought or only in name—allows an idea or a shade of any difference, and entrusted to the One, who is denuded of all quantity and difference, in whom also God the Father, God the Son and the Holy Ghost lose and are stripped of all differences and attributes, and are One and in One. And this One makes us blessed, and the further away we are from the One, the less we are sons and the Son, and the less perfectly the Holy Spirit springs up in us and flows from us. But according as we are nearer to the One, we are all more truly sons of God and the Son and also there flows from us God and the Holy Spirit. This is the meaning of the words spoken by our Lord, God's Son in the Deity: 'Whosoever drinks of the water that I shall give, in him a well of water will arise, which springs up to eternal life.' And St. John tells us that He said this of the Holy Spirit.

In accordance with His attributes, the Son in the Deity gives nothing else than sonship, or being born as God, the fountain, origin and source of the Holy Spirit, of the love of God, the full, true, entire image of the One, of the heavenly Father. Therefore the Father's voice spoke from heaven to the Son saying: 'Thou art My beloved Son, in whom I am beloved and well-pleased.' For undoubtedly no one loves God sufficiently and purely unless he is God's son. For love, the Holy Spirit, originates in and flows from the Son, and the Son loves the Father for His own sake, the Father in Himself and Himself in the Father. Therefore our Lord says: 'Blessed are the poor in spirit', that is, those who have nothing of their own and of human spirit and come naked to God. St. Paul says: 'God has revealed it to us in His Spirit.'

St. Augustine says that he understands the Scriptures best who stripped of all intellect, seeks the sense and truth of the Scriptures in the Scriptures themselves, that is, in the Spirit in which they were written and spoken, in the Spirit of God. St. Peter says that all saintly men spoke in the Spirit of God. St. Paul says: 'No man can know what is in man, save the spirit that is in man, and no one can know what the Spirit of God and in God is, save the Spirit which is of God and is God.' Therefore, as is very well said in a theological work, a gloss, no one can understand nor teach St. Paul's writings unless he has the spirit in which St. Paul spoke and wrote. And this is always my whole complaint that ignorant people who are devoid of the spirit of God and possess nothing of it, wish to judge by their ignorant human understanding what they hear or read in the Scriptures, which was spoken and written by and in the Holy Spirit, and they do not consider that it is written: 'What is impossible with men is possible with God.' And also, in general and in the natural sphere, what is impossible for the lower nature is usual and natural for the higher nature.

Therefore, you should understand in addition what I have just said, namely that a good man, as a son of God born in God, loves God for His own sake and in Himself, and many other words I have previously said. To understand it even better, one should know, as I have often said, that a good man born of goodness and in God enters into all the properties of the Divine nature. Now according to the words of Solomon, it is a property of God that God does all things for Himself, that is to say, that He does not look for any 'Why' outside Himself, but only for what is for His own sake. He loves and works all things for His own sake. Therefore, when man loves Him Himself and all things and does all his works not for reward, for honour or happiness, but only for the sake of God and His glory, that is a sign that he is a son of God.

Furthermore, God loves for His own sake and does all things for His own sake, that is, He loves for the sake of love and He acts for the sake of action. For undoubtedly God would never have begotten His only Son in eternity unless 'having begotten' were not the same as 'begetting'. Hence the saints say that the Son was eternally begotten in such a way that He is being begotten without intermission. Also, God would never have created the world unless 'having been created' were not the same as 'being created'. Hence God created the world in such a way that He is still continually creating it. Everything that is past and what is future is alien to God and remote from Him. Therefore, whoever is born of God as a son of God loves God for His sake, that is to say, he loves God for the sake of loving God and does all his work for the sake of working. God is never weary of loving and working, and also everything that He loves is all one love. Therefore it is true that God is love. Therefore I said above that the good man wishes and would fain be suffering at all times for the sake of God, and would not like to have suffered. While suffering he has what he loves. He loves suffering for the sake of God, and he suffers because of God. Therefore and therein he is a son of God, formed in His image and in Him, who loves for Himself, that is to say, He loves for the sake of love, works for the sake of work, and therefore God loves and works uninterruptedly. God's work is His nature, His being, His life, His happiness. Thus indeed, for the son of God, a good man, in so far as he is a son of God, to suffer for God's sake, to work for God's sake, is his being, his life, his work, his happiness. For our Lord said: 'Blessed are they who suffer for righteousness' sake.'

I say further, thirdly, that a good man, in so far as he is good, has God's attitude not only in that he loves and works everything that he loves and works for the sake of God, whom he loves and for whose sake he works, but also he who loves and works for his own sake too. For that which he loves is God the Father unbegotten and He who loves is God the Son begotten. Now the Father is in the Son and the Son in the Father. Father and Son are one. As to the way in which what is innermost and highest in the soul draws in and receives the Son of God and the birth of God's Son in the bosom and heart of the heavenly Father, see towards the end of this book, where I write: 'Of the Nobleman who went away to a far country to receive for himself a kingdom, and to return.'

One should also know, however, that in nature the impress and inflow of the uppermost nature and of the highest is to everyone more blissful and joyful than his own nature and being. Water flows downhill because of its own nature, and its being depends on this. Yet owing to the impression and influence of the moon in the sky above, it denies and forgets its own nature and flows uphill, and the flood-tide is much easier for it than the ebb. From this man should know whether it would be right that he should be happy and joyful to leave and to forsake his natural will and to forsake himself entirely in everything that God wills that man should suffer. This is the meaning, in a good sense, of our Lord's words 'If any man will come to me, let him deny himself and take up his cross', that is, he should lay down everything and get rid of everything that is a cross and a sorrow. For indeed, if anyone had forsaken himself and had denied himself altogether, nothing could be a cross or sorrow or suffering to him. It would all be happiness, joy and gladness, and he would come and truly follow God. For, as God cannot make anyone sad or sorrowful, in the same way, nothing could make such a man unhappy or sad. Therefore, the words of our Lord, 'If any man will come to me, let him deny himself and take up his cross and follow Me', are not only a command, as one usually says and believes, but they are also a promise and a Divine teaching, telling us how all man's suffering, all his works, all his life become happy and joyful, and these words are a promise of reward rather than a command. For a man who is so constituted has everything he wants, and he does not want anything evil, and this is blessedness. Therefore indeed our Lord says: 'Blessed are they who suffer for the sake of righteousness.'

Also, when our Lord, the Son, says 'Let him deny himself and take up his cross and come to Me', that means 'Become a son, as I am a Son, born as God, and the same One as I am, whom I receive, indwelling, remaining within the Father's bosom and heart'. 'Father,' says also the Son, 'I will that he who follows Me should be where I am.' No one really comes to the Son, as Son, except him who becomes a son, and no one is where the Son is, who in the Father's bosom and heart is one in One, except him who is a son.

'I', says the Father, 'shall lead her into the wilderness and speak to her heart there.' Heart to heart, one in one; God loves that. Everything that is alien to and remote from this is hated by God. God allures and draws to the One. All creatures seek One, even the lowest creatures seek the One, and the One is perceived by the highest. Drawn beyond their nature and transformed, they seek the One in One in Himself. It is perhaps for this reason that the Son says: 'In the Son of the Deity in the Father, where I am, there shall he be who serves Me, who follows Me, who comes to Me.'

There is still another consolation. One should know that it is impossible for the whole of nature to break, or spoil, or even touch anything in which she does not aim at a higher good for the thing which she touches. It does not suffice for her to make something equally good; she always wishes to make something better. How is this? A wise physician never touches the diseased finger of a man in such a way as to hurt him, unless he can make the finger itself better, or the whole man, and make him comfortable. If he can cure the man and also his finger, he does so. If he cannot, he cuts the finger off, in order to cure the man. It is much better to lose only a finger and to save the man than that both the finger and the man should perish. One loss is preferable to two, especially when one is incomparably greater than the other.

One should also know that the finger and the hand and every limb naturally loves the man of which it is a limb much more than itself and it submits gladly and unhesitatingly and cheerfully to hardship and loss for the sake of the man. I speak with assurance and truthfully: this limb does not love itself at all except for the sake of the whole and in the whole, of which it is a limb. Therefore it would be quite reasonable, and as a matter of course it would be right, that we should not love ourselves at all except for the sake of God and in God. And if it were so, everything that God wanted of us and in us would be easy and a joy to us, especially if we were certain that God could tolerate any deficiency or loss much less if He did not know and intend that there should be a much greater advantage in it. Indeed, if anyone does not trust God [to do this] it is certainly right that he should have suffering and pain.

There is further consolation. St. Paul says that God chastens all those whom He accepts and receives as His sons. In order to be a son it is essential that one should suffer. As the Son of God could not suffer in the Deity, nor in eternity, the heavenly Father sent Him into the world that He might become man and that He might suffer. If then you would be a son of God and yet you are not willing to suffer, you are quite in the wrong. In the Book of Wisdom it is written that God examines and tests to find out who is just, as one examines and tests gold in a furnace. It is a sign that the king or a prince trusts a knight completely if he sends him into the battle. I have seen a nobleman who sometimes, when he had accepted a man as a member of his retinue, sent him out at night and rode out to attack him and fought him. And once it happened that he was very nearly killed by a man whom he wished to put to the test in this way, and he afterwards esteemed this retainer much more highly than before.

We read that St. Antony in the desert on one occasion in particular suffered cruelly because of evil spirits, and when he had overcome his trials, our Lord appeared to him visibly and blissfully. Then the holy man said: 'Ah, dear Lord, where wert Thou just now, when I was in great distress?' Then our Lord spoke: 'I was here, just as I am now. But I wanted and had a desire to see how brave you were.' A piece of silver or gold is indeed pure, but when one wishes to make a goblet out of it, from which the king is to drink, it is smelted much more carefully than another piece. Hence it is written that the Apostles were glad to be found worthy of suffering dishonour for the sake of God.

He who was the Son of God by nature wanted to become man by grace in order that He might suffer for your sake, and you want to become a son of God and not a man so that you cannot and do not need to suffer for the sake of God or for your own sake?

Also, if man were to be aware and to consider how much joy God Himself really has in His own fashion, and all the angels and all those who know and love God, in the patience of man when he suffers pain and loss for the sake of God, he would certainly be rightly consoled by that alone. For a man gives his possessions and suffers pain in order to give pleasure to his friend and to render him a kindness.

But one should also consider that if a man had a friend who was in distress on his account and in sorrow and pain, it would indeed be quite fitting that he should be with his friend and that he should encourage him with his presence and with such comfort as he could give him. Hence our Lord says in the Psalter of a good man that He will be with him in his suffering. From these words one can derive seven lessons and seven kinds of consolation.

First, there is what St. Augustine says, that patience in suffering for the sake of God is better, more precious, higher and nobler than anything that one can take away from a man against his will, that is all external possessions. Assuredly, one could not find any lover of this world who would not willingly and gladly suffer great pain, and moreover suffer for very long, in order that he might later become the powerful ruler of the whole world.

Secondly, not only do I draw my conclusion from the words that God says, namely that He is with man in his sufferings, but from these very words I deduce it and say: If God is with me in suffering, what more do I desire and what else can I desire? After all, I want nothing else; I want nothing more than God, if I am rightly disposed. St. Augustine says: 'He who is not satisfied with God is very avaricious and unwise', and elsewhere he says: 'How can man be satisfied with God's external or internal gifts if he is not satisfied with God Himself?' And for this reason he says again elsewhere: 'Lord, if Thou turnest us away from Thee, give us another Thee, for we want nothing but Thee'.

324

Therefore the Book of Wisdom says: 'With God, the eternal Wisdom, all good things have come together with one another.' That means, in one sense, that nothing is good, or can be good, that comes without God, and everything that comes with God is good, and it is good only because it comes with God. Of God I will be silent. But if one were to take away from all creatures of this world the being that God gives, they would remain a mere nothing, repulsive, worthless and hateful. The words 'All good comes with God' have many other precious meanings, which it would take too long to mention now.

Our Lord says: 'I am with man in trouble.' St. Bernard says on this text: 'Lord, if Thou art with us in trouble, give me trouble at all times, in order that Thou mayest be with me at all times, so that I shall have Thee at all times.'

Thirdly, I say that 'God is with us in trouble' means that He Himself suffers with us. Indeed, he who recognizes the truth knows that I am speaking truthfully. God suffers with man, indeed He suffers in His way before and incomparably more than the man who suffers for His sake. Now I say, if then God Himself is willing to suffer, it is quite right that I should suffer, for if I am well disposed, I will what God wills. I pray every day, and God bids me pray, 'Lord, Thy will be done', and yet, when God wills suffering, I will complain about the suffering. This is quite wrong. I also say confidently that God suffers so gladly with us and for our sakes that, if we suffer for the sake of God alone, He suffers without suffering. Suffering is so blissful to Him that for Him suffering is not suffering. Therefore, if we were well disposed, suffering would not be suffering for us; it would be happiness and consolation.

In the fourth place, I say that the sympathy of a friend naturally diminishes this suffering. If then I can be comforted by the suffering which a man feels for me, I ought to be comforted much more by God's sympathy.

In the fifth place, if I should and would suffer with a man whom I loved and who loved me, then I ought gladly and quite rightly to suffer with God, who suffers with me, and suffers for my sake through the love which He has for me.

Sixthly, I say that, if it is the case that God has suffered previously, before I suffer, and if I suffer for the sake of God, then indeed all my sufferings will easily become comfort and joy to me, however great and varied they are. If it is true in the natural course of things that if a man does one work for the sake of another work, then the purpose for which he does it is nearer to his heart, and that which he does is further from his heart, except for the sake of that which is his motive for doing it. If someone is building and cutting the wood and chiselling the stone to the end and purpose of making a house as a protection against the heat of the summer and the frost of the winter, his object is primarily and entirely the house, and he would never cut the stone, nor do the work, if it were not for the sake of the house. We see quite well, if a sick man drinks sweet wine, that it seems to him and he also says that it is bitter, and this is true, for the wine loses its sweetness outside in the bitterness of the tongue before the wine can go inside, where the soul knows and judges the taste. Similarly, and in a much higher degree and more truly, when man does all his works for the sake of God, then God is in these works the medium and that which is nearest to the soul. Nothing can touch the soul and the heart of man which for the sake of God and His sweetness does not lose, and necessarily lose, its bitterness and become pure sweetness before it can ever touch the heart of the man.

There is another example and illustration: the masters say that under the sky there is fire in all directions and therefore no rain or wind nor any kind of storm or tempest can approach the sky so near from below that anything could touch it at all. Everything is burnt and destroyed by the heat of the fire before it reaches the sky. Hence I say, everything that one suffers and works for the sake of God, all becomes sweet in the sweetness of God before it reaches the heart of the man who works and suffers for the sake of God. For that is the meaning of the words 'for the sake of God', because it never reaches the heart except when flowing through the sweetness of God, in which it loses its bitterness. It is also burnt by the ardent fire of the Divine love, which has enclosed the heart of the good man entirely within it.

Now one can clearly recognize how fittingly and in how many ways a good man is on all hands comforted in suffering, in pain and in activity. It is in one way when he suffers and works for the sake of God, in another when he is in Divine love. Also man can know and recognize whether he does all his works for the sake of God, and whether he is in the love of God. For certainly wherever man finds himself suffering and comfortless, to this extent his work was not done for the sake of God alone, look, and to this extent it is not entirely done in the love of God. A fire, says King David, comes with God and goes before Him, burning everything round about, which God finds against Him or unlike Him, that is, pain, despair, unrest and bitterness.

There is still a seventh meaning in the text that God is with us in suffering and sympathizes with us, namely, that God's nature should powerfully comfort us because He is pure unity without any non-essential multiplicity of difference even in the abstract. Everything that is in Him is God Himself. And since this is true, I say that everything a good man suffers for the sake of God he suffers in God, and God is with him, suffering in his suffering. If my suffering is in God and God sympathizes with me, how can suffering be painful to me then, if suffering loses its pain, and my pain is in God and my pain is God? Indeed as God is truth, and wherever I find truth I find my God, the Truth, in the same way also, neither more nor less, when I find pure suffering for the sake of God and in God, there I find God, my suffering. Whoever does not recognize this, should lament his blindness, not me or the Divine truth and loving kindness.

Suffer therefore in this manner for the sake of God, since it brings such great pain and blessedness. 'Blessed are they', said our Lord, 'which suffer for righteousness' sake'. How can God, who loves goodness, permit that His friends, who are good people, are not always suffering without interruption? If a man had a friend who was able to suffer for a short time, in order to obtain as a result great benefits, honour and happiness, and long enjoy these things; if he wanted to prevent this, or if it was his wish that someone else should prevent it, then one would not say that he was his friend or that he loved him. It is therefore possible that God could not in any way permit that His friends, who are good people, should ever be without suffering, unless they were able to suffer without pain. All the goodness of external suffering comes and flows from the goodness of the will, as I have written above. Therefore, everything that the good man would wish to suffer and is prepared and desirous to suffer for the sake of God, he suffers all this before the face of God and for the sake of God in God.

King David says in the Psalter: 'I am ready in all distress and my pain is continually present in my heart, before my face.' St. Jerome says that a piece of pure wax, that is very soft and suitable for modelling into whatever one chooses, has enclosed in it anything that one can make out of it, even although no one makes anything visible out of it. I have also written above that a stone is not less heavy when it does not lie visibly on the ground. All its weight is completely contained in its capacity to incline downwards and to be prepared in itself to fall downwards. In the same way, I have said above that the good man has already done everything in heaven and on earth that he wanted to do, and in this respect also he is like God.

Now one can know and recognize the ignorance of people who are as a rule amazed when they see good people suffering pain and distress, and often the thought and idea occurs to them that it is due to their secret sins. Such people say sometimes: 'Ah, I thought he was quite a good man. How is it that he suffers such great pain and distress, and I thought he lacked nothing!' And I agree with them and say: 'Certainly, if it was really pain, and if it was pain and unhappiness to them to suffer, then they would not be good, nor without sin. But if they are good the suffering is not pain or unhappiness to them, but it is a great happiness and blessedness.'

'Blessed', said God, the Truth, 'are they which suffer for righteousness' sake.' Hence the Book of Wisdom says that 'The souls of the righteous are in the hands of God. Foolish persons think and believe that they die and go to ruin, but they are in peace', in bliss and happiness. In the passage in which St. Paul tells of many saints suffering manifold great trials, he says that the world was unworthy of it. These words have a threefold meaning for him who is properly disposed. The first is, that this world is unworthy of the presence of many good people. The second meaning is better, and it signifies that the goodness of the world is hateful and worthless. God alone is worthy, therefore they are worthy to God and worthy of God. The third meaning is the one I now have in mind, namely, that this world, that is the people who love this world, are unworthy of suffering pain and distress for the sake of God. Hence it is written that the holy Apostles rejoiced that they were found worthy to suffer pain for the sake of the name of God.

Let this now suffice, since in the third part of this book I shall write about many kinds of consolation by means of which a good person should and could be comforted in his sufferings, and how this is to be found not only in the words of good and wise persons but also in their works.

III

In the Book of Kings one reads that a man cursed King David and deeply insulted him. Then one of David's friends said that he would slay this bad dog. But the King said: 'No, for perchance God will return good to me for this insult.'

We read in the *Lives of the Fathers* that a man complained to a holy father that he was in trouble. Then the father said: 'Son, do you wish me to pray to God to take this away from you?' Then the other said: 'No, Father, for it is helpful to me; I recognize this quite well. But ask God to give me His grace that I may bear it willingly.'

A sick man was once asked why he did not pray to God to cure him. Then the man answered that he did not wish to do this for three reasons. The first was that he wanted to be certain that God, who is love, could never permit him to be ill unless it was for his good. The second reason was that, if a man is good, then he wills everything that God wills, rather than that God should will what the man wills; that would be quite wrong. And so if He wills that I should be sick—for if He did not will it, then it would not be so—then I should not wish to be well. For undoubtedly, if it could happen that God cured me without willing it, it would be worthless and undesirable that He should make me well. Willing comes from love, not-willing from lack of love. It is much more desirable, better and more beneficial to me that God should love me and that I should be ill, than that I should be well physically and that God should not love me. What God loves is something; what He does not love is nothing, as the Book of Wisdom says. It is also true that everything that God wills is good in and because of the fact that God wills it. Indeed, humanly speaking, I should prefer to be loved by a rich, powerful man, such as a king, even if he left me for a time without gifts, rather than that he should immediately order something to be given to me and that he should not really love me. I should prefer it if he did not give me anything at all from love and hence gave me nothing now because he wanted to reward me more abundantly and generously later. Yet I suppose that the man who loves me and gives me nothing now, is not thinking of giving me anything later, but perhaps he will think better of it later and give me something. I ought to wait patiently, especially because his gift is an act of grace and undeserved. Also it is certain that if I do not heed a man's love and if my will is opposed to his will, unless I receive a gift from him, then it is quite fitting that he should give me nothing, and also that he should hate me and leave me unfortunate.

The third reason why it would be unworthy and hateful for me to pray to God to cure me is this: I do not wish, nor ought I to ask the powerful, loving, generous God for so slight a thing. Let us suppose that I were to go to the Pope from one hundred or two hundred leagues away, and then I entered his presence and said: 'My Lord, Holy Father, I have come a good two hundred leagues on rough roads and at great expense, and I ask you— for which reason I have come here to see you—to give me a bean.' Then indeed he himself and anyone who heard it would say, and quite rightly, that I was a great fool. Now I am certainly speaking the truth when I say that every good, and indeed all creatures, are smaller in comparison with God than a bean as compared with the whole of this physical world. Therefore I should rightly despise myself, if I was a good, wise man, for praying to be cured.

In this connection I add that it is a sign of a faint heart if a man is either cheerful or sad on account of the transient things of this world. One ought to be heartily ashamed before God and His angels and before men that one ever took any notice of them. One is so greatly ashamed of a disfigurement in the face that people can see outwardly. Why should I say more? The books of the Old and New Testament and also of the saints and even the books of the pagans are full of examples of pious persons who for the sake of God and also through natural virtue gave up their lives and willingly denied themselves.

Meister Eckhart

A heathen master, Socrates, says that virtue makes impossible things possible and even easy and pleasant. Also I will not omit to add that the holy woman of whom the Book of Maccabees tells, saw one day before her eyes extraordinary torments, inhuman and horrible to hear, done and inflicted on her seven sons. She saw them cheerfully, supporting and particularly exhorting them, not to be afraid and to give up body and soul willingly for the sake of the justice of God. Herewith this book ends. Yet I will say two things more.

The first is this: a good and godly man should indeed be very deeply and thoroughly ashamed of ever being moved by suffering, if we see how a merchant for the sake of making a small profit and an uncertain one at that, will often travel such great distances, on such rough roads, over hill and dale, desert and seas, infested with robbers and murderers of life and property, suffering great lack of food and drink, of sleep, and other hardships. Yet he will gladly and willingly forget it all for the sake of such a trifling and uncertain gain. A knight in battle risks his property, his body and soul for the sake of fleeting and brief honours, and yet it seems so hard for us to suffer a little for the sake of God and eternal blessedness.

The second thought that I have in mind is that many ignorant persons will say that much of what I have written in this book and elsewhere is not true. To them I answer as did St. Augustine in the second book of his *Confessions*. He says that God has already made everything that is still to come, even thousands and thousands of years hence, if the world is to endure so long, and that He is to make today everything that passed many thousands of years ago. What is it to me if anyone does not understand? And he says again elsewhere that the man loves himself too openly who wishes to blind other people in order that his blindness may be concealed. It suffices for me that what I say and write should be true in me and in God. If anyone sees a stick thrust into water, the stick seems to him to be crooked, although it is quite straight. This is due to the fact that the water is a coarser medium than air. Yet the stick is both straight and not crooked in itself and also in the eye of the man who sees it only in the clarity of the air.

St. Augustine says that whoever without any kind of thought, any kind of physical medium, or images knows within what is conveyed there by no external sight, he knows that it is true. But he who knows nothing of this will laugh and sneer at me, and I shall be sorry for him. But such persons want to see and to feel eternal things and divine works and to stand in the light of eternity, and yet their hearts are still fluttering about in yesterday and tomorrow.

A pagan master, Seneca, says: 'One should speak of great and lofty things with a great and lofty mind and with a sublime soul.' People will also say that such a doctrine should not be spoken or written for the unlearned. To this I reply: if one is not to teach the unlearned, then no one will ever be learned and no one will be able to teach or to write. For one teaches the unlearned to the end that from unlearned persons they may become learned ones. If there were nothing new, nothing would ever become old. 'They who are whole', said our Lord, 'have no need of medicine.' The physician exists for the purpose of making the sick healthy. But if there should be anyone who misunderstands these words, is that the fault of the man who rightly says these words which are right? St. John said his holy Gospel to all believers and also to all unbelievers, in order that they might become believers, and yet he began his Gospel with the loftiest thoughts that man could ever express here concerning God. His words also, and those of our Lord, have been wrongly understood.

May the God of love and mercy, the Truth, grant to me, and to all those who are to read this book, that we may find and become aware of the truth in ourselves. Amen.

Thomas à Kempis
1380-1471

The Imitation of Christ *is one of the most widely known books in world literature. Since the time of its writing around 1427, it has been one of the major documents in the library of Christian spirituality. Though its authorship has been and continues to be debated, the name of Thomas à Kempis is the one almost universally identified with it.*

Both Thomas à Kempis and The Imitation *come from a period of great tension and confusion. The medieval period of history had come to an end and what lay ahead for Christianity was not at all clear. There were tensions between church and civil authorities, struggles within the church to seize papal power, disorder in monasteries and convents. In the face of all this, small groups of devout Christians sought to rediscover the basic teachings of the gospels and to revivify the religion that was their heritage. One of the groups, rising up in the Netherlands around the end of the fourteenth century, developed a life-style that took on the title of the* Devotio Moderna. *As distinct from the "old" spirituality of the thirteenth century with its highly scholastic and speculative approach, the "new" spirituality was marked by emphasis on imitation of Christ's life and virtues, self-knowledge as the foundation for perfection, self-denial, anti-intellectualism, anti-humanism, a highly developed interior life, flight from the world and meditative reading of the Sacred Scriptures.*

Thomas à Kempis was part of this movement. He was born in Kempen, near Düsseldorf in the Rhineland. As a youth of twelve or thirteen, he went to Deventer in the Netherlands to study. Eventually he entered the Canons Regular of St. Augustine and was ordained in 1413. His life was one of study, prayer, manuscript copying and composition of spiritual works. Because of The Imitation of Christ, *he is the outstanding representative of the* Devotio Moderna.

From its opening lines, the message of The Imitation *is clear. "He who follows Me, says Christ our Savior, walks not in darkness, for he will have the light of life." The four books that make up* The Imitation *are designed to assist the individual to arrive at perfection, at union with God, by steeping himself in the life and teachings of Christ. Book I, from which the following selection is taken, contains admonitions that are useful for a spiritual life. Book II guides the reader through various themes essential to the interior life, such as recognition of one's defects, purity of intention, pure conscience, love of Jesus, thanksgiving and the Cross. Book III develops what is called the inward speaking of Christ to a faithful soul. Book IV treats the role of the sacrament of the Eucharist in the spiritual life.*

The Imitation of Christ *has known both praise and serious adverse criticism. That it is highly inspiring and a significant contribution to Christian spirituality cannot be denied. At the same time, it must be recognized that the absence of a sound doctrinal structure limits its value. Kept within the context of the times during which* The Imitation *was written, the themes of negation, fear, self-denial, excessive individualism, and the like are comprehensible. The reader should accept* The Imitation *as a work that offers great insights to the spiritual life but which constantly needs re-orientation through other aspects of the Christian tradition.*

THE IMITATION OF CHRIST

1. OF THE IMITATION OR FOLLOWING OF CHRIST AND THE DESPISING OF ALL VANITIES OF THE WORLD

He who follows Me, says Christ our Saviour, walks not in darkness, for he will have the light of life. These are the words of our Lord Jesus Christ, and by them we are admonished to follow His teaching and His manner of living, if we would truly be enlightened and delivered from all blindness of heart.

Let all the study of our heart be from now on to have our meditation fixed wholly on the life of Christ, for His holy teachings are of more virtue and strength than the words of all the angels and saints. And he who through grace has the inner eye of his soul opened to the true beholding of the Gospels of Christ will find in them hidden manna.

It is often seen that those who hear the Gospels find little sweetness in them; the reason is that they do not have the spirit of Christ. So, if we desire to have a true understanding of His Gospels, we must study to conform our life as nearly as we can to His.

What avail is it to a man to reason about the high, secret mysteries of the Trinity if he lack humility and so displeases the Holy Trinity? Truly, it avails nothing. Deeply inquisitive reasoning does not make a man holy or righteous, but a good life makes him beloved by God. I would rather feel compunction of heart for my sins than merely know the definition of compunction. If you know all the books of the Bible merely by rote and all the sayings of the philosophers by heart, what will it profit you without grace and charity? All that is in the world is vanity except to love God and to serve Him only. This is the most noble and the most excellent wisdom that can be in any creature: by despising the world to draw daily nearer and nearer to the kingdom of heaven.

It is therefore a great vanity to labor inordinately for worldly riches that will shortly perish or to covet honor or any other inordinate pleasures or fleshly delights in this life, for which a man after this life will be sorely and grievously punished. How great a vanity it also is to desire a long life and to care little for a good life; to heed things of the present and not to provide for things that are to come; to love things that will shortly pass away and not to haste to where joy is everlasting. Have this common proverb often in your mind: The eye is not satisfied or pleased with seeing any material things, nor the ear with hearing. Study, therefore, to withdraw the love of your soul from all things that are visible, and to turn it to things that are invisible. Those who follow their own sensuality hurt their own cause and lose the grace of God.

2. AGAINST VAIN, SECULAR LEARNING, AND OF A HUMBLE KNOWLEDGE OF OURSELVES

Every man by nature desires to know, but of what avail is knowledge without the fear of God? A humble farm laborer who serves God is more acceptable to Him than an inquisitive philosopher who, considering the constellations of heaven, willfully forgets himself. He who knows himself well is mean and abject in his own sight, and takes no delight in the vain praise of men. If I knew all things in this world, but knew without charity, what would it avail me before God, who judges every man according to his deeds? Let us, therefore, cease from the desire of such vain knowledge, for often great distraction and the deceit of the enemy are found in it, and so the soul is much hindered and blocked from the perfect and true love of God.

Those who have great learning desire generally to seem to be accounted wise in the world. But there are many things whose knowedge brings but little profit and little fruit to the soul; he is most unwise who gives heed to any other thing except what will profit him to the health of his soul. Words do not feed the soul, but a good life refreshes the mind, and a clean conscience brings a man to a firm and stable trust in God. The more knowledge you have, the more grievously will you be judged for its misuse, if you do not live according to it. Therefore, do not lift yourself up into pride, because of any skill or knowledge that is given you, but have the more fear and dread in your heart—for it is certain that, hereafter, you must yield a stricter accounting. If you think that you know many things and have great learning, then know for certain that there are many more things you do not know. So with true wisdom you may not think yourself learned, but ought rather to confess your ignorance and folly. Why will you prefer yourself in knowledge before another, since there are many others more excellent and more wise than you and better learned in the Law? If you would learn anything and know it profitably to the health of your soul, learn to be unknown and be glad to be considered despicable and as nothing.

The highest and most profitable learning is this: that a man have a truthful knowledge and a full despising of himself. More, not to presume of himself, but always to judge and think well and blessedly of another, is a sign and token of great wisdom and of great perfection and of singular grace. If you see any person sin or commit any great crime openly before you, do not judge yourself to be better than he, for you know not how long you shall persevere in goodness. We are all frail, but you shall judge no man more frail than yourself.

3. OF THE TEACHING OF TRUTH

Happy and blessed is he whom truth teaches and informs, not by symbols and deceitful voices, but as the truth is. Our opinion, our intelligence, and our understanding often deceive us, for we do not see the truth. Of what use is the knowledge of such things as will neither help us on the day of judgment if we know them, nor hurt us if we do not know them? It is, therefore, great folly to be negligent of such things as are profitable and necessary to us, and to labor for such things as are worthless and to be condemned. Truly, if we so act, we have eyes but see not.

And of what avail is knowledge of the variety and operations of creatures? Truly, nothing. He to whom the everlasting Word, that is, Jesus, speaks, is freed of many vain opinions. From that Word all things proceed and all things openly show and cry that He is God. Without Him, no man understands the truth, or judges rightly. But a person to whom all things are one, and he who draws all things into one and establishes all things in one and desires nothing but one, may quickly be made firm in heart and fully at peace in God.

O Truth that is God, make us one with You in perfect charity, for all that I read, hear, or see without You is grievous to me; in You is all that I will or can desire! Let all learned ones be quiet in Your presence and let all creatures keep themselves in silence and do You only, Lord, speak to my soul. The more a man is one with You, and the more he is gathered together in You, the more he understands without labor high secret mysteries, for he has received from above the light of understanding. A clean, pure and constant heart is not broken or easily overcome by spiritual labors, for he does all things to the honor of God, because he is clearly mortified to himself. Therefore, he desires to be free from following his own will. What hinders you more than your own affections not fully mortified to the will of the spirit? Truly, nothing more.

A good devout man so orders his outward business that it does not draw him to love of it; rather, he compels his business to be obedient to the will of the spirit and to the right judgment of reason. Who wages a stronger battle than he who labors to overcome himself? And it should be our daily desire to overcome ourselves, so that we may be made stronger in spirit and go daily from better to better. Every perfection in this life has some imperfection attached to it, and there is no knowledge in this world that is not mixed with some blindness or ignorance. Therefore, a humble knowledge of ourselves is a surer way to God than is the search for depth of learning.

Well-ordered learning is not to be belittled, for it is good and comes from God, but a clean conscience and a virtuous life are much better and more to be desired. Because some men study to have learning rather than to live well, they err many times, and bring forth little good fruit or none. Oh, if they would be as busy to avoid sin and plant virtues in their souls as they are to dispute questions, there would not be so many evil things seen in the world, or so much evil example given to the people, or so much dissolute living in religion. On the day of judgment we will not be asked what we have read, but what we have done; not how well we have discoursed, but how religiously we have lived.

Tell me, where now are all the great students and famous scholars whom you have known? When alive, they flourished greatly in their learning, but now, others have succeeded to their posts and promotions, and I cannot tell whether their successors give them a thought. In their lifetime they were considered great in the world; now, little is spoken of them. Oh, how swiftly the glory of this world, with all its false, deceitful pleasures, passes away. Would to God their life had accorded well with their learning, for then would they have studied and read well. How many perish daily in this world by vain learning who care little for a good life and for the service of God. And because they desire to be great in the world rather than to be humble, they vanish away in their learning as smoke in the air.

He is truly great who has great charity. And he is great who is little in his own sight and who sets at naught all worldly honor. And he is very wise who accounts all worldly pleasures as vile dung, so that he may win Christ. And he is very well taught who forsakes his own will and follows the will of God.

4. THAT EASY CREDENCE IS NOT TO BE GIVEN TO WORDS

It is not good, truly, to believe every word or impression that comes; they ought to be pondered and considered advisedly and leisurely, so that Almighty God may not be offended through our fickleness. But alas, for sorrow, we are so frail that we quickly believe evil of others sooner than good. Nevertheless, perfect men are not so ready to give credence, for they well know that the frailty of man is more prone to evil than to good, and that he is very unstable in words. It is great wisdom, therefore, not to be hasty in our deeds, not to trust much in our own wits, not readily to believe every tale, not to show straightway to others all that we hear or believe.

Always take counsel of a wise man, and desire to be instructed and governed by others rather than to follow your own ingenuity. A good life makes a man wise toward God and instructs him in many things a sinful man will never feel or know. The more humble a man is in himself and the more obedient he is to God, the more wise and peaceful will he be in everything he will have to do.

5. ON THE READING OF HOLY SCRIPTURE

Charity and not eloquence is to be sought in Holy Scripture, and it should be read in the same spirit with which it was first made. We ought also to seek in Holy Scripture spiritual profit rather than elegance of style, and to read simple and devout books as gladly as books of high learning and wisdom. Do not let the authority of the author irk you, whether he be of great learning or little, but let the love of every pure truth stir you to read. Ask not: Who said this; but heed well what is said. Men pass lightly away, but the truth of God endures forever.

Almighty God speaks to us in His Scriptures in various manners, without regard for persons, but our curiosity often hinders us in reading Scripture when we reason and argue things we should humbly and simply pass over. If you will profit by reading Scripture, read humbly, simply, and faithfully, and never desire to gain by your reading the name of learned. Ask gladly and heed humbly the sayings of saints, and do not disdain the parables of the ancient Fathers, for they were not spoken without great cause.

6. OF INORDINATE AFFECTIONS

When a man desires anything inordinately, he is at once unquiet in himself. The proud and covetous man never has rest, but the humble man and the poor in spirit lives in great abundance of rest and peace. A man not mortified to himself is easily tempted and overcome by little and small temptations. And he who is weak in spirit and is yet somewhat carnal and inclined to worldly things can with difficulty withdraw himself from worldly desires; when he does withdraw himself from them, he often has great grief and heaviness of heart and rebels if any man resists him. And if he obtains what he desires, he is disquieted by remorse of conscience, for he has followed his passion which has not helped at all in winning the peace he desired. By resisting passion, and not by following it, the truest peace of heart is won. There is, therefore, no peace in the heart of a carnal man or in the heart of a man who gives himself all to outward things. But in the heart of spiritual men and women who have their delight in God great peace and inward quiet are found.

7. THAT VAIN HOPE AND ELATION OF MIND ARE TO BE FLED AND AVOIDED

He is vain who puts his trust in man or in any created thing. Be not ashamed to serve others for the love of Jesus Christ, and to be poor in this world for His sake. Trust not in yourself, but set all your trust in God: do all in your power to please Him and He will well assist your good will. Trust not in your own wisdom or in the wisdom or plans of any living creature, but instead, in the grace of God who helps humble persons and allows those who presume of themselves to fall until they are humbled. Glory not in your riches, or in your worldly friends, because they are mighty; let all your glory be in God only, who gives all things and desires to give Himself above all things.

Exult not in the strength or fairness of your body, for by a little sickness it may soon be disfigured. Rejoice not in your ability or readiness of wit, lest you displease God, of whose free gift comes all that you have. Do not think yourself better than others, lest perhaps you be thereby belittled in the sight of God who knows all that is in man. Be not proud of your good deeds, for the judgments of God are different from the judgments of man, and what pleases man often displeases God. If you have any goodness or virtue, believe firmly that there is much more goodness and virtue in others, so that you may always keep yourself in humility. No harm comes if you hold yourself worse than any other, though it may not in truth be so, but much harm results if you prefer yourself above any other, even if he is ever so great a sinner. Great peace is with the humble man, but in the heart of a proud man are always envy and anger.

8. THAT MUCH FAMILIARITY IS TO BE AVOIDED

Open not your heart to every person, but only to him who is wise, discreet, and reverent. Go seldom among strangers; neither flatter the rich nor bear yourself as an equal among the great. Keep company with the humble and the simple in heart, who are devout and of good deportment, and treat with them of things that may edify and strengthen your soul. Be not familiar with any woman, but commend all good women to God. Desire to be familiar only with God and with His angels; have a care to avoid the familiarity of man as much as you can. Charity is to be had toward all; familiarity is not expedient.

Sometimes it happens that an unknown person, whose good reputation commended him much, does not appeal to us when afterwards we meet him. We think sometimes to please others by our presence, but we displease them instead by all the evil manners and evil conditions they see and will consider in us.

9. OF HUMBLE SUBJECTION AND OBEDIENCE AND THAT WE SHOULD GLADLY FOLLOW THE COUNSEL OF OTHERS

It is a great thing to be obedient, to live under authority and to seek our own liberty in nothing. It is a much surer way to stand in the state of obedience than in the state of authority. Many are under obedience more out of necessity than of charity and they have great pain and easily murmur and complain; they will never have liberty or freedom of spirit until they submit themselves wholly to their superiors. Go here and there where you will, you will never find perfect rest, save in humble obedience, under the governance of your proper superior. Dreaming of a change of place has deceived many a person in religion.

It is certainly true that many a person in religion is disposed to act after his own will and can agree best with those who follow his own ways, but, if we desire that God be among us, we must sometimes set aside our own will (though it seem good) so that we may have love and peace with others. Who is so wise that he can fully know all things? No one, surely. Therefore, trust not too much in your own judgment, but gladly hear the advice of others. And if, perhaps, the thing you would have done might be good and profitable, and yet you set aside your own will with regard to it and follow another's will, you will thereby find much profit. I have often said that to hear and take counsel is a more sure way than to give it. It is good to hear every man's counsel; not to agree with it, when reason demands agreement, is a sign of a great isolation of mind and of much inward pride.

10. THAT WE SHOULD AVOID SUPERFLUITY OF WORDS AND THE COMPANY OF WORLDLY-LIVING PERSONS

Flee the company of worldly-living persons as much as you can, for the treating of worldly matters greatly hinders the fervor of spirit, even though it be done with a good intention. We are soon deceived by the vanity of the world and in a manner are made a slave to it, unless we take good heed.

I would I had held my peace many times when I spoke and that I had not been so much among worldly company as I have been. But why are we so glad to speak and commune together, since we so seldom depart without some harm to our conscience? This is the cause: By communing together we think to comfort each other and to refresh our hearts when we are troubled by vain imaginations, and we speak most gladly of such things as we most love, or else of things that are most irksome to us. But alas, for sorrow, all we do is vain, for this outward comfort is no little hindrance to the true inward comfort that comes from God.

It is necessary, therefore, that we watch and pray that time does not pass away from us in idleness. If it is lawful and expedient, speak, then, of God and of such things as are edifying to your soul and your neighbor's. Bad habits and neglect of our spiritual profit often make us take little heed how we should speak. Nevertheless, a devout communing on spiritual things sometimes greatly helps the health of the soul, especially when men of one mind and spirit in God meet and speak and commune together.

11. THE MEANS TO GET PEACE, AND OF DESIRE TO PROFIT IN VIRTUES

We might have much peace if we would not meddle with other men's sayings and doings that do not concern us. How can he long live in peace who willfully meddles with other men's business and who seeks occasions for it straightway in the world and seldom or never gathers himself together in God? Blessed by the true, simple, and humble people, for they shall have a great plentitude of peace.

Why have many saints been so perfectly contemplative? Because they studied always to mortify themselves from worldly desires, that they might freely, with all the power of their heart, tend to our Lord. But we are occupied with our passions and are much busied with transitory things, and it is very seldom that we may fully overcome any one vice. And we are not at all quick to the performance of our duties, so we remain cold and slow to devotion. If we were perfectly mortified to the flesh and to the world, and were inwardly purified in soul, we should soon have a taste for heavenly things, and should to some degree experience heavenly contemplation. The greatest hindrance to heavenly contemplation is that we are not yet clearly delivered from all passions and concupiscence. We do not force ourselves to follow the way that holy saints have taken before us, but when any little adversity comes to us, we are at once cast down, and turn all too soon to seek human comfort. But if, like strong men and mighty champions, we would fight strongly in this spiritual battle, we should undoubtedly see the help of God come in our need, for He is always ready to help all who trust in Him. And He brings about occasions for such battles so that we may overcome and win the victory, and in the end have the greater reward.

If we place the end and perfection of our religion in outward observances, our devotion will soon be ended; and so we must set our axe deep to the root of the tree, so that, purged from all passion, we may have a quiet mind. If we would every year overcome one vice, we should soon come to perfection; but I fear rather, to the contrary, that we were better and more pure at the beginning of our conversion than we were many years after we were converted. Our fervor and desire for virtue should daily increase in us as we increase in age, but it is now thought a great thing if we may hold a little spark of the fervor that we had first. If we would at the beginning break the evil inclination we have to ourselves and to our own will, we should afterwards do virtuous works easily.

It is a hard thing to leave evil customs and it is harder to break our own will, but it is most hard forever to lie in pain and forever to lose the joys of heaven. If you do not overcome small and light things, how shall you then overcome the greater? Resist quickly at the beginning your evil inclinations and leave off wholly all your evil customs, lest, perhaps, by little and little they afterwards bring you greater difficulty. Oh, if you would consider how great inward peace you would have yourself, and how great gladness you would cause in others by behaving yourself well, I truly believe you would be much more diligent to profit in virtue than you have been before this.

12. OF THE PROFIT OF ADVERSITY

It is good that we sometimes have griefs and adversities, for they drive a man to behold himself and to see that he is here but as in exile, and to learn thereby that he ought not put his trust in any worldly thing. It also is good that we sometimes suffer contradiction, and that we be thought of by others as evil and wretched and sinful, though we do well and intend well; such things help us to humility, and mightily defend us from vainglory and pride. We take God better to be our judge and witness when we are outwardly despised in the world and the world does not judge well of us. Therefore, a man ought to establish himself so fully in God that, whatever adversity befall him, he will not need to seek any outward comfort.

When a good man is troubled or tempted, or is disquieted by evil thoughts, then he understands and knows that God is most necessary to him, and that he may do nothing that is good without God. Then the good man sorrows and weeps and prays because of the miseries he rightly suffers. Then the wretchedness of this life burdens him, too, and he yearns to be dissolved from this body of death and to be with Christ, for he sees that there can be no full peace or perfect security here in this world.

13. OF TEMPTATIONS TO BE RESISTED

As long as we live in this world we cannot be fully without temptation, for, as Job says, the life of man upon earth is a warfare. Therefore, every man should be well on guard against his temptations, and watch in prayer so that his spiritual enemy, who never sleeps but always goes about seeking whom he may devour, may find no time or place to deceive him.

There is no man so perfect or so holy in this world that he does not sometimes have temptations, and we cannot be fully without them. Though they be for a time very grievous and painful, yet if they are resisted they are very profitable, for by them a man is made more humble and is purified and instructed in various manners which he would never have known save through the experience of such temptations. All the blessed saints who are now crowned in heaven grew and profited by temptations and tribulations; those that could not well bear temptations, but were finally overcome, are held perpetual prisoners in hell.

There is no station so holy or any place so secret that it is fully without temptation, and there is no man fully free from it here in this life, for in our corruptible body we bear the matter whereby we are tempted, that is, our inordinate concupiscence with which we were born. As one temptation goes, another comes; and so we shall always have something to suffer, and the reason is that we have lost our innocence.

Many people seek to flee temptation and fall the more deeply into it, for by merely fleeing we cannot win the victory, but by humility and patience we may be made stronger than all our enemies. He who merely flees the outward occasions and does not cut away the inordinate desires hidden inwardly in his heart shall gain little; temptation will easily come to him again and grieve him more than it did at first. Little by little, with patience and fortitude, and with the help of God, you will sooner overcome temptations than with your own strength and persistence. In your temptation it is good often to ask counsel. It is good not to be severe on any person who is tempted; rather, be glad to comfort him as you would be glad to be comforted.

The beginning of all evil temptations is inconstancy of mind and too little trust in God. As a ship without a rudder is driven hither and thither by every storm, so an unstable man who soon leaves his good purpose in God is variously tempted. Fire proves gold, and temptation proves the righteous man.

Many times we know not what we can bear, but temptation shows plainly what we are, and what virtue is in us. It is necessary at the beginning of every temptation to be well aware, for the enemy is soon overcome if he is not allowed to enter the heart, but is resisted and shut out as soon as he attempts to enter.

As medicine for the body is administered too late when the sickness has been allowed to increase by long continuance, so it is with temptation. First, an unclean thought comes to the mind, then follows a strong phantasm, then pleasure in it and various evil motions, and at the end follows a full consent; so, little by little, the enemy gains full entrance, because he was not wisely resisted at the beginning. The slower a man is in resisting, the weaker he is to resist, and the enemy is daily stronger against him.

Some people have their greatest temptation at the beginning of their conversion, some at the end, and some after a fashion are troubled with temptations all their life, and there are many who are but lightly tempted. And all this comes from the great wisdom and righteousness of God, who knows the state and merit of every person, and ordains all things for the best and for the everlasting health and salvation of His elect and chosen ones.

Therefore, we shall not despair when we are tempted, but shall the more fervently pray to God, that of His infinite goodness and fatherly pity He may vouchsafe to help us in every need; and that, according to the saying of St. Paul, He may so go before us with His grace in every temptation that we may be able to bear it. Let us, then, humble ourselves under the strong hand of Almighty God, for He will save and exalt all who are here meek and lowly in spirit.

In temptations and tribulations a man is proved, and how much he has gained is shown, and his merit is thereby the greater in the sight of God, and his virtues the more openly manifest. It is no great marvel if a man is fervent and devout when he feels no grief. But if he can suffer patiently in the time of temptation or other adversity and, despite it, stir himself also to fervor of spirit, it is a token that he will advance greatly thereafter in virtue and grace. Some people are kept from any great temptations, and yet are daily overcome in little and small occasions; that happens because the great goodness and patience of God would keep them in humility, so that they will not trust or presume of themselves, since they see themselves daily overcome so easily and in such little things.

14. THAT WE WILL NOT TOO EASILY JUDGE OTHER MEN'S DEEDS, OR CLING MUCH TO OUR OWN WILL

Always have a good eye to yourself, and be careful not to judge other men too easily. In judging others a man often labors in vain, often errs, and carelessly offends God, but in judging himself and his own deeds he always labors fruitfully and to his spiritual profit. We often judge according to our own heart and affections, and not according to the truth. We lose true judgment through love of ourselves. But if God were always the whole intent of our desires, we should not so easily err in our judgments, or be so readily troubled because our own will has been resisted. But commonly there is in us some inward inclination or some outward affection which draws our heart along with them away from true judgment.

Many persons, through a secret love that they have for themselves, work indiscreetly according to their own will and not according to the will of God, yet they do not know it. They seem to stand in great inward peace when things go according to their own mind, but if anything happens contrary to their mind, they are soon moved with impatience and are quite downcast and melancholy.

From diversity of opinion dissension between friends and neighbors often springs, and also between religious and devout persons. An old habit is not easily broken, and no man will readily be moved from his own will; but if you cling more to your own will or to your own reason than to the humble obedience of Jesus Christ, it will be long before you are a man illumined by grace. Almighty God wills that we be perfectly subject and obedient to Him, and that we rise high above our own will and our own reason by a great burning love and a complete desire for Him.

15. OF WORKS DONE IN CHARITY

Not for anything in the world or for the love of any created thing is evil to be done. But sometimes, for the need and comfort of our neighbor, a good deed may be deferred or turned into another good deed. Thereby the good deed is not destroyed, but is changed into better.

The outward deed without charity is little to be praised, but whatever is done from charity, even if it be ever so little and worthless in the sight of the world, is very profitable before God, who judges all things according to the intent of the doer, not according to the greatness or worthiness of the deed. He does much who loves God much, and he does much who does his deed well, and he does his deed well who does it rather for the common good than for his own will. A deed sometimes seems to be done in charity and from a love of God, when it is really done out of worldly and fleshly love, rather than out of a love of charity. Commonly, some worldly inclination toward our friends, some inordinate love of ourselves, or some hope of a temporal reward or desire of some other gain moves us to do the deed, and not the pure love of charity.

Charity does not seek itself in what it does, but it desires to do only what will honor and praise God. Charity envies no man, for it loves no personal love. Charity will not joy in itself, but desires above all things to be blessed in God. Charity knows well that no goodness begins originally from man, and therefore charity refers all goodness to God, from whom all things proceed, and in whom all the blessed saints rest in everlasting fruition. Oh, he who has a little spark of this perfect charity should feel in his soul with certain truth that all earthly things are full of vanity.

16. OF BEARING OTHER MEN'S FAULTS

Such faults as we cannot amend in ourselves or in others we must patiently suffer until our Lord of His goodness will dispose otherwise. And we shall think that perhaps it is best for the testing of our patience, without which our merits are but little to be considered. Nevertheless, you shall pray heartily that our Lord, of His great mercy and goodness, may vouchsafe to help us to bear such burdens patiently.

If you admonish any person once or twice, and he will not accept it, do not strive too much with him, but commit all to God, that His will may be done, and His honor acknowledged in all His servants, for by His goodness He can well turn evil into good. Study always to be patient in bearing other men's defects, for you have many in yourself that others suffer from you, and if you cannot make yourself be as you would, how may you then look to have another regulated in all things to suit your will?

We would gladly have others perfect, yet we will not amend our own faults. We desire others to be strictly corrected for their offenses, yet we will not be corrected. We dislike it that others have liberty, yet we will not be denied what we ask. We desire that others should be restrained according to the laws, yet we will in no way be restrained. And so it appears evident that we seldom judge our neighbors as we do ourselves.

If all men were perfect, what would we then have to put up with in our neighbors, for God's sake? Therefore, God has so ordained that each one of us shall learn to bear another's burden, for in this world no man is without fault, no man without burden, no man sufficient to himself, and no man wise enough of himself. And so it behooves each one of us to bear the burden of others, to comfort others, to help others, to counsel others, and to instruct and admonish others in all charity. The time of adversity shows who is of most virtue. Occasions do not make a man frail, but they do show openly what he is.

17. WHAT SHOULD BE THE LIFE OF A TRUE RELIGIOUS PERSON

It behooves you to break your own will in many things, if you would have peace and concord with others. It is no little thing to be in monasteries and in religious congregations, to continue there without complaining or speaking amiss, and faithfully to persevere there until the end. Blessed are they who there live well and come to a good end. If you would stand surely in grace, and profit much in virtue, consider yourself as an exile and a pilgrim here in this life, and be glad, for the love of God, to be considered in the world as a foolish and an unworthy person, as you are.

The religious habit and the tonsure help little; the changing of one's life and the mortifying of passions make a person perfectly and truly religious. He who seeks any other thing in religion than God alone and the salvation of his soul will find nothing there but trouble and sorrow; he will not remain there long in peace and quiet who does not labor to be the least, and subject to all.

It is good, therefore, to remember often that you came to religion to serve and not to be served, and that you are called in religion to suffer and to labor, and not to be idle or to tell vain tales. In religion, a person shall be proved as gold in a furnace, and no person in religion can remain long in grace and virtue unless he will humble himself with all his heart for the love of God.

St. Ignatius of Loyola
1491-1556

St. Ignatius Loyola, founder of the Society of Jesus and author of the famous Spiritual Exercises, *was born in Spain in 1491. Throughout his youth and during the years prior to his religious conversion in 1521-22, his life was involved with nobility and the military. The account of his battle wounds in 1521 and the period of convalescence during which he slowly oriented his entire existence toward God and Jesus Christ is one of the better known conversion stories in Christianity. This period was followed by years of study, penance, prayer and apostolic activity. The twofold goal that evolved for Ignatius was the greater promotion of God's glory and the education of men that they might know and achieve their true destiny. He was convinced that the Society, founded in 1539-40, would achieve these goals to its love of the Church and its obedience to the papacy. Ignatius was the general of the Society from the time of its foundation until his death in 1556. He was canonized in 1622. The impact he has had on the history of Christianity by way of the Society of Jesus is immeasurable.*

Besides a life of organization and administration, Ignatius lived a very rich spiritual life which led him to the heights of mysticism. The spiritual writings of Ignatius reveal much of his interior life. It shows how he was totally permeated with the mystery of the Trinity. Ignatius was caught up in both the internal dynamism of the Persons of the Trinity and the external communication of the Trinity through the mystery of the Incarnation. This led him to an incredible love for and service of the ordinary, everyday world. Rather than detaching him from the suffering and sorrow of his fellow man, his mystical life enabled him to be at home with any human situation. He actually beheld at the center of human fragility and weakness the wonderful triune God of all creation. Ignatius was clearly a most unusual man.

His Spiritual Exercises *are the fruit of his life of prayer. No doubt the methodology contained in the* Exercises *was influenced by the spiritual authors with whom Ignatius was familiar. But what he took from predecessors he interiorized and personalized. By way of the* Exercises, *mental prayer or meditation took on a central role in the spiritual life. The underlying assumption was that a disciplined, organized life of meditation would lead a person to an enriched spiritual state. The method was anchored in solid Christian doctrine. It enabled a person to move in two directions, both toward an interior reflection on a given aspect of the Christian mystery in order more fully to grasp the truth of the Christian life and toward an exterior, concrete application of the reflection. The two were necessarily interdependent. One can see here the same dual movement that sustained Ignatius himself.*

The following selections from the writings of Ignatius present various aspects of his spiritual growth process. The letter to St. Francis Borgia, particularly, is an amazing summary of much of Ignatius' teaching. It reveals both his tremendous thirst for a mystical life in God and his common sense approach to everyday details. His basic message is clear: whatever we do, seek, or desire, all should be for God's greater glory.

ST. IGNATIUS' OWN STORY

CHAPTER 3

E very day he begged alms in Manresa. He ate no meat, drank no wine, although both were offered him. On Sundays he did not fast, and he drank the little wine that was given him. Because he had been quite delicate about caring for his hair, which in those days was quite the vogue—and he had a good head of hair—he made up his mind to neglect it and to let it grow wild, without combing or cutting it or covering it either day or night. For the same reason he allowed the nails of his hands and feet to grow, because here too he had been excessive. While he was in this hospital, it often happened to him in broad daylight to see something in the air close to him, which gave him great consolation because it was very beautiful. He could not make out clearly what the thing was, but somehow it appeared to have the form of a serpent. It was bright with objects that shone like eyes, although they were not eyes. He found great delight and consolation in looking at this thing, and the more he saw it the greater grew his consolation. When it disappeared it left him displeased.

Up to this time he had continued in the same interior state of great and undisturbed joy, without any knowledge of the inner things of the soul. Throughout the days when this vision lasted, or a little before it began, for it went on for many days, there occurred to him a rather disturbing thought which troubled him by representing to him the difficulty of the life he was leading, as though he heard a voice within him saying: "How can you stand a life like this for the seventy years you have yet to live?" But this he answered also interiorly with great strength, feeling that it was the voice of the enemy: "You poor creature! Can you promise me even one hour of life?" In this way he overcame the temptation and remained at peace. This is the first temptation that came to him after what has been said above. It happened while he was entering the church in which he heard high Mass daily, as well as vespers and compline, which were always sung, and in which he found great spiritual comfort. As a rule he read the passion during the Mass, always preserving his serenity of soul.

But soon after the temptation just now related, he began to experience great changes in his soul. Sometimes his distaste was so great that he found no relish in any of the prayers he recited, or in hearing Mass, or in any kind of prayer he made. At other times everything was just the contrary, and so suddenly, that he seemed to have got rid of the sadness and desolation pretty much as one removes a cloak from the shoulders of another. Here he began to marvel at these changes which he had never before experienced, saying to himself: "What new kind of life is this that we are now beginning?" At this time he still spoke occasionally with a few spiritual persons who had some regard for him and liked to talk with him. For although he had no knowledge of spiritual things, he showed much fervor in his talk and a great desire to go forward in the service of God. There was in Manresa at that time a woman of many years, who for a long time had been a servant of God. She was known as such in many parts of Spain, so much so that the Catholic King had called her once to tell her something. This woman, meeting one day with this new soldier of Christ said to him: "May our Lord Jesus Christ appear to you some day!" He was surprised at this and, giving a literal meaning to her words, asked, "And how would Jesus Christ appear to me?" On Sundays he never missed his weekly confession and communion.

But at this time he had much to suffer from scruples. Although the general confession he had made at Montserrat had been entirely written out and made carefully enough, there still remained some things which from time to time he thought he had not confessed. This caused him a good deal of worry, for even though he had confessed it, his mind was never at rest. He began, therefore, to look for some spiritual man who would cure him of his scruples, but without success. Finally a doctor of the Cathedral Church, a very spiritual man who preached there, told him one day in confession to write out all he could remember. He did so. But after confessing it his scruples returned, each time becoming more minute, so that he became quite upset, and although he knew that these scruples were doing him much harm and that it would be good to be rid of them, he could not shake them off. Sometimes he thought the cure would be for the confessor to tell him in the name of Jesus Christ never to mention anything of the past, and he wished that his confessor would so direct him, but he did not dare tell the confessor so.

But without his having said a word to him, his confessor told him not to confess anything of his past life unless it was something absolutely clear. As he thought that everything was quite clear, this direction was of no use to him and he remained always with his trouble. At this time he was in a small room which the Dominicans had given him in their monastery, where he continued with his seven hours of prayer on his knees, rising faithfully every midnight, and performing all the other exercises already mentioned. But none of them provided him with a cure for his scruples, although it was now some months that they had been afflicting him. One day, when he was especially tormented, he began to pray and to call aloud to God, crying out in his fervor: "Help me, O Lord, since I find no help from men or from any creature. No trial would be too great for me to bear if I thought there was any hope of finding that help. Do you, Lord, show me where I can find it, and even though I should have to follow a little dog to find it, I would do so."

While these thoughts were tormenting him he was frequently seized with the temptation to throw himself into an excavation close to his room and adjacent to the place where he did his praying. But, knowing that it was a sin to do away with himself, he cried again: "Lord, I will do nothing to offend you," frequently repeating these words as he did the first. Here he recalled the story of a saint who to obtain from God something he much desired, went many days without eating until he got what he wanted. Giving a good deal of thought to this fact, he finally made up his mind to do the same thing, telling himself that he would neither eat nor drink until God did something for him, or he saw that death was approaching. For, if he saw himself reduced to the extremity of having to die if he did not eat, in that case he would ask for bread and food (as though in that extremity, he could either ask for it or even eat it).

He resorted to this one Sunday after having received communion, and went through the whole week without putting a morsel of food into his mouth. He omitted none of his ordinary exercises, even going to the divine office and praying on his knees from midnight on, and so forth. But on the following Sunday, which was his confession day, as he was accustomed to be very detailed with his confessor, he told him also that he had eaten nothing that week. The confessor bade him give up this abstinence, and although he was still strong, he obeyed his confessor, and that day and the next found himself delivered from his scruples. But on the third day, which was Tuesday, while he was praying he began to recall his sins, and so went on thinking of his past sins, one after the other, as though one grew out of another, till he felt that it was his bounden duty to confess them once again. As a sequel to these thoughts, he was seized with a disgust of the life he was leading and a desire to be done with it. It was our Lord's way of awakening him as it were from sleep. As he now had some experience of the different spirits from the lessons he had received from God, he began to look about for the way in which that spirit had been able to take possession of him. He therefore made up his mind, which had become very clear on the matter, never to confess his past sins again, and from that day on he remained free of those scruples, holding it a certainty that our Lord in His mercy had liberated him.

Besides his seven hours of prayer, he busied himself with certain souls who came looking for him to discuss their spiritual interests. All the rest of the day he spent thinking of divine things, those especially which he had either read or meditated that day. But when he went to bed he received great illuminations and spiritual consolations which made him lose much of the time he had set aside for sleep, and that was not much. He looked into this matter a number of times and gave it some thought. Having set aside so much time for dealing with God, and besides that even all the rest of the day; he began to doubt whether these illuminations came from the good spirit. He concluded that he had better not have anything to do with them, and give the time determined on to sleep. And this he did.

While he was carrying out his abstinence from meat, without any thought of changing it, one morning as he got up, a dish of meat appeared before him as though he actually saw it with his eyes. But he had no antecedent desire for it. At the same time he felt within himself a great movement of the will to eat it in the future. Although he remembered his former resolve, he could not hesitate to make up his mind that he ought to eat meat. Relating this to his confessor later, the confessor told him that he ought to find out whether this was a temptation. But he, examine it as he would, could never have any doubt about it.

At this time God treated him just as a schoolmaster treats a little boy when he teaches him. This perhaps was because of his rough and uncultivated understanding, or because he had no one to teach him, or because of the firm will God Himself had given him in His service. But he clearly saw, and always had seen that God dealt with him like this. Rather, he thought that any doubt about it would be an offense against His Divine Majesty. Something of this can be gathered from the five following points.

First. He had a great devotion to the Most Holy Trinity, and thus daily prayed to the Three Persons distinctly. While he was also praying to the Most Holy Trinity, the objection occurred to him as to how he could say four prayers to the Trinity. But this thought gave him little or no trouble, as being something of only slight importance. One day while he was reciting the Hours of our Lady on the steps of the same monastery, his understanding began to be elevated as though he saw the Holy Trinity under the figure of three keys. This was accompanied with so many tears and so much sobbing that he could not control himself. That morning he accompanied a procession which left the monastery and was not able to restrain his tears until dinner time. Nor afterwards could he stop talking about the Most Holy Trinity. He made use of many different comparisons and experienced great joy and consolation. The result was that all through his life this great impression has remained with him, to feel great devotion when he prays to the Most Holy Trinity.

Second. Another time there was represented to his understanding with great spiritual delight the manner in which God had created the world. It had the appearance of something white out of which rays were coming, and it was out of this that God made light. But he did not know how to explain these things, nor did he remember well the spiritual illumination which at that time God impressed upon his soul.

Third. At Manresa also, where he remained almost a year, after he began to feel God's consolations and saw the fruit produced in the souls with whom he dealt, he gave up those outward extremes he formerly adopted, and trimmed his nails and hair. One day, in this town, when he was hearing Mass in the church of the monastery already mentioned, during the elevation he saw with the inner eyes of the soul something like white rays that came from above. Although he cannot explain this after so long a time, yet what he clearly saw with his understanding was how Jesus Christ our Lord is present in that most holy sacrament.

Fourth. When he was at prayer, he often and for a long time saw with the inner eyes the humanity of Christ. The shape which appeared to him was like a white body, not very large or very small, but he saw no distinction of members. He often saw this in Manresa. If he were to say twenty, or even forty times, he would not venture to say that it was an untruth. He saw it another time when he was in Jerusalem, and still another when he was on the road near Padua. He has also seen our Lady in like form, without distinction of parts. These things which he saw gave him at the time great strength, and were always a striking confirmation of his faith, so much so that he has often thought to himself that if there were no Scriptures to teach us these matters of faith, he was determined to die for them, merely because of what he had seen.

Fifth. Once out of devotion he was going to a church which was about a mile distant from Manresa, and which I think was called St. Paul. The road ran along close to the river. Moving along intent on his devotion, he sat down for a moment with his face towards the river which there ran deeply. As he sat, the eyes of his understanding began to open. He beheld no vision, but he saw and understood many things, spiritual as well as those concerning faith and learning. This took place with so great an illumination that these things appeared to be something altogether new. He cannot point out the particulars of what he then understood, although they were many, except that he received a great illumination in his understanding. This was so great that in the whole course of his past life right up to his sixty-second year, if he were to gather all the helps he had received from God, and everything he knew, and add them together, he does not think that they would equal all that he received at that one time.

After this had lasted for some time he went to kneel at a nearby cross to give thanks to God, where again appeared that vision which he had often seen and which he had never understood, that is, the object described above, which he thought very beautiful and which seemed to have many eyes. But he noticed that as it stood before the cross it did not have that beautiful color as heretofore, and he understood very clearly, with a strong assent of his will, that it was the evil one. Later it often appeared to him for a long time, but he drove it away with the pilgrim's staff he held in his hand and a gesture of contempt.

Once in Manresa he was ill with a high fever which brought him to death's door, and he felt sure that his soul was about to leave his body. At this moment the thought occurred to him that he was a just man. It annoyed him to such an extent that he did nothing but resist it and place his sins before his eyes. He had more trouble with this thought than with the fever itself, but he could not overcome it no matter how he tried to get the better of it. However, as the fever abated a little and he was no longer in immediate danger of death, he began to cry out to certain ladies who had come to visit him that for the love of God if ever they saw him at the point of death again, they should cry out and remind him that he was a sinner and should remember the offenses he had committed against God.

On another occasion, when he was on his way from Valencia to Italy by sea, the rudder of the ship was broken by a mighty storm, and matters came to such a pass that in his own judgment and that of many other passengers they could not in the ordinary course of events escape death. He examined himself carefully and prepared for death, but could not have any fear because of his sins, or of being condemned. He had rather great confusion and sorrow for not having made a proper use of the gifts and graces that God our Lord had bestowed upon him.

Again in the year 1550 he was very ill, and he and many others thought that his last hour had come. This time, thinking about death, he found so much joy and so much spiritual consolation in the thought of dying that he melted into tears. This became so common with him that he often turned his thoughts away from death to avoid having so much of this consolation.

At the beginning of winter (1522), he came down with a very severe illness, and the town placed him in the house of the father of a certain Ferrera, who was later in the service of Baltasar de Faria. Here he was very attentively cared for, and many prominent ladies of the town came to watch over him at night out of the devotion they felt for him. But even after his recovery from this illness, he remained quite weak with frequent stomach pains. For this reason, and also because the winter was very severe, they insisted that he dress properly, wear shoes and a hat, two dark gray jackets of a rough sort of cloth, with a headpiece that was half bonnet and half cap. At this time there were many days when he was very eager to hold forth on spiritual things, and to find those who were likewise interested in them. But the time was drawing near that he had set for his departure for Jerusalem.

Therefore, at the beginning of the year 1523, he left for Barcelona to take ship, and although several offered to accompany him, he preferred to travel by himself, since his whole purpose was to have God alone for refuge. One day he was beset by many who argued with him to take some companions on the grounds that he did not know Italian or Latin, and a companion would be of great help to him. He answered that even if the companion was the son or the brother of the Duke of Cardona he would not travel in his company. He desired, he said, three virtues, faith, hope and charity. If he had a companion he would expect help from him when he was hungry, and he would thus trust in him, and be drawn to place his affection in him, when he wanted to place all this confidence and affection and hope in God alone. He spoke thus out of the fullness of his heart. In this state of mind he wished to embark, not merely alone, but without any provisions for the voyage. When they discussed the cost of passage, he obtained free passage from the shipmaster, since he was without money. But he was expected to bring aboard enough ship's biscuit to keep him, and would not be taken aboard on any other condition.

When it came time to arrange for this biscuit he suffered great scruples. "Was this the faith and the hope that you had in God, of His not failing you?" The thought caused him a great deal of annoyance, and at length, now knowing what to do, as there were probable reasons on both sides, he made up his mind to place himself in the hands of his confessor. Thus, he made known how great was his desire for perfection, and for the greater glory of God, and the reasons which caused him to doubt whether he should bring along anything for his support. The confessor decided that he should ask what was necessary and take it along with him. Asking it of a lady, she enquired where he was going. For a moment he doubted whether he should tell her, and finally did not dare tell her more than that he was going to Italy and Rome. Taken by surprise, she said, "You want to go to Rome? Why, there's no telling how they return who go there," meaning to say that they who go to Rome get little spiritual profit from it. His reason for not saying that he was Jerusalem bound was his fear of vainglory, a fear that so afflicted him that he never dared to say what land he came from or to what family he belonged. Finally, he got on board with his biscuit. But when he came to the seashore, finding five or six *blancas* in his pockets, all that was left of what he had begged from door to door, as this was the way he used to get along, he left them on a bench there on the seashore.

He went aboard, having been in Barcelona a little more than twenty days. While he was still in Barcelona before embarking, he sought out as usual all spiritual persons, even those who were living at a distance in hermitages, to hold conversation with them. But neither in Barcelona, nor in Manresa, could he find anyone to help him as much as he wished. Except in Manresa, that woman mentioned above, who said that she asked God that Jesus Christ appear to him, was the only one who to him seemed to be deeply versed in the spiritual life. Therefore, after leaving Barcelona he lost for good this eagerness to seek out spiritual persons.

CHAPTER 10

During those days in Venice he spent some time giving the Exercises and in other spiritual associations. The more important people to whom he gave them were Masters Peter Contarini and Gaspar De Doctis, and a Spaniard called Rojas. There was also another Spaniard who was called the Bachelor Hocez, who had a good deal to do with the pilgrim and also with the bishop of Ceuta. Although he had some desire to make the Exercises he never carried it into execution. Finally, however, he made up his mind to make them, and after the third or fourth day, opened his mind to the pilgrim to tell him that he had been afraid that some wicked doctrine was taught in the Exercises. Someone in fact had told him as much. It was for this reason that he had brought with him certain books which he could use as protection, if he happened to want to impose these doctrines on him. He found great help in the Exercises, and when they were over he resolved to follow the pilgrim's way of life. He was also the first to die.

In Venice also another persecution was begun against the pilgrim. There were many who said that his likeness had been burned in Spain and in Paris. Matters came to such a pass that a trial was held and sentence rendered in favor of the pilgrim.

The nine companions arrived at Venice in the beginning of 1537. There they separated to serve the sick in the different hospitals. After two or three months they all went to Rome to get the Pope's blessing before setting out on their journey to Jerusalem. The pilgrim did not go with them, because of Doctor Ortiz and the Theatine Cardinal who had just been created. The companions returned from Rome with drafts for two or three hundred *scudi* which they were given as alms to help them on their way to Jerusalem. They did not wish to receive the money, except in checks, and since they did not go to Jerusalem later, they returned the checks to those who had given them.

The companions returned to Venice just as they had left it, that is, on foot and begging, but divided into three parties, which were always made up of different nationalities. Those who were not priests were ordained in Venice, and received faculties from the Nuncio, who was in Venice at the time, and who was later called Cardinal Verallo. They were ordained under the title of poverty, all taking the vows of poverty and chastity.

During that year they could not find a ship for the Near East, because Venice had broken with the Turks. When they saw their hopes diminishing, they dispersed throughout the Domain of Venice, with the intention of waiting out the year they had decided upon, and then if there was no chance of getting passage, they would return to Rome.

It fell to the pilgrim to go with Faber and Laynez to Vicenza. There they found a house outside the city limits, which had neither door nor window, where they slept on a little straw they brought with them. Two of the three went twice daily to ask alms, and brought back so little that they could hardly subsist. Usually they ate a little toasted bread when they had it, prepared by the one whose lot it was to remain at home. In this manner they spent forty days intent on nothing but their prayers.

After the forty days, Master John Codure arrived, and the four of them decided to preach. They went to four different piazzas on the same day and at the same hour, and began to preach, first by shouting out to the people and waving their hats at them. This style of preaching started a great deal of talk in the city; many were moved to devotion and supplied their physical needs with greater abundance.

While he was in Vicenza he had many supernatural visions and much ordinary consolation, just the opposite of what he experienced in Paris. These consolations were specially given while he was preparing for ordination in Venice and getting ready to say his first Mass. In all his journeys he had great supernatural visitations of the kind he used to have when he was at Manresa. While he was in Vicenza, he learned that one of his companions who was staying at Bassano was sick and at death's door. He himself at the time was ill with a fever. Nevertheless, he started off and walked so fast that Faber, his companion, could not keep up with him. In that journey he was given the certainty by God, and so told Faber, that the companion would not die of that illness. When the pilgrim arrived at Bassano, the sick man was much consoled and soon got well.

All then returned to Vicenza, where all ten remained some days. Some went to seek alms in the towns adjacent to Vicenza.

As the year went by and they found no passage to Jerusalem, they decided to go to Rome, even the pilgrim, because the two persons about whom he doubted showed themselves very kindly disposed on the other occasion when his companions had gone there.

They went to Rome in three or four groups, the pilgrim with Faber and Laynez, and in this journey he received many special favors from God.

He had made up his mind after taking orders to wait a year before saying Mass, preparing himself and praying our Lady to place him with her Son. One day, a few miles before they reached Rome, while he was praying in a church, he felt such a change in his soul, and saw so clearly that God the Father placed him with Christ His Son, that he would not dare to doubt that the Father had placed him with His Son.

(I who am writing these things told the pilgrim when he narrated this, that Laynez had recounted this occurrence with some added details. He told me that whatever Laynez said was true, because he did not recall all the particulars in such detail. But he added: "When I told him that, I knew for certain that all I told him was true." He made the same statement to me about other things.)

Arriving at Rome, he observed to his companions that he noticed that all the windows were closed, meaning by that that they would have to suffer many contradictions. He also said: "We must walk very carefully and hold no conversations with women, unless they are well known." What happened to Master Francis is very pertinent here. At Rome he heard a woman's confession and visited her occasionally to talk about her spiritual life. She was later found to be pregnant. But it pleased God that the responsible party was caught. The same thing happened to John Codure whose spiritual daughter was caught with a man.

CHAPTER 11

From Rome the pilgrim went to Monte Cassino to give the Exercises to Doctor Ortiz, and was there for forty days, during which he one day saw the Bachelor Hocez entering heaven. He had many tears and deep spiritual consolation at this, and he saw this so clearly that if he said that he did not he would feel that he was lying. From Monte Cassino he brought Francis de Strada back to Rome with him.

Back at Rome, he worked helping souls, and still living at the vineyard he gave the Spiritual Exercises to different people at one and the same time, one of whom lived near St. Mary Major, and the other near the Ponte Sesto.

Persecutions now began, and Michael started to be annoying and to speak ill of the pilgrim, who had him summoned to the governor's court, first showing the governor a letter of Michael's which praised the pilgrim highly. The governor examined Michael, and put an end to the proceedings by banishing him from Rome.

Mudarra and Barreda opened their campaign of persecution. They alleged that the pilgrim and his companions were fugitives from Spain, Paris and Venice. In the end, both confessed in the presence of the governor and the legate who at the time was in Rome, that they had nothing wrong to say against them, either in their conduct or their teaching. The legate imposed silence in the case, but the pilgrim was not satisfied with that, declaring that he wanted a definitive sentence. This was pleasing neither to the legate nor the governor nor those who at first favored the pilgrim. But after a few months, the Pope finally returned to Rome, and the pilgrim went to Frascati to speak with him, and gave him a number of reasons. The Pope, being thus informed, commanded that sentence be pronounced, which which was done in favor of the pilgrim and his associates.

With the help of the pilgrim and his companions some works of piety were founded in Rome, such as the house of catechumens, the house of Santa Maria, and the orphanage. Master Nadal will be able to tell you all the rest.

After this recital, about October 20th, I asked the pilgrim about the Exercises, the Constitutions, wishing to learn how he drew them up. He answered that the Exercises were not composed all at one time, but things that he had observed in his own soul and found useful and which he thought would be useful to others, he put into writing—the examination of conscience, for example, with the idea of lines of different length, and so on. The forms of the election in particular, he told me, came from that variety of movement of spirits and thoughts which he experienced at Loyola, while he was still convalescing from his shattered leg. He said that he would speak to me about the Constitutions that evening.

That same day he called me before supper. He seemed to be more recollected than usual. He made a kind of protestation, the sum of which was to show the intention and the simplicity with which he had narrated these matters. He said that he was certain that he did not tell me anything beyond the facts, and that he had frequently offended our Lord after he had begun to serve Him, but that he had never given consent to a mortal sin. His devotion always went on increasing, that is, the ease with which he found God, which was then greater than he had ever had in his life. Whenever he wished, at whatever hour, he could find God. He also said he still had many visions, especially that in which he saw Christ as a sun, as mentioned above. This often happened to him, especially when he was speaking of matters of importance, and came to confirm him in his decision.

He also had many visions when he said Mass, and very frequently when he was drawing up the Constitutions. This he could affirm the more easily because he had the habit of setting down his thought every day, and these writings he had then found. He showed me a rather large bundle of collected writings, a large part of which he read to me. The larger part of the visions he saw in confirmation of some of the Constitutions, seeing now the Father, now all Three Persons of the Trinity, sometimes our Lady who interceded for him and sometimes confirmed what he had written.

In particular he told me of a decision on which he spent forty days, saying Mass each day, and each day shedding many tears. What he wanted to decide was whether our churches should have an income, and whether the Society could accept help from it.

His method of procedure, when he was drawing up the Constitutions, was to say Mass every day, and to lay the point he was treating before God, and to pray over it. He always made his prayer and said his Mass with tears.

I wanted to see all the papers dealing with the Constitutions, and I asked him to let me see them for a moment. But he would not.

LETTER TO ST. FRANCIS BORGIA

The Duke of Gandia was by this time a professed member of the Society of Jesus. By virtue of a papal brief, he continued with the administration of his estates, and in his palace led the life of a saint. In one of his letters to the Founder of the Society, he had given his opinion on his own exercises of prayer and penance. In the following letter St. Ignatius gives him rules that are full of wisdom to help him arrive at the proper mean in these exercises.

Rome, September 20, 1548

IHS

May the perfect grace and everlasting love of Christ our Lord be always in our favor and help.

When I hear how harmoniously you have reconciled your spiritual and temporal interests and directed them to your spiritual progress, I find fresh reason, I assure you, for rejoicing in our Lord, and while giving thanks to His Eternal Majesty I can attribute my joy only to His Divine Goodness, which is the source of all our blessings. And yet, I realize in our Lord that at one time we may be in need of certain exercises, spiritual as well as physical, and at another time we will need others: because those which for a season have proved profitable may cease to be so later, I will tell you what I think in His Divine Majesty on this subject, since your Lordship has asked for my views.

First. I should think that the time devoted to these exercises, both interior and exterior, should be reduced by half. We ought to increase these exercises, both interior and exterior, when our thoughts arise from ourselves, or are suggested by our enemy, and lead us to fix our attention on objects that are distracting, frivolous or forbidden, if we wish to prevent the will from taking any satisfaction in them or yielding any consent. I say that as a rule we ought to increase these exercises, both interior and exterior, the more these thoughts are multiplied, in order to conquer them, keeping in mind the character of the individual and the varying nature of the thoughts and temptations, and being careful to measure the exercises to the capacity of the individual. Contrariwise, when these thoughts lose their strength and cease, their place will be taken by holy thoughts and inspirations, and to these we must give the utmost welcome by opening to them all the doors of the soul. Consequently there will be no further need of so many weapons to overthrow the enemy.

From what I can judge of your Lordship in our Lord, it would be better if you were to devote to study about half the time that you now give to these exercises. In the future learning will always be very necessary, or certainly useful, and not only that which is infused, but that also which is acquired by study. Some of your time should be given to the administration of your estates and to spiritual conversation. Try to keep your soul always in peace and quiet, always ready for whatever our Lord may wish to work in you. It is certainly a more lofty virtue of the soul, and a greater grace, to be able to enjoy the Lord in different duties and places than in one only. We should, in the divine Goodness, make a great effort to attain this.

Secondly. As to fasts and abstinences, I would advise you to be careful and strengthen your stomach for our Lord, and your other physical powers, rather than weaken them. My reason is that, in the first place, when a soul is so disposed to lose its own life rather than offend God's Majesty by even the slightest deliberate sin, and is moreover comparatively free from the temptations of the world, the flesh and the devil (a condition of soul which I am sure your Lordship by God's grace enjoys), I should like very much to see your Lordship imprint in your soul the truth that as both body and soul are a gift from your Creator and Lord, you should give Him a good account of both. To do this you must not allow your body to grow weak, for if you do, the interior man will no longer be able to function properly. Therefore, although I once highly praised fasting and abstinence even from so many ordinary foods, and for a certain period was pleased with this program, I cannot praise it for the future, when I see that the stomach, because of these fasts and abstinences, cannot function naturally or digest any of the ordinary meats or other items of diet which contribute to the proper maintenance of the body. I should rather have you seek every means of strengthening the body. Eat, therefore, whatever food is allowed and as often as you find it convenient. But it should be done without offence to the neighbor. We should love the body in so far as it is obedient and helpful to the soul, since the soul with the body's help and service is better disposed for the service and praise of our Creator and Lord.

Thirdly. Concerning the ill treatment of the body for our Lord's sake, I would say, avoid anything that would cause the shedding even of a drop of blood. If His Divine Majesty has given you the grace for this and for all that I have mentioned (it is my conviction that He has), it would be better for the future without reasons or arguments, to drop this penance, and instead of trying to draw blood, seek more immediately the Lord of all, or what comes to the same thing, seek His most holy gifts, such as the gift of tears. This could be 1) because of our own sins or the sins of others; or 2) while contemplating the mysteries of the life of Christ, either here on earth or in heaven; or 3) from a loving consideration of the Three Divine Persons. Thus, the higher our thoughts soar the greater will be their worth. The third is more perfect in itself than the second, and the second than the first. But, for a given person that level will be much better on which our Lord communicates more of Himself in His holy graces and spiritual gifts, because He sees and knows what is best for you. Like one who knows all He points out the way to you. On our part, with the help of His grace, we will learn by making trial of many methods, so that we may advance along the way that stands out clearest, which will be for us the happiest and most blessed in this life, leading us directly by ordered paths to that other everlasting life, after having united us in a close embrace with His most holy gifts.

By these gifts I understand those that are beyond the reach of our own powers, which we cannot attain at will, since they are rather a pure gift of Him Who bestows them and Who alone can give every good. These gifts, with His Divine Majesty as their end, are faith, hope and charity, joy and spiritual repose, tears, intense consolation, elevation of mind, divine impressions and illuminations together with all other spiritual relish and understanding which have these gifts as their objects, such as a humble reverence for our holy Mother the Church, her rulers and teachers. Any of these holy gifts should be preferred to exterior and visible manifestations which are good only when they have one or other of these higher gifts as their object. I do not mean to say that we should seek them merely for the satisfaction or pleasure they give us. We know, however, that without them all our thoughts, words and actions are of themselves tainted, cold, disordered, while with them they become clear and warm and upright for God's greater service. It is for this reason that we should desire these gifts, or some of them, and spiritual graces; that is, in so far as they are a help to us, to God's greater glory. Thus, when the body falls ill because of excessive effort, it is the most reasonable thing to seek these gifts by acts of the understanding and other more moderate exercises. For it is not the soul alone that should be healthy. If the mind is healthy in a healthy body, all will be healthy and much better prepared to give God greater service.

As to how you should act in individual cases, I do not think it wise in the Lord to speak in detail. It is my hope that the same Divine Spirit Who has hitherto guided your Lordship will continue to guide you and rule you in the future, to the greater glory of His Divine Majesty.

Rome, September 20, 1548.

St. Teresa of Avila
1515-1582

The Christian spiritual tradition, both in its development and in its literature, is dominated by men. Though countless numbers of women have, through the centuries, generously dedicated their lives to the ideals of Christian perfection, few are the women who have been recognized as leaders of the tradition.

Teresa of Avila is clearly not only one of the leaders, but one of the greatest. She has the distinction of being called a Doctor of the Church. Teresa was a person with rare qualities—dynamic, extroverted, intelligent, sensitive. She was a member of the Carmel in Avila, Spain, which she entered in 1535. Her life, both before and after entering the Carmel, was marked by periods of illness, loneliness, sadness, and a feeling of mediocrity. Slowly and steadily she grew into a rich spiritual personality. Interiorly, she matured through a life of profound prayer, to the point of the gift of spiritual marriage with Christ. Exteriorly, she was a reformer of Carmel and foundress of the Discalced Carmelites, a lifetime activity which demanded that she give her attention to all the details that are part of founding an organization.

Her spiritual growth process is best understood by journeying through her major writings, her Life *(written by herself),* The Way of Perfection, The Book of Foundations, *and* The Interior Castle. *Teresa's writings are an analysis of her interior* states. *Though the subject matter includes the virtues, prayer, perfection, union with God, and other spiritual themes, she always writes from the point of view of her own personal experiences. Thus, rather than meeting a theory of spirituality as a kind of object, the reader discovers the reality of spirituality as lived by a very unusual woman. Her literary style actually became a dominant mode in spiritual literature.*

The particular work from which the following selection is taken, The Way of Perfection, *was written for the sisters of one of Teresa's foundations. She wanted them to love prayer, to love it to the point of consuming their lives in it. This, she was convinced, would lead them most effectively to a life of perfection. After an introduction, in which Teresa speaks of the breakdown of strict religious observance in her time, and the need for the virtue of poverty in order to reverse the trend, Teresa turns to the subject of prayer. Love, detachment and humility are essential to the life of prayer. They will lead the soul to true freedom and sovereignty. Every aspect of prayer is explored, its joys and sorrows, its victories, the illusions related to it, the problem of sin. The final chapters of the book are a commentary on the Lord's Prayer.*

The Way of Perfection *is the most comprehensible of Teresa's writings. It successfully presents some of the most profound aspects of mystical theology in a clear and simple terminology. For that reason, it serves as an excellent introduction to the writings of a woman who, through her apostolic activity and mystical life, is one of the most influential personalities within the entire Christian spiritual tradition.*

THE WAY OF PERFECTION

CHAPTER XVI

DESCRIBES THE DIFFERENCE BETWEEN PERFECTION IN THE LIVES OF
CONTEMPLATIVES AND IN THE LIVES OF THOSE WHO ARE CON-
TENT WITH MENTAL PRAYER. EXPLAINS HOW IT IS SOMETIMES
POSSIBLE FOR GOD TO RAISE A DISTRACTED SOUL TO PERFECT
CONTEMPLATION AND THE REASON FOR THIS. THIS CHAPTER
AND THAT WHICH COMES NEXT ARE TO BE NOTED CAREFULLY.

I hope you do not think I have written too much
about this already; for I have only been placing the
board, as they say. You have asked me to tell you
about the first steps in prayer; although God did not lead me by
them, my daughters, I know no others, and even now I can
hardly have acquired these elementary virtues. But you may be
sure that anyone who cannot set out the pieces in a game of
chess will never be able to play well, and, if he does not know
how to give check, he will not be able to bring about a checkmate. Now you will reprove me for talking about games, as we
do not play them in this house and are forbidden to do so. That
will show you what kind of a mother God has given you—she
even knows about vanities like this! However, they say that the
game is sometimes legitimate. How legitimate it will be for us to
play it in this way, and, if we play it frequently, how quickly
we shall give checkmate to this Divine King! He will not be able
to move out of our check nor will He desire to do so.

It is the queen which gives the king most trouble in this
game and all the other pieces support her. There is no queen
who can beat this King as well as humility can; for humility
brought Him down from Heaven into the Virgin's womb and
with humility we can draw Him into our souls by a single hair.
Be sure that He will give most humility to him who has most
already and least to him who has least. I cannot understand how
humility exists, or can exist, without love, or love without
humility, and it is impossible for these two virtues to exist
save where there is great detachment from all created things.

You will ask, my daughters, why I am talking to you about virtues when you have more than enough books to teach you about them and when you want me to tell you only about contemplation. My reply is that, if you had asked me about meditation, I could have talked to you about it, and advised you all to practise it, even if you do not possess the virtues. For this is the first step to be taken towards the acquisition of the virtues and the very life of all Christians depends upon their beginning it. No one, however lost a soul he may be, should neglect so great a blessing if God inspires him to make use of it. All this I have already written elsewhere, and so have many others, who know what they are writing about, which I certainly do not: God knows that.

But contemplation, daughters, is another matter. This is an error which we all make: if a person gets so far as to spend a short time each day in thinking about his sins, as he is bound to do if he is a Christian in anything more than name, people at once call him a great contemplative; and then they expect him to have the rare virtues which a great contemplative is bound to possess; he may even think he has them himself, but he will be quite wrong. In his early stages he did not even know how to set out the chess-board, and thought that, in order to give checkmate, it would be enough to be able to recognize the pieces. But that is impossible, for this King does not allow Himself to be taken except by one who surrenders wholly to Him.

Therefore, daughters, if you want me to tell you the way to attain to contemplation, do allow me to speak at some length about these things, even if at the time they do not seem to you very important, for I think myself that they are. If you have no wish either to hear about them or to practise them, continue your mental prayers all your life; but in that case I assure you, and all persons who desire this blessing, that *in my opinion* you will not attain true contemplation. I may, of course, be wrong about this, as I am judging by my own experience, but I have been striving after contemplation for twenty years.

I will now explain what mental prayer is, as some of you will not understand this. God grant that we may practise it as we should! I am afraid, however, that, if we do not achieve the virtues, this can only be done with great labour, although the virtues are not necessary here in such a high degree as they are for contemplation. I mean that the King of glory will not come to our souls—that is, so as to be united with them—unless we strive to gain the greatest virtues. I will explain this, for if you once catch me out in something which is not the truth, you will believe nothing I say—and if I were to say something untrue intentionally, from which may God preserve me, you would be right; but, if I did, it would be because I knew no better or did not understand what I said. I will tell you, then, that God is sometimes pleased to show great favour to persons who are in an evil state [and to raise them to perfect contemplation], so that by this means He may snatch them out of the hands of the devil. It must be understood, I think, that such persons will not be in mortal sin at the time. They may be in an evil state, and yet the Lord will allow them to see a vision, even a very good one, in order to draw them back to Himself. But I cannot believe that He would grant them contemplation. For that is a Divine union, in which the Lord takes His delight in the soul and the soul takes its delight in Him; and there is no way in which the Purity of the Heavens can take pleasure in a soul that is unclean, nor can the Delight of the angels have delight in that which is not His own. And we know that, by committing mortal sin, a soul becomes the property of the devil, and must take its delight in him, since it has given him pleasure; and, as we know, his delights, even in this life, are continuous torture. My Lord will have no lack of children of His own in whom He may rejoice without going and taking the children of others. Yet His Majesty will do what He often does—namely, snatch them out of the devil's hands.

Oh, my Lord! How often do we cause Thee to wrestle with the devil! Was it not enough that Thou shouldst have allowed him to bear Thee in his arms when he took Thee to the pinnacle of the Temple in order to teach us how to vanquish him? What a sight it would have been, daughters, to see this Sun by the side of the darkness, and what fear that wretched creature must have felt, though he would not have known why, since God did not allow Him to understand! Blessed be such great pity and mercy; we Christians ought to feel great shame at making Him wrestle daily, in the way I have described, with such an unclean beast. Indeed, Lord, Thine arms had need to be strong, but how was it that they were not weakened by the many [trials and] tortures which Thou didst endure upon the Cross? Oh, how quickly all that is borne for love's sake heals again! I really believe that, if Thou hadst lived longer, the very love which Thou hast for us would have healed Thy wounds again and Thou wouldst have needed no other medicine. Oh, my God, who will give me such medicine for all the things which grieve and try me? How eagerly should I desire them if it were certain that I could be cured by such a health-giving ointment!

Returning to what I was saying, there are souls whom God knows He may gain for Himself by this means; seeing that they are completely lost, His Majesty wants to leave no stone unturned to help them; and therefore, though they are in a sad way and lacking in virtues, He gives them consolations, favours and emotions which begin to move their desires, and occasionally even brings them to a state of contemplation, though rarely and not for long at a time. And this, as I say, He does because He is testing them to see if that favour will not make them anxious to prepare themselves to enjoy it often; if it does not, may they be pardoned; pardon Thou us, Lord, for it is a dreadful thing that a soul whom Thou hast brought near to Thyself should approach any earthly thing and become attached to it.

For my own part I believe there are many souls whom God our Lord tests in this way, and few who prepare themselves to enjoy this favour. When the Lord does this and we ourselves leave nothing undone either, I think it is certain that He never ceases from giving until He has brought us to a very high degree of prayer. If we do not give ourselves to His Majesty as resolutely as He gives Himself to us, He will be doing more than enough for us if He leaves us in mental prayer and from time to time visits us as He would visit servants in His vineyard. But these others are His beloved children, whom He would never want to banish from His side; and, as they have no desire to leave Him, He never does so. He seats them at His table, and feeds them with His own food, almost taking the food from His mouth in order to give it them.

St. Teresa of Avila

Oh, what blessed care of us is this, my daughters! How happy shall we be if by leaving these few, petty things we can arrive at so high an estate! Even if the whole world should blame you, *and deafen you with its cries,* what matter so long as you are in the arms of God? He is powerful enough to free you from everything; for only once did He command the world to be made and it was done; with Him, to will is to do. Do not be afraid, then, if He is pleased to speak with you, for He does this for the greater good of those who love Him. His love for those to whom He is dear is by no means so weak: *He shows it in every way possible.* Why, then, my sisters, do we not show Him love in so far as we can? Consider what a wonderful exchange it is if we give Him our love and receive His. Consider that He can do all things, and we can do nothing here below save as He enables us. And what is it that we do for Thee, O Lord, our Maker? We do hardly anything [at all] —just make some poor weak resolution. And, if His Majesty is pleased that by doing a mere nothing we should win everything, let us not be so foolish as to fail to do it.

O Lord! All our trouble comes to us from not having our eyes fixed upon Thee. If we only looked at the way along which we are walking, we should soon arrive; but we stumble and fall a thousand times and stray from the way because, as I say, we do not set our eyes on the true Way. One would think that no one had ever trodden it before, so new is it to us. It is indeed a pity that this should sometimes happen. *I mean, it hardly seems that we are Christians at all or that we have ever in our lives read about the Passion. Lord help us—that we should be hurt about some small point of honour! And then, when someone tells us not to worry about it, we think he is no Christian. I used to laugh—or sometimes I used to be distressed—at the things I heard in the world, and sometimes, for my sins, in religious Orders.* We refuse to be thwarted over the very smallest matter of precedence: apparently such a thing is quite intolerable. We cry out at once: "Well, I'm no saint"; *I used to say that myself.*

God deliver us, sisters, from saying "We are not angels", or "We are not saints", whenever we commit some imperfection. We may not be; but what a good thing it is for us to reflect that we can be if we will only try and if God gives us His hand! Do not be afraid that He will fail to do His part if we do not fail to do ours. And since we come here for no other reason, let us put our hands to the plough, as they say. Let there be nothing we know of which it would be a service to the Lord for us to do, and which, with His help, we would not venture to take in hand. I should like that kind of venturesomeness to be found in this house, as it always increases humility. We must have a holy boldness, for God helps the strong, being no respecter of persons; *and He will give courage to you and to me.*

I have strayed far from the point. I want to return to what I was saying—that is, to explain the nature of mental prayer and contemplation. It may seem irrelevant, but it is all done for your sakes; you may understand it better as expressed in my rough style than in other books which put it more elegantly. May the Lord grant me His favour, so that this may be so. Amen.

CHAPTER XVII

HOW NOT ALL SOULS ARE FITTED FOR CONTEMPLATION AND HOW SOME TAKE LONG TO ATTAIN IT. TRUE HUMILITY WILL WALK HAPPILY ALONG THE ROAD BY WHICH THE LORD LEADS IT.

I seem now to be beginning my treatment of prayer, but there still remains a little for me to say, which is of great importance because it has to do with humility, and in this house that is necessary. For humility is the principal virtue which must be practised by those who pray, and, as I have said, it is very fitting that you should try to learn how to practise it often: that is one of the chief things to remember about it and it is very necessary that it should be known by all who practise prayer. How can anyone who is truly humble think herself as good as those who become contemplatives? God, it is true, by His goodness and mercy, can make her so; but my advice is that she should always sit down in the lowest place, for that is what the Lord instructed us to do and taught us by His own example. Let such a one make herself ready for God to lead her by this road if He so wills; if He does not, the whole point of *true* humility is that she should consider herself happy in serving the servants of the Lord and in praising Him. For she deserves to be a slave of the devils in hell; yet His Majesty has brought her here to live among His servants.

I do not say this without good reason, for, as I have said, it is very important for us to realize that God does not lead us all by the same road, and perhaps she who believes herself to be going along the lowest of roads is the highest in the Lord's eyes. So it does not follow that, because all of us in this house practise prayer, we are all *perforce* to be contemplatives. That is impossible; and those of us who are not would be greatly discouraged if we did not grasp the truth that contemplation is something given by God, and, as it is not necessary for salvation and God does not ask it of us before He gives us our reward, we must not suppose that anyone else will require it of us. We shall not fail to attain perfection if we do what has been said here; we may, in fact, gain much more merit, because what we do will cost us more labour; the Lord will be treating us like those who are strong and will be laying up for us all that we cannot enjoy in this life. Let us not be discouraged, then, and give up prayer or cease doing what the rest do; for the Lord sometimes tarries long, and gives us as great rewards all at once as He has been giving to others over many years.

I myself spent over fourteen years without ever being able to meditate except while reading. There must be many people like this, and others who cannot meditate even after reading, but can only recite vocal prayers, in which they chiefly occupy themselves *and take a certain pleasure*. Some find their thoughts wandering so much that they cannot concentrate upon the same thing, but are always restless, to such an extent that, if they try to fix their thoughts upon God, they are attacked by a thousand foolish ideas and scruples and doubts *concerning the Faith.* I know a very old woman, leading a most excellent life —*I wish mine were like hers*— a penitent and a great servant of God, who for many years has been spending hours and hours in vocal prayer, but from mental prayer can get no help at all; the most she can do is to dwell upon each of her vocal prayers as she says them. There are a great many other people *just* like this; if they are humble, they will not, I think, be any the worse off in the end, but very much in the same state as those

who enjoy numerous consolations. In one way they may feel
safer, for we cannot tell if consolations come from God or are
sent by the devil. If they are not of God, they are the more
dangerous; for the chief object of the devil's work on earth is
to fill us with pride. If they are of God, there is no reason for
fear, for they bring humility with them, as I explained in my
other book at great length.

Others walk in humility, and *always* suspect that if they
fail to receive consolations the fault is theirs, and are always
most anxious to make progress. They never see a person shedding a tear without thinking themselves very backward in God's
service unless they are doing the same, whereas they may perhaps be much more advanced. For tears, though good, are not
invariably signs of perfection; there is always greater safety in
humility, mortification, detachment and other virtues. There
is no reason for fear, and you must not be afraid that you will
fail to attain the perfection of the greatest contemplatives.

Saint Martha was holy, but we are not told that she was a
contemplative. What more do you want than to be able to grow
to be like that blessed woman, who was worthy to receive
Christ our Lord so often in her house, and to prepare meals
for Him, and to serve Him and *perhaps* to eat at table with
Him? If she had been absorbed in devotion [all the time], as
the Magdalen was, there would have been no one to prepare a
meal for this Divine Guest. Now remember that this *little*
community is Saint Martha's house and that there must be people of all kinds here. Nuns who are called to the active life must
not murmur at others who are very much absorbed in contemplation, for contemplatives know that, though they themselves may be silent, the Lord will speak for them, and this,
as a rule, makes them forget themselves and everything else.

Remember that there must be someone to cook the
meals and count yourselves happy in being able to serve like
Martha. Reflect that true humility consists to a great extent in
being ready for what the Lord desires to do with you and happy
that He should do it, and in always considering yourselves unworthy to be called His servants. If contemplation and mental
and vocal prayer and tending the sick and serving in the house
and working at even the lowliest tasks are of service to the

Guest who comes to stay with us and to eat and take His re-creation with us, what should it matter to us if we do one of these things rather than another?

I do not mean that it is for us to say what we shall do, but that we must do our best in everything, for the choice is not ours but the Lord's. If after many years He is pleased to give each of us her office, it will be a curious kind of humility for you to wish to choose; let the Lord of the house do that, for He is wise and powerful and knows what is fitting for you and for Himself as well. Be sure that, if you do what lies in your power and prepare yourself for *high* contemplation with the perfection aforementioned, then, if He does not grant it you (and I think He will not fail to do so if you have true detachment and humility), it will be because He has laid up this joy for you so as to give it you in Heaven, and because, as I have said elsewhere, He is pleased to treat you like people who are strong and give you a cross to bear on earth like that which His Majesty Himself always bore.

What better sign of friendship is there than for Him to give you what He gave Himself? It might well be that you would not have had so great a reward from contemplation. His judgments are His own; we must not meddle in them. It is indeed a good thing that the choice is not ours; for, if it were, we should think it the more restful life and all become great contemplatives. Oh, how much we gain if we have no desire to gain what seems to us best and so have no fear of losing, since God never permits a truly mortified person to lose anything except when such loss will bring him greater gain!

CHAPTER XVIII

CONTINUES THE SAME SUBJECT AND SHOWS HOW MUCH GREATER ARE THE TRIALS OF CONTEMPLATIVES THAN THOSE OF ACTIVES. THIS CHAPTER OFFERS GREAT CONSOLATION TO ACTIVES.

I tell you, then, daughters—those of you whom God is not leading by this road [of contemplation]—that, as I know from what I have seen and been told by those who are following this road, they are not bearing a lighter cross than you; you would be amazed at all the ways and manners in which God sends them crosses. I know about both types of life and I am well aware that the trials given by God to contemplatives are intolerable; and they are of such a kind that, were He not to feed them with consolations, they could not be borne. It is clear that, since God leads those whom He most loves by the way of trials, the more He loves them, the greater will be their trials; and there is no reason to suppose that He hates contemplatives, since with His own mouth He praises them and calls them friends.

To suppose that He would admit to His close friendship pleasure-loving people who are free from all trials is ridiculous. I feel quite sure that God gives them much greater trials; and that He leads them by a hard and rugged road, so that they sometimes think they are lost and will have to go back and begin again. Then His Majesty is obliged to give them sustenance—not water, but wine, so that they may become inebriated by it and not realize what they are going through and what they are capable of bearing. Thus I find few true contemplatives who are not courageous and resolute in suffering; for, if they are weak, the first thing the Lord does is to give them courage so that they may fear no trials *that may come to them.*

I think, when those who lead an active life occasionally see contemplatives receiving consolations, they suppose that they never experience anything else. But I can assure you that you might not be able to endure their sufferings for as long as a day. The point is that the Lord knows everyone as he really is and gives each his work to do—according to what He sees to be most fitting for his soul, and for His own Self, and for the good of his neighbour. Unless you have omitted to prepare yourselves for your work you need have no fear that it will be lost. Note that I say we must all strive to do this, for we are here for no other purpose; and we must not strive merely for a year, or for two years or ten years, or it will look as if we are abandoning our work like cowards. It is well that the Lord should see we are not leaving anything undone. We are like soldiers who, however long they have served, must always be ready for their captain to send them away on any duty which he wants to entrust to them, since it is he who is paying them. And how much better is the payment given by our King than by people on this earth! *For the unfortunate soldiers die, and God knows who pays them after that!*

When their captain sees they are all present, and anxious for service, he assigns duties to them according to their fitness, *though not so well as our Heavenly Captain.* But if they were not present, He would give them neither pay nor service orders. So practise mental prayer, sisters; or, if any of you cannot do that, vocal prayer, reading and colloquies with God, as I shall explain to you later. Do not neglect the hours of prayer which are observed by all the nuns; you never know when the Spouse will call you (do not let what happened to the foolish virgins happen to you) and if He will give you fresh trials under the disguise of consolations. If He does not, you may be sure that you are not fit for them and that what you are doing is suitable for you. That is where both merit and humility come in, when you really think that you are not fit for what you are doing.

Go cheerfully about whatever services you are ordered to do, as I have said; if such a servant is truly humble she will be blessed in her active life and will never make any complaint save of herself. *I would much rather be like her than like some contemplatives.* Leave others to wage their own conflicts, which are not light ones. The standard-bearer is not a combatant, yet none the less he is exposed to great danger, and, inwardly, must suffer more than anyone, for he cannot defend himself, as he is carrying the standard, which he must not allow to leave his hands, even if he is cut to pieces. Just so contemplatives have to bear aloft the standard of humility and must suffer all the blows which are aimed at them without striking any themselves. Their duty is to suffer as Christ did, to raise the Cross on high, not to allow it to leave their hands, whatever the perils in which they find themselves, and not to let themselves be found backward in suffering. It is for this reason that they are given such an honourable duty. Let the contemplative consider what he is doing; for, if he lets the standard fall, the battle will be lost. Great harm, I think, is done to those who are not so far advanced if those whom they consider as captains and friends of God let them see them acting in a way unbefitting to their office.

The other soldiers do as best they can; at times they will withdraw from some position of extreme danger, and, as no one observes them, they suffer no loss of honour. But these others have all eyes fixed on them and cannot move. Their office, then, is a noble one, and the King confers great honour and favour upon anyone to whom He gives it, and who, in receiving it, accepts no light obligation. So, sisters, as we *do not understand ourselves and* know not what we ask, let us leave everything to the Lord, *Who knows us better than we know ourselves. True humility consists in our being satisfied with what is given us.* There are some people who seem to want to ask favours from God as a right. A pretty kind of humility that is! He Who knows us all does well in seldom giving things to such persons; He sees clearly that they are unable to drink of His chalice.

If you want to know whether you have made progress or not, sisters, you may be sure that you have if each of you thinks herself the worst of all and shows that she thinks this by acting for the profit and benefit of the rest. Progress has nothing to do with enjoying the greatest number of consolations in prayer, or with raptures, visions or favours [often] given by the Lord, the value of which we cannot estimate until we reach the world to come. The other things I have been describing are current coin, an unfailing source of revenue and a perpetual inheritance—not payments liable at any time to cease, like those favours which are given us and then come to an end. I am referring to the great virtues of humility, mortification and an obedience so *extremely* strict that we never go an inch beyond the superior's orders, knowing that these orders come from God since she is in His place. It is to this duty of obedience that you must attach the greatest importance. It seems to me that anyone who does not have it is not a nun at all, and so I am saying no more about it, as I am speaking to nuns whom I believe to be good, or, at least, desirous of being so. So well known is the matter, and so important, that a single word will suffice to prevent you from forgetting it.

I mean that, if anyone is under a vow of obedience and goes astray through not taking the greatest care to observe these vows with the highest degree of perfection, I do not know why she is in the convent. I can assure her, in any case, that, for so long as she fails in this respect, she will never succeed in leading the contemplative life, or even in leading a good active life: of that I am absolutely certain. And even a person who has not this obligation, but who wishes or tries to achieve contemplation, must, if she would walk safely, be fully resolved to surrender her will to a confessor who is himself a contemplative *and will understand her.* It is a well-known fact that she will make more progress in this way in a year than in a great many years if she acts otherwise. As this does not affect you, however, I will say no more about it.

I conclude, my daughters, [by saying] that these are the virtues which I desire you to possess and to strive to obtain, and of which you should cherish a holy envy. Do not be troubled because you have no experience of those other kinds of devotion: they are very unreliable. It may be that to some people they come from God, and yet that if they came to you it might be because His Majesty had permitted you to be deceived and deluded by the devil, as He has permitted others: *there is danger in this for women.* Why do you want to serve the Lord in so doubtful a way when there are so many ways of [serving Him in] safety? Who wants to plunge you into these perils? I have said a great deal about this, because I am sure it will be useful, for this nature of ours is weak, though His Majesty will strengthen those on whom He wishes to bestow contemplation. With regard to the rest, I am glad to have given them this advice, which will teach contemplatives humility also. *If you say you have no need of it, daughters, some of you may perhaps find it pleasant reading.* May the Lord, for His own sake, give us light to follow His will in all things and we shall have no cause for fear.

CHAPTER XIX

BEGINS TO TREAT OF PRAYER. ADDRESSES SOULS WHO CANNOT REASON
WITH THE UNDERSTANDING.

It is a long time since I wrote the last chapter and I have had no chance of returning to my writing, so that, without reading through what I have written, I cannot remember what I said. However, I must not spend too much time at this, so it will be best if I go right on without troubling about the connection. For those with orderly minds, and for souls who practise prayer and can be a great deal in their own company, many books have been written, and these are so good and are the work of such competent people that you would be making a mistake if you paid heed to anything about prayer that you learned from me. There are books, as I say, in which the mysteries of the life of the Lord and of His *sacred* Passion are described in short passages, one for each day of the week; there are also meditations on the Judgment, on hell, on our own nothingness and on all that we owe to God, and these books are excellent both as to their teaching and as to the way in which they plan the beginning and the end of the time of prayer. There is no need to tell anyone who is capable of practising prayer in this way, and has already formed the habit of doing so, that by this good road the Lord will bring her to the harbour of light. If she begins so well, her end will be good also; and all who can walk along this road will walk restfully and securely, for one always walks restfully when the understanding is kept in restraint. It is something else that I wish to treat of and help you about if the Lord is pleased to enable me to do so; if not, you will at least realize that there are many souls who suffer this trial, and you will not be so much distressed at undergoing it yourselves at first, *but will find some comfort in it.*

There are some souls, and some minds, as unruly as horses not yet broken in. No one can stop them: now they go this way, now that way; they are never still. *Although a skilled rider mounted on such a horse may not always be in danger, he will be so sometimes; and, even if he is not concerned about his life, there will always be the risk of his stumbling, so that he has to ride with great care.* Some people are either like this by nature or God permits them to become so. I am very sorry for them; they seem to me like people who are very thirsty and see water a long way off, yet, when they try to go to it, find someone who all the time is barring their path—at the beginning of their journey, in the middle and at the end. And when, after all their labour—and the labour is tremendous—they have conquered the first of their enemies, they allow themselves to be conquered by the second, and they prefer to die of thirst rather than drink water which is going to cost them so much trouble. Their strength has come to an end; their courage has failed them; and, though some of them are strong enough to conquer their second enemies as well as their first, when they meet the third group their strength comes to an end, though perhaps they are only a couple of steps from the fountain of living water, of which the Lord said to the Samaritan woman that whosoever drinks of it shall not thirst again. How right and *how very* true is that which comes from the lips of Truth Himself! In this life the soul will never thirst for anything more, although its thirst for things in the life to come will exceed any natural thirst that we can imagine here below. How the soul thirsts to experience this thirst! For it knows how very precious it is, and, grievous though it be and exhausting, it creates the very satisfaction by which this thirst is allayed. It is therefore a thirst which quenches nothing but desire for earthly things, and, when God slakes it, satisfies in such a way that one of the greatest favours He can bestow on the soul is to leave it with this longing, so that it has an even greater desire to think of this water again.

Water has three properties—three relevant properties which I can remember, that is to say, for it must have many more. One of them is that of cooling things; however hot we are, water tempers the heat, and it will even put out a large fire, except when there is tar in the fire, in which case, *they say*, it only burns the more. God help me! What a marvellous thing it is that, when this fire is strong and fierce and subject to none of the elements, water should make it grow fiercer, and, though its contrary element, should not quench it but only cause it to burn the more! It would be very useful to be able to discuss this with someone who understands philosophy; if I knew the properties of things I could explain it myself; but, though I love thinking about it, I cannot explain it—perhaps I do not even understand it.

You will be glad, sisters, if God grants you to drink of this water, as are those who drink of it now, and you will understand how a genuine love of God, if it is really strong, and completely free from earthly things, and able to rise above them, is master of all the elements and of the whole world. And, as water proceeds from the earth, there is no fear of its quenching this fire, which is the love of God; though the two elements are contraries, it has no power over it. The fire is absolute master, and subject to nothing. You will not be surprised, then, sisters, at the way I have insisted in this book that you should strive to obtain this freedom. Is it not a funny thing that a poor *little* nun of Saint Joseph's should attain mastery over the whole earth and all the elements? What wonder that the saints did as they pleased with them by the help of God? Fire and water obeyed Saint Martin; even birds and fishes were obedient to Saint Francis; and similarly with many other saints. *Helped as they were by God, and themselves doing all that was in their power, they could almost have claimed this as a right.* It was clear that they were masters over everything in the world, because they had striven so hard to despise it and subjected themselves to the Lord of the world with all their might. So, as I say, the water, which springs from the earth, has no power over this fire. Its flames rise high and its source is in nothing so base as the earth. There are other fires of love for God—small ones, which may be quenched by the least little thing. But this fire will most certainly not be so quenched. Even should a whole sea of temptations assail it, they will not keep it from burning or prevent it from gaining the mastery over them.

Water which comes down as rain from Heaven will quench the flames even less, for in that case the fire and the water are not contraries, but have the same origin. Do not fear that the one element may harm the other; each helps the other and they produce the same effect. For the water of genuine tears—that is, tears which come from true prayer—is a good gift from the King of Heaven; it fans the flames and keeps them alight, while the fire helps to cool the water. God bless me! What a beautiful and wonderful thing it is that fire should cool water! But it does; and it even freezes all worldly affections, when it is combined with the living water which comes from Heaven, the source of the above-mentioned tears, which are given us, and not acquired by our diligence. Certainly, then, nothing worldly has warmth enough left in it to induce us to cling to it unless it is something which increases this fire, the nature of which is not to be easily satisfied, but, if possible, to enkindle the entire world.

The second property of water is that it cleanses things that are not clean already. What would become of the world if there were no water for washing? Do you know what cleansing properties there are in this living water, this heavenly water, this clear water, when it is unclouded, and free from mud, and comes down from Heaven? Once the soul has drunk of it I am convinced that it makes it pure and clean of all its sins; for, as I have written, God does not allow us to drink of this water *of perfect contemplation* whenever we like: the choice is not ours; this Divine union is something quite supernatural, given that it may cleanse the soul and leave it pure and free from the mud and misery in which it has been plunged because of its sins. Other consolations, excellent as they may be, which come through the intermediacy of the understanding, are like water running all over the ground. This cannot be drunk directly from the source; and its course is never free from clogging impurities, so that it is neither so pure nor so clean as the other. I should not say that this prayer I have been describing, which comes from reasoning with the intellect, is living water—I mean so far as my understanding of it goes. For, despite our efforts, there is always something clinging to the soul, through the influence of the body and of the baseness of our nature, which we should prefer not to be there.

I will explain myself further. We are meditating on the nature of the world, and on the way in which everything will come to an end, so that we may learn to despise it, when, almost without noticing it, we find ourselves ruminating on things in the world that we love. We try to banish these thoughts, but we cannot help being slightly distracted by thinking of things that have happened, or will happen, of things we have done and of things we are going to do. Then we begin to think of how we can get rid of these thoughts; and that sometimes plunges us once again into the same danger. It is not that we ought to omit such meditations; but we need to retain our misgivings about them and not to grow careless. In contemplation the Lord Himself relieves us of this care, for He will not trust us to look after ourselves. So dearly does He love our souls that He prevents them from rushing into things which may do them harm just at this time when He is anxious to help them. So He calls them to His side at once, and in a single moment reveals more truths to them and gives them a clearer insight into the nature of everything than they could otherwise gain in many years. For our sight is poor and the dust which we meet on the road blinds us; but in contemplation the Lord brings us to the end of the day's journey without our understanding how.

The third property of water is that it satisfies and quenches thirst. Thirst, I think, means the desire for something which is very necessary for us—so necessary that if we have none of it we shall die. It is a strange thing that if we have no water we die, and that we can also lose our lives through having too much of it, as happens to many people who get drowned. Oh, my Lord, if only one could be plunged so deeply into this living water that one's life would end! Can that be? Yes: this love and desire for God can increase so much that human nature is unable to bear it, and so there have been persons who have died of it. I knew one person who had this living water in such great abundance that she would almost have been drawn out of herself by raptures if God had not quickly succoured her. *She had such a thirst, and her desire grew so greatly, that she realized clearly that she might quite possibly die of thirst if something were not done for her.* I say that she would almost have been drawn out of herself because in this state the soul is in repose. So intolerable does such a soul find the world that it seems to be overwhelmed, but it comes to life again in God; and in this way His Majesty enables it to enjoy experiences which, if it had remained within itself, would perforce have cost it its life.

Let it be understood from this that, as there can be nothing in our supreme Good which is not perfect, all that He gives is for our welfare; and, however abundant this water which He gives may be, in nothing that He gives can there be superfluity. For, if His gift is abundant, He also bestows on the soul, as I have said, an abundant capacity for drinking; just as a glassmaker moulds his vessels to the size he thinks necessary, so that there is room for what he wishes to pour into them. As our desires for this water come from ourselves, they are never free from fault; any good that there may be in them comes from the help of the Lord. But we are so indiscreet that, as the pain is sweet and pleasant, we think we can never have too much of it. We have an immeasurable longing for it, and, so far as is possible on earth, we stimulate this longing: sometimes this goes so far as to cause death. How happy is such a death! And yet by living one might perhaps have helped others to die of the desire for it. I believe the devil has something to do with this: knowing how much harm we can do him by living, he tempts us to be indiscreet in our penances and so to ruin our health, which is a matter of no small moment to him.

I advise anyone who attains to an experience of this fierce thirst to watch herself carefully, for I think she will have to contend with this temptation. She may not die of her thirst, but her health will be ruined, and she will involuntarily give her feelings outward expression, which ought at all costs to be avoided. Sometimes, however, all our diligence in this respect is unavailing and we are unable to hide our emotions as much as we should like. Whenever we are assailed by these strong impulses stimulating the increase of our desire, let us take great care not to add to them ourselves but to check them gently by thinking of something else. For our *own* nature may be playing as great a part in producing these feelings as our love. There are some people *of this type* who have keen desires for all kinds of things, even for bad things, but I do not think such people can have achieved great mortification, for mortification is always profitable. It seems foolish to check so good a thing as this desire, but it is not. I am not saying that the desire should be uprooted—only checked; one may be able to do this by stimulating some other desire which is equally praiseworthy.

In order to explain myself better I will give an illustration. A man has a great desire to be with God, as Saint Paul had, and to be loosed from this prison. This causes him pain which yet is in itself a great joy, and no small degree of mortification will be needed if he is to check it—in fact, he will not always be able to do so. But when he finds it oppressing him so much he may almost lose his reason. I saw this happen to someone not long ago; she was of an impetuous nature, but so accustomed to curbing her own will that, from what I had seen at other times,

I thought her will was completely annihilated; yet, when I saw her for a moment, the great stress and strain caused by her efforts to hide her feelings had all but destroyed her reason. In such an extreme case, I think, even did the desire come from the Spirit of God, it would be true humility to be afraid; for we must not imagine that we have sufficient charity to bring us to such a state of oppression.

I shall not think it at all wrong (if it be possible, I mean, for it may not always be so) for us to change our desire by reflecting that, if we live, we have more chance of serving God, and that we might do this by giving light to some soul which otherwise would be lost; as well as that, if we serve Him more, we shall deserve to enjoy Him more, and grieve that we have served Him so little. These are consolations appropriate to such great trials: they will allay our pain and we shall gain a great deal by them if in order to serve the Lord Himself we are willing to spend a long time here below and to live with our grief. It is as if a person were suffering a great trial or a grievous affliction and we consoled him by telling him to have patience and leave himself in God's hands so that His will might be fulfilled in him: it is always best to leave ourselves in God's hands.

And what if the devil had anything to do with these strong desires? This might be possible, as I think is suggested in Cassian's story of a hermit, leading the austerest of lives, who was persuaded by the devil to throw himself down a well so that he might see God the sooner. I do not think this hermit can have served God either humbly or efficiently, for the Lord is faithful and His Majesty would never allow a servant of His to be blinded in a matter in which the truth was so clear. But, of course, if the desire had come from God, it would have done the hermit no harm; for such desires bring with them illumination, moderation and discretion. This is fitting, but our enemy and adversary seeks to harm us wherever he can; and, as he is not unwatchful, we must not be so either. This is an important matter in many respects: for example, we must shorten our time of prayers, however much joy it gives us, if we see our bodily strength waning or find that our head aches: discretion is most necessary in everything.

Why do you suppose, daughters, that I have tried, *as peo-ple say,* to describe the end of the battle before it has begun and to point to its reward by telling you about the blessing which comes from drinking of the heavenly source of this living water? I have done this so that you may not be distressed at the trials and annoyances of the road, and may tread it with courage and not grow weary; for, as I have said, it may be that, when you have arrived, and have only to stoop and drink of the spring, you may fail to do so and lose this blessing, thinking that you have not the strength to attain it and that it is not for you.

Remember, the Lord invites us all; and, since He is Truth Itself, we cannot doubt Him. If His invitation were not a general one, He would not have said: "I will give you to drink." He might have said: "Come, all of you, for after all you will lose nothing by coming; and I will give drink to those whom I think fit for it." But, as He said we were all to come, without making this condition, I feel sure that none will fail to receive this living water unless they cannot keep to the path. May the Lord, Who promises it, give us grace, for His Majesty's own sake, to seek it as it must be sought.

CHAPTER XX

DESCRIBES HOW, IN ONE WAY OR ANOTHER, WE NEVER LACK CONSOLA-TION ON THE ROAD OF PRAYER. COUNSELS THE SISTERS TO IN-CLUDE THIS SUBJECT CONTINUALLY IN THEIR CONVERSATION.

In this last chapter I seem to have been contradicting what I had previously said, as, in consoling those who had not reached the contemplative state, I told them that the Lord had different roads by which they might come to Him, just as He also had many mansions. I now repeat this: His Majesty, being Who He is and understanding our weakness, has provided for us. But he did not say: "Some must come by this way and others by that." His mercy is so great that He has forbidden none to strive to come and drink of this fountain of life. Blessed be He for ever! What good reasons there would have been for His forbidding me!

But as He did not order me to cease from drinking when I had begun to do so, but caused me to be plunged into the depths of the water, it is certain that He will forbid no one to come: indeed, He calls us publicly, and in a loud voice, to do so. Yet, as He is so good, He does not force us to drink, but enables those who wish to follow Him to drink in many ways so that none may lack comfort or die of thirst. For from this rich spring flow many streams—some large, others small, and also little pools for children, which they find quite large enough, for the sight of a great deal of water would frighten them: by children, I mean those who are in the early stages. Therefore, sisters, have no fear that you will die of thirst on this road; you will never lack so much of the water of comfort that your thirst will be intolerable; so take my advice and do not tarry on the way, but strive like strong men until you die in the attempt, for you are here for nothing else than to strive. If you always pursue this determination to die rather than fail to reach the end of the road, the Lord may bring you through this life with a certain degree of thirst, but in the life which never ends He will give you great abundance to drink and you will have no fear of its failing you. May the Lord grant us never to fail Him. Amen.

Now, in order to set out upon this aforementioned road so that we do not go astray at the very start, let us consider for a moment how the first stage of our journey is to be begun, for that is the most important thing—or rather, every part of the journey is of importance to the whole. I do not mean to say that no one who has not the resolution that I am going to describe should set out upon the road, for the Lord will gradually bring her nearer to perfection. And even if she did no more than take one step, this alone has such virtue that there is no fear of her losing it or of failing to be very well rewarded. We might compare her to someone who has a rosary with a bead specially indulgenced: one prayer in itself will bring her something, and the more she uses the bead the more she will gain; but if she left it in a box and never took it out it would be better for her not to have it. So, although she may never go any farther along the same road, the short distance she has progressed will give her light and thus help her to go along other roads, and the farther she goes the more light she will gain. In fact, she may be sure that she will do herself no kind of harm through having started on the road, even if she leaves it, for good never leads to evil.

So, daughters, whenever you meet people and find them well-disposed and even attracted to the life of prayer, try to remove from them all fear of beginning a course which may bring them such great blessings. For the love of God, I beg you always to see to it that your conversation is benefiting those with whom you speak. For your prayers must be for the profit of their souls; and, since you must always pray to the Lord for them, sisters, you would seem to be doing ill if you did not strive to benefit them in every possible way.

If you would be a good kinswoman, this is true friendship; if you would be a good friend, you may be sure that this is the only possible way. Let the truth be in your hearts, as it will be if you practise meditation, and you will see clearly that love we are bound to have for our neighbours. This is no time for child's play, sisters, and these worldly friendships, good though they may be, seem no more than that. Neither with your relatives nor with anyone else must you use such phrases as "If you love me", or "Don't you love me?" unless you have in view some noble end and the profit of the person to whom you are speaking. It may be necessary, in order to get a relative—a brother or some such person—to listen to the truth and accept it, to prepare him for it by using such phrases and showing him signs of love, which are always pleasing to sense. He may possibly be more affected, and influenced, by one kind word, as such phrases are called, than by a great deal which you might say about God, and then there would be plenty of opportunities for you to talk to him about God afterwards. I do not forbid such phrases, therefore, provided you use them in order to bring someone profit. But for no other reason can there be any good in them and they may even do harm without your being aware of it. Everybody knows that you are nuns and that your business is prayer. Do not say to yourselves: "I have no wish to be considered good," for what people see in you is bound to bring them either profit or harm. People like nuns, on whom is laid the obligation to speak of nothing save in the spirit of God, act very wrongly if they dissemble in this way, except occasionally for the purpose of doing greater good. Your intercourse and conversation must be like this: let any who wish to talk to you learn your language; and, if they will not, be careful never to learn theirs: it might lead you to hell.

It matters little if you are considered ill-bred and still less if you are taken for hypocrites: indeed, you will gain by this, because only those who understand your language will come to see you. If one knows no Arabic, one has no desire to talk a great deal with a person who knows no other language. So worldly people will neither weary you nor do you harm—and it would do you no small harm to have to begin to *learn and* talk a new language; you would spend all your time learning it. You cannot know as well as I do, for I have found it out by experience, how very bad this is for the soul; no sooner does it learn one thing than it has to forget another and it never has any rest. This you must at all costs avoid; for peace and quiet in the soul are of great importance on the road which we are about to tread.

If those with whom you converse wish to learn your language, it is not for you to teach it to them, but you can tell them what wealth they will gain by learning it. Never grow tired of this, but do it piously, lovingly and prayerfully, with a view to helping them; they will then realize what great gain *it brings*, and will go and seek a master to teach it them. Our Lord would be doing you no light favour if through your agency He were to arouse some soul to obtain this blessing. When once one begins to describe this road, what a large number of things there are to be said about it, even by those who have trodden it as unsuccessfully as I have! *I only wish I could write with both hands, so as not to forget one thing while I am saying another.* May it please the Lord, sisters, that you may be enabled to speak of it better than I have done.

CHAPTER XXI

DESCRIBES THE GREAT IMPORTANCE OF SETTING OUT UPON THE PRACTICE OF PRAYER WITH FIRM RESOLUTION AND OF HEEDING NO DIFFICULTIES PUT IN THE WAY BY THE DEVIL.

Do not be dismayed, daughters, at the number of things which you have to consider before setting out on this Divine journey, which is the royal road to Heaven. By taking this road we gain such precious treasures that it is no wonder if the cost seems to us a high one. The time will come when we shall realize that all we have paid has been nothing at all by comparison with the greatness of our prize.

Let us now return to those who wish to travel on this road, and will not halt until they reach their goal, which is the place where they can drink of this water of life. *Although in some book or other—in several, in fact—I have read what a good thing it is to begin in this way, I do not think anything will be lost if I speak of it here.* As I say, it is most important—all-important, indeed—that they should begin well by making an earnest and most determined resolve not to halt until they reach their goal, whatever may come, whatever may happen to them, however hard they may have to labour, whoever may complain of them, whether they reach their goal or die on the road or have no heart to confront the trials which they meet, whether the very world dissolves before them. Yet again and again people will say to us: "It is dangerous", "So-and-so was lost through doing this", "Someone else got into wrong ways", "Some other person, who was always praying, fell just the same", "It is bad for virtue", "It is not meant for women; it may lead them into delusions", "They would do better to stick to their spinning", "These subtleties are of no use to them", "It is quite enough for them to say their Paternoster and Ave Maria."

With this last remark, sisters, I quite agree. Of course it is enough! It is always a great thing to base your prayer on prayers which were uttered by the very lips of the Lord. People are quite right to say this, and, were it not for our great weakness and the lukewarmness of our devotion, there would be no need for any other systems of prayer or for any other books at all. I am speaking to souls who are unable to recollect themselves by meditating upon other mysteries, and who think they need special methods of prayer; some people have such ingenious minds that nothing is good enough for them! So I think I will start to lay down some rules for each part of our prayer—beginning, middle and end—although I shall not spend long on the higher stages. They cannot take books from you, and, if you are studious and humble, you need nothing more.

I have always been fond of the words of the Gospels and have found more recollection in them than in the most carefully planned books—especially books of which the authors were not fully approved, and which I never wanted to read. If I keep close to this Master of wisdom, He may perhaps give me some thoughts which will help you. I do not say that I will explain these Divine prayers, for that I should not presume to do, and there are a great many explanations of them already. Even were there none, it would be ridiculous for me to attempt any. But I will write down a few thoughts on the words of the Paternoster; for sometimes, when we are most anxious to nurture our devotion, consulting a great many books will kill it. When a master is himself giving a lesson, he treats his pupil kindly and likes him to enjoy being taught and does his utmost to help him learn. Just so will this heavenly Master do with us.

Pay no heed, then, to anyone who tries to frighten you or depicts to you the perils of the way. What a strange idea that one could ever expect to travel on a road infested by thieves, for the purpose of gaining some great treasure, without running into danger! Worldly people like to take life peaceably; but they will deny themselves sleep, *perhaps* for nights on end, in order to gain a farthing's profit, and they will leave you no peace either of body or of soul. If, when you are on the way to gaining this treasure, or to taking it by force (as the Lord says the violent do) and are travelling by this royal road—this safe road trodden by our King and by His elect and His saints—if even then they tell you it is full of danger and make you so afraid, what will be the dangers encountered by those who think they will be able to gain this treasure and yet are not on the road to it?

Oh, my daughers, how incomparably greater must be the risks they run! And yet they have no idea of this until they fall headlong into some real danger. Having *perhaps* no one to help them, they lose this water altogether, and drink neither much nor little of it, either from a pool or from a stream. How do you suppose they can do without a drop of this water and yet travel along a road on which there are so many adversaries to fight? Of course, sooner or later, they will die of thirst; for we must all journey to this fountain, my daughters, whether we will or no, though we may not all do so in the same way. Take my advice, then, and let none mislead you by showing you any other road than that of prayer.

I am not now discussing whether or no everyone must practise mental or vocal prayer; but I do say that you yourselves require both. For prayer is the duty of religious. If anyone tells you it is dangerous, look upon that person himself as your principal danger and flee from his company. Do not forget this, for it is advice that you may possibly need. It will be dangerous for you if you do not possess humility and the other virtues; but God forbid that the way of prayer should be a way of danger! This fear seems to have been invented by the devil, who has apparently been very clever in bringing about the fall of some who practise prayer.

See how blind the world is! It never thinks of all the thousands who have fallen into heresies and other great evils through yielding to distractions and not practising prayer. As against these multitudes there are a few who did practise prayer and whom the devil has been successful enough at his own trade to cause to fall: in doing this he has also caused some to be very much afraid of virtuous practices. Let those who make use of this pretext to absolve themselves from such practices take heed, for in order to save themselves from evil they are fleeing from good. I have never heard of such a wicked invention; it must indeed come from the devil. Oh, my Lord, defend Thyself. See how Thy words are being misunderstood. Permit no such weakness in Thy servants.

There is one great blessing—you will always find a few people ready to help you. For it is a characteristic of the true servant of God, to whom His Majesty has given light to follow the true path, that, when beset by these fears, his desire not to stop only increases. He sees clearly whence the devil's blows are coming, but he parries each blow and breaks his adversary's head. The anger which this arouses in the devil is greater than all the satisfaction which he receives from the pleasures given him by others. When, in troublous times, he has sown his tares, and seems to be leading men everywhere in his train, half-blinded, and [deceiving them into] believing themselves to be zealous for the right, God raises up someone to open their eyes and bid them look at the fog with which the devil has obscured their path. (How great God is! To think that just one man, or perhaps two, can do more by telling the truth than can a great many men all together!) And then they gradually begin to see the path again and God gives them courage. If people say there is danger in prayer, this servant of God, by his deeds if not by his words, tries to make them realize what a good thing it is. If they say that frequent communion is inadvisable, he only practises it the more. So, because just one or two are fearlessly following the better path, the Lord gradually regains what He had lost.

Cease troubling about these fears, then, sisters; and never pay heed to such matters of popular opinion. This is no time for believing everyone; believe only those whom you see modelling their lives on the life of Christ. Endeavour always to have a good conscience; practise humility; despise all worldly things; and believe firmly in the teaching of our Holy Mother [the Roman] Church. You may then be quite sure that you are on a [very] good road. Cease, as I have said, to have fear where no fear is; if any one attempts to frighten you, point out the road to him in all humility. Tell him that you have a Rule which commands you, as it does, to pray without ceasing, and that that rule you must keep. If they tell you that you should practise only vocal prayer, ask whether your mind and heart ought not to be in what you say. If they answer "Yes"—and they cannot do otherwise—you see they are admitting that you are bound to practise mental prayer, and even contemplation, if God should grant it you. [Blessed be He for ever.]

CHAPTER XXII

EXPLAINS THE MEANING OF MENTAL PRAYER

You must know, daughters, that whether or no you are practising mental prayer has nothing to do with keeping the lips closed. If, while I am speaking with God, I have a clear realization and full consciousness that I am doing so, and if this is more real to me than the words I am uttering, then I am combining mental and vocal prayer. When people tell you that you are speaking with God by reciting the Paternoster and thinking of worldly things—well, words fail me. When you speak, as it is right for you to do so, with so great a Lord, it is well that you should think of Who it is that you are addressing, and what you yourself are, if only that you may speak to Him with proper respect. How can you address a king with the deference due to him, or how can you know what ceremonies have to be used when speaking to a grandee, unless you are clearly conscious of the nature of his position and of yours? It is because of this, and because it is the custom to do so, that you must behave respectfully to him, and must learn *what the custom is, and not be careless about such things,* or you will be dismissed as a simpleton and obtain none of the things you desire. *And furthermore, unless you are quite conversant with it, you must get all necessary information, and have what you are going to say written down for you. It once happened to me, when I was not accustomed to addressing aristocrats, that I had to go on a matter of urgent business to see a lady who had to be addressed as "Your Ladyship". I was shown that word in writing; but I am stupid, and had never used such a term before; so when I arrived I got it wrong. So I decided to tell her about it and she laughed heartily and told me to be good enough to use the ordinary form of polite address, which I did.*

How is it, my Lord, how is it, my Emperor, that Thou canst suffer this, *Prince of all Creation?* For Thou, my God, art a King without end, and Thine is no borrowed Kingdom, *but Thine own, and it will never pass away.* When the Creed says "Whose Kingdom shall have no end" the phrase nearly always makes me feel particularly happy. I praise Thee, Lord, and bless Thee, *and all things praise Thee* for ever—for Thy Kingdom will endure for ever. Do Thou never allow it to be thought right, Lord, for those who *praise Thee and* come to speak with Thee to do so with their lips alone. What do you mean, Christians, when you say that mental prayer is unnecessary? Do you understand what you are saying? I really do not think you can. And so you want us all to go wrong: you cannot know what mental prayer is, or how vocal prayers should be said, or what is meant by contemplation. For, if you knew this, you would not condemn on the one hand what you praise on the other.

Whenever I remember to do so, I shall always speak of mental and vocal prayer together, daughters, so that you may not be alarmed. I know what such fears lead to, for I have suffered a certain number of trials in this respect, and so I should be sorry if anyone were to unsettle you, for it is very bad for you to have misgivings while you are walking on this path. It is most important that you should realize you are making progess; for if a traveller is told that he has taken the wrong road, and has lost his way, he begins to wander to and fro and the constant search for the right road tires him, wastes his time and delays his arrival. Who can say that it is wrong if, before we begin reciting the Hours or the Rosary, we think Whom we are going to address, and who we are that are addressing Him, so that we may do so in the way we should? I assure you, sisters, that if you gave all due attention to a consideration of these two points before beginning the vocal prayers which you are about to say you would be engaging in mental prayer for a very long time. For we cannot approach a prince and address him in the same careless way that we should adopt in speaking to a peasant or to some poor woman like ourselves, whom we may address however we like.

The reason we sometimes do so is to be found in the humility of this King, Who, unskilled though I am in speaking with Him, does not refuse to hear me or forbid me to approach Him, or command His guards to throw me out. For the angels in His presence know well that their King is such that He prefers the unskilled language of a humble peasant boy, knowing that he would say more if he had more to say, to the speech of the wisest and most learned men, however elegant may be their arguments, if these are not accompanied by humility. But we must not be unmannerly because He is good. If only to show our gratitude to Him for enduring our foul odour and allowing such a one as myself to come near Him, it is well that we should try to recognize this at once when we approach Him, just as we do when we visit the lords of the earth. Once we are told about their fathers' names and their incomes and dignities, there is no more for us to know about them; for on earth one makes account of persons, and honours them, not because of their merits but because of their possessions.

O miserable world! Give hearty praise to God, daughters, that you have left so wretched a place, where people are honoured, not for their own selves, but for what they get from their tenants and vassals: if these fail them, they have no honour left. It is a curious thing, and when you go out to recreation together you should laugh about it, for it is a good way of spending your time to reflect how blindly people in the world spend theirs.

O Thou our Emperor! Supreme Power, Supreme Goodness, Wisdom Itself, without beginning, without end and without measure in Thy works: infinite are these and incomprehensible, a fathomless ocean of wonders, O Beauty containing within Thyself all beauties. O Very Strength! God help me! Would that I could command all the eloquence of mortals and all wisdom, so as to understand, as far as is possible here below, that to know nothing is everything, and thus to describe some of the many things on which we may meditate in order to learn something of the nature of this our Lord and God.

When you approach God, then, try to think and realize Whom you are about to address and continue to do so while you are addressing Him. If we had a thousand lives, we should never fully understand how this Lord merits that we behave toward Him, before Whom even the angels tremble. He orders all things and He can do all things: with Him to will is to perform. It will be right, then, daughters, for us to endeavour to rejoice in these wondrous qualities of our Spouse and to know Whom we have wedded and what our lives should be. Why, God save us, when a woman in this world is about to marry, she knows beforehand whom she is to marry, what sort of a person he is and what property he possesses. Shall not we, then, who are already betrothed, think about our Spouse, before we are wedded to Him and He takes us home to be with Him? If these thoughts are not forbidden to those who are betrothed to men on earth, how can we be forbidden to discover Who this Man is, Who is His Father, what is the country to which He will take me, what are the riches with which He promises to endow me, what is His rank, how I can best make Him happy, what I can do that will give Him pleasure, and how I can bring my rank into line with His. If a woman is to be happy in her marriage, it is just those things that she is advised to see about, even though her husband be a man of very low station.

Shall less respect be paid to Thee, then, my Spouse, than to men? If they think it unfitting to do Thee honour, let them at least leave Thee Thy brides, who are to spend their lives with Thee. A woman is indeed fortunate in her life if her husband is so jealous that he will allow her to speak with no one but himself; it would be a pretty pass if she could not resolve to give him this pleasure, for it is reasonable enough that she should put up with this and not wish to converse with anyone else, since in him she has all that she can desire. To understand these truths, my daughters, is to practise mental prayer. If you wish to learn to understand them, and at the same time to practise vocal prayer, well and good. But do not, I beg you, address God while you are thinking of other things, for to do that is the result of not understanding what mental prayer is. I think I have made this clear. May the Lord grant us to learn how to put it into practice. Amen.